Sacrilege versus Civility

Muslim Perspectives on *The Satanic Verses* Affair

Edited by
M.M. AHSAN and A.R. KIDWAI

The Islamic Foundation

ISBN 0-86037-210-3 (Paperback)
ISBN 0-86037-211-1 (Hardback)

Cover Design: Anwar Cara

The Arabic calligraphy on the title cover refers to the Qur'ānic verse 'And We have exalted your (the Prophet's) fame' – *Al Sharḥ* 94:4.

Published by
The Islamic Foundation,
Markfield Dawah Centre,
Ratby Lane,
Markfield,
Leicester LE6 0RN,
United Kingdom

Quran House,
P.O. Box 30611,
Nairobi,
Kenya

P.M.B. 3193,
Kano,
Nigeria

British Library Cataloguing in Publication Data

A Catalogue record for this book
is available from the British Library

Printed and bound by
Cromwell Press Ltd., Broughton Gifford, Wiltshire

Contents

Acknowledgements

We gratefully acknowledge the copyright permission granted to us by the following:

Impact International, London; *Focus on Christian-Muslim Relations,* Leicester; UK Action Committee on Islamic Affairs, London; *The Islamic Horizons; The Message International; The Independent; The Guardian; The Bookseller; Africa Events; The Daily Telegraph; The Sunday Express; The Times; Discernment,* London; *Index on Censorship;* Edwin Mellen Press; Charles Taylor, *Public Culture; New Statesman and Society;* Commission for Racial Equality; Richard Webster, Orwell Press; Faber & Faber; Islamic Circle of North America, Jamaica, NY; Dr. M.A. Anees; Quill Publishers, Kuala Lumpur; Bishop Lesslie Newbigin; Rev. Kenneth Cragg; Mr. Keith Vaz MP; Professor Bhikhu Parekh; Professor Michael Dummet; Mr. Anthony Burgess; Mr. G.B. Bentley; Professor Norman Stone; Lord Jacobovits, Chief Rabbi.

Preface

This book is an attempt to place the Satanic Verses Affair in the Muslim perspective with sidelights on the variety of responses it evoked. A spate of books have already been published on the Affair, as is evident from our fairly long Bibliography. We nevertheless felt the need for an updated work documenting and analysing the Affair as Muslims see it. For, the coverage in the books published so far stops at mid- or late-1989. We, therefore planned it for publication in early 1991. This plan proved, in a sense, providential in that it enabled us to cover a significant 'twist' in the Affair – Rushdie's 'embracing' of Islam on the 24th December, 1990. We believe the discussion on this latest, unpredictable and ambivalent aspect of the Affair should make this book stand out above others. Seeking permission to reproduce some extracts, particularly from national dailies, revealed to us the other face of the much-vaunted ideal of the freedom of expression. The very champions of this freedom who had supported Rushdie with all their might in presenting a sheer distortion of Islam literally prevented us from even representing what had been published day in and day out in their newspapers and magazines. Hardly had we expected such 'thou shall not-ism' of the Liberal establishment.

This book emanates from our belief in the primacy of civility over sacrilege. To our dismay and bewilderment, we noted the voice of civility being stifled in the din and furore engendered by the literati, liberals, secularists, racists and media, each contributing its part. With passions calming down and the restoration of some semblance of sanity and reason, particularly in the media, we believe it is now time to listen and respond to the voice of civility.

The detailed Chronology provides a synoptic account of almost all relevant events. Chapter 1, 'The Muslim Perspective', offers a dense, coherent treatment of the Affair, ranging from the sacrilegious contents of *The Satanic Verses,* the Muslim response including the *fatwā,* to Rushdie's reported conversion to Islam. Chapter 2 recapitulates Rushdie's own postures on the genesis and design of *The Satanic Verses,* apart from a piece full of insights into his mind. In the fierce battle between sacrilege and civility there were voices of all sorts – hysterical and abusive as well as sane and rational. With a view to recording such material in the broader context of the West *vis-à-vis* Islam/Muslims, a selection of writings, mostly extracts, is presented in Chapters 3 and 4 entitled 'In Defence of Sacrilege' and 'Voices of Civility' respectively. As already indicated, the original plan was to include a fairly large selection of such material, particularly in Chapter 3. However, the refusal of copyright permission forced us to drop several pieces. What was published elsewhere without any qualms was deemed unsuitable for reproduction in our book by the custodians of free speech! Had this material been so 'hot' it should not have been published in the first place.

The discussion broached in Chapter 1 is resumed and elaborated by several writers in Chapter 5, 'The Muslim Argument'. It reflects the depth, range and passion of the Muslim response to the sacrilege embodied in Rushdie's work. We have tried our best to avoid the repetition of any argument but being a collection of articles some overlapping was inevitable in this Chapter. Appended to the book are several significant documents with bearings on the Affair. Another useful element of the book is an extensive and annotated bibliography of relevant material in books and journals. For obvious constraints of space we had to exclude from the Bibliography the plethora of material on the Affair in national dailies, of which some extracts are, however, quoted in Chapters 3 and 4.

Though some of the extracts reproduced in the book did require language editing, we have quoted them verbatim. The headings of excerpts in italic are our own, while the original heading is specified in the source

We hope this book will help appreciate better the Muslim position on the Affair, which far from betraying any 'militancy' or 'fundamentalism' consists in their preference for civility over sacrilege.

Several colleagues and friends helped us in preparing this book, to whom we are extremely grateful for comments and suggestions.

It is impossible to mention them all by name. However, we would like to record our thanks to Mr. M.H. Faruqi for going through part of the manuscript and giving invaluable suggestions for improvements. We are also grateful to Muslim and non-Muslim friends for allowing us to reproduce their writing in part or full. Our thanks are also due to Mr. Zaheeruddin, President, ICNA, New York, Mrs. Motaharunnisa Omar, Madras (India), Mr. Ekramul Haque, former editor of *The Message,* USA and Mr. Iqbal Sacranie, Joint Convenor, UK Action Committee on Islamic Affairs, for providing us with useful material. Mrs. K. Barratt and Mr. E.R. Fox deserve our special thanks for respectively typing the manuscript and seeing the book through the press.

Leicester, **Editors**
June 1991

Chronology

26th September, 1988	Viking/Penguin, London, publish Salman Rushdie's *The Satanic Verses* despite its own Editorial Consultant, Mr. Khushwant Singh's repeated warning that it would cause offence to Muslims.
3rd October, 1988	Objectionable passages from the book brought to the attention of Muslim organizations, mosques, and Muslim ambassadors in the UK. Penguin officials contacted for immediate withdrawal of this offensive work.
3rd–10th October, 1988	Thousands of letters and phone calls to the publisher demanding that the offensive work be withdrawn. The publisher does not reply.
5th October, 1988	The Government of India takes the lead in banning *The Satanic Verses.*
11th October, 1988	The UK Action Committee on Islamic Affairs, representing major Muslim organizations, mosques and scholars in the UK, formed in London in order to mobilize public opinion against this sacrilegious and unwarranted attack on the Islamic sanctities.
	The Riyadh-based World Assembly of

	Muslim Youth, representing over 500 Muslim youth organizations the world over, condemns the offensive book and demands a world ban.
21st October, 1988	Hundreds of thousands of Muslims sign the petition protesting against the publication of *The Satanic Verses,* and calling for its withdrawal. Again, the publisher pays no heed to the Muslims' demand.
5th November, 1988	The 46-nation Organization of the Islamic Conference General Secretariat asks member states to take strong action against the publisher and the author if they fail to withdraw the work.
	Bangladesh bans *The Satanic Verses.*
21st November, 1988	Al-Azhar, the 1,000-year-old most venerated Islamic seminary in Egypt, brands *The Satanic Verses* as blasphemous and calls on the 45 Muslim countries to take concerted action.
22nd November, 1988	Sudan bans *The Satanic Verses.*
24th November, 1988	South Africa bans *The Satanic Verses* in response to the South African Muslims' protest.
1st December, 1988	Mr. Ken Hargreaves, MP, moves an Early Day Motion in the House of Commons, regretting the distress caused to Muslims in the UK by the publication of *The Satanic Verses.*
10th December, 1988	A massive protest rally in London organized by the Islamic Defence Council against the publication of *The Satanic Verses.*

14th December, 1988	Sri Lanka bans *The Satanic Verses.*
19th December, 1988	A delegation of Muslim ambassadors in London call on the British Home Minister to protest against *The Satanic Verses.*
23rd December, 1988	The British Attorney General gives the official legal opinion that British law precluded any action against the publisher.
28th December, 1988	Oman blacklists Penguin, the publisher in accordance with the OIC resolution.
December, 1988 onwards	Massive protest rallies in every British town with a sizeable Muslim population in protest against the publication of the blasphemous book.
14th January, 1989	Muslims in Bradford, Yorkshire (UK) burn symbolically a copy of *The Satanic Verses* in order to draw attention to their long unacknowledged protest against the blasphemous book. The media picks on the event without any concern for the anguish suffered by the Muslims.
16th January, 1989	W.H. Smith, Britain's biggest bookseller, withdraws *The Satanic Verses* from sale in its shops.
1st February, 1989	Mr. Douglas Hurd, the British Home Secretary, addressing a Muslim gathering in Birmingham, rules out any change in the blasphemy law and instead asks the British Muslims to join 'the mainstream'.
12th February, 1989	Ten peaceful Muslim protesters in Islamabad (Pakistan) shot dead by the Pakistan police outside the US Embassy.

	Public demonstrations against the book held in almost all major towns in Pakistan.
13th February, 1989	Five Muslim protesters killed and others injured in Srinagar, Kashmir, India.
14th February, 1989	Ayatollah Khomeini proclaims that Salman Rushdie, being an apostate, deserves the death penalty.
15th February, 1989	Big demonstrations outside the British Embassy in Tehran. Iran blacklists all Penguin/Viking publications. Rushdie goes into hiding.
18th February, 1989	Rushdie issues a non-apology purporting to say that 'Muslims in many parts of the world are genuinely distressed by the publication of *The Satanic Verses.*' Yet there is no word about the withdrawal of the offensive book.
21st February, 1989	Iran withdraws ambassadors from the EEC countries.
23rd February, 1989	WCXR-FM, a radio station outside Washington, DC withdraws albums by Yusuf Islam, the former pop singer, and decides not to play them in future for Yusuf Islam's condemnation of *The Satanic Verses.*
	Cardinal Albert Decourtray, Head of the French Roman Catholic Church, remarks on the publication of *The Satanic Verses:* 'Once again believers have been offended in their faith.'
24th February, 1989	Bombay police open fire on a peaceful Muslim procession, killing at least 13.

26th February, 1989	Thousands of American Muslims protest in New York against the publication of *The Satanic Verses.*
27th February, 1989	A British Muslim delegation calls on Mr. John Patten, Minister of State, Home Office. He, however, rejects the Muslims' plea for equal treatment for all faiths under the blasphemy law.
1st March 1989	Kenya bans *The Satanic Verses.*
3rd March, 1989	More than 10,000 Muslims stage a rally against *The Satanic Verses* in Dhaka (Bangladesh). About 100 people injured when the police open fire on the procession.
	Mrs. Thatcher, the British Prime Minister and Sir Geoffrey Howe, the Foreign Secretary, concede that *The Satanic Verses* is 'offensive'.
4th March, 1989	A big protest rally against *The Satanic Verses* in Istanbul, Turkey.
7th March, 1989	Thailand bans *The Satanic Verses.*
	Iran severs diplomatic ties with the UK.
13th March, 1989	Tanzania bans *The Satanic Verses.*
	Indonesia bans *The Satanic Verses.*
14th March, 1989	Singapore bans *The Satanic Verses.*
16th March, 1989	The Organization of Islamic Conference (OIC) in Riyadh (Saudi Arabia) resolves to ban Penguin publications in 45 Muslim countries in protest at the company's refusal to withdraw the offensive book.

17th March, 1989	A massive demonstration by the Sudanese Muslims in Khartoum against *The Satanic Verses*.
22nd March, 1989	Poland decides not to publish *The Satanic Verses*.
28th March, 1989	A delegation of Tehrik Tahaffuzi-Namoos-i-Risalat, Action Committee in Pakistan against *The Satanic Verses* presents a memorandum to the British Foreign Secretary for banning the blasphemous book.
1st April, 1989	The Muslim Institute, London, holds a conference on the Rushdie Affair. In his keynote address, Dr. Kalim Siddiqui, Director, Muslim Institute, defends the *fatwā* and outlines the implications of the Rushdie affair for Muslims in Britain.
27th May, 1989	A massive demonstration by British Muslims organized by the British Muslim Action Front in London in protest against the blasphemous book.
29th May, 1989	Two Labour MPs call for withdrawal of *The Satanic Verses*.
15th June, 1989	Venezuela bans *The Satanic Verses*.
17th June, 1989	The Bradford Council of Mosques charts out a 10-point action programme against the publisher and the blasphemous book.
20th June, 1989	The British High Court grant the Muslim Action Front leave to challenge an earlier court ruling in March, refusing to issue summonses for a private prosecution.

4th July, 1989	Mr. John Patten, British Minister of State at the Home Office, writes to influential Muslims on issues confronting British Muslims and speaks of difficulties and problems in extending legal protection to non-Anglican sanctities.
28th July, 1989	The French edition of *The Satanic Verses* is published.
July, 1989	The UK Action Committee, London, propose to launch a National Petition to the House of Commons, expressing revulsion at *The Satanic Verses*.
1st August, 1989	The BBC turns down the Archbishop Dr. Runcie's plea to shelve Tony Harrison's 'The Blasphemous Banquet', its programme related to *The Satanic Verses,* which attacks religious belief and is particularly abusive of Iran's late leader, Ayatollah Khomeini.
11th September, 1989	The UMO Conference considers the continued publication of *The Satanic Verses* as the most important issue facing British Muslims. Mr. Neil Thorne, Conservative MP, calls for the book to be withdrawn.
30th September, 1989	Mr. Ahmad Deedat, the South African Muslim scholar, holds a week-long British tour, campaigning for banning *The Satanic Verses*. He addresses huge meetings in Bradford, Blackburn, Leicester, Glasgow, Birmingham and London.
20th October, 1989	A Harris Poll conducted for BBC Television shows that four out of five British

	Muslims want some kind of action taken against Rushdie.
June–October, 1989	Protest rallies by British Muslims against *The Satanic Verses* continue in UK towns.
16th December, 1989	The Association of Sunni Muslims reaffirms its determination to continue the campaign until *The Satanic Verses* is withdrawn.
	Muslims at 1,000 mosques in the UK raise their hands in a 'show of solidarity' for their campaign against *The Satanic Verses.*
8th–12th January, 1990	British Muslims representing all parts of the country conduct a 5-day vigil outside Penguin/Viking offices, London. A letter stating their demands delivered to Penguin. As in the past, Penguin refuses to consider any of these demands.
21st January, 1990	A representative meeting of 200 Muslim community leaders, held in Coventry, organized by the International Muslims Organization, resolves to conduct a united campaign against the blasphemous book.
3rd February, 1990	UMO Winter Conference held in Gwent (Wales) presses for extension of the blasphemy law to cover Islam.
4th February, 1990	Writing a long, malicious piece, 'In Good Faith', in *The Independent,* Rushdie claims that he has never been a Muslim.

5th February, 1990	Rushdie presses Penguin/Viking to bring out the paperback edition of *The Satanic Verses,* though more than one million copies of the novel in hardback have already been sold. Of these, 740,000 were sold in the USA.
7th February, 1990	British Muslim leaders dismiss Rushdie's Read Memorial Lecture and his press statements, as 'publicity stunts'.
10th February, 1990	Ayatollah Ali Khamenei, Iran's supreme leader, endorses the *fatwā* passed a year ago against Rushdie for his blasphemous work.
16th February, 1990	The UK Action Committee observes a Solidarity Day of Prayer and Dedication to the Muslim martyrs of Islamabad, Bombay and Srinagar, who sacrificed their lives in February 1989 while protesting against the publication of *The Satanic Verses.*
27th February, 1990	The Council for the British Muslim Action Front argues in the London High Court for equality in law. It is pointed out also that the demonstrations against *The Satanic Verses* have already cost 30 Muslim lives in different parts of the world.
6th March, 1990	Lord Hutchinson and Lord Harris urge prosecutions against the British Muslims for their protests over *The Satanic Verses.*
9th April, 1990	The Queen's Bench Divisional Court, under Section 4(1) of the Public Order Act 1986, dismisses the British Muslims'

	application for issuing a summons against Penguin/Viking, publisher of *The Satanic Verses* for causing public disorder.
10th April, 1990	The British Muslim Action Front seeks leave to appeal to the House of Lords for protecting Islam against blasphemy.
28th April, 1990	Rushdie, speaking on BBC Radio 4, expresses surprise that no Muslim has been prosecuted for 'threats against him'.
8th May, 1990	According to a Gallup Poll, published in *The Daily Telegraph,* the majority of respondents say that Rushdie should apologize.
	A group of Conservative MPs call on Rushdie to compromise.
25th May, 1990	The High Court refuses British Muslims leave to appeal to the House of Lords against the judgement that the law of blasphemy applies only to Christianity.
16th July, 1990	The Muslim Institute holds a conference in London on the Rushdie Affair.
31st July–4th August, 1990	The 19th Islamic Foreign Ministers Conference meeting in Cairo adopts a mandatory resolution calling on all member states to take all necessary steps, including economic sanctions, against the publisher of *The Satanic Verses,* and its holding company, Pearson.
2nd August, 1990	In a conciliatory gesture to Iran Mr. Douglas Hurd, the British Foreign Sec-

	retary, reiterates Britain's great respect for Islam.
28th September, 1990	Iran and Britain resume diplomatic links. The agreement makes no reference to Ayatollah Khomeini's *fatwā* against Rushdie.
30th September, 1990	In an ITV programme Rushdie speaks of his experiences during the last 18 months.
27th November, 1990	British Muslim leaders refute Rushdie's claim of his negotiations with Muslim leaders. Unless *The Satanic Verses* is withdrawn, and an unqualified apology tendered to Muslims of the world, they insist they will continue their campaign until these demands are met.
24th December, 1990	Rushdie claims to have 'embraced' Islam in the presence of the Egyptian Minister for *Awqāf* and some Egyptian officials. He says he will not publish the paperback edition of *The Satanic Verses* or permit its translation into other languages *while any risk of further offence exists.*
	British Muslim leaders cautiously greet the reported 'conversion' of Rushdie and demand the immediate withdrawal of the hardback edition.
26th December, 1990	The Iranian supreme leader, Ayatollah Ali Khamenei, reaffirms the *fatwā* against Rushdie, stating that the *fatwā* pronounced by Imam Khomeini is irrevocable.

In a press statement, Shaikh Jamal Manna, who was present at Rushdie's meeting with Egyptian officials, refutes Rushdie's claim that the book is not offensive. He again urges Rushdie to withdraw the hardback edition of the sacrilegious book.

The UK Action Committee on Islamic Affairs holds that Rushdie has not addressed the central issue of the total withdrawal of the offensive book and says that it is his 'religious duty' to do so in a genuine spirit of repentance for the offence caused.

28th December, 1990 In his article 'Why I have Embraced Islam' (*The Times*), Rushdie insists that *The Satanic Verses* will not be totally withdrawn for he cannot betray his readers and that it is not a deliberate insult to Islam. Once again he states that the Egyptian scholars did not regard his book as offensive.

29th December, 1990 Members of the UK Action Committee on Islamic Affairs, representing major Muslim organizations, institutions and scholars, in a press conference at the Islamic Cultural Centre, London view the latest attempt by Rushdie to 'embrace' Islam as an apparent ploy to get him 'off the hook'. They believe that he has taken no steps to suggest that his conversion to Islam is genuine and that he is not seriously committed to removing the offence being perpetrated through the continued publication and circulation of the sacrilegious book worldwide. They vow to continue their campaign until the book is totally withdrawn, an unqualified apology tendered to the Muslims and payment of damages made to an Islamic charity.

31st December, 1990 — Speaking on BBC Radio 4's Sunday Programme, Rushdie goes back on his earlier pledge, made at the time of his affirmation of Islam on 24th December, not to publish the paperback edition or further translations of *The Satanic Verses* and says that 'these would go ahead when it could *happen safely*'.

Rushdie claims to have received blessings from the Egyptian officials and scholars and an invitation to meet Shaikh Gad el-Haq Ali Gad el-Haq, the Grand Shaikh of al-Azhar in Cairo.

1st January, 1991 — An Egyptian government spokesman refutes Rushdie's claim of having been invited to Egypt as 'absolutely without foundation'.

4th January, 1991 — Francis Bennion, the author, barrister, former Oxford University law lecturer and one of the prominent members of the Committee of writers and human rights campaign supporting Salman Rushdie, dissociates himself from the novelist saying he was 'not worth defending'. Several other members of the committee such as Arnold Wesker, the playwright, are also reported to have been angry and disappointed at the reported conversion of the author to Islam and the temporary stoppage of the publication of the paperback edition of the book.

6th January, 1991	In a phone-in programme of *Sunrise Radio,* London, Rushdie once again insists that he would not withdraw *The Satanic Verses* and the book 'should remain around to be the basis of a serious analysis and discussion'. But he offers to make a contribution to the families of those killed in protest demonstrations against his sacrilegious book in 1989 'if a fund were set up'.
17th January, 1991	In an interview with Akbar S. Ahmad (*The Guardian,* 17th January), Rushdie once again evades the real issue of the withdrawal of the offensive book by offering three ingenious 'reasons'. He wants to meet the members of the UK Action Committee on Islamic Affairs to 'talk about it'.
23rd January, 1991	Mrs. Angela Rumbold, Home Office Minister, meets the delegation of the UK Action Committee on Islamic Affairs and discusses the government's move 'to find a way forward' about legal provisions for protecting religious sensitivities.
11th February, 1991	The Oxford University Press drops the plan for inclusion in a forthcoming English language teaching book, a 'too sensitive' and offensive passage from Rushdie's earlier novel, *Midnight's Children.*
14th February, 1991	Following the recent resumption of diplomatic relations between Iran and the UK and Rushdie's reported embracing of Islam, there was a general expectation in the West that the *fatwā* would be lifted on its second anniversary. The Iranian religious authorities, however, reaffirmed the *fatwā*.

CHAPTER 1

The Muslim Perspective

Perhaps no other book has ever caused so much anger, fury and revulsion amongst Muslims the world over as the publication by Viking/Penguin in September 1988 of Salman Rushdie's *The Satanic Verses*. No other book has been used in the same way as *The Satanic Verses* has as a pretext to launch an attack against Islam and the Muslim community in the West. Indeed, no other book has caused so many deaths and injuries in the Muslim world as this outrageous publication. And, no book has caused so much misunderstanding and hostility against Islam in the West as *The Satanic Verses*. What should have been seen as a simple issue of blasphemy and profanity has been turned into a clash between Muslim and Western liberal culture. Ironically, instead of trying to understand the offence *The Satanic Verses* has caused to Islam and Muslims and instead of listening to authentic Muslim points of view, the entire establishment in the West, with a few exceptions, has turned against Islam and hounded the Muslim community with all its might and contempt. What should have been seen as a genuine Muslim reaction of anger and protest has been misdirected to issues of freedom of expression and censorship.

Once again the media has taken its revenge on Islam, turning the victims into criminals, the oppressed into oppressors, the innocent into the guilty. A smokescreen of confusion, vilification and malice was created in an effort to mislead the people and to scare Muslims into submission. Hardly anyone tried to understand why Muslims reacted so angrily to the book's publication, why there were so many demonstrations and protests, why more than 20 people in India and Pakistan gave their lives and scores more sustained serious injuries, why Imam Khomeini issued the *fatwā,* why Iran broke off diplomatic relations with Britain and then had to face the indignation and hostility of the European community.

In this essay, we shall attempt to evaluate the Muslim perspective on the Rushdie affair. We shall further assess why the publication of this novel provoked the anger of the Muslim community, examine how the Muslim community launched and sustained their campaign against the book and with what consequences.

The British Muslim Campaign

Although several reviews appeared in leading British newspapers soon after the book's publication and the author himself explained some of its contents on the BBC Network East programme, it was not until late September that the Muslim community in Britain came to appreciate fully the blasphemous nature of the work. It was Rushdie's interview with *India Today* (15th September 1988) that alerted and shocked the Muslim community in India. It was they who launched the first movement to have the book banned in their own country and it was their efforts which turned the book into an international issue. Soon the news had travelled to Britain, sending a shock-wave of revulsion and indignation among rank and file Muslims up and down the country. The Muslim community's first reaction was one of disbelief, seeing this as yet another literary attack on Islam in the tradition of the Orientalists and their medieval predecessors. But disbelief turned to dismay and outrage when it was seen through the excerpts circulated by Muslim organizations in Britain and India that *The Satanic Verses* was a deliberate attempt to malign and ridicule Islam and Muslim belief and practices in the most foul and vulgar manner. There is no precedent for this in modern literature no matter what the language of publication. Overwhelmed with pain, outrage and anger, the leaders of the Muslim community assembled at the Islamic Cultural Centre to discuss how they should react to this *fitna* (outrageous issue) and what action they could possibly take to redress their pain and grief occasioned by the book's publication. With one voice and with an extreme sense of urgency on 11th October 1988 the 'UK Action Committee on Islamic Affairs' was formed to combat the *fitna* and to guide the Muslim community in their efforts to express their anger and hurt, through democratic means, and to ensure that their protest stayed within the framework of the law.

An appeal was made to the Muslim community to vehemently protest against the publication of the book through letters, telephone calls and representations to the publishers, the author and the British government demanding that the book be withdrawn from circulation, that a public apology be made, that a pledge be given that the book would not be republished in any form or language and that compensation be made for injuring the feelings of Muslims the world over. A signature campaign outlining the four-point demand was launched and some 60,000 signatures were submitted to Viking/Penguin urging them to realize their 'mistake' and to take the necessary measures to redress the Muslims' grievances. For a few days, Viking/Penguin's telephone exchange was jammed by Muslim protesters and thousands of letters of protest were sent to their headquarters. An attempt was made to meet Peter Meyer, Penguin's Managing Director and the man behind the book's publication, but to no avail. The publisher's delayed response was arrogant in the extreme, with no appreciation of the extent of the injury to Muslims' feelings. To add insult to injury they also announced that they planned to translate and publish the book in at least nine other languages. Penguin continued to refuse to see any Muslim delegation on the issue and meanwhile the book had earned great acclaim from the literati in the West and was nominated for the prestigious Booker Prize. Naturally, Muslim frustration, bewilderment and anger intensified with the continuing insensibility of both the publishers and the British government. But the Muslim community resolved to steadfastly continue its campaign.

Islam and Freedom of Expression

Islam has neither advocated the suppression of freedom of expression nor encouraged censorship of healthy and useful material. Indeed, its historians and scholars have built up a unique tradition of recording knowledge, provided it came through a sound chain of authority. Had Islam wanted to censor materials or suppress information, malicious stories like the so-called 'Satanic Verses' would not have found a mention in the early

Muslim writings of Ṭabarī or Ibn Sa'd. The stand which Muslims have taken over the publication of Rushdie's novel is not one which seeks to suppress freedom of expression but rather one which refuses to give licence for such abuse, ridicule and vulgar attack on Islam and on the values which Muslims hold sacred and regard dearer than their lives and properties.

Muslims are not angry because Rushdie has criticized Islam nor that he presented an academic refutation of some of its beliefs and practices which non-Muslim scholars, Orientalists, have been doing for centuries but because he has deliberately blasphemed against Islam and skilfully disguised this abuse in the form of a dream, a fictional dream, of a deranged mind. He not only abused the Qur'ān, the Prophet, his Companions, his wives, but also the Prophet Abraham, the Patriarch common to Islam, Christianity and Judaism, the Hindus, the Sikhs and in so doing did not spare the Queen, the British Prime Minister and white women in general. The iniquitous four-letter word has been used so profusely that it occurs more than fifty times in the book, and other derisive and offensive remarks appear page after page. It is for this reason that Muslims consider Rushdie's book a piece of the most profane literature – a religious pornography.[1] The list of offensive sentences and ideas recorded in the book is so long that to record and analyse them properly would amount to writing a book the size of Rushdie's own. It will be sufficient to discuss some of the most flagrant insinuations, innuendoes and abuses hurled against the Prophet, some of Islam's institutions and some of its personalities.

The Sacrilege of *The Satanic Verses*

Very few people realize that the name 'Satanic Verses' however innocent it may seem, is itself a great blasphemy, a sacrilege asserting that the Qur'ān is not immune from external manipulation and interpolation as God has proclaimed but that it was influenced and manipulated by Satan. The accusation cuts at the very root of Muslim belief that the Qur'ān is the unique revelation of God preserved in the same language and diction as was revealed to the Prophet through the agency of the Angel Gabriel 1400 years ago, unalloyed by any interpolation, change or editing.

The malicious story of the 'Satanic Verses' was initiated by

Orientalists on the basis of a misleading account of *Gharānīq al-'Ulā* (the high-soaring ones) which Satan is alleged to have inserted in *Sūra al-Najm,* the 53rd chapter of the Qur'ān. According to this preposterous story, the Prophet was unable to detect the Satanic manipulation and so recited the 'Satanic Verses' in his prayers for days, if not months, without realizing their Satanic origin. This continued until the Angel Gabriel came one evening, rebuked the Prophet for his mistake, and changed the satanic verses for more appropriate ones.[2] As part of the story was mentioned in the earliest books of Muslim history such as those by Ibn Sa'd and Ṭabarī, non-Muslim scholars such as Nöldeke, Muir and Watt have taken great relish in narrating the story with their usual embellishments, malice and innuendoes. However, most discerning scholars, both past and present, such as Ibn Isḥāq, Ibn Hishām, Ibn Kathīr, al-Rāzī, al-Qurṭubī, Mawdūdī, Sayyid Quṭb and Haikal, have exposed the false nature of the story and regard it as a preposterous and malicious fabrication designed to cast serious doubt on the authenticity of the Qur'ān and its message. Some Western scholars, such as the Italian Caetani and the Briton John Burton, have also regarded the story as pure fabrication and without foundation. Ordinary readers in the West who have no knowledge about the story do not realize that Rushdie by naming his novel *The Satanic Verses* has tried to kill, as it were, two birds with one stone – firstly, to discredit the Prophet and secondly, to make Muslims question their belief in the authenticity of the Qur'ān, and so undermine the very basis of Islam. It needs an ingenious but malicious mind like that of Rushdie's to conjure up a plot like this!

Abuse against the Prophet's Companions *(Ṣaḥāba)*

Rushdie not only plants the outrageous story of the Satanic Verses in his novel but brands one of the greatest and most beloved Companions of the Prophet, Salman the Persian, as a cheat and a manipulator of the Qur'ānic revelations, despite the fact that Salman was neither an Arab nor a scribe as he embraced Islam not in Makka but in Madina. According to Rushdie, the Prophet not only failed to realize Salman's initial manipulation but also approved the interpolations in good faith. This disgusted Salman and made him forsake not only the Prophet but also Islam itself. This is how Rushdie builds up the scenario:

> Little things at first. If Mahound recited a verse in which God was described as *all-hearing, all-knowing,* I would write, *all-knowing, all-wise.* Here's the point: Mahound did not notice the alterations. So there I was, actually writing the Book, or re-writing, anyway, polluting the word of God with my own profane language . . .
>
> So the next time I changed a bigger thing. He said *Christian,* I wrote down *Jew.* He'd notice that, surely; how could he not? But when I read him the chapter he nodded and thanked me politely, and I went out of his tent with tears in my eyes (pp. 367–8).

Disillusioned with the Prophet and Islamic *Sharī'a,* so asserts Rushdie, Salman the Persian became an apostate, went back to the hedonistic metropolis of *Jāhiliyya* and launched a bitter ideological assault on Islam. For example, Rushdie asserts that Salman narrated his experience with the Prophet to the anti-Islamic poet Baal, saying: 'Mahound had no time for scruples . . . no qualms about ends and means' that 'the closer you are to a conjurer, the easier to spot the trick' (p. 363) and again Mahound 'laid down the law and the angel would confirm it afterwards' (p. 365). Rushdie regards the rules of Islamic law as 'revelations of convenience' (p. 365) with bizarre and obnoxious statements like 'sodomy and the missionary position were approved of by the archangel, whereas the forbidden postures included all those in which the female was on top' (p. 364). What further proof do we need of a deranged and perverted mind!

Another leading Companion and the first Muezzin of Islam, Bilal the Abyssinian, has been abused as 'scum', 'an enormous black monster, this one, with a voice to match his size' (p. 101) – an abuse of monstrous proportions indeed! Rushdie abuses other Companions of the Prophet, Khalid, Bilal and Salman, as 'this trinity of scum', 'that bunch of riff-raff' (p. 101), 'stupid drunk' (p. 117), 'those *goons* and – those f... *clowns*' (p. 101).

Abuse against the Prophet Muḥammad (peace be upon him)

The worst target of Rushdie's invective and gratuitous attack is the Prophet Muḥammad (peace be upon him) himself. Not only is the Prophet depicted as incapable of distinguishing between revelation from an Angel and inspiration from the Devil, he has also been presented as a devil incarnate, the Mahound. 'Our mountain-climbing, prophet-motivated solitary', derides Rushdie, 'is to be the medieval baby-frightener, the Devil's synonym: Mahound' (p. 93). The deliberate use of the medieval stereotype for the Prophet Muḥammad (peace be upon him) whom Muslims love and revere more than their parents and their own selves is not only highly provocative, but derogatory in the extreme and without justification. The epithet 'Mahound' and its different variants in medieval times were used by Christian clerics to deride the Prophet who was accused of being an impostor, an anti-Christ, a devil and a licentious person who used the wives of other men to satisfy his lust and who brought revelations to justify his promiscuous conduct.

Rushdie further ridicules the Prophet, deriding him as 'the businessman-turned-prophet, Mahound, is founding one of the world's great religions; and . . . There is a voice whispering in his ear: *'what kind of idea are you? Man-or-mouse?'* (p. 95). He is also alleged to have said: 'writers and whores, I see no difference here' (p. 392). At another place the Prophet is accused of lying naked and unconscious in the tent of Hind with a 'bursting headache'. Hind 'sits close to him on the bed . . . and strokes his chest' (pp. 119–21). When he asked Hind how he happened to be there, Hind answered: 'I was walking the city streets last night, masked, to see the festivities, and what should I stumble over but your unconscious body? Like a drunk in the gutter, Mahound. I sent my servants for a litter and brought you home' (p. 120).

In another sensuous scene, Hind is shown licking the Prophet's feet 'in excessive, sensual adoration' (p. 374). The Prophet is also described as wrestling with Gibreel in the cave stark naked, with a vivid and intimate description (p. 122). The Prophet has not only been called 'a small bastard' but a debauchee, who, after the death of his wife, slept with so many women that 'they turned his beard half-white in a year' (p. 366). Rushdie further derides the Prophet, saying: 'He went for mothers and daughters, think of his first wife and then Ayesha: too old and too young, his two loves. He didn't like to pick on someone his own size' (p. 366). There are several other offensive and obscene remarks about the Prophet, not even sparing the four-letter word (pp. 366; 367; 381; 386).

It is true that the Prophet's contemporary arch-enemies, the polytheists of Makka, called him a liar, said he was possessed of Jinn and insane and that the medieval Christian detractors applied all sorts of abusive epithets to him, but Rushdie with his obscenity, vulgarity and the intensity of his hatred has surpassed them all. One wonders whether these vulgar attacks on the life of the Beloved Prophet are an attempt to rewrite history, albeit from a secular perspective, as he has claimed in one of his earlier interviews, or whether it is a deliberate effort to injure Muslims' feelings and incite them to violence and desperate reactions. Rushdie must have known that a malicious story published in a Bangalore newspaper, *The Deccan Herald,* in December 1986, entitled 'Muhammad the Idiot' with no direct reference to the Prophet caused widespread violence and riots resulting in the death of some 50 people in India. The mere fact that the name Muhammad was used in the fiction for the deaf mute boy and he was further called an idiot was enough to rouse the feelings of ordinary Muslims who overwhelmed with anger and outrage did not hesitate to sacrifice their lives in order to protect the dignity and honour of the Prophet. Rushdie should also know that in India again, as early as 1924, the person responsible for publishing a blasphemous and provocative book in Urdu entitled *Rangīla Rasūl* (The Licentious Prophet) was murdered in the courtroom by an illiterate Muslim, Ghazi Ilmuddin, who sacrificed his life to save the honour of the Prophet and who proudly embraced a death sentence issued by the then British administration.[3]

Rushdie should also have known that some 50 years ago, when the British historian, H.G. Wells, depicted an unflattering portrait of the Prophet in his *Short History of the World* (originally published in 1922 and reprinted by Penguin in 1946) not in any way comparable to Rushdie's blasphemy, it occasioned great fury and resentment in the Muslim world. Protest rallies were held not only in London but in Kenya (Mombasa, Nairobi) and Uganda (Kampala) and demands were made to ban it throughout the British Empire. Muslims, as James Piscatori[4] informs us, 'demanded the severe punishment of the author for offending the religious sensibilities of millions of British subjects, and otherwise peaceful people'. The Muslims' anger did not subside until Lord Zetland, the then Secretary of State for India, expressed regrets at the injury caused to Muslims by the publication of the book.

It is no wonder that with the publication of Rushdie's offensive and outrageous book, Muslims all over the world became outraged and showed their anger through protest marches and demonstrations. The governments of Pakistan and India unfortunately panicked and handled the situation with the utmost inefficiency and brutality. The police opened fire on unarmed demonstrators, and caused the unnecessary and unfortunate deaths of over 20 people (at least 7 in Islamabad, 2 in Srinagar, and 13 in Rushdie's own birthplace, Bombay) and injury to hundreds more. Despite this, Muslims still regard this as a small price if their martyrdom can bring the *fitna* to an end. But it has been proved beyond any doubt that to the British government and the publishers of Rushdie's work the life of the blasphemer is more important and sacred than the lives of these people.

Abuse against the Prophet's Family

Rushdie not only reviles the Prophet in the most vulgar ways, but also portrays the Prophet's wives in the most shameful and indecent manner. The Prophet's wives, according to Qur'ānic parlance, are the 'Mothers of the Faithful' and are respected by Muslims in the same way that the Prophet is revered. By calling the brothel a 'curtain' and locating it in the Ka'ba, Rushdie on the one hand, ridicules the Islamic tradition of *Ḥijāb* (Muslim women's dress) and on the other, defiles the sanctity of the Ka'ba, the House of God, the symbol of Muslim unity, towards which Muslims the world over face in their five daily prayers. Rushdie compounds the blasphemy by giving the prostitutes the names of the Prophet's wives. This is how Rushdie pours out his venom against the Prophet's family and how, one by one, he abuses the Mothers of the Faithful:

> When the news got around Jahilia that the whores of The Curtain had each assumed the identity of one of Mahound's wives, the clandestine excitement of the city's males was intense . . . The fifteen-year-old whore 'Ayesha' was the most popular with the paying public, just as her namesake was with Mahound . . . The oldest, fattest whore, who had taken the name of 'Sawdah', would tell her visitors – and she had plenty, many of the men of Jahilia seeking her out for her maternal and also grateful charms – the story of how

> Mahound had married her and Ayesha, on the same day, when Ayesha was just a child. . . . The whore 'Hafsah' grew as hot-tempered as her namesake, and as the twelve entered into the spirit of their roles the alliances in the brothel came to mirror the political cliques at the Yathrib mosque; 'Ayesha' and 'Hafsah', for example, engaged in constant, petty rivalries against the two haughtiest whores, who had always been thought a bit stuck-up by the others and who had chosen for themselves the most aristocratic identities, becoming 'Umm Salamah the Makhzumite', and the snootiest of them all, 'Ramlah', whose namesake, the eleventh wife of Mahound, was the daughter of Abu Simbel and Hind. And there was a 'Zainab bint Jahsh', and a 'Juwairiyah', named after the bride captured on a military expedition, and a 'Rehana the Jew', a 'Safia' and a 'Maimunah' and, most erotic of all the whores, who knew tricks she refused to teach to competitive 'Ayesha': the glamorous Egyptian, 'Mary the Copt'. Strangest of all was the whore who had taken the name of 'Zainab bint Khuzaimah', knowing that this wife of Mahound had recently died (pp. 381–2).

Rushdie also ridicules the sacred act of *ṭawāf* in the *Ḥajj* and *'Umra* by saying the clients 'curled around the innermost courtyard of the brothel rotating about its centrally positioned fountain of love much as pilgrims rotated for other reasons around the ancient pillar of stone' (p. 381). Can one think of anything more outrageous in its profanity than the book Rushdie has produced, considered by some as a specimen of fine literature worthy of receiving the highest literary award, the Booker Prize? When Muslims protest at such profanity and abuse they become reactionary, fundamentalist and uncivilized, yet if Rushdie vomits such profligacy he becomes a champion of freedom of expression. What a unique pronouncement of Western secular liberalism!

Abuse against Islamic Institutions

Islamic law or *Sharī'a* to Rushdie is a jumbled up set of rules which relates to 'every damn thing', 'if a man farts, let him turn his face to the wind, a rule about which hand to use for the purpose of cleaning one's behind . . . The revelation – the *recitation* told the faithful how much to eat, how deeply they should sleep, and which sexual positions had received divine sanction' (pp. 363–4). Even the institution of *Wuḍū'* (ablution) and prayer has not escaped Rushdie's ridicule and derision. Note how he makes fun of these: 'Ablutions, always ablutions, the legs up to the knees, the arms down to the elbows, the head down to the neck. Dry torsoed, wet-limbed and damp-headed, what eccentrics they look! Splish, splosh, washing and praying. On their knees, pushing arms, legs, heads back into the ubiquitous sand, and then beginning again the cycle of water and prayer' (p. 104). The Muslim ritual of slaughtering the animal to obtain *halāl* meat also receives derisive comment, saying: 'animals to be killed slowly, by bleeding, so that by experiencing their deaths to the full they might arrive at an understanding of the meaning of their lives' (p. 364).

Muslims could have forgiven him for giving the two main characters in the novel the names of the Angel Gabriel (as Gibreel Farishta) and the Muslim hero Ṣalāḥuddīn Ayyūbī (as Saladin Chamcha) albeit in a derogatory form meaning a sycophant, a spoony. (It is to be noted that the Angel Jibrīl is one of the leading-most angels responsible for bringing down the revelation to all the Prophets, and Ṣalāḥuddīn Ayyūbī is the great champion of Islamic *Jihād* who defeated the Crusaders and liberated the *Masjid Al-Aqṣā* from the Christians.) However, they cannot forgive the gratuitous and obscene attack on the life of the Prophet, his family and Companions.

In condemnation of such profanity, Muslims of all shades, with the exception of a few of Rushdie's friends like Tariq Ali and Hanif Qureshi, have come forward with one voice, with great solidarity and unison. It is not surprising that an open-minded Muslim like Dr. Zaki Badawi – who evoked the scathing criticism and even wrath of the Muslim community for his offer of asylum to Rushdie and who on Christmas Eve 1990 took part in the drama whereby Rushdie embraced Islam at the hands of the Egyptian Minister of Endowment – regards Rushdie's book 'like a knife being dug into you – or being raped yourself'.[5] He further holds that what Rushdie has written is 'far worse to Muslims than if he's raped one's own daughter'.[6] Similarly, the Tanzanian scholar, Professor Ali Mazrui, during his visit to Pakistan in November 1988, was particularly struck by the analogy given by some

Pakistanis to the blasphemy contained in Rushdie's book: 'It's as if Rushdie had composed a brilliant poem about the private parts of his parents, and then gone to the market place to recite that poem to the applause of strangers, who invariably laughed at the jokes he cracks about his parents' genitalia – and he's taking money for doing it.'[7] It is also in this spirit that Shabbir Akhtar wrote: 'Any Muslim who fails to be offended by Rushdie's book ceases on account of the fact to be a Muslim.'[8]

In a similar tone, Ziauddin Sardar and Merryl Wyn Davies were obliged to write: 'By reducing the Prophet to a caricature, embodied in the persona of an object of fear and loathing, by abusing him and his Sunnah in the most vicious and violent manner, he has tried to destroy the sanctity of the Prophet as a paradigm of behaviour; *it is as though he has personally assaulted and raped every single believing Muslim man and woman!*[9] (italics ours).

It is clear from the above that it is not freedom of expression or freedom to question or even freedom to criticize or offend that Muslims are objecting to. It is rather the sheer slander, the abuse, the use of obscene and foul language, and the outrageous liberties which Rushdie has taken with Islam and its Prophet that has distressed and outraged Muslims. This is what has compelled them to take their own desperate steps of protest. It is in the nature of their faith that Muslims must not abuse or injure the feelings of others, nor should they tolerate any provocative and obnoxious attack on the person of the Prophet, his family members and his Companions. The love of the Prophet is not only the main criteria of *Īmān* (faith), it is the *raison d'être* for the existence of every Muslim. The Prophet is not loved superficially by paying lip service; his *Sunna* (the way of life) is internalized in every Muslim's behaviour.

The question is if Rushdie wanted to write on the theme of 'migration, metamorphosis, divided selves, love, death, London and Bombay', why did he provocatively name the book *'The Satanic Verses'*? Why did he, as Faruqi says, devote six out of nine chapters to an Islamic theme, Islamic symbolism and with real Islamic characters only thinly disguised by a mix of fantasy and the absurd? Why did he compound the blasphemy by using the derogatory synonym, coined in the European Middle Ages, of Mahound for the Prophet Muḥammad which by his own admission meant medieval baby-frightener and devil?[10] Could he not have spared his readers all this rubbish and filth? What else apart from a deliberate attempt to ridicule Islam and abuse the Prophet and everything sacrosanct to Muslims can explain the purpose of Rushdie's book? Not only Muslims but several non-Muslim scholars and critics also regarded Rushdie's book as filthy and non-readable. The *Washington Times* reviewer (13 February 1989) for example wrote: 'But having discovered no literary reason why Mr. Rushdie chose to portray Muhammad's wives as prostitutes, the Koran as the work of Satan and the founders of the faith as roughnecks and cheats, I had to admit to a certain sympathy with the Islamic leaders' complaints. True or not, slander hurts the slandered, which makes 'The Satanic Verses' not simply a rambling and trivial book, but a nasty one as well.'

Exposing Rushdie's blasphemy and calculated insult with malicious intent, Sardar and Davies rightly inform us that: 'Dreams are Rushdie's stratagem for presenting his own ideas about religion, monotheism, prophethood and, specifically, about Islam and its Prophet, without having to acknowledge the limits of propriety, respect for the sensitivity of others or the complexity of the historical record. Most of all, the dream stratagem enables him to play a game with historical fact, spicing the novel with a grand sufficiency of historical detail to establish his credentials without having to be responsible to accuracy, or honesty, in handling these facts.'[11]

It is claimed that the sequences Muslims found so objectionable in the novel happened in dreams to a character suffering a psychotic breakdown. But one wonders if the same things had happened to Christian and Jewish believers and their faiths, how such insults would be stomached? Would they let them go unchallenged in the name of freedom of expression? For example, if the Virgin Mary (God forbid) was portrayed as a prostitute and Jesus as an illegitimate child of one of her sexual clients and the Disciples of Jesus as a gang of homosexuals (given to gay orgies in the Garden of Gethsemane) or if Hitler was depicted as the Saviour of the Jews, would the Christian and Jewish communities tolerate, let alone passionately patronize such publications? Similarly, if the Queen was projected as a prostitute, and members of the Royal Family as debauchees with no morals, how would the British public react? As Professor Mazrui puts it admirably: 'It would be interesting to speculate which ones of the leading Western writers would march in a procession in defence of the rights of such a novelist.'[12]

Are we prepared to give such authors the right to blaspheme under the right to freedom of expression? Why then, one may ask, is Islam judged by a different yardstick? When a fictional film under the title 'International Guerilla' is released in Pakistan and is requested to be shown on British television, why is there such a hue and cry against it? Why did the distributor have to take recourse to the courts and why did it take several months for him to win his right to distribute the video in the UK? Is it not true that not long ago, in 1987, the management of London's Royal Court Theatre faced with the protests of some members of the Jewish community, abandoned its plan to stage Jim Allen's play *Perdition* which questioned the account of the Holocaust and injured the feelings of the Jewish community?[13] Have the present directors and administrators of Penguin publishing house forgotten that a whole Penguin edition of the French cartoonist Sines' book *Massacre* was literally burned by Allen Lane, one of Penguin's former chiefs, and declared out of print, as soon as he was told the book was regarded as blasphemous and offensive?[14] Why is it then, one may ask, when Penguin's Indian literary referee, Mr. Khushwant Singh, who is not a Muslim, let alone a fundamentalist, advised Penguin about the lethal nature of *The Satanic Verses* and recommended that it not be published, and if *The Independent*'s report is to be believed some British referees also endorsed this view, Viking/Penguin published this book? Is it that there is one rule for Islam and another for the non-Islamic world? Echoing a similar concern and supporting the voices of civility, Prof. John Vincent of Bristol University, as early as 2nd March, 1989 when the Muslim campaign was in its early stages, in *The Times* made the following incisive comments: 'In the case of blasphemy, that [the equality of law] is strictly untrue. We deny Islamic fellow subjects a remedy at law; we then chide them for contemplating remedies outside it. For Christians, the courts are open; to Muslims, suffering identical grievances, they are shut. It is a strange way to show the British sense of fair play.'

The Muslims' demand to withdraw the filthy book is not something unreasonable or unprecedented in civilized history.

Despite the sacred right to freedom of expression and freedom to publish, every civilized society enacts laws that restrict their freedom and keep it within the bounds of decency and fair play. Unbridled use or abuse of freedom has never been accepted as a norm by any civilized government or society. Among the many letters published in British newspapers during the controversy on *The Satanic Verses* Affair, one may quote a few lines from the perceptive remarks of Dr. Edward de Bono, which appeared in *The Times,* on 12th February, 1990: 'Civilisation is not solely defined by freedom, but by the way freedom is limited by responsibility, duties, compassion, and, when these prove inadequate, the law. The jungle is free – civilisation is not. Those who want the freedom of the jungle must also accept the retribution of the jungle without yelping.

The freedom to insult is matched by the freedom to feel insulted. Those who exercise power without restraint are bullies. Unlimited freedom to insult is not the mark of civilisation that is so strenuously claimed under the misleading banner of "freedom".'

It is no wonder that the final sentence of the concluding paragraph in the international PEN Charter of the World Association of Writers clearly holds: 'And since freedom implies voluntary restraint, members pledge themselves to oppose such evils of a free press as mendacious publication, deliberate falsehood and distortion of facts for political and personal ends.' Perhaps keeping this principle in view, Michael Ignatieff once commented that 'Freedom is not a holy belief, nor even a supreme value'.[15] It is in this vein that Shabbir Akhtar asked the question: 'Does the secular clergy have the right to canonise freedom of speech as an absolute value overriding all other relevant considerations?'[16] The answer cannot be but in the negative. Otherwise the whole range of restrictions on free speech in the UK such as 'the law on patents, copyright, contracts in restraint of trade, protection of trade secrets, intellectual property, misleading or dangerous advertisements and consumer protection, libel, slander, treason, conspiracy to commit crimes, incitement to commit crimes, official secrets, breach of confidence, obscenity, blasphemy, and incitement to racial hatred'[17] will be preposterous. Restrictions on publications such as *Spycatcher* in England, cancellation of plays like *Perdition,* suppression of Sinn Fein's voice over British radio and television, burning of loads of hard-core pornographic materials by customs officials and similar acts in the interest of public order, civility and government requirements are not unknown in the West. In fact such restrictions are regarded as necessary not only to maintain law and order, but decency, and peace in society. One of the recent examples set by the publishing magnate, Robert Maxwell, in pulping 20,000 copies of an offensive and blasphemous book, *True Faith,* is highly instructive. The book was supposed to be a comic-strip novel by Garth Ennis that offensively described God as 'a blockage in the world's toilet'. This was not only offensive and sacrilegious to Christians but also to Muslims and any believer who retained a belief in God. However, in this case, a letter of protest from the Evangelical Alliance was sufficient for Robert Maxwell to order Fleetway, one of his publishing companies, to pulp the entire stock and redress the grievance of the Christian group.[18] The recent controversy over *American Psycho,* the latest novel by B. E. Ellis, offending feminists in the United States, is also a case in point. One of the great champions of free speech and supporters of Salman Rushdie, astonishingly, Fay Weldon could not help voicing her protest against this *offensive* book. The perceptive comments of James Tweed on Robert Maxwell's willingness to withdraw the offensive book by G. Ennis without fuss or comment and the intransigent attitude of Viking/Penguin about withdrawing Rushdie's most outrageous book is worth mentioning.

'The Evangelical Alliance's letter could just as easily have been written by Muslim leaders about *The Satanic Verses.* What would have happened, one wonders, if Robert Maxwell had been Salman Rushdie's publisher?'[19]

The British Media and the Muslims

The Western media in general and the British media in particular, with rare exceptions, played a very negative game against Muslims and took the Rushdie saga as a golden opportunity to settle some old scores. In criticizing Islam they exceeded all norms of decency and vied with each other in painting an obnoxious picture conjuring up all the much-maligned images reminiscent of the Crusades. Its rage against Islam, as Bhikhu

Parekh puts it, 'escalated step by even sillier step to a wholly mindless anger first against *Bradford* Muslims, then against all *British* Muslims, then against all *Muslims,* and ultimately against *Islam* itself'.[20] Or as John Michell suggests, 'first the Muslims were inflamed against the West; hate-filled Western propaganda was then propelled against Islam'.[21]

Although the Muslims' campaign against the sacrilegious book from October 1988 onward evoked criticism and sometimes scathing remarks from the media, it was the book-burning incident on 14th January, 1989 in Bradford that ignited the hate campaign against British Muslims and Islam which was further accentuated by the late Ayatollah Khomeini's *fatwā* or death sentence on the author on 14th February, 1989. It is to be noted that Rushdie's book was also burned in Bolton on 2nd December (before the Bradford incident) but the media did not care to report it. Bradford turned out to be a special case. It is now amply documented that the Bradford incident was staged by certain sections of the media and a London solicitor was behind the 'arrangement'.[22] Naturally the 'ceremony' was properly filmed and broadcast the world over with vicious comments comparing Muslims with Nazis and labelling them as 'barbarians', 'uncivilized', 'fanatics', 'ignorant', 'bloodthirsty bigots' and 'medieval fundamentalists'. The people in the media knew very well that the Muslims' act of burning a copy of *The Satanic Verses* bore no resemblance to the Nazi burning of libraries and harassment of intellectuals and it was more in the nature of a desperate attempt to draw the attention of the media than an act of intolerance; they did not show any let-up in their campaign of vilification and denunciation of Islam and Muslims. It was painfully one-way traffic and all attempts by Muslim spokesmen to clarify the situation and present the Muslim viewpoint in the print and electronic media were frustrated. Both the tabloid and quality papers joined hands in mocking the Muslims, accusing them of intolerance and, as Bhikhu Parekh puts it, 'wondered if a tolerant society should tolerate the intolerant'.[23] The London literati, in the words of Malise Ruthven, 'shared a crusading outrage at Muslim desecration of the temple of free speech',[24] and consequently planned to hurl all sorts of calumnies against Islam and disparage the British Muslims. In an article entitled 'The New Appeasers Who Bow to Mecca', Stephen Vizinczey (*The Sunday*

Telegraph, 19th March, 1989), for example, accuses: 'booksellers all over Europe and North America are being terrorised into hiding the novel', and further asserted, 'what is at issue is the militant Islamic right to dictate to us what we can read, write, print, distribute and display.'

Clifford Longley, the respected religious correspondent of *The Times* (29th December, 1990) asserted that the paradox of Islam is that it 'knows how to treat minorities – but it does not know how to be a minority'. He did not hesitate to give a *fatwa* on British Muslims, saying: 'They need to be able to incorporate into the Islamic tradition of religious tolerance the Western (and by no means un-Islamic) principle that to compel a man against his conscience, or to punish him for his religious thought, is one of the most abhorrent of crimes. Once past that watershed, Islam has a healthy future as a Western religion. *If not, it has no future here at all*' (italics ours).

An appalling example of the madness shown by the self-appointed standard-bearers of 'reason', 'tolerance', and 'objectivity' is typified in *The Times* editorial 'A Greater Evil' (6th February, 1990). Apart from accusing in a hysterical tone the Muslim campaign leaders of acting on behalf of 'foreign (read Iran) paymasters' it goads the British government with all the urgency at its command to stiffen immediately laws for punishing the Muslim campaigners. Since even this would not placate the hurt ego and the suggested legislation might take some time, here is the interim solution offered without any qualms of conscience: 'Meanwhile any Muslim troublemaker without full British citizenship should be expelled from the country.'

Not surprisingly, the editorial contains not a single reference to the outraged Muslim sensitivities.

In an earlier editorial, 'Race, Religion and Rushdie', *The Times* (25th July, 1989) emphasizing learning of English for British Muslims, pronounced the following edict: 'British Muslim children should know their Koran: of course, but *they should also know their Shakespeare*' (italics ours). As if Muslim children were not going to the same school, following the same syllabus with English as one of the core subjects.

About the Muslim demand for abandoning the paperback edition of *The Satanic Verses,* the loaded imagery employed in *The Independent* (6th February, 1990) is worth noting: 'Without doubt it would be an *intolerable victory* for the *book-burners* if Mr. Rushdie or his publishers were to be *bullied* or *morally blackmailed* into abandoning publication against their will.'

Robert Kilroy-Silk, a regular columnist in *The Times,* holds the unenviable distinction of consistently provoking both the British public and government for a tougher, harsher stand against British Muslims whom he brands as 'resident Ayatollahs'. For him there is nothing racist in his belief that 'if Muslim immigrants cannot and will not accept British values and laws then there is no reason at all why the British should feel any need, still less compulsion, to accommodate theirs' ('Defending Ethnic Majorities', *The Times,* 17th February, 1989). Needless to say, the tenor of such utterances smacks not only of racism but of fascism too.

Anthony Burgess in *The Independent* (16th February, 1989) did not hesitate in comparing Muslims to Nazis who, according to him, shame Britain 'through the vindictive agency of bonfires'. In a patronizing tone he advised them to 'fly to the arms of the Ayatollah or some self-righteous guardian of strict morality', rather than staying in secular Britain.

In line with the media assault on the British Muslims was its hounding of Dr. Runcie, the then Archbishop of Canterbury, for his appeal to the BBC to not show Harrison's offensive 'The Blasphemous Banquet'. *The Daily Telegraph* (11th August, 1989) was quick to exhort Dr. Runcie that the Church 'cannot in any circumstances counsel accommodation with evil' (read the British Muslims' protest against *The Satanic Verses*).

Against this backdrop how ironic looks this patently self-deceptive statement: 'tolerance is now the prevailing code of West European society' (*The Independent,* 20th July, 1989). For who on earth can reconcile this flaunted spirit of tolerance with Norman Stone's impassioned war cry: 'The Mahdi is the enemy of mankind, and particularly of womankind, and we need all the allies we can get. The world as a whole must unite to make sure that fundamentalist Islam does not get away with it' ('We Need Russian Help Against Islam', *The Sunday Telegraph,* 19th February, 1989).

Even all these hysterical pieces pale into insignificance as one reads the delirious writings of Fay Weldon, a British novelist of a sort, now better known as a notorious activist on Rushdie's behalf. Her venomous raving about Islam, the Qur'ān and

Muslims falls nothing short of sheer abuse uttered with mindless crudity. Take these excerpts from Weldon as instances in point: 'The Koran is food for no-thought. It is not a poem on which society can be safely or sensibly based. It forbids change, interpretation, self-knowledge or even art, for fear of treading on Allah's creative toes . . . (The Qur'ān) gives weapons and strength to the thought police . . . My great complaint [is] against the God of Islam, this God of vengeance, wrath and occasional forgiveness, who rules by terror and threat . . . The Koran, the extraordinary piece of verse gives the believer permission to hate the unbeliever. *The Satanic Verses,* the other extraordinary piece of poetry, does not, oddly enough, give permission to hate' (Fay Weldon, *Sacred Cows,* London, Chatto & Windus, 1989).

In a similar crusading tone but full of venom and rancour one can see the *Daily Star* (21st February, 1989) screaming about the Ayatollah in foul language: 'Isn't the world getting sick of the ranting that pours non-stop from the disgusting foam-flecked lips of the Ayatollah Khomeini? Clearly this Muslim cleric is stark raving mad. And more dangerous than a rabid dog. Surely the tragedy is that millions of his misguided and equally potty followers believe every word of hatred he hisses through those yellow-stained teeth. The terrifying thing is not that a lot of these crackpots actually live here among us in Britain, but that we are actually becoming frightened of them. The whole thing is crazy. And it has to stop.'

To conclude this discussion it will not be inappropriate to quote a paragraph from Prof. Bhikhu Parekh's insightful and perceptive evaluation of 'The Rushdie Affair and the British Press': 'As happens so often in "tribal" England', he commented, 'it [the national press] instinctively ganged up against the Muslims, mocking, abusing, ridiculing and morally bludgeoning them into silence. With several honourable exceptions, the racism of many a journalist was just below the surface. They attacked not just the protest, which they were entitled to do, but the entire Muslim community as barbarians unfit to be citizens of a civilized society. The widely used and never clearly defined term "fundamentalism" became a popularly accepted disguise under which racism masqueraded itself. Catholic, Jewish and Anglican fundamentalism were acceptable, but not Muslim. Every Muslim parent who disapproved of sexual permissiveness, mixed sports or girls wearing shorts was dismissed as a fundamentalist. The term became a devious device for blackmailing Muslims into rejecting their values. Hardly any liberal realized that in countering Muslim "fundamentalism", they were setting up a rival fundamentalism of their own and corrupting the great liberal tradition. Historically speaking, whenever liberalism has felt frightened and nervous, it has tended to become aggressive and intolerant. The Rushdie affair was no exception.'[25]

The Story of Rushdie's 'Conversion' to Islam

On Christmas Eve, 24th December 1990, Rushdie dramatically declared his acceptance of Islam at the hands of six Egyptian Muslim scholars led by the Egyptian Minister of *Awqāf* Dr. Muhammad Ali Mahgoub. For several weeks prior to this news had filtered through of Rushdie's discussions with some unnamed Muslim leaders, who had apparently assured him that the Iranian *fatwā* could be lifted and that the matter would be resolved to Rushdie's satisfaction. Muslim leaders up and down the country denounced this report as 'malicious propaganda' and as an attempt to dent Muslim unity.

However, following the Muslim community's demand, a Harley Street dentist, Dr. Hesham el-Essawy, emerged from 'hiding' and claimed in the newspapers that he had had a very interesting and frank discussion with Mr. Rushdie over the telephone and that Mr. Rushdie's views about Islam had undergone considerable change. It was Dr. el-Essawy who prompted Rushdie to embrace Islam and set up the 'stage' in which two Egyptian Imams, of London's Regents Park Central Mosque, were also involved. The other Muslim 'scholars' involved were Dr. Zaki Badawi, the first secretary of the Egyptian Embassy in London and el-Essawy himself. Hesham el-Essawy also asked Dr. A.A. Mughram Al-Ghamdi, the Director General of the Central Mosque and the Islamic Cultural Centre, to allow him to stage the 'ceremony' in the Central Mosque. Dr. Ghamdi, being the Chairman of the UK Action Committee on Islamic Affairs and the Central Mosque being the headquarters of the Action Committee, could not but give a scornful refusal. The ceremony, however, is reported to have taken place in a hotel and the following statement purporting to affirm Islam was released by Rushdie and countersigned by the six witnesses present:

'In the presence of His Excellency the Egyptian Secretary of State for Endowment and the Head of the Supreme Council of Scholars of Islamic Affairs, Dr. Muhammad Ali Mahgoub, and a group of Islamic scholars:

1. To witness that there is no God but Allah and that Muhammad is His last Prophet.
2. To declare that I do not agree with any statement in my novel *The Satanic Verses* uttered by any of the characters who insult the Prophet Muhammad or who cast aspersions upon Islam or who question the authenticity of the Holy Qur'ān, or who reject the divinity of Allah.
3. I undertake not to publish the paperback edition of *The Satanic Verses* or to permit any further agreements for translation into other languages, *while any risk of further offence exists.*
4. I will continue to work for a better understanding of Islam in the world, as I have always attempted to do in the past.'

Under normal circumstances, Muslims would have rejoiced at Rushdie's return to Islam and at seeing a conclusion to this painful episode. Indeed, the Muslim community initially welcomed the news, regarding it as a step in the right direction, but soon their joy turned into dismay when they discovered that there was no mention of the hardback edition of the offensive book and that the statement regarding the non-publication of the paperback edition was hedged round an ingenious ploy – 'while any risk of further offence exists'. Their dismay was further heightened when they saw Rushdie not only defending the hardback edition of *The Satanic Verses* but also giving a completely false statement on BBC1 Television (News at Nine, 24th December, 1990) to the effect that the Egyptian Muslim scholars did not regard his book as offensive, and implying that had they done so, he would have considered withdrawing it from circulation.

It is on record, however, that not only did those same Muslim 'scholars' regard Rushdie's book as highly offensive, but that they also asked him during the course of their meeting to withdraw the hardback edition as well. He lied to them, saying he could not withdraw the book as it rests within the domain of the publisher and he had no control over its sale and distribution. Shaikh Jamal Manna Ali Solaiman, the Chief Imam of the Central

Mosque, London, who was one of the witnesses to Rushdie's conversion, was obliged, the following day, to issue a 'statement of clarification' declaring categorically that 'at no time in the meeting was it accepted that the novel was inoffensive to Islam' and that 'he strongly urged the publishers and all concerned to withdraw that offensive novel from circulation'.[26]

Rushdie, on the other hand, was not only apologetic but evasive in his reply in the same News programme. John Humphries asked him about his conversion to Islam. Rather than simply saying 'Yes', he replied in a long-winded answer that he had 'moved closer and closer to an engagement with religious faith' and that he had 'no quarrel with the central tenets of Islam'. Perhaps this prompted Frances de Souza, the Chairwoman of the Rushdie Defence Committee, to state (*The Times,* 27th December, 1990) that 'Salman Rushdie feels very strongly that he has not necessarily changed his position' and that is why 'he has talked about embracing the religion. Conversion is not the word he has used.'

Faced by criticism from friend and foe alike, Rushdie published an 'apology' the following day (i.e. Friday, 28th December) in the form of a clarification in *The Times* with the title 'Why I have embraced Islam'. Once again he played with words, showed his mastery of jugglery, and repeated the same lies he had expressed on television. In short, he showed no remorse at the offence caused by the publication of his sacrilegious book. He tried to dupe the readers once again by saying that '*The Satanic Verses* was never intended as an insult; that the story of Gibreel is a parable of how a man can be destroyed by the loss of faith'. And again, 'the six scholars and I agreed that the controversy of *The Satanic Verses* was based on a tragic misunderstanding, and we must all now work to explain to Muslims everywhere that neither I nor my work have ever been inimical to Islam. As to the question of total withdrawal of the book, I would say this. In spite of everything, *The Satanic Verses* is a novel that many of its readers have found to be of value. I cannot betray them. Even more important is the recognition of Muslim scholars that the book is not a deliberate insult. Had they felt otherwise, I might well have thought again. As it is, I believe the book must continue to be available, so that it can gradually be seen for what it is.'

Seven days after Rushdie's embracing of Islam, his friend Hesham el-Essawy arranged an interview in London with Yasir

Farhan, an Egyptian correspondent of *al-Muslimūn,* the weekly magazine published from Saudi Arabia (18th January, 1991, issue No. 311). Instead of giving clear-cut and straightforward answers to the questions about whether or not he had embraced Islam, Rushdie once again gave long-winded and apologetic answers and refused to acknowledge that the book was in any way offensive. He not only refused to withdraw the book from circulation but denied having committed any offence through writing the sacrilegious book. The journalist who, with great hope, came to meet a repentant Rushdie, was naturally shocked and disappointed to see a defiant and apostate Rushdie.

To those Muslims who gave him the benefit of the doubt in his reported affirmation of Islam, it has now become crystal clear that Rushdie intended to play a dual game. On the one hand, seeking to please his supporters, an assorted group of secular intellectuals, by not withdrawing the hardback edition, and on the other the Muslims, by promising not to publish the paperback edition and further translations of his offensive book. His friends, Hesham el-Essawy and Zaki Badawi, have both told Muslims that since the act of one's 'embracing Islam' nullifies his past sins, Rushdie has now become 'pure' and that moreover he has made a great monetary sacrifice, £4–5 million, by undertaking not to publish the paperback edition. However, every Muslim knows, [as we made clear in the letters column of *The Independent* (Friday, 4th January, 1991)] that the author cannot be automatically absolved of the offence following his 'conversion' to Islam if the book remains in circulation and the author does not repent of having written it. Indeed, his affirmation of Islam becomes meaningless and the offence he has committed by writing and publishing *The Satanic Verses* continues if the book stays in circulation in the form of hardback and translations.

This is why the UK Action Committee on Islamic Affairs and other organizations regarded Rushdie's conversion and statements as 'a disingenious ploy to bail out the unrepentant author . . . without meeting any of the concerns of the Muslim community and indeed dismissing it and mocking it as causing a "furore" over nothing'. As the Muslim community rightly explained, whereas Rushdie previously sought to achieve his means through the pen of an 'unbeliever', he now seeks the same ends as a self-appointed member of the Muslim community.

Faced with such a clear response from the Muslim community which, unequivocally, dismissed his conversion to Islam and rejected also by some of his erstwhile literati supporters, who not only regarded his Islam as a betrayal under compulsion but also as a reconciliation with that 'bigoted' creed which sentenced him to death, Rushdie rolled his dice once again. His attempt to ride on two horses has landed him nowhere.

To countenance his secular friends, he in effect refuted his pledge, hardly one week old, not to publish the paperback edition or further translations – he announced on BBC Radio 4's Sunday programme that 'these would go ahead when it could happen safely'. In his efforts to regain the Muslim community's sympathy he gave the glad tidings that he had not only received blessings from the Grand Shaikh of al-Azhar, the 'leader' of the Sunni Muslims of the world, but that he had also been invited by the Government of Egypt to receive these blessings in person, in Cairo. He also tried to appease Iran, by pleading his 'innocence' through the BBC world service Persian programme. Being frustrated in this attempt he tried to belittle the importance of Iran by reference to the Shi'a community, saying that it represents no more than 10 per cent of Muslims and that as such its intransigence matters little.

Rushdie's attempts to mislead the Muslim community were frustrated once again however when the official Egyptian Government spokesman on 1st January, 1991, refuted Rushdie's invitation claim as 'absolutely without foundation'. Confounded by this rebuff from the Egyptian Government and by the Muslim community's rebuke labelling his Islam 'as a ploy to get him off the hook', Rushdie, on Sunday, 6th January, 1991, made further overtures on an Asian radio phone-in programme broadcast by Sunrise Radio. Faced with extremely tough questioning by the callers, Rushdie was obliged to regret his earlier remark to the effect that he wished his book had offended Muslims more. In an obvious bid to placate the Muslim community, he offered to make a monetary contribution to the families of those that had been killed in the 1989 protest demonstrations against his sacrilegious book *if a fund were to be set up*.

On 17th January, 1991, *The Guardian* published a full-page interview of Rushdie with Dr. Akbar Ahmad, the visiting Iqbal Fellow at Cambridge University, England. Although there was nothing much new in the interview, it did appear that Rushdie is desperate to get out of the predicament as for the first time he expressed his 'difficulties' in withdrawing the hardback edition. He gave the following excuses for not being able to withdraw the book.

> First, in the real world, the book as an idea and entity cannot be withdrawn and, as it circulates more freely, to try 'to turn back the clock is unrealistic'.
>
> Secondly, after signing the contract with the publishers, Rushdie does not have the power to withdraw the book. It is therefore unreasonable to ask him to do something over which he has no control.
>
> Thirdly, if the book is withdrawn, it would 'be a celebrity' and become 'fantastically prominent again' and 'there would almost certainly be illegal, pirated paperback editions which would be impossible to control'.
>
> Moreover, in withdrawing the book, his 'reputation as a serious person in this country and in this civilization would be destroyed' and he would no longer be able to vociferously support Muslim rights 'ranging from Kashmir to Pakistan to racism in Britain'.
>
> And, most importantly, the withdrawal of the book could bring nothing but a 'catastrophic victory' for some leaders. The effect of the withdrawal, in Rushdie's view, 'would be to unleash against the Muslim community in this country a degree of hostility which would make everything that's happened in the last two years look like nothing'. He also forecast that the 'damage would last not for a week or two but for decades'.

Taking advantage of the statement of the two Imams of the Central Mosque, London (3rd May, 1991) who once again categorically rejected Rushdie's conversion and declared that Rushdie was and is an apostate who cannot be accepted as a Muslim until he has totally withdrawn the offensive book, Rushdie again through the letters column of *The Independent* (9th May, 1991) pleaded that his Islam was a matter of conscience and it was not for any human being to question it. He attacked the two

Imams for their statement alleging that they have done so 'under coercion and to save their jobs'. As far as his book is concerned since it is 'the product of a mixed tradition and seriously intended work of art', its 'withdrawal would be a disaster' and it will 'bring the controversy back to fever pitch'. He also revealed that on 24th December he agreed to suspend the paperback edition 'in the name of peace' and not by way of any repentance, as some people may have deduced.

Muslims regarded his 'explanations' for not withdrawing the offensive book as totally unacceptable and a clever attempt to confuse the Muslim mind. Rather than addressing the central issue of forthright withdrawal of the book squarely and unequivocally, which is a constant source of anguish in the Muslim community and against which they have been campaigning ever since its publication, once again the author tried to evade the issue and made it look so complicated. There cannot be any dialogue with Rushdie over the issue whether the book should be withdrawn or not. That the book is highly offensive and the author has committed the crime of abusing the Prophet *(sabb al-Nabī/Shatm al-Rasūl)* is not only maintained by Iran but also by more than 46 member states of the Organization of Islamic Conference (OIC) at the Foreign Ministers' Conference held in Riyadh in March 1989. The fact that almost all Muslim and several non-Muslim countries have banned this outrageous book is yet another proof in support of the Muslim demand. As the Muslim community have made clear time and again, far from absolving his sin, Rushdie's crime becomes all the more grave if he claims to be a Muslim and continues to insult the Prophet and Islam through the continued circulation of the book in hardcover and translations.

It is interesting to note that Marianne Wiggins, Rushdie's wife, in an interview with *The Sunday Times* (31st March, 1991) accused him of being 'vain and self obsessed'. She said 'the only cause he had promoted in his two years in hiding was himself. While others campaigned in his name for freedom of expression, he was concerned solely with his career'. She further revealed that 'on the eve of war in the Gulf, he was talking of greeting Colonel Gadaffi of Libya in an attempt to save his life'. Referring to his 'conversion' to Islam, she said 'this is a man who announced his very, very private religious conversion in an extraordinarily public way and then takes umbrage and exacts an emotional price from anyone who speaks about him in public. He is not the bravest man in the world but will do anything to save his life', she said. There is hardly anything strange in this as in an earlier article in *The Times* (11th February, 1990) we have seen Robert Harris commenting about an unpleasant smell of money hanging over all this. 'Mr. Rushdie', Harris rightly wrote, 'has made well over £1m from *The Satanic Verses.* To cash in on his predicament by asking exorbitant fees to defend his right to speak does not help his case, especially given the enormous sums already demanded of the British taxpayer for his round-the-clock protection . . . Unfortunately one of the characteristics of his "brilliant polemic" is to drip vitriol on anyone – writers, bishops, journalists, historians, politicians – who dared criticise him. Such raw sensitivity to offence is, to put it mildly, curious in a man who reserves the right to offend 800m Muslims and who cheerily pins on people names like "Mrs. Torture" ' [a reference to Mrs. Thatcher].

However, Rushdie's overtures remain meaningless unless his sacrilegious book is completely withdrawn and Rushdie has proved by his actions that he is a genuine believer in Islam and the Prophet's honour. Otherwise, as a *Newsweek* report puts it, his 'embrace of Islam flummoxed both friend and foe' (14th January 1991, p. 53), and would remain an exercise in futility.

The *Fatwā* and the Law of Sacrilege

For Muslims of all times and all places the Prophet Muḥammad (peace be upon him) stands out as a model *par excellence* – his life *(Sīra)* being the ideal to approximate, his sayings *(Ḥadīth)* to follow and his practices *(Sunna)* the paradigm to emulate. Utmost devotion to and fervent love of the Prophet has consistently been a prominent trait of every Muslim, from the Prophet's Companions *(Ṣaḥāba)* in early Islam to present-day Muslims. Since the Prophet through his word and deed demonstrated what the Divine Will fundamentally is, his example is a basic source of Islam, next only to the Qur'ān. In the Islamic scheme of things, to follow the Prophet is synonymous with obeying God and thus the way for attaining success in the Hereafter.

Of the numerous Qur'ānic verses describing the exalted position of the Prophet, a few are quoted below:

(i) The Prophet is closer to believers than their own selves. (*al-Aḥzāb* 33: 6.)

(ii) Whoever is an enemy to Allah and His angels and prophets, to Gabriel and Michael, Allah is an enemy to those who reject Faith. (*al-Baqara* 2: 98.)

(iii) Those who annoy Allah and His Messenger, Allah has cursed them in this world and in the Hereafter, and has prepared for them a humiliating punishment. (*al- Aḥzāb* 33: 57.)

The Islamic religious texts abound in exhortations to follow and honour the Prophet as much as a Muslim can possibly do. The love of the Prophet is ingrained so deeply and indelibly on a Muslim's heart that any disrespect to him is simply unacceptable, nay unimaginable. And any Muslim would be proud to sacrifice his life, his precious possessions and all that he has in defending the Prophet's honour, should it be demanded of him. Indeed in one of the Traditions of the Prophet, the perfection of faith has been made conditional upon the love of the Prophet which takes precedence over the love of one's parents and even one's own self.

In view of the pivotal position the Prophet holds in both theoretical and practical varieties of Islam, Islamic law prescribes a deterrent penalty – death, for the loathsome crime of abuse or insult hurled at the Prophet (*sabb al-Nabī* or *Shatm al-Rasūl*). And this crime is regarded as such a heinous one that, according to some schools of Islamic law, the *Shātim* (one who abuses the Prophet) cannot be reprieved, even if he repents and resolves not to repeat his crime. The remarkably categorical tenor of the punishment for this offence is worth noting, for in other cases involving murder, the convicted person stands a chance of being pardoned by the victim's heirs.

Against this background, it is understandable why Muslims the world over felt so outraged at the publication of Salman Rushdie's *The Satanic Verses.* Immediately after the publication of the offensive book in September, 1988, Muslims in Britain and elsewhere launched their campaign against the book under the auspices of the UK Action Committee on Islamic Affairs and other representative bodies. This was a clear proof that the book had hurt the feelings of Muslims and they found it not only deeply offensive but sacrilegious. Hence they were justified in demanding that the book should be withdrawn and a public apology by the publisher and the author be given and the remaining copies be pulped with the undertaking that it would not surface again in any form or language. Exercising their democratic right they protested to the publisher through telephone messages, letters and finally through peaceful and dignified demonstrations followed by memorandum and vigil. Muslims were determined to keep their campaign within the law and not be provoked by any incitement or external interference which was proved by the very fact that there was not a single threat on record to Rushdie or the publisher by the Muslim community prior to the issuance of the *fatwā* by Ayatollah Khomeini on 14th February, 1989.

In the initial period of four months of protest before Rushdie went into hiding, Muslims in Britain were restrained in their resentment against the book and kept their protests within the boundary of the British law and generally remained calm even after the Iranian *fatwā*. However, in a few demonstrations staged by Muslims, some people did shout abuse against Rushdie, but these were in the nature of symbolic outbursts of anger of some individual Muslims which were more in protest against the apathy of the British government in not taking serious note of the Muslim protests than anything else.

Though the timing of Imam Khomeini's *fatwā* on 14th February, 1989 was a surprise to British Muslims, its substance was not. For, the leaders of the Muslim community and the *'ulamā'* new very well that according to Islamic law, abuse and insult of the Prophet (*sabb al-Nabī* or *Shatm al-Rasūl*) was a crime, a capital offence punishable by law. This crime is considered as transgressing the limits *(ḥudūd)* and is worse than treason which clearly constitutes a *ḥadd* offence.

There is some difference of opinion among jurists on the issue whether or not a true repentance of the blasphemer nullifies the death sentence or *ḥadd*. According to the Ḥanafī and Shāfi'ī schools of law, the offender may be given a chance to repent and if he does so sincerely, the sentence may be waived. However, they emphasize that if the blasphemer is found committing the same crime again, his fate is sealed as there is no scope for the reprieve of such a person for a second time. According to the Mālikī and Ḥanbalī schools of *fiqh,* the offender must be given the *ḥadd* punishment irrespective of whether he makes any repentance *(tawbā)* or not. The same view has been held by Imam Ibn Taimiyya who holds that even if the *Shātim al-Rasūl* (blasphemer) repents, or converts to Islam in the case of a non-Muslim, he should not be reprieved.[27] The position from the Shī'a point of view has been made clear by the *fatwā* of Imam Khomeini. The government and *'ulamā'* in Iran have made it clear time and again that even though the author of the sacrilegious book converts and becomes the most pious person on earth, the death sentence pronounced by the Imam cannot be lifted. They have emphasized that repentance or *tawba* is strictly a matter of the *ākhira* (Hereafter) depending upon the sincerity of the repentance and acceptance of it by Allah *(subḥānahū wata'ālā)*. As far as this world is concerned the crime of sacrilege and profanity should not go unpunished.

It was also common knowledge as prescribed by Islamic law, that the sentence was only applicable where the jurisdiction of Islamic law applies. Moreover, the sentence has to be passed by an Islamic court and executed by the state machinery through the due process of the law. Even in Islamic countries, let alone in non-Muslim lands, individuals cannot take the law into their own hands. The sentence when passed, must be carried out by the state through the usual machinery and not by individuals. Indeed it becomes a criminal act to take the law into one's own hands and punish the offender unless it is in the process of self-defence.[28] Moreover the offender must be brought to the notice of the court and it is the court who should decide how to deal with him.[29] This law applies equally to Muslim as well as non-Muslim territories. Hence, on such clarification from the *'ulamā'*, Muslims in Britain before and after Imam Khomeini's *fatwā* made it very clear that since Islamic law is not applicable to Britain, the *ḥadd* punishment cannot be applied here.

As British citizens, Muslims are subject to British law and they have all along promised to keep their campaign within the framework of the law. It was the British media and people like Kilroy-Silk who provoked the Muslim community and labelled them as violent and bloodthirsty. Despite such provocation, Muslims remained calm and dignified and tried to express their anger and frustration within the framework of the law of the land. However, they have made it clear that as far as the legal position of the *fatwā* is concerned, they are not in a position to compromise or condemn it. They will neither take the law into their own hands, nor will they condone violation of the law on British soil. Even the unofficial spokesman of the Iranian revolution, Dr. Kaleem Siddiqi, has clarified more than once that under British law Imam Khomeini's edict cannot be implemented here and he himself would not attempt to kill the blasphemer.

The British and Western media violently abused the Muslim community and did not allow the authentic Muslim viewpoint to be voiced. A smokescreen of vilification and intimidation was created and the false impression was given to the world that the two million Muslims in Britain were up in arms and determined to kill Rushdie, who is not only a British subject, but a great champion of the freedom of expression and liberal values. Once again the power of the media prevailed and falsehood was so skilfully propagated that the British public was mesmerized into believing it. Hardly anybody cared to think that the Muslim community has long been under 'siege' and even their legitimate and democratic demands, such as the establishment of voluntary-aided schools, have not only been refused but frowned upon. Why is it so, Muslims ask, that there are over 2,430 voluntary-aided schools for Catholics, over 2,140 for Anglicans and over 20 for the Jewish community, and not a single voluntary-aided school for Muslims? What else except, perhaps, the policy of discrimination and intimidation can explain this unfortunate situation.

In *The Satanic Verses* affair, Muslims wanted to take recourse to the court but were told that the law of blasphemy is reserved for Anglicans and that it could not be extended to anybody else let alone to Muslims. Despite this, the British Muslim Action Front took the issue to court. The initial hope notwithstanding, the Muslim community was plainly told that they should not try to interfere with the blasphemy law as there is no way that their grievances can be redressed under British law. It remains to be seen whether the European Court of Human Rights entertains the case and makes any attempt to redress the Muslim grievances.

In one media manoeuvre, it was projected that it was Iran alone that condemned the book and the author and asked for appropriate steps to be taken and no other Muslim country or organization shared this view. It should be noted that long before the Iranian *fatwā,* the Grand Shaikh of al-Azhar, Shaikh Gad el-Haq Ali Gad el-Haq, in early December 1988 not only condemned the book as sacrilegious but called on the 46 member organizations of Islamic Conference to take action against this 'distortion of Islamic history'. He also appealed to Islamic organizations in Britain 'to join in taking legal steps to prevent the book's circulation'. Similarly, the Islamic Fiqh (jurisprudence) Council of the Muslim World League in late February 1989 described the language contained in the book as the most repulsive and abhorrent ever directed against Islamic beliefs and called for its global ban. The Council declared that the ideas expressed by the author do not fall within the ambit of freedom of thought but are a vicious attack and violation of all that is sacrosanct and as such a breach of law in all countries that respect the rights of others. Dr. Abdullah Naseef, Secretary General of the Muslim World League, called on the Organization of Islamic Conference to sue the author and publishing houses that print the book.

Although these leading organizations and the OIC Conference in Riyadh (March 1989) did not directly pronounce a *fatwā* they made it very clear in their deliberations that apostasy and vicious abuse of the Prophet does constitute a capital offence. Rushdie tried to avoid the punishment of apostasy by declaring that he was not a Muslim. However, it is not the crime of apostasy, but *Shatm al-Rasūl* (blasphemy against the Prophet) to which Rushdie remains accountable. Although, as mentioned earlier, there is some difference of opinion among different schools of Islamic law whether true repentance nullifies the punishment, there is no difference on applying the punishment to a blasphemer whether he is a Muslim or non-Muslim. Indeed the gravity of the crime becomes more serious if the *Shātim al-Rasūl* (one who abuses the Prophet) happens to be a Muslim and continues to abuse the Prophet and his family through circulating and translating the sacrilegious book.

The only prospect for Rushdie would seem to be true repentance followed by an immediate and unconditional withdrawal of the book from circulation. If there is genuine repentance there should not be any hesitation in offering an unqualified apology to Muslims and seeking forgiveness from God Almighty. As far as the death sentence is concerned, there may be a possibility that if circumstances completely change and the matter is referred to the *'ulamā'*, they might consider a fresh ruling, especially when the Ḥanafī and Shāfi'ī schools keep the door of *tawbā* open. It is the domain of the qualified scholars and *mujtahids* alone to pronounce a new judgement if necessary and guide the Muslim community. It is certainly not for the individual or Muslim leaders to lift the sentence, as it is not within their jurisdiction and it was not they who issued the *fatwā* in the first place.

Notes

1. See, among others, Atam Vetta, 'A contract with the Devil', *Impact International,* 23rd February – 8th March, 1990, pp. 5–8; Ziauddin Sardar and Merryl Wyn Davies, *Distorted Imagination: Lessons from the Rushdie Affair,* London, 1990, Chapter Six, 'Deconstructing Satan', pp. 142–83; Shabbir Akhtar, *Be Careful with Muhammad: The Salman Rushdie Affair,* London, 1989, pp. 13–36; Malise Ruthven, *A Satanic Affair: Salman Rushdie and the Rage of Islam,* London, 1989, pp. 16–53; Ali A. Mazrui, *The Satanic Verses or A Satanic Novel?: The Moral Dilemmas of the Rushdie Affair,* New York, 1989, pp. 1–34.

2. For a full exposition of this outrageous story, see pp. 131–41 in this book where full reference to relevant sources has been provided. See also Ziauddin Sardar and Merryl Wyn Davies, *op. cit.,* pp. 147–53.

3. Annemarie Schimmel, *And Muhammad is His Messenger: The Veneration of the Prophet in Islamic Piety,* North Carolina, 1985, p. 66; Malise Ruthven, *op. cit.,* pp. 87–8; Shabbir Akhtar, *op. cit.,* p. 5; Ali A. Mazrui, *op. cit.,* who quotes the letter by H.V. Ravinder, *New York Times,* February 26th, 1989, 'The Week in Review', p. 22. For further details, see Gene R. Thursby, 'Rushdie, Rajpal and Religious Controversy in British India', *Proceedings of the Eleventh International Symposium on Asian Studies, 1989,* Hong Kong, 1990, pp. 423–34. The author also mentions two other blasphemous publications – one in Hindi entitled *Vichitra Jivan* (The Colourful Life: Some Strange and Mysterious Incidents from the Life of Muhammad Sahib), Agra, 1923; and an Urdu essay published in the Amritsar monthly journal *Risala-i-Vartman,* with the title 'Sair-i-Dozakh' (A Trip to Hell), May, 1927. Both publications along with the *Rangīla Rasūl* were confiscated and banned in British India by the Government.

4. James Piscatori, 'The Rushdie Affair and the Politics of Ambiguity', *International Affairs,* Cambridge, Vol. 66, No. 4, 1990, pp. 267ff.

5. *The Guardian,* 27th February, 1989.

6. *Ibid.*

7. Ali A. Mazrui, *op. cit.,* reproduced in Munawar A. Anees, *The Kiss of Judas: Affairs of a Brown Sahib,* Kuala Lumpur, 1989, p. 61.

8. Shabbir Akhtar, *op. cit.,* p. 35.

9. Ziauddin Sardar and Merryl Wyn Davies, *op. cit.,* p. 165.

10. M.H. Faruqi, 'Publishing Sacrilege is Not Acceptable', *Impact International,* 28th October – 10th November, 1988, pp. 12–14.

11. Ziauddin Sardar and Merryl Wyn Davies, *op. cit.,* pp. 157–8.

12. Ali A. Mazrui, *op. cit.,* p. 71.

13. G. Kaufman, *The Independent,* 1st March, 1989; Shabbir Akhtar, *op. cit.,* p. 124. For a detailed and insightful account of the suppression of Jim Allen's play *Perdition,* see. F. el-Manssoury, 'The Stranger-than-Fiction Case of Jim Allen's Suppressed Play', *International Journal of Islamic and Arabic Studies,* 4/2, 1987, pp. 63–7. It is intriguing to note that the same theatre which under Jewish pressure refused to stage the play *Perdition* proudly staged the offensive play *Iranian Nights* by Tariq Ali and Howard Brenton. This too at the height of the Rushdie affair and despite vehement protests from Muslims.

14. See Appendix IV, *The Position Statement of the UK Action Committee on Islamic Affairs.*

15. *The Observer*, 2nd April, 1989.

16. Shabbir Akhtar, 'Is Freedom Holy to Liberals? Some Remarks on the Purpose of Law' in *Free Speech.* Discussion Papers No. 2, CRE, London, 1990, p. 25.

17. Simon Lee, 'Free Speech and Religious Freedom' in *Law, Blasphemy and the Multi-Faith Society.* Discussion Papers No. 1, CRE, London, 1990, p. 4.

18. For a detailed account of this event, see James Tweed's report in *New Statesman and Society,* London, Vol. 4, No. 138, 1991, p. 19.

19. *Ibid.* Robert Maxwell is not the only example to record. In March 1989, a Chinese publishing house published a book entitled *Sexual Customs* in which the authors, Ke Le and Sang Ya, preposterously argued that minarets of mosques were phallic symbols, domes represented female breasts and the main purpose of a pilgrim's visit to Makka is to commit bestiality with camels. Following demonstrations and strong protests from Chinese Muslims, the Chinese government immediately banned the book and brought the saga to a peaceful conclusion (see for details, report in the national newspapers, also Shabbir Akhtar, *Be Careful with Muhammad,* p. 125).

In May 1991, Sa'id Habib, an Arab columnist of the London-based newspaper *Al-'Arab* outraged the Muslim community by impudently comparing Saddam Hussein with the Prophet, some of his Companions and the Prophet Jesus. As soon as a Muslim delegation under the auspices of the UK Action Committee on Islamic Affairs met the columnist and editor of the newspaper, they realized their mistake and immediately offered their unqualified apology for unwittingly offending the feelings of Muslims. The columnist not only resigned from his post, but published an apology in the same newspaper thereby closing the door of further speculation and misunderstanding (see *Al-'Arab,* 8th May, 1991; also the press release of UKACIA, 10th May, 1991).

20. Bhikhu Parekh, 'The Rushdie Affair and the British Press: Some Salutary Lessons', in *Free Speech,* Report of a Seminar, Discussion Papers No. 2, CRE, London, 1990, p. 65.

21. John Michell, *Rushdie's Insult,* London, 1989, p. 5.

22. Bhikhu Parekh, *ibid.*, p. 62. M.H. Faruqi, 'The Author as the Stooge', *Impact International,* 23rd February–8th March, 1990, p. 17.

23. Bhikhu Parekh, *ibid.*, p. 62.

24. Malise Ruthven, *A Satanic Affair,* London, 1990, p. 131.

25. Bhikhu Parekh, *ibid.*, pp. 71–2.

26. Indeed, later on, when the Muslim community advised the two Imams to disassociate themselves from Rushdie's so-called conversion to Islam and declare categorically that his conversion was not genuine, they did so on Friday, 3rd May, 1991 before a large congregation at the Central Mosque, London. They not only apologized for their mistake in witnessing the ceremony of Rushdie's conversion to Islam but clearly said that 'what Salman Rushdie has done [by embracing Islam] has not changed the previous judgement on him as an apostate for he has expressed no real and honest repentance translated into good deeds' (see the report in *The Independent,* 3rd and 4th May, 1991).

27. For a detailed analysis of the viewpoint of different schools of Islamic law on this issue see Qāḍī 'Iyāḍ, *Al-Shifā' bi-ta'rīf Ḥuqūq al-Muṣṭafā* and Shaikh al-Islām Ibn Taimiyya, *al-Ṣārim al-Maslūl 'alā Shātim al-Rasūl,* 1st edition, Hyderabad, Deccan, n.d.; Ibn 'Ābidīn, *Ḥāshiya Radd al-Muḥtār,* Dār al-Fikr, 1979 and 'Abd al-Qādir 'Awda, *al-Tashrī' al-Jinā'ī al-Islāmī,* Vol. I, Beirut, n.d. For an Orientalist's detailed response to the *fatwā* and related issues, see Bernard Lewis, 'Behind the Rushdie Affair', *American Scholar* (Washington, D.C.), Spring, 1991, pp. 185–96.

28. If a Muslim driven by his zeal to protect the honour of the Prophet takes the law into his own hands and kills the blasphemer, the Islamic law of *qiṣāṣ* or punishment for deliberate murder will not apply to him. He will however be punished for taking the law into his own hands and the Islamic court will decide what punishment should be meted out to such an offender.

29. However Islamic law allows Muslim governments to seek extradition of the one abusing the Prophet under the international law of extradition of criminals.

CHAPTER 2

Salman Rushdie: The Man and His Mind

"My Theme is Fanaticism"

by Salman Rushdie

Excerpts from his interview with Principal Correspondent, Madhu Jain.

Q. *When did you actually begin* The Satanic Verses?

A. Parts of the novel have been in my head since I first began to study Islamic history at the university 20 years ago. But I started work on the book in early 1984. I stopped after my first draft. I wasn't very happy with it and the Nicaragua trip came as a godsend. It gave me the chance to get away from my own internal situation. When I returned the problems jamming me had gone away.

Q. *The novel appears to be quite a fierce critique of Islamic fanaticism . . . .*

A. Actually, one of my major themes is religion and fanaticism. I have talked about the Islamic religion because that is what I know the most about. But the ideas about religious faith and the nature of religious experience and also the political implications of religious extremism are applicable with a few variations to just about any religion. In the beginning and the end of the novel there are other kinds of fundamentalism also. . . .

Q. *Some of the names you use are straight out of the Book, based on real characters in Islamic tradition; but others are made up. Why did you do that?*

A. I have changed names. I have given the name of an Egyptian temple, Abu Simbel, to the leader of Mecca. . . .

. . . The book is really about the fact that an idea or a new thing in the world must decide whether to compromise or not. Beyond that, the image out of which the book grew was of the prophet going to the mountain and not being able to tell the difference between the angel and the devil. . . .

Q. *Do you fear a backlash from the mullahs?*

A. Even *Shame* was attacked by fundamentalist Muslims. I cannot censor. I write whatever there is to write.

Source: *India Today* (New Delhi), 15th September 1988 – ' "My Theme is Fanaticism" '.

Read 'Satanic Verses' Before Condemning It

by Salman Rushdie

Dear Rajiv Gandhi: On Oct. 5, the Indian Finance Ministry announced the banning of my novel, "The Satanic Verses," under Section 11 of the Indian Customs Act. Many people around the world will find it strange that it is the Finance Ministry that gets to decide what Indian readers may or may not read. But let that pass, because at the end of the notification of the ban an even stranger statement appeared.

The ministry – I am quoting from the Press Trust of India's report – "added that the ban did not detract from the literary and artistic merit of Rushdie's work." To which I can only reply: Thanks for the good review.

The book was banned after representations by two or three Muslim politicians, including Syed Shahabuddin and Khurshid Alam Khan, both members of Parliament. These persons, whom I do not hesitate to call extremists, even fundamentalists, have attacked me and my novel while stating that they had no need actually to read it. That the government should have given in to such figures is profoundly disturbing.

A further official statement was brought to my notice. This explained that "The Satanic Verses" had been banned as a pre-emptive measure. Certain passages had been identified as susceptible to distortion and misuse, presumably by unscrupulous religious fanatics and such. The banning order had been issued to prevent this misuse. Apparently, my book is not deemed blasphemous or objectionable in itself, but is being proscribed for, so to speak, its own good!

This really is astounding. It is as though, having identified an innocent person as a likely target for assault by muggers or rapists, you were to put that person in jail for protection. This is no way, Mr. Gandhi, for a free society to behave. Clearly, your government is feeling a little ashamed of itself and, Sir, it has much to be ashamed about. It is not for nothing that just about every leading Indian newspaper has deplored the ban.

It is not for nothing that such eminent writers as Kingsley Amis, Harold Pinter and Tom Stoppard have joined International PEN and India's association of publishers and book sellers in condemning the decision. The right to freedom of expression is at the foundation of any democratic society, and at present, all over the world, Indian democracy is becoming something of a laughing-stock.

When Syed Shahabuddin and his fellow self-appointed guardians of Muslim sensibilities say that "no civilized society" should permit the publication of a book like mine, they have got things backward. The question raised by the book's banning is precisely whether India, by behaving in this fashion, can any more lay claim to the title of a civilized society.

Let us try to distinguish truth from falsehood in this matter. Like my zealous opponents, you will probably not have read "The Satanic Verses." So let me explain a few simple things. I am accused of having "admitted" that the book is a direct attack on Islam. I have admitted no such thing, and deny it strongly. The section of the book in question (and let us remember that the book is not actually about Islam, but about migration, metamorphosis, divided selves, love, death, London and Bombay) deals with a prophet – who is not called Muhammad – living in a highly fantastical city made of sand (it dissolves when water falls upon it).

He is surrounded by fictional followers, one of whom happens to bear my own first name. Moreover, this entire sequence happens in a dream, the fictional dream of a fictional character, an Indian movie star, and one who is losing his mind, at that. How much further from history could one get?

In this dream sequence I have tried to offer my view of the phenomenon of revelation and the birth of a great world religion; my view is that of a secular man for whom Islamic culture has been of central importance all his life.

Can the Finance Ministry really be saying that it is no longer permissible in modern supposedly secular India, for literature to treat such themes? If so, things are more serious than I had believed. From where I sit, *Mr Gandhi, it looks very much as if your government has become unable or unwilling to resist pressure from more or less any extremist religious grouping; that, in short, it is the fundamentalists who now control the political agenda.*

You know, as I know, that the real issue is the Muslim vote. I deeply resent my book being used as a political football; what should matter to you more than my resentment is that you come out of this looking not only Philistine and anti-democratic but opportunistic.

Mr. Prime Minister, I can't bring myself to address finance ministries about literature. In my view, this is now a matter between you and me. I ask you this question: What sort of India do you wish to govern? Is it to be an open or a repressive society?

Your action in the matter of "The Satanic Verses" will be an important indicator for many people around the world. If you confirm the ban, I'm afraid I, and many others, will have to assume the worst. If, on the other hand, you should admit your government's error and move swiftly to correct it, I will be the first to applaud your honorable deed.

[This widely published letter appeared in October 1988.]

Source: *Illustrated Weekly of India* – 'Please, Read 'Satanic Verses' Before Condemning It'. (Italics ours.)

'Simon Rushton' aka Salman Rushdie

Kashmiri ancestry, born in Bombay, a pale-skinned boy arrives at a Rugby public school at the age of 13. His father, Anis Rushdie, had brought him up 'in a very Anglophile and Anglocentric way'. Pale-skinned, back home he 'could easily pass for white among his compatriots', but Rugby was to prove a terrible shock to his 'very English obsession'.

He did not know how to eat the kipper in his breakfast. Everyone is watching and no one tells him how to handle this spiky fish. He takes a piece and chokes on bones. 'Suddenly in England I became Indian.' Not that he wanted to. Educated in a Bombay missionary school, he had come to England to shed his 'Indianness' and not to be told that no matter how pale your skin you are a 'b . . . . y Indian'.

This fishy initiation (apparently he had had no trouble with pork, ham or bacon) was to produce an everlasting scar on the young boy, Salman Rushdie's personality. He was determined to 'show them all' and his career has since been a continuous strip-tease, from soft to hard to harder and ever harder porn. He will not stop as long as the music and footlights were on. He will not only do what the Romans do, he would out-Roman them. He was also out to take revenge: on himself and his peers. 'Like in any American Jewish novel', his way of revenge was 'to be three times as clever'. And dirty!

Rushdie mastered the artless art of eating kipper and went on to develop his 'snobbish' and 'conservative' childhood personality. In 1965 he moved to King's, Cambridge. 'It was a very good time to be at Cambridge, 1965 to 1968. It started with sex and drugs and rock 'n' roll and ended with *les evenements*. I ceased to be a conservative under the influence of Vietnam war and dope,' Rushdie told Brian Appleyard.

Little has been said about his family background. From Rushdie's account, his father, Anis, had been a businessman who had inherited 'quite a lot of money and spent the rest of his life losing it'. When he died last year, apparently not quite happy with his celebrity son, there was little left in the bank. The son admits to having had a sometimes bloody relationship with his father and sharing a bad temper with him.

After graduating, Rushdie went on a visit to Pakistan. His parents had moved to Karachi for 'all kinds of terrible reasons' and 'half reasons . . . like finding husbands for my sisters', because 'they were beginning to sense discrimination in India'. Rushdie had been in England for seven years. 'He was beginning to lose his grip on his homeland' and 'felt nothing for Pakistan. In England he still felt like an alien'. Pakistan seemed worth trying.

The visit ended in dismay and frustration and he returned with a badly hurt ego. 'Full of Cambridge confidence' Rushdie had tried his luck with both television and journalism, but they would not let him use the word 'sex' or use pig as a character, he says. His first impressions of Pakistan had been rejected by the press censors. It must have been in terrible bad taste because those were the libertine days of Yahya Khan. Sad and rejected, Rushdie returned 'home'. He had one more cause to disprove that he was neither an Indian nor a Pakistani.

Rushdie now wanted to be a writer; not being one as yet, he earned his living by acting in fringe theatre, at the Oval House in Kennington, and by doing casual work with advertising agencies. We do not know about his theatrical achievements but in advertising 'he tended to submit more or less the same copy over and over again. He was felt to be heavy-going'. Or so they said, although he was also credited with coining the line 'Naughty but nice' for cream cakes. The slogan was rejected by the manufacturers because it seemed to link cream with obesity.

(A letter in *The Sunday Times,* 9th October 1988, said: The phrase is some 100 years old, and of American origin. The song entitled "It's naughty but it's nice" was popularised by Minnie Schult in the 1880s, and the catchphrase itself reached Britain soon after.)

Acting and experimenting with words, Rushdie met an English girl, Clarissa Luard. She had been working in what her 'mother would call fun things' – fashion, rock and pop. At that time both Rushdie and Luard 'were living with others' and 'for two years, they conducted a secret affair until, finally, they moved in together' into a house which belonged to Mrs Luard. They married in 1976.

Enter a lodger, Liz Calder, who worked in publishing at Gollancz. She mothered Rushdie's first published novel, *Grimus* in 1975. It proved a flop receiving dismissive reviews, but Rushdie has not yet 'showed them all'. Nor did he intend to give up. He finished *Midnight's Children* in 1979. Calder had moved to Cape.

Published in 1981, the *Children* was an instant success. You did not need a Kipling, a Foster or even Katherine Mayo, Colonel Blimp himself had arrived. An Indian and a more 'authentic' Colonel Blimp. The *Children* won Rushdie the $10,000 Booker Prize. He had been discovered and he had been launched.

There was a little mishap though about *Midnight's Children.* The late Indian Prime Minister Mrs Indira Gandhi had to be given a public apology by both Rushdie and his publishers in answer to her libel action. They also paid costs and gave an undertaking to remove from all future editions under their control the passages objected to by her.

Rushdie tried to do better in *Shame.* He took an aim on Pakistan, its political characters, its culture and its religion. Some you enjoyed, some you loathed and much you did not understand. Rushdie's style is dense and its import as clothed as a strip-tease dancer. 'There exists in London something called The Page 15 Club. It consists of literary editors, journalists, academics, novelists who have got no further than page 15 with Rushdie's books.'

Yet these things mattered little because he had been given the certificate of success. He had hoped to win the Booker Prize once more. He was cross when he did not and set about putting together his *Satanic Verses.* Combining all his skills in writing, acting and imagining and remembering his credo 'I will show them all', he has achieved an enormous success in outrage and sacrilege. If he does not get the Booker Prize, a second time this year, he can look forward to winning the Nobel Prize, next year or the year after that. There is no reason to assume that he is incapable of producing something, yet more filthy than his *Satanic Verses.*

Rushdie – 'His detractors anglicise his name to Simon Rushton' – has also been mobile with his women. The marriage with Clarissa Luard, mother of his nine-year-old son, Zafar, 'actually ended' in 1984, although they were formally divorced in 1987. He left Liz Calder who had launched him as a published novelist as well as his original agent Deborah Rogers.

From Cape he went to Viking-Penguin who will give him '$850,000 for two novels as an advance against royalties.' Rushdie also sacked his literary agent in America, Elaine Markson and replaced her with Andrew Wylie. Leaving Clarissa, he had an affair with an Australian writer, Robyn Davidson and is currently married to an American novelist, Marianne Wiggins.

Rushdie thinks 'there are two Salman Rushdies walking around town . . . and frequently when I meet people, I have to kill the one they think they know before they can see him'. Two into one like Salahuddin Chamcha and Gibreel Farishta, implying that *per se,* there is no evil and no good either. That is what *The Satanic Verses* is all about.

(Sources: 1, Salman Rushdie: 'Caught between two worlds' by Lloyd Grove, *The Guardian,* London, 26th May 1986. 2, 'Fishing for Salman' by Mark Lawson, *The Independent,* London, 10th September, 1988. 3, 'Portrait of the novelist as a hot property' by Brian Appleyard, *The Sunday Times Magazine,* 11th September 1988.)

Source: *Impact International,* 18/20, 28th October–10th November 1988 – ' "Simon Rushton" aka Salman Rushdie'.

The Satanic Mind

Throughout the Affair, particularly after Imam Khomeini's *fatwā,* Salman Rushdie was the focus of the Western media. Whatever he said, no matter how frivolous, was reported dutifully on prime time TV and figured quite prominently in the British dailies. As to the genesis of *The Satanic Verses* Rushdie offered often contradictory, rather opportunistic stances. Before the protest over its sacrilegious contents, Rushdie took great delight and pride in having taken up Islam and fundamentalism in his novel for he 'knew the most about it'. This stance is reflected at its best in his interview with the *Bandung File,* a Channel 4 TV programme, recorded on 27th January, 1989, that is before Imam Khomeini's *fatwā* but broadcast on 14th February, 1989, the day Imam Khomeini issued his *fatwā.* In his reply to the question how far his novel was based on the Qur'ānic text or Islamic history, Rushdie had the audacity to say: 'Almost entirely. Almost everything in these sections [the Chapter in *The Satanic Verses* dealing with Islam] starts from an historical or quasi-historical basis.' For as a historian studying Islam he had discovered in the case of Muḥammad (peace be upon him) his 'brief flirtation with a possible compromise about monotheism'. And here is how Rushdie the historian pieces together what transpired between the Prophet and Gibreel, the archangel who brought him revelations: 'When Gibreel comes to Mohammad and tells him that these verses are Satanic verses and should be removed – and here are the real verses – he forgave him. He [Gibreel] said, "Never mind, it is understandable, things like this have happened before" '. This great historian does not, however, indicate how he managed to retrieve this dialogue between the archangel and the Prophet after 1400 years. He is, however, quick enough to condemn his critics for such fanciful and pernicious ravings in the name of history. For he says: 'It seems that Gibreel is more tolerant than some of these people attacking the book'. Quite unequivocally he once again states the historical origin of *The Satanic Verses* rooted in Islamic history: 'At the very beginning of Islam you find a conflict between the sacred text and the profane text, between revealed literature and imagined literature . . . So that's what I was doing, exploring'.

He was brazen enough to claim: 'I get letters every day from Muslims who do like the book.'[1] He denounced the 'mullahs' for stage-managing the protest: 'I knew that very theocratic, medievalist Islam that is being pushed through the mosques was not likely to take very kindly to the book I was writing, but I didn't foresee a reaction on this scale. If you don't believe, and I don't, that some kind of disembodied supreme being sent an angel to dictate a book to a seventh century businessman named Mohammed, you are in trouble.'[2] He said if he had known that this book was going to produce such a reaction by Muslims, he would have penned a stronger and more 'critical' book on Islam. What he meant was that he would have gone even further in his insult and mockery of Islamic sanctities.

After the *fatwā* one notes a sea-change in Rushdie's position. Take this recanting of his word as an example: 'I recognise that many Muslims have felt shocked and pained, too.' Abandoning the self-appointed role of a historian of Islam in writing *The Satanic Verses,* he started invoking the privileges and protection of an artist. Look at his version of the freedom of expression: 'What is freedom of expression? Without the freedom to offend, it ceases to exist . . . Muslims are accustomed to satire as anyone else, why must a novel be proscribed for doing the same?' Entitled 'In Good Faith', Rushdie's piece is full of vendetta against things Islamic. Here is his harangue, distorting, discrediting and dismissing the Islamic law: ' . . . I would ask the following question: are all the rules laid down at a religion's origin immutable for ever? How about the penalties for prostitution (stoning to death) or thieving (mutilation)? How about the prohibition of homosexuality? How about the Islamic law of inheritance, which allows a widow to inherit only an eighth of share, and which gives to sons twice as much as it does to daughters? What of the Islamic law of evidence, which makes a woman's testimony worth only half that of a man? Are these too, to be given unquestioning respect.' It is followed by the declaration: 'I am a modern, and modernist, urban man, accepting uncertainty as the only constant, change as the only sure thing. I believe in no god, and have not done so since I was a young adolescent . . . To put it as simply as possible: I am not a Muslim.'[3] Then there was another somersault in that on 24th December 1990, he announced his 'embracing' of Islam in these words: ' . . . religion for me has always meant Islam . . . I am able now to say that I am a Muslim.'[4]

Notes and References

1. The complete text of this interview is published in *The Rushdie File* edited by Lisa Appignanesi and Sara Maitland, pp. 27–31.
2. 'The Devil Made Him Do It', *Newsweek,* 6th February, 1989.
3. 'In Good Faith', *The Independent on Sunday,* 4th February, 1990.
4. 'Why I have Embraced Islam', *The Times,* 28th December, 1990.

Divorce for Rushdie

by Graham Lord

Salman Rushdie is "very, very depressed" by his two-year captivity, says his estranged wife, American novelist Marianne Wiggins, who tells me she and Rushdie will divorce later this year. . . .

"He's so depressed, extremely down. He's isolated himself from his former friends and he's developed a very thin skin recently and can't take criticism.

"The man's career is incredibly operatic and he's very volatile . . . "

She denies that she now has a new man but says: "The rumours are rife about Salman, that he has several new women friends – and why not? . . . "

One friend who speaks to Rushdie once a week on the telephone admits: "He's not in too good a shape. He's far worse than he was and in greater difficulties now than he's ever been. . . . "

Source: *Sunday Express,* 24th March 1991 – 'Divorce Ahead for Rushdie After His Wife's Year of Pain'.

For further reading:

- Laura Shapiro with Donna Foote, 'The Devil Made Him Do It', *Newsweek,* 6th February, 1989.
- Salman Rushdie, 'In Good Faith', *The Independent,* 4th February, 1990.
- 'An Exclusive Talk With Salman Rushdie', *Newsweek,* 12th February, 1990.
- Salman Rushdie, 'Why I Have Embraced Islam', *The Times,* 28th December, 1990.
- Tim Rayment, 'Salman is Vain and Self-Obsessed, says Mrs. Rushdie', *The Times,* 31st March, 1991.

CHAPTER 3

In Defence of Sacrilege

Muslims – Nazis of Britain?

If members of Britain's community of some two million Muslims do not want to read Salman Rushdie's novel *The Satanic Verses,* all they have to do is abstain from buying it or taking it out of the local library. They should not seek to impose their feelings about its contents – or, more probably, what they have been told about them – on the rather larger non-Islamic part of the population. Their campaign to have the book banned, on the grounds that it blasphemes Islam, led to a demonstration over the weekend in Bradford in which, following the example of the Inquisition and Hitler's National Socialists, a large crowd of Muslims burnt some copies of the book. . . .

Source: ©*The Independent,* 16th January 1989 – 'Dangers of a Muslim Campaign'.

Not the Book but the Muslim Protest is Distasteful

If members of Britain's Moslem community wish to pay £12.95 for the privilege of burning a copy of Mr Salman Rushdie's The Satanic Verses in the privacy of their own homes, that is a matter for them. Many Christians who have struggled with Mr Rushdie's impenetrable novels will warm their hands at the fireside. But *the public campaign to expunge the offending work from the bookshops of Britain has aroused the widest dismay and distaste.* We may not be able to follow all that Mr Rushdie writes, but we defend absolutely his right to be read. It is doubly regrettable, therefore, that a chain of the size and influence of W H Smith should announce that it is withdrawing the book from two of its shops, except on special order.

Booksellers are perfectly at liberty to decline to stock books they themselves find blasphemous. But Sir Simon Hornby, for Smith's, makes no claim on that score. Nor is it a case that public appetite for the novel is slackening, since it continues to appear in the fiction best-seller lists, and we do not imagine that its presence there will be impeded by the present furore. W H Smith's talk of the risks to its premises and staff suggests, instead, the prospect of some kind of Islamic *jihad* against its shop windows.

The scenes in Bradford over the weekend presented an image of Moslem sentiment in Britain of the most unhelpful possible kind to race relations. In reality, we know that it is atypical. We note the hard work and enterprising spirit of the Moslem minority, their piety and devotion to family values. But the religious intolerance displayed by some factions is ominous. Salman Rushdie will not be the greatest author to provoke a religious backlash: compare the reaction, in 1643, to Milton's Tetrachordon, advocating divorce and polygamy. *Islamic religious leaders have two obligations: first, to maintain a sense of proportion about any perceived threat to their religion posed by Mr Rushdie; and second, to recall that, as citizens or residents of this country, they have a responsibility to respect the British tradition of free speech, not to react in the fashion of the ayatollahs.* W H Smith has the protection of the law. If it wishes to maintain the honourable name of booksellers in the community, then it has a duty to sell books that are lawful, and in demand from a far larger section of the community than that which seeks to banish them.

Source: ©*The Daily Telegraph,* 17th January 1989 – 'Right to be Read'. (Italics ours.)

Islam's Gangster Tactics

by Anthony Burgess

Evidently, there is a political element in the attack on *The Satanic Verses* which has killed and injured good if obstreperous Muslims in Islamabad, though it may be dangerously blasphemous to suggest it. The Ayatollah Khomeini is probably within his self-elected rights in calling for the assassination of Salman Rushdie, or of anyone else for that matter, on his own holy ground. To order outraged sons of the Prophet to kill him, and the directors of Penguin Books, on British soil is tantamount to a *jihad.* It is a declaration of war on citizens of a free country, and as such it is a political act. It has to be countered by an equally forthright, if less murderous, declaration of defiance.

Islam, like Genevan Calvinism, accepts the theocratic principle. The law of the state is the law of God: there are no crimes of purely secular import. If a thief is caught, he must suffer the severance of the hand that stole because the Koran says so. (The Koran also recommends mercy, a grace on which Khomeini insists rather little).

Great Britain has allowed the secular virtue of tolerance to prevail over religious rigour. This explains why our Muslims are permitted freely to exercise their faith so long as its code of behaviour does not conflict with civil law. We want no hands cut off here. For that matter, we want no ritual slaughter of livestock, though we have to put up with it.

I gain the impression that few of the protesting Muslims in Britain know directly what they are protesting against. Their Imams have told them that Mr Rushdie has published a blasphemous book and must be punished. They respond with sheeplike docility and wolflike aggression. They forget what the Nazis did to books – or perhaps they do not: after all, some of their co-religionists approved of the Holocaust – and they shame a free country by denying free expression through the vindictive agency of bonfires.

They have no right to call for the destruction of Mr Rushdie's book. If they do not like secular society, they must fly to the arms of the Ayatollah or some other self-righteous guardian of strict Islamic morality. They cannot have the privileges of a theocratic state in a society which, as they knew when they entered it, grants total tolerance to all faiths so long as those faiths do not conflict with that very principle of tolerance.

What applies to the United Kingdom applies equally to the United States. What a secular society thinks of the prophet Mohamed is its own affair, and reason, apart from law, does not permit aggressive interference of the kind that has brought shame and death to Islamabad.

Logic would seem to demand that the whole corpus of anti-Islamic literature in English should be placed in the hands of incendiary Muslims: the Guild Plays of the Middle Ages, for instance, in which Mohamed appears – as in *The Satanic Verses* – as Mahound, an atheistic force loosely identified with both King Herod and the Devil. If Muslims want to attack the Christian or humanistic vision of Islam contained in our literature, they will find more vicious travesties than Mr Rushdie's.

They had better look, for instance, at Edward Fitzgerald's *Rubáiyát of Omar Khayyám*. But nobody is interested in this issue historically or philosophically.

There is a little too much political opportunism in this picking on a recently published book which neither Iran nor Pakistan would read even if it could. One doubts the sincerity of protest that is secondhand and unjustified by argument, thought or anything more intellectual than the throwing of stones and the striking of matches.

It is not for me to question the manner in which Islamic theocracy conducts affairs on its own ground. I feel about Khomeini as I felt about Hitler before 1939: I may not like his domestic policy, but I have no grounds, other than those of common humanitarianism, for protest. I am within my rights, I think, in regretting that both his brand of Islamic fundamentalism and the equally intolerant fundamentalism of the American South have remembered nothing of the medieval subtleties of Averroës on the one hand and St Thomas Aquinas on the other. Neither religion used to be as crude as this. And I am even more within my rights in inveighing against an aggressiveness which denies to a free society its privilege of allowing its citizens to speak their minds without fear of brutal reprisal.

I do not think that even our British Muslims will be eager to read that great vindication of free speech, which is John Milton's

Areopagitica. Oliver Cromwell's Republic proposed muzzling the press, and Milton replied by saying, in effect, that the truth must declare itself by battling with falsehood in the dust and heat. Mohamed is presumably great enough to report a spiritual victory over misrepresentation by both theologians and novelists. *Islam once did intellectual battle. Now it prefers to draw blood. It seems to have lost its major strength only to resort to the tactics of the gangster.* This is unworthy of a major religion.

One wonders if even major religions, however sincerely held, should be allowed to prevail over those secular beliefs that no longer owe anything to theology – tolerance, charity, a sense of humour and a great deal of goodwill. There is something not very likeable about a faith that is so quick to order assassination.

I would much prefer that Khomeini argued rationally with the infidel West in the manner of the great medieval Arabs. But, instead of arguing, he declared a holy war against argument. His insolence is an insult to Islam.

Source: ©*The Independent,* 16th February 1989 – 'Islam's Gangster Tactics'. (Italics ours.)

Unite Against Islam!

by Norman Stone

. . . Islam is the religion, after all, of the ferocious Ayatollahs, of suicide-bombings and hostage-taking; of the Afghan sects, who, no doubt, will soon be meting revenge on collaborators with the Soviets. Salman Rushdie has learned this, in a very hard way. . . .

. . . The Mahdi is the enemy of mankind, and particularly of womankind, and we need all the allies we can get. The world as a whole must unite to make sure that fundamentalist Islam does not get away with it. . . .

Source: ©*The Daily Telegraph,* 19th February 1989 – 'We Need Russian Help Against Islam'.

Limits of Tolerance

There are few more difficult tasks, even or perhaps especially in a liberal democracy, than to define the limits of tolerance. A year after the Ayatollah Khomeini first pronounced sentence on Mr Salman Rushdie, the difficulties for the author, his publishers, and our own society have become no easier to reconcile. Mr Rushdie himself, with his huge conceit, fastidious distaste for Thatcherite Britain and impenetrable literary style, is an implausible hero for any save the likes of Mr Harold and Lady Antonia Pinter. Yet to almost all of us, Mr Rushdie's right to publish his book was, and remains, beyond dispute. If has been dismaying to behold British Moslems publicly echoing the murderous threats of the Iranians. Only a month or two ago, several hundred Moslems gathered in Walthamstow to vote that the death sentence against the author should "remain in place". One Dr Kalim Siddiqui has been strongly and openly associated with the call for Mr Rushdie's death.

To many of us, it has been acutely dismaying to see Moslems making threats in a fashion which, there can be little doubt, would have caused them to be prosecuted for incitement were they members of the more extreme white groups, such as the National Front. By adopting a "softly, softly" approach, the Government and the police have plainly sought to avoid a head-on confrontation. Yet it seems important to leave minority groups in Britain in no doubt about the limits of tolerance for behaviour of this sort. *If Moslem fundamentalism, and its bloodier manifestations, gain any hold in this country, they will have to be suppressed, employing the full vigour of the laws which were introduced to protect minority communities from racial harassment.*

We may all wish that Mr Rushdie had not written his book. But he has done so, and we should continue to defend his rights, as Mrs Thatcher and her Government have done with such credit. British publishers should encourage Penguin to proceed with the paperback edition. To flinch from publication now would be a surrender to those forces of fanaticism with which we cannot compromise, if we are to sustain the traditional values and licence of our own society. It is those values to which British Moslems must subscribe, however unwillingly, if they are to play a full part in British life, as we all wish that they should.

Source: ©*The Daily Telegraph,* 6th February 1990 – 'Limits of Tolerance'. (Italics ours.)

An Islamicist's Nightmare!

by Daniel Easterman

. . . Islamic law is not democratic: it is a system rooted in a series of supposedly infallible and unchallengeable texts, established by an elite body of scholars long since dead, and today interpreted and implemented by a similar elite. Shi'ite law is, if anything, less democratic than its Sunni equivalent: mujtahids achieve their positions, not by election, but by scholastic achievement. . . .

What would happen, then, if the law did allow the Muslim case against *The Satanic Verses* . . . fundamentalist zeal could draw up an ever-expanding list of additional titles for the attention of the courts. . . .

Now, what does that mean? For one thing, it means that books by Muslim heretics could be cited as blasphemous and banned in Britain. Studies by Muslim scholars challenging received wisdom about the Qur'an, *hadith,* Prophet, or law would meet the same censorship here as they already do in Iran, Saudi Arabia, or Egypt. Books by Baha'is – a group universally hated throughout the Muslim world – could be taken off the shelves in London or Edinburgh. Academic works on Islam would be scrutinized and, where found wanting, removed from university reading lists or libraries or bookshops. Older European texts deemed unflattering to Islam or Muhammad – Dante, Gibbon, Carlyle, Voltaire – could appear in bowdlerized editions.

Remember, this is not paranoia on my part: books like these are already banned in most Muslim countries on the grounds of blasphemy. Why on earth would anyone stop at *The Satanic Verses* if they had the power to regulate anything and everything written about Islam? . . .

Source: *Index on Censorship,* 4/90, pp. 9–11 – 'A Sense of Proportion'.

Rushdie Shemozzle is Attempt to Blackmail

Mary Kenny was last week surely mistaken for once. The Rushdie shemozzle is not just a matter of freedom of expression versus censorship. *Islam is trying to blackmail us, with its preposterous death sentence and hints that hostages might be freed and diplomatic relations be restored if we ceased to protect Mr Rushdie from its hit-men or at least consigned his book to oblivion.*

Why should Muslims expect their religion to be protected from attack? Christianity is frequently assailed, sometimes blasphemously, but we do not respond by threatening murder and burning books and bookshops. Indeed we expect our religion to be spoken ill of, since Jesus himself warned us that it would be. The proper reaction, we know, is to pity the blasphemer and pray for his salvation.

The lesson of the Rushdie affair is that it was unwise to let Muslim communities establish themselves in our midst. People talk glibly about a "multicultural society", but the expression is a contradiction in terms, since social cohesion depends on cultural consensus. Introduce alien cultures resistant to assimilation and you ask for trouble.

Society splits up into culturally disparate communities that are only held together by the State. Conflict may lie dormant for a time, but then something happens that puts the cat among the pigeons. The publication of Mr Rushdie's book was such a happening, and it let the cat out of the bag – in more senses than one.

G.B. Bentley,
5 The Cloisters,
Windsor Castle, Berkshire

Source: ©*The Sunday Telegraph,* 24th June 1990 – 'Rushdie Shemozzle is Attempt to Blackmail'. (Italics ours.)

The Philistines' Chapter and Verse

by Hilary Mantel

. . . What is more important is that without requiring any guarantees of Rushdie's safety, our government has recently resumed diplomatic relations with Iran. That is to say, it has shaken hands with the would-be murderers. Its attitude has always been suspect; now it is shameful. . . .

. . . And the rest of us, who thought that as we were British and under the protection of the law we were therefore free to speak and write as we liked, have been properly put in our place. "From now on, no one will ever dare to insult our holy prophet nor our dear Islamic values." . . .

Source: ©*The Independent on Sunday,* 30th December 1990 – 'The Philistines' Chapter and Verse'.

For further reading:

- Robert Kilroy-Silk, 'Meeting the Mob Half Way', *The Times,* 27th January, 1989.
- ——, 'Defending Ethnic Majorities', *The Times,* 17th February, 1989.
- 'Talking to Muslims', *The Times,* 27th February, 1989.
- Stephen Vizinczey, 'The New Appeasers Who Bow to Mecca', *The Sunday Telegraph,* 19th March, 1989.
- 'Race, Religion and Rushdie', *The Times,* 25th July, 1989.
- Robert Kilroy-Silk, 'When Will Christians Stop Being So Craven?' *The Times,* 1st September, 1989.
- 'A Greater Evil', *The Times,* 16th February, 1990.
- Clifford Longley, 'Rushdie to the Rescue', *The Times,* 29th December, 1990.
- Margarette Driscoll, 'Religious Terrorists Have Won, say Rushdie Supporters', *The Times,* 30th December, 1990.
- Michael Knowles, 'Labour's Shame on Muslim Tolerance', *The Daily Telegraph,* 31st December, 1990.

CHAPTER 4

Voices of Civility

Deliberate Provocation

by J.P. Dixit et al.

Two important arguments against the banning of Salman Rushdie's book "the Satanic Verses," are: (1) The idea that individual expression in art cannot have any social and judicial limitation, and less seriously, (2) That those who support the ban have not read the book.

To take the second point first, do we know enough about the book already to form a judgement, perhaps not of literary and other merits, but of its ability to outrage the sentiments of all who believe in Islam?

The author is quite clear, "Actually, one of my major themes is religion and fanaticism. I have talked about Islamic religion because that is what I know best." (India Today, Sept. 15, 1988). How does he *talk* about this religion? Its founder is named Mahound. Mr. Rushdie has not invented this name. This was the name given to Prophet Muhammad by his European detractors as a term of abuse (*Ma* from *Mahomet* added to and *hound*) used frequently in various European ecshatologies as a creature belonging to the lowest depths of Hell, as the devil himself.

How has Rushdie treated the other pillars of the Islamic faith? Ayesha, the youngest wife of the Prophet and the one who is regarded as one of the highest authorities of tradition, is shown, in the words of Madhu Jain (India Today, ibid) as "clad only in butterflies" leading "an entire village, lemming-like into the Arabian Sea." The Ka'aba, regarded by the Muslims as the only consecrated spot on earth is treated no better. Disguised as the "Tent of Black Stone called The Curtain," it has twelve prostitutes with the names of the twelve wives of Mahound to add "the tempting spices of profanity." These "tempting spices" were apparently necessary to increase the number of pilgrims.

Then what else remains of the basic core of Islamic faith? The Prophet is the Devil, the law-givers are sexual perverts, and the Ka'aba and the Haj examples of depravity and greed. The Koran is of course only a collection of Satanic verses. Are these not sufficient to, in the words of our law, "outrage the religious feelings of a section of people"? Soli Sorabjee seems to think that it is just a matter of "adverse criticism of religions or derogatory references to its (sic) founder." This shows an inability to see the difference between reasoned discourse and the search for the sensational.

Most liberals and socialists believe that the freedom of artistic expression can have certain reasonable restrictions according to social and historical circumstances. Even where religious faith is vibrant and at the center of identity, it may certainly be opposed by reason and precept but not by means that outrage the faithful into trauma and pain. The pain of scurrilous intrusion into the religions of the sacred is not felt by the so-called fundamentalists only, but it is the common experience of the whole, besieged minority. While there can be rational opposition to their faith, there should be no outraging of it by obscenity and slander.

We, the undersigned, are all not Muslims. We are, therefore, obviously not subscribers to the Islamic faith. We believe that any critique of that faith has to be restrained, reasoned and full of the spirit of respecting diverse cultures and faiths. India's unity and harmony demands it. It is for such harmony and unity that we demand that the ban on this book be not lifted.

J.P. Dixit
Nissim Ezekiel
Jean Kalgutkar
Vrinda Nabar
Vaskar Nandy
Vasanthi Raman
Ashim Roy

Source: *Indian Express,* 17th October 1988 – 'You Knew That You Were Courting Trouble'.

The West's Arrogant Disdain

by Nicholas Ashford

. . . Freedom of expression, like all freedoms, carries its own responsibilities and conditions. In a civilised society we try, either by imposing the minimum of restrictions or through voluntary self-restraint, to ensure that right is not abused. I wonder whether Viking/Penguin would have claimed a similar right of freedom of expression to publish books which were anti-Semitic or inflamed racial hatred. And would Harold Pinter and his literary colleagues have lobbied 10 Downing Street in support of an author whose life was being threatened for writing a novel in which Hitler was a hero rather than a villain? Almost certainly not. . . .

. . . the Rushdie row has fuelled the fires of anti-Muslim sentiment in this country, and elsewhere in the West. Such feelings are never far below the surface. Popular newspapers trot out stereotypes of Muslims as people who are fanatical in speech and intolerant in thought. Islam is presented as a primitive, narrow-minded religion still anchored in the Middle Ages, which places more emphasis on the punishment than forgiveness of sinners . . .

I have long suspected that the West's arrogant disdain of Islam is based in part on the realisation that the growth and increased assertiveness of the Islamic faith (of which fundamentalism is undoubtedly a part) is taking place at a time when Christianity is in decline. But that is another story . . . perhaps one which Rushdie might care to take his pen to next.

Source: ©*The Independent,* 18th February 1989 – 'Freedom of the Press Also Means Responsibility'.

Blasphemy: A Mere Joke!

Dear Sir,

May I, as a Christian, ask the courtesy of your columns to make six points about *The Satanic Verses* affair?

1. I sympathise with Muslims in their anger at what is perceived as blasphemy against God and his messenger.

2. Blasphemy has become a meaningless concept in contemporary British society because it is not seriously believed that God exists. The supreme reality on which we rely for welfare is the nation state. To betray the interests of the nation is therefore the supreme crime, but blasphemy is a joke.

3. The blasphemy laws were not designed, as you have suggested "to protect the Christian religion". They were an acknowledgement of the fact that since God is the author and sustainer of our being, to blaspheme him is to inject poison into public life, a poison with more deadly long-term effects than anything offered by the drug merchants.

4. Christians in this country have become accustomed to hearing their faith blasphemed. They are not permitted to respond as the Ayatollah has done, because the centre of their faith is at the point where the Lord himself accepted death on a charge of blasphemy. Whether the silence of contemporary British Christians in the face of blasphemy is due to an understanding of their faith, or to indifference, only God can judge.

5. Freedom to do and say what one likes is not a human right. We prohibit the sale of harmful drugs to those who want to use them, and we punish harmful speech when it injures a particular individual. We do not punish speech when it poisons the whole of public life; we watch entrepreneurs making profit out of it. We do not and ought not to authorise governments to censor speech, but we (and here the churches have a heavy responsibility) can bear witness to the fact that poison is poison.

6. The present controversy could lead to enmity against the Muslims in Britain. That would be tragic. It could, on the other hand, provide an opportunity for Christians to consider how seriously they believe what they profess.

Yours faithfully,
Bishop Lesslie Newbigin
Birmingham

Source: ©*The Independent,* 21st February 1989 – ' "The Satanic Verses": Blasphemy *v* Freedom of Speech'.

Rushdie's Insensitivity

by Christopher S. Taylor

. . . As a professional writer, Salman Rushdie knows the importance and power of words. He knows both the good and the evil that words can arouse in the hearts and souls of men. His special circumstance, which makes him a part of two very different worlds, entail a special obligation to know and weigh the impact of his words in both of those worlds. The great potential of Rushdie is that because he stands at the inter-section of two worlds, one modern and secular and the other traditional and religious, he has much to offer both worlds in terms of mutual understanding or at least an acceptance of each other . . .

The trouble with his latest work arises from two chapters involving a series of dream sequences that have deeply offended the Muslim world. That the chapters in question refer to the Prophet Muhammad cannot seriously be disputed by anyone familiar with the Islamic religious tradition. Rushdie's recent protests to the contrary are as disingenuous as they are self-serving.

The problem is less that Rushdie has expressed his own doubt about faith it is the technique he has employed to articulate that doubt. This essentially involves an insulting depiction of Muhammad, which can hardly be anything but deeply offensive to a true believer, even the most tolerant, educated or Westernized among them. Rushdie cannot claim ignorance of the world he has so deeply offended. The fact that Rushdie has chosen to use the technique that he did raises serious issues of his responsibility and sensitivity as a writer. To communicate one's own self is one thing but to do so by deliberately debasing and demeaning what others still cherish as sacred is to cross an altogether different line.

What has enraged Muslims is the way Rushdie has chosen to articulate his doubt by insensitively degrading and devaluing what millions of believing Muslims continue to perceive as sacrosanct. Most of Rushdie's Western readers will not understand what he has done, or appreciate why it is so offensive to Muslims. But the life of the prophet is so familiar and sacred to devout Muslims that Rushdie's treatment of it cannot help offending.

In light of this situation, is it not fair to ask how responsibly Rushdie has exercised the treasured right of free expression guaranteed him in the world he has adopted his own? In questioning his own faith, was it truly necessary for him to depict the prophet of Islam as a lying licentious misogynist and fraud? In searching of our own truths, how much must be destructively trampled on and degrade the faith of other? Why at a time when the mutual understanding between the Islamic tradition that he was born into, and the western secular tradition he has adopted, is so clearly lacking, was it necessary to excite this type of anger?

What exactly is to be gained from the further ignorant ridicule of the Muslim world, on the part of the Western audience that does not understand Islam, or the profound humiliation and resentment of the audience that believes very sincerely and deeply in Islam? When the discourse between our two traditions is already so strained, garbled, do we really need this provocative and inflammatory approach? Is the light it shed worth the pain and now blood, that it has cost? . . .

The anger in the Islamic world provoked by Rushdie's book arises from a profound sense of pain caused by calculated and senseless ridicule. The hurt caused by this work may be a powerful force in making it a best seller but they are not particularly useful in helping us to better understand either ourselves or the common humanity we need to recognize in each other, especially in the frightening complexity of the contemporary age. In our world, Salman Rushdie has a right to do what he has done.

But we, as part of a large collective humanity, also have rights. We have a right to expect more sensitivity from our writers. We have a right to expect our writers to know the power of the written word, and to exercise their right to use the written word in a responsible manner. We have a right to expect more from our writers. We have a right to expect them to use their talent to help us understand ourselves and each other. Finally, we have a right to feel disappointed when they let us down.

Source: *The Christian Science Monitor,* 3rd March 1989 – 'Rushdie's Insensitivity'.

Rushdie and the Freedom of Speech

From Lord Shawcross, QC

Sir, The Government hardly needed the support of the members of the Society of Authors (some more known than others) who signed the letter about *The Satanic Verses* (February 28). The Prime Minister has, as one would expect, made it abundantly clear that the Ayatollah Khomeini's writ, itself a violation of the rule of law and the comity of nations, will not run in this country.

The writers of the letter might however have been better advised to emphasize that the privilege of freedom of speech which we enjoy in this country depends, as do all privileges, upon responsibility in its exercise.

As to that, I would wish to record my complete agreement with the letter you published from Mr Roald Dahl on the same day. The irresponsibility of Mr Rushdie in publishing a sensational novel which he knew full well would cause immense offence to millions of Muslims all over the world does indeed, as Mr Dahl says, put some strain . . . on our right to say what we like.

This is already demonstrated by the many voices which urge that our law of blasphemy should be extended to protect all theistic religions or at least those satisfying the criteria suggested by the Archbishop of York in his letter (March 1).

Muslims form a very large section of our fellow human beings and I have great respect for their religion. There is much in the teaching of Muhammad which commends itself to all of us and most Muslims follow their religion with an explicit devotion far exceeding that which I fear many of us show towards our own established religion here.

The Rushdie book has done incalculable harm to the interests of all people, not with any intention of contribution to scholarship (as Mr Yaqub Zaki's important article (February 28) shows) but in order to sensationalise a novel in the hope of securing its better sale. It is a deplorable abuse of the freedom which he shares with the rest of us, but which we must nonetheless defend.

Hartley Shawcross, QC
House of Lords.
March 1.

Source: *The Times,* 3rd March 1989 – 'Rushdie and the Freedom of Speech'.

Sheer Effrontery: Rushdie's Book Is An Insult

by Jimmy Carter

In preparation for the Middle East negotiations that led up to Camp David and the Israeli-Egyptian peace treaty, I tried to learn as much as possible about the Muslim faith. . . .

"The Satanic Verses" goes much further in vilifying the Prophet Mohammad and defaming the Holy Koran. The author, a well-versed analyst of Muslim beliefs, must have anticipated a horrified reaction throughout the Islamic world. . . .

While Rushdie's First Amendment freedoms are important, we have tended to promote him and his book with little acknowledgement that it is a direct insult to those millions of Muslims whose sacred beliefs have been violated and are suffering in restrained silence the added embarrassment of the Ayatollah's irresponsibility.

This is the kind of intercultural wound that is difficult to heal. Western leaders should make it clear that in protecting Rushdie's life and civil rights, there is no endorsement of an insult to the sacred beliefs of our Muslim friends. . . .

Source: *Are You Being Kept in the Dark: The Satanic Verses – Rushdie's Dilemma,* Jamaica NY, Islamic Circle of North America, 1989, p. 6. (To be referred to as ICNA booklet.)

Who is Fanatic?

by Keith Vaz

The adjustment made by immigrant communities to their so-called "hosts" is greater than the ability of the host community to accommodate them. The right to belong is more important than the right to be different. This assertion of difference, this protection of culture, has manifested itself indelibly on the British. The monuments to the new communities may not all be as grand as the Central Mosque in Birmingham or the Sanatan Mandir in Leicester or the great Gudwaras in Southall but they exist.

British history has until now known only two great religious powerhouses, Canterbury and Rome. The "new religions" are at once an object of interest and a threat. First, many are in fact old religions whose histories rival Christianity. Second, the Christian religion has less and less meaning in the lives of ordinary people – because of the policies of this Government. Third, there is no understanding of the role that the new religions play in the lives of the new communities.

The great error of the supporters of Salman Rushdie has been their total failure to grasp the role of Islam in the lives of Muslims. The words that have provoked the greatest reaction at rallies and demonstrations have not been – as the media and Fay Weldon would have us believe – "Kill, kill, kill!" but the much more emphatic "Nara-et-Akbar?" ("Who is great?") [sic] producing the response "Allah-o-Akbar" ("God is great").

Devotion is described as fanaticism. Those who have opposed Rushdie's decision to publish a book steeped in intolerance and religious abuse are branded as supporters of the fanatics. *All* those who pray and believe are by their nature fanatics. How strong is your belief in your religion if you don't believe in its fundamental values? Faith is something to be respected and revered: not to be used as an opportunity to humiliate.

We owe a debt of gratitude to Rushdie for the thoughts he has provoked. A remarkable coalition of all classes and shades of opinion will not kowtow to book and effigy burners so long as the book is *The Satanic Verses* and the effigies are of Rushdie. Yet Scottish councillors burning poll tax notices and Hampshire residents burning an effigy of the Secretary of State for the Environment are not ticked off. No questions are asked here about fanatics and fundamentalists.

Last week 12,000 worthies rallied to defend Rushdie. They were lecturing the new religions and new communities by reasserting fundamental principles. To be British is to accept the rule of law; this is a fundamental principle. Yet in exchange for British citizenship, the new Britons are to be stripped of not just culture but also religion. They must be sanitised from a thousand years of their history. Women above all must be liberated.

The liberation of Asian and especially Muslim women has

become a great cause for the Rushdie defenders. The hypocrisy is extraordinary and the arrogance is breathtaking. I am sure that I went to a synagogue recently in which women were placed in a different part of the room from men. I saw no demonstrations outside urging the Jewish religion to liberate its women.

Fay Weldon is the new, self-appointed liberator. Her pamphlet, *Sacred Cows,* declares that the Koran has enslaved Muslim women. Living, as we all do, in a society that is supposed to be enlightened but which tolerates and encourages sexism and the suppression of women in abundance, it is the ultimate cheek to lecture Muslim women about liberation and Muslim men about sexism.

An international conference held in Kuwait in 1980 and sponsored by the International Commission of Jurists recognised that the equal rights of women is a vital teaching of the Koran. There was no question of second-class status. During the recent Pakistani elections, observers noted the huge personal vote generated to elect the first woman leader of an Islamic state. It is impossible to under-estimate the impact of this event on Muslim women.

To mock and goad the new religions is to rob them of their roots and their sensitivities. They must be left to develop in their own way: aware that they are not in their countries of origin; that they are minority religions; that they are in another place which has less tolerance and understanding than they were entitled to expect.

Source: ©*The Independent,* 29th July 1989 – 'Lecturing is the Ultimate Cheek'.

No Authorship Without Responsibility!

. . . If book-burning kindles the righteous abhorrence of our culture for the excesses of Islam, the Rushdie affair has also brought out the worst in Western liberalism. In the name of tolerance we cry for a total autonomy of the arts. The slogan seems to be: "If we will we may." Does not authorship have responsibility to social well-being? Is there to be nothing like a "highway code" of community above commodity by which we freely take account of "the common good" and – so doing – both curtail our liberties and ensure our freedoms?

The Right Rev Kenneth Cragg

Source: ©*The Independent,* 8th August 1989 – 'Western Views of Islam'.

Lay Off the Sacred

by Charles Taylor

. . . We tend to think that freedom of speech is indivisible, that either it applies to everything or it doesn't exist at all. . . .

But why give such a special status to religion? . . . Even looking at it from a secular humanist point of view, the fact that someone's religion is the locus of his/her stand on the deepest and most fundamental issues – death, evil, the meaning of life – seems to justify giving it exceptional protection. This all still seems obvious outside of the West, but no longer so clear here. . . .

. . . Let unbelievers explore their views; only let them lay off the symbols, stories, figures, books which are sacred to religious traditions. Couldn't Kanzantzakis have made his point without bringing in Christ's sex life? Couldn't Rushdie without the insulting story about Mahound? . . .

. . . To live in this difficult world, the western liberal mind will have to learn to reach out more.

Source: *Public Culture,* 2/1, Fall 1989 – 'The Rushdie Controversy'.

What Freedom?

. . . Frances D'Souza's letter (27th October) advances the broad proposition that the Publishers Association represents the interests of various groups which "must and do have a legitimate interest in freedom of expression". The PA in fact only represents publishers, but on the question of freedom of expression, one has to ask "Whose freedom?" and, especially, "What freedom?"

Is it the freedom to be malicious and scurrilous about women, blacks, Jews, homosexuals and, for example, Jeffrey Archer, Robert Maxwell and Sonia Sutcliffe? And if we recognise that we are not free in this sense due to various legal pitfalls and the power of self-censorship, should we therefore be free to traduce what are well known to be essential articles of religious faith? These last are a soft target: we can defy religious zealots to do their worst with a self-righteousness that simply cannot be deployed on groups protected by the liberal consensus if not by law, or on libelled individuals.

The Muslims have fought back and are absolutely right to do so. Their beliefs are the very fabric of their community and identity, and if we, of other religions or none, are not merely unable to understand this but self-righteously condemn them for their desire to see *The Satanic Verses* extirpated, we are betraying the ethos of our society, which is still one of tolerance and courtesy: in this case the burden of toleration is on us, the host society. We may never be able to grasp exactly why they find the book intolerable, but can we not now give them the benefit of any doubt?

This wretched book has caused death and mayhem, and yet there have been triumphalist demands for its publication in paperback (as if the cased edition had not sold enough copies), just so that the cup of "freedom" can be drunk to its lees. With superb unconcern, the knife is given another twist inside the wound.

Publishers should stand together in the face of threats, blatant or insidious, to their basic freedom to publish. But this togetherness loses much of its force when the cause is dubious. To a publisher in a country where there is no political freedom, the freedom to blaspheme must seem a very odd cause in which to go to the battlements.

Christopher Hurst
London WC2.

Source: *The Bookseller,* 17th November 1989 – 'The Satanic Verses'.

Living Without The Sacred

by Lesslie Newbigin

. . . A society which has finally lost the sense of the sacred, in which there is nothing worthy of reverence, must eventually dissolve into nihilism. In such a society no meaning can finally be affirmed. Art and literature, as well as behaviour must eventually be meaningless. Because freedom degenerates into idiocy if it loses contact with reality, a free society cannot be sustained forever without the commitment of its people, or at least some of them, to something which is sacred, for which life itself may be surrendered. I think British people must be grateful to Muslims for challenging a false idea of freedom. . . . Both Christians and Muslims can, however, join in unmasking a false concept of freedom, in warning against its consequences, in bearing witness to the reality of the sacred, and in protesting when that which is sacred is treated with contempt or ridicule. Among ourselves, both in the internal discussions of matters of faith within the Christian and Muslim communities, and in dialogue between them, we shall always need to use our critical faculties in serious discussion with one another. But it will be done with reverence for the sacred, even when we differ in our understandings. For, as has been well said, it is no more possible to understand the reality by which we are surrounded and sustained without reverence, than it is to penetrate the secrets of the galaxies without a telescope.

Source: *Discernment* (London), 4/2, 1990, p. 17 – 'Blasphemy and the Free Society'.

Without Any Faith!

by Bhikhu Parekh

Salman Rushdie's suggestively entitled "In Good Faith" . . . is a polemical not a reflective statement, conceived in a combative not contemplative mood. It defends *The Satanic Verses* against criticisms rather than analysis, and reflects on their content, cultural context and provenance.

Rushdie does not inquire why his book has provoked such strong reaction and what deep nerves it has disturbed; he is convinced that it is all a result of political manipulation, massive misunderstanding or egregious ignorance. He does not ask why his critics include not just mullahs and their gullible flock, but also decent and fair-minded Muslims – such intelligent Muslim writers as Ali Mazrui and Edward Said, many a non-Muslim and even a few a-religious sceptics, atheists and Marxists. . .

The Muslims ask why he mixed up religion and sex, which Islam so radically separates, and why he thought it fit to discuss fantasised Islam with a generous helping of the four-letter word and other "abusive" epithets. They want to know what gives the artist the right to plunder and reduce the deepest experiences and memories of a community to a mere raw material to be used as he pleases, and why the community does not enjoy the equal right to fight back in defence of what gives meaning to its existence.

However mistaken these questions might be, they deserve answers. To conceptualise them in terms of a clash between art and religion, or between imagination and faith, is wholly to misunderstand them. Rushdie's subsequent Herbert Read Memorial Lecture sets up false antinomies, misdefines transcendence and sacredness, and skirts important issues. In spite of these and other limitations, Rushdie's "In good faith" is a most important and welcome contribution. That he should have made it at all is an earnest of his anguish at the tragic events of the past year.

Although he is not wholly convincing, he takes great pains to explain the intricate structure of the book. In deeply moving words he expresses his pain at the racist abuse hurled at Muslims, pleads for a "way forward" through the "mutual recognition of mutual pain", affirms his "good-faith", "regrets" the unintended offence, and grieves at his separation from "my community, from India".

Source: ©*The Independent on Sunday,* 11th February 1990 – 'Towards Mutual Understanding'.

An Open Letter

Dear Mr Rushdie,

I am extremely glad that the first Muslim responses, published in last Monday's *Independent,* to your article "In good faith" have been so generous. My own reaction, I am sorry to say, is less generous. After a year in which to reflect upon it, is that all that you could manage to say?

The "Rushdie affair" has done untold damage. It has intensified the alienation of Muslims here and in other Western countries from the society around them, in reaction to the uncomprehending liberal chorus of support for you. Racial hostility towards them, where overt, has been inflamed, and, where latent, has been aroused. All hope of any relaxation of Iranian rigour has been destroyed, and, with it, any relief for the wretched hostages, whose far more severe imprisonment than yours you do not mention.

A great part of the blame of course rests with the Ayatollah Khomeini, not least for obscuring the fact that there would still have been a Rushdie affair without his intervention. His *fatwa,* which I assume Sunni Muslims have no duty to respect, was an abominable act, supplying to all those prejudiced against Islam a legitimate ground of accusation. Yet more shocking even than Khomeini's call for your assassination was his subsequent statement that, even if you were to repent and become a model Muslim, you would still burn in hell, implying of course, that there are sins which Allah, the Compassionate, the Merciful, does not forgive even the repentant. If this accorded with sound Muslim theology, the religion would not deserve respect. We should not be perturbed, however, that so few Muslim authorities have repudiated the statement. That is sufficiently explained by the fate of the imam in Belgium, whom you do not think worth mentioning and everyone else seems to have forgotten, who spoke out against Khomeini and actually was assassinated.

What worried me most in what you say is that you do not seem to have understood what the affair has done to you; here we can only say, what have you done to yourself. Before *The Satanic Verses* was published, you were a hero among members of the ethnic minorities, far beyond the circle of those who had read your books, for your forceful television broadcast denouncing British racism. (You did me the honour to quote with approval something I had written, which constitutes my only qualification for now writing to you.) It was your status as a hero that made your book appear so great a betrayal. Much as you might want to, you can never again play that role: you can never again credibly assume the stance of denouncer of white prejudice. For now you are one of us. You have become an honorary white: merely an honorary white intellectual, it is true, but an honorary white all the same.

Some of your defenders so far forgot themselves as to declare that, if Muslims cannot abide free speech they should go back where they came from. You round on them, affecting to suppose them to be telling you to go back where you came from. They were not addressing you, Mr Rushdie: they were *defending* you. You will remain there as long as you cannot bring yourself to repudiate what you did, and, as a first, least step, to cease insisting on your right to have as many readers for your book as possible.

You protest the falsity of the accusation, "He must have known". No one could have foreseen all that would happen; but I incline to think that, if you really did not grasp the offence you would give to believing Muslims, you were not qualified to write upon the subject you chose. In any case, no one escapes responsibility for the consequences of a bad action by having failed to foresee them; moreover, you know now, yet you still insist on your right to wider publication.

Rhetoric about free speech always obscures the evident distinction between whether there should be legal restraints on what is said, and whether there are moral constraints on what ought to be said. It is, in my view, a disgusting thing to defile what other men regard as holy; and no literary intention, however lofty, can excuse it. You have imbibed the assumption of Western intellectuals that religious believers may properly be affronted, indeed deserve to be affronted. Those in the West who have no religious belief are oblivious to the depth of pain caused to those who have by what they perceive as blasphemy: lacking so much as the concept of some things being holy, they lack the will to grasp the magnitude of the affront, although they could begin to imagine it if there is anything they hold dear or in respect. It is unimaginative to say, "They don't have to read or watch it if they don't want to": in some cases (like yours), they can't escape hearing about it; in others, it is encountered quite unexpectedly.

The ground for the law against blasphemy is different, now this is no longer a Christian country as such; and the case for its extension is sound. If there had been such a law, the Rushdie affair would not have occurred; we can hardly afford another such. We rightly do not extend the principle of free speech to cover incitement to racial hatred or contempt; no sacred principle would be breached by withdrawing its protection from writings grossly offensive to believers in non-Christian religions, as opposed to seriously reasoned argument. I have no doubt that, under such a law, you could have found a way of expressing yourself that did not breach it. Free speech enthusiasts warn us that, if we censor pornography or blasphemy, we shall be opening the doors to political censorship; that this warning is a sham is shown by their lack of concern about the political censorship already in existence (the suppression some years ago of the news of the man who incinerated himself outside 10 Downing Street, for instance).

Certainly it is said that anyone should be able publicly to threaten murder with impunity; that is the price our law pays for not prohibiting what a whole community views as an intolerable insult. It is to the credit of this country that some have shown an understanding of the nature of the affront you gave, instead of reacting as Americans did to an insult to the First Amendment of *their* holy book; your attributing this solely to a desire for votes shows that you have not yet understood what you did. Until you do, and probably even if you do, its reverberations will continue.

Michael Dummett
New College, Oxford

Source: ©*The Independent on Sunday,* 11th February 1990 – 'An Open Letter'.

Who Killed the Writer?

I was deeply saddened to read Salman Rushdie's attack on me in the course of a magnificent defence of the liberal position. But now I feel at the very least I have put on record why my play *Who Killed the Writer?* has not appeared in public.

I wrote the play very quickly in the weeks following the *fatwa,* believing writers should immediately do what they could to express support, and, more importantly, draw the lessons from the event.

Through a confrontation between the assassin and a political journalist, I wanted to show that the West, particularly the British and American secret services, deliberately brought down the democratically elected Iranian government headed by Mossadeq in 1953, and installed the appalling regime of the Shah, which used its secret police to terrorise all opposition.

I did not send the play to Mr Rushdie "in case he needed something to read". As I explained in the covering letter, "I want to give you the opportunity to see this play before the title becomes known in the hope that it will reassure you that, while I have used your appalling predicament, I have not exploited it. . . . I have only one hope for the play and that is by widening the debate about Muslim (or any other) fundamentalism, I may contribute to a general lessening of tensions in the world. I want to show that though your condemnation by the Ayatollah was wicked and unacceptable in any kind of world order we can tolerate, it did not arrive out of the blue but that the Western powers have helped to create the monster which now threatens to devour us."

Mr Rushdie responded by leaving a message on my answer-phone saying that he was appalled that I would think the play which postulated his death could in any way be acceptable to him, that he would resist its being performed.

As Mr Rushdie is nowhere portrayed or even named in the play it was easy to change the title to *Who Killed the Writer?* (though it would be disingenuous to pretend the play was not predicated on his position). But I was shocked to be in receipt of a letter from Mr Rushdie's agent saying that if we intended production we should send him a formal note so that he could "establish Salman's legal rights".

The irony of Mr Rushdie wishing to suppress a play because it offended him was so obvious that it became clear to me he could not be thinking well. I decided not to go ahead with production. No note was sent. It is hard now not to feel that my act of self-censorship was misguided.

Brian Clark
London N1

Source: ©*The Independent on Sunday,* 11th February 1990 – 'Who Killed the Writer?' Since *The Independent on Sunday* did not have the forwarding address of Mr Brian Clark we could not seek his permission to reproduce the above letter, though the *Independent* stated that they had no objection to our using it. If we are able to trace Mr Clark's address, the necessary steps would be taken for the second edition.

Compromise That Rushdie Will Have to Make

Some kind of reciprocal understanding is going to be the only way out of Salman Rushdie's distressing situation, but he does himself little service in claiming a sort of infallibility in all points of detail, nit-picking his way through the one-sidedly sympathetic media.

As one who admires his work with some reservations, but believes it deserving of publication in all available forms, I am a little dismayed by his postures of self-righteousness and self-importance: in particular in claiming that the novel in general – and presumably his own in particular – is now the best substitute for formal religion.

Any artist would do well to take a second look at his understanding of humanity if he is blind to the fact that there are areas of sensibility and attack which initiates will still, even in the modern world, defend to the death. In Britain treason against the state is still a capital offence though some right-minded individuals who have suffered unnecessarily and painfully during the past decade, might be forgiven for doubting the unmitigated wisdom of that law. Punishment by death is always barbaric, but its demand should not surprise the perceptive mind who is willing to understand the variety of human responses.

Salman Rushdie's attitude appears to be one of unrelenting astonishment, in which case his naivete in these matters should have encouraged him to look deeper and harder before committing his pen to paper. Or if he did guess the likely response that his book would provoke, his present situation should not surprise him.

From him, a statement that he can see and understand at least a little of the point of view of the other side and less self-justification at all cost might begin to help. Most of all, we should bear in mind that he has written not some valuable though suppressed treatise on human rights, but a derivative novel of debated merit, whose publication is likely to change nothing in terms of the human condition or its amelioration.

Ian Flintoff,
22 Chaldon Road,
London SW6.

Source: ©*The Guardian,* 19th February 1990 – 'Compromise That Rushdie Will Have to Make'.

A Contract With the Devil

by Atam Vetta

. . . Mr Rushdie and his friends allege that the critics of his book are radical Muslims. Some of them are but others are not. I am one of the latter. I am not even a Muslim and if I am forced to subscribe to a religion it will have to be the Hindu religion and an agnostic Hindu at that. I believe it is the duty of those non-Muslims who feel equally offended by *The Satanic Verses* to speak up.

The inability of the Western literary world to comprehend the anger and frustration that most Muslims and Hindus feel at the publication of the book is exemplified by the issue of the World Statement. The signatories deceive themselves by pretending that they are 'also involved in the publication' of the book. This they assert is because they 'defend the right to freedom of opinion and expression'. The implication is that those, perhaps, like myself, who believe that the book should be withdrawn do not or would not defend these rights. This implication I reject with utmost contempt as would the signatories if only they would allow their common sense to take precedence over irrational anger. Freedom of expression is not a licence and must be exercised in conjunction with other freedoms. It is this failure i.e. taking account of other freedoms, of the Western literary world which, in the final analysis, resulted in the issuing of the *Fatwa.* Had the book been withdrawn there would have been no need of the *Fatwa.* It is doubtful if most of the signatories of the World Statement have either read or understood the book.

Origins of the Book

It is generally accepted that Mr Rushdie may have got the idea of the book from his paper Muhammad, Islam and the Rise of Caliphs which he wrote while at King's College, Cambridge for Part II of his history Tripos ('The Sunday Times', 19 February). He is reputed to have been paid $850,000 in advance royalties by his publishers. Viking Penguin then asked their editorial consultant Mr Khushwant Singh for his expert opinion on the manuscript. He advised that the book was 'lethal' ('The Times', 20 February 1989) and rejected it. He is reported by the 'Times' to have said, 'I must say "I told you so". I read the manuscript carefully and I was positive that it would cause a lot of trouble. There are several derogatory references to the Prophet and to the Koran and Muhammad is made out to be a small-time imposter".'

Mr Singh's statement indicates that, at least, the publishers Viking Penguin were aware of the tragic possibilities. It needs to be stated firmly that any reasonable person from the Indian subcontinent would have realised that the publication of the book may create serious problems in India and Pakistan. Therefore, it is not correct to say that 'Rushdie could not have calculated the effect of what he wrote, because the effect came almost as an after thought' ('The New Statesman', 21 March 1989).

The criticism against The Satanic Verses is that it is pornographic and it is blasphemous. Besides it insults the different ethnic groups and British women.

Choice of the Name 'Mahound'

Mahound was the name given to the Prophet Muhammad by Christian crusaders. In the war between the two religions they wanted to denigrate and disparage Muslims. Their chosen name Mahound, means a lustful and profligate false prophet and an idolater. It is a word of abuse. Mr Rushdie acknowledges that 'long ago, (it) was indeed used as derogatory term'. He, however, defends his choice of the name by saying that his novel tries in all sorts of ways to reoccupy negative images, to reposses pejorative language, and on page 93 explains 'To turn insults into strengths, whigs, tories, Blacks all chose to wear with pride the names they were given in scorn; likewise, our mountain climbing, prophet-motivated solitary is to be . . . Mahound'. Mr Rushdie omits to quote himself fully. Actually, he continues, '(to be) the medieval baby frightener, the Devil's synonym: (Mahound)'. Does he really expect us to accept the 'the demon-tag (Mahound) the frangis' wished to hang around our necks? We have rejected it for nearly a thousand years. His description of the Prophet is far from flattering. There is no attempt on page 93 to pretend that he is talking about any one other than the Prophet Muhammad. Indeed, it is evident from his article in the 'Observer' that he is talking about Muhammad. Mr Rushdie's Mahound is, in fact, the Prophet Muhammad.

Mahound is asked 'What kind of idea are you? Man or mouse?' (p.95).

In Britain 'bastard' is not now regarded to be such an abusive word but on the Indian subcontinent it is a degrading form of abuse and its use may result in a rather serious affray resulting in bodily injuries. Mr Rushdie describes Ibrahim as a bastard.

Muhammad had, in Christian terminology, three 'disciples'. Their names were Khalid who was a water carrier (beheshti), Salman who was of Persian origin and Bilal who was a freed black slave. The three companions of the Prophet are treated with respect by Muslims. Mr Rushdie describes Khalid as the 'despised water carrier' (p.95). He describes Salman as a 'bum from Persia' and Bilal as 'an enormous black monster'. The three are described as 'this trinity of scum'; 'idlers' and 'a bunch of riff raff'. They are also described as 'goons' and 'those f...... clowns' (p.101). I wonder what would be the reaction of most British people if the disciples of Jesus were described in this manner. He describes Muhammad and the three companions as "Mahound with his raggle-taggle gang" (p.102).

Concerning Muhammad's ideas and philosophy, he says 'If Mahound's ideas were worth anything, do you think they would only be popular with trash like you (i.e. the three companions)'.

Further '. . . . unpopular Prophet and his wretched followers' (p.113).

Mr Rushdie makes archangel Gibreel say 'Mahound comes to me for revelation, asking me to choose between monotheist and henotheist alternatives, and I am just some idiot actor having a bhaenchod (sister f.....) nightmare, what the f... do I know, yaar (friend), what to tell you, help. Help' (p.109).

He continually describes Muhammad as 'Prophet Messenger Businessman' (p.118). He states that Mahound 'had no time for scruples . . . no qualms about end and means' (p.363).

Concerning the early followers of Islam, he says, 'The faithful lived by lawlessness, but in those years Mahound – or should one say the Archangel Gibreel? – should one say Al-lah?' (p.363) – became obsessed by law. . . .

Muhammad's Personal Life

Concerning Muhammad's personal life: ' . . . but after his wife's death Mahound was no angel, you understand my meaning. But in Yathrib he almost met his match. Those women up there: they turned his beard half-white within a year' (p.366).

"The point about our Prophet, my dear Baal, is that he did not like his women to answer back, he went for mothers and daughters, think of his first wife and then Ayesha: too old and too young (p.366). Who would not find this abusive?

'No wonder the two of you did not hit off: she wouldn't be your mother or your child' (p.369).

He recounted a quarrel between Mahound and Ayesha. 'That girl could not stomach it that her husband wanted so many other women. He talked about necessity, political alliances and so on, but she was not fooled. Who can blame her? Finally he went into – what else? – one of his trances, and out he came with a message from the archangel. Gibreel had recited verses giving him full divine support. God's own permission to f... as many women as he liked. So there: what could poor Ayesha say against verses of God? You know what she did say? This: "Your God certainly jumps to it when you need him to fix things up for you" (p.386).

'The sexual aspect of Submission (the religion of Mahound) is "unhealthy", pronounced Salman.

'Safwan brought Ayesha back to Yathrib safe and sound; at

which point tongues began to wag, not least in the harem. . . . The two young people had been alone in the desert for many hours, and it was hinted at . . . might not she therefore have been attracted to someone closer to her own age? "Quite a scandal". . . . (Mahound) saw his pet, the archangel, and then informed one and all that Gibreel had exonerated Ayesha. . . . the lady didn't complain about the convenience of the verses'.

'Mahound said "Writers and whores. I see no difference" (p.392).

'Hind won't be happy till she has ripped out your (Mahound's) tongue, to say nothing of my balls, excuse me' (p.125).

Pornography

The book is pornographic in its excessive use of the four letter words and descriptions which stimulate sexual excitement. Indeed, one of the demands made by some critics is that if it is to be made available in a public library then it should be catalogued under pornography. Mr Rushdie is aware of this. He says 'The zealots also attack me by false analogy, comparing my book to pornography and demanding a ban on both. Many Islamic spokesmen have compared my work to antisemitism. But intellectual dissent is neither pornographic nor racist' ('Observer', 22 January 1989).

Regrettably, the judgement whether a book is a work of art, an intellectual dissent or pornography is intensely personal. No criteria exist which enable us to make the decision objectively. The days when the occurrence of the four letter word in a book was sufficient for it to be declared pornographic are long past. I can do no better than to itemise the phrases and sentences which have led many to dub it as pornographic.

(Dr Atam Vetta provides quotes from 47 pages where the four-letter word is used generally as well as in relation to 'white women', 'this country', 'this nation', 'communists' etc.)

The Satanic Verses uses the word penis and its different names some of which were not known to the authors of the *Kama Sutra* or *The Perfumed Garden.* (14 page references are cited.). . . .

Racism

Chinese – 'the little yellow buggers . . . ' (p.196). 'Goddamn Chinese' (p.197).

African Britons – Seeing black men and women in a church the reaction of one of his characters is interesting. He says 'Hubshees' . . . Troublemakers and savages he called them. 'I feel sorry for you' he pronounced. "Every morning you have to look yourself in the mirror, and see, staring back, the darkness, the stain, the proof that you are the lowest of the low' (p.255).

Sikhs – 'Sikh Kebab' (p.440).

The English – 'Those bastards (Londoners) down there won't know what hit them' (p.1).

Mrs Chamchawala advises her son 'Don't go dirty like those English', she warned him. 'They wipe their bee tee em with paper only. Also they get into each other's dirty bathwater' (p.39).

'The trouble with the English was that they were English: damn cold fish! – Living underwater most of the year, in days the colour of night' (p.352).

' . . . the moral fuzziness of the English was meteorologically induced . . . when the land is not drier than the sea, then clearly a people will lose their power to make distinctions . . . ' (p.354).

' . . . the poison of this devil island had infected her baby girls' (p.250).

'Plus also they had come to the demon city (London) in which anything could happen' (p.250).

'Yes a land of phantom imps' (Britain) (p.250).

' . . . (famous) for his predilections for white women with enormous breasts and plenty of rump' (p.261).

And the Queen

' . . . he found himself dreaming of the Queen, of making tender love to the Monarch. She was the body of Britain, the avatar of the State, and he had chosen her joined with her; she was his beloved, the moon of his delight' (p.169).

Intellectual Dissent?

Mr Rushdie as quoted above says that intellectual dissent is not pornography. I agree with him. Neither is pornography necessarily intellectual dissent. I am told that Mr Rushdie's contribution to the English novel is not based on the excessive use of four and five letter words in different languages. Pornographic words and phrases quoted above should not ordinarily evoke comment. The problem arises because they are used in the context of the Prophet Muhammad and his close associates and companions. Many fellow human beings hold him in high regard.

Mr Rushdie fails to understand this simple point and says that 'They have turned Muhammad into a perfect being,' his life into a perfect life, his revelation into the unambiguous, clear event it originally was not. One may not discuss Muhammad as if he were human, with human virtues and weaknesses. One may not discuss Islam as a historical phenomenon, as an ideology born out of its time. These are the taboo against which *The Satanic Verses* has transgressed . . . ('Observer', 22 January 1989).

He is wrong. One may do all these. He has done none of these. His transgression is that he has surrounded the Prophet and the revelations with pornography. There is no legitimate reason for this. It is odd that neither he nor his Liberal and Literati backers understand this simple fact.

Surrealist Satire?

Mr Rushdie says 'Of all the European artistic movements, surrealism is the one I most respond to, the idea that you have to make the world fresh, scratching away at the surface of expectation and habit.

I subscribe to the modernist belief that there is no longer an agreed definition of the universe or even of society. And when the consensus breaks down, you can't write a realistic novel any more.' ('The Independent Magazine,' 10 September, 1988, p.60.) This has led some writers to conclude as did Mr John Calder that 'The novel *(The Satanic Verses)* is basically a surrealist satire' ('The Guardian', 11 March 1989).

In the Bandung File interview on Channel 4, Mr Rushdie was asked 'The controversy, in a sense, has been on your acting on the historic text of the Qur'an and playing with that. How much was that based on historical fact?' His answer was: 'Almost entirely . . . The interesting thing about Muhammad is that there *is* objective information about him other than in the sacred text . . . and the relationship between people involved is absolutely fascinating' ('The Guardian', 15 February 1989). He goes on to say, 'So I thought, let us not try and pretend to be writing a history. Let us take the themes I am interested in and fantasise them and fabulate them and all that . . . ' His fantasy turns into obscenity. Maybe this is surrealism. . . .

Dev Assur Sanghram (Battle Between Good and Evil)

The ancient Hindus also knew about the battle between 'the light and the dark'. For they invented the concept of *Dev Assur Sanghram* which simply translated means a battle between Good and Evil. This is a continuous battle. The *devas* for Mr Rushdie are all those who support his association of pornography with Muhammad and *Assurs* are those who complain against it. I am probably an *assur* in his eyes.

In his 'Observer' article he says that his book 'is a clash of faiths, in a way. Or more precisely, it is a clash of languages'. On this he is right. It is a clash of faiths. A clash between his faith and mine, between his values and mine. His faith which tramples on the faith of others and mine which respects their faith in the knowledge that there are few absolute truths. His certainty which can only be conveyed by extensive use of pornography and my doubt, where pornography has no place and a sexual act is a totally personal affair. His faith in his own freedom of expression which requires that the freedom of expression of others be curtailed. Specifically, the Labour leadership should respond by 'disowning (the) initiative' of Brian Sedgemore MP, Max Madden MP, Bernie Grant MP and Councillor Mohammad Ajeeb in asking that the blasphemy law be extended to cover Islam. If you do not agree with Mr Rushdie you are on the side of the Mullahs who are the 'contemporary thought police'. In the struggle between 'light and dark', you have then chosen the dark (quotes from 'Observer', 22 January 1989).

Mr Rushdie's 'Mullahs' are not slow to respond. For example, Dr Shabir Akhtar's concept of a Muslim in the present context is rather interesting. He says that 'Anyone who fails to be offended by Rushdie's book *ipso facto* ceases to be a Muslim' (The Guardian' 27 February 1989). I do hope that the converse is not true because I have no intention of becoming a Muslim. I totally reject the idea that only a Muslim will feel offended by insults to the Prophet and am confident that Dr Akhtar does not imply that.

Mr Rushdie and the Mullahs

Mr Rushdie is clear in his mind that he was writing against the taboos imposed by 'a powerful tribe of clerics'. He is not the first to do so. In Urdu poetry there is a strong and respected tradition of poking fun at clerics. The poets, however, did not indulge in pornography and did not insult the Prophet and people closely associated with him. I am not one of Martin Amis' ('New Statesman', 30 March, 1989) 'career clerics and self-ghettosing community leaders' (perhaps he will tell me who the latter are as I have not met any) but, like him, I am convinced that Mr Rushdie knew what he was doing. I am, however, less certain whether Martin Amis does.

Mr Rushdie is simply trying to stereotype Mullahs. The latter, like any other human beings, also have political and social convictions.

Freedom of Speech

It is a pity that Mr Rushdie's character Swatilekha, who announced that battle lines are being drawn in India today is not an Asian Briton.

Otherwise she would have noticed that in Britain a battle line separates those who believe that the *freedom of speech* is the only sacred thing in life and those who would grant the status of sacredness to other things including religious faiths of fellow human beings and the life itself, whether it belongs to a protesting Indian or Pakistani Muslim or a Briton. It divides those who believe with Mr Rushdie that 'the offence done to our principles (by the Bradford flames) is as great as any offence caused to those who burned my book' from those, like myself, who *are* offended by the Bradford flames but nonetheless believe that the offence caused by his book is immeasurably greater. The divide between those who have turned the Freedom of Speech into a new goddess and its worship into a most exalted religion and those, like myself, who remain agnostic even in the presence of this new goddess or, like many Muslims who regard their own creed superior to the new creed.

For an immigrant, life is a struggle and being accepted on equal terms in the new homeland appears to be an impossible task.

Businesses, universities, publishers are all controlled by others. It is very tempting, for the sake of being accepted 'to die first' and then 'to be born again'. Most Asian Britons have resisted this temptation, because as Rushdie's Mahound says, 'Writers and prostitutes, I see no difference'.

The world media is controlled by people who are not particularly sympathetic to views people like myself hold. The play Perdition is not acceptable, not because it portrays the weaknesses of humans faced with an impossible situation but because those humans happen to be Zionists.

The Satanic Verses is acceptable because it maligns a religion which Europeans have maligned for centuries. The interesting question is would Viking Penguin have published the book had it been an Indian controlled company with headquarters in Delhi and a branch office in London?

Some purists believe that the freedom of speech of an individual is at stake. They claim the right to be able to read and judge for themselves. I have profound respect for this position, provided it is espoused with consistency. Anyone who has not opposed censorship in other situations eg against the IRA, against the Zionist pressures to ban a play like Perdition, etc. is not a purist. Being a Gandhite, I cannot and do not support the violence perpetrated by the IRA. I am also against the publication of speeches, articles, books etc, which insult any ethnic group. I am not a purist. I believe that an individual's freedom of speech is constrained by other freedoms and also by freedoms of others. It is not a licence to insult.

The Satanic Verses is a pornographic insult to the Prophet Muhammad and people associated with him. It also insults other individuals.

I am totally opposed to the issuing of the *Fatwa* and we must endeavour to have it withdrawn. We also need to have the book withdrawn because it is a continuing provocation.

Islam has a long tradition of civilised debate about its origins and its culture. No Muslim will shirk from a discussion of these. Profanity, however, is different and The Satanic Verses is profane.

Source: *Impact International,* 20/4, 23rd February–8th March 1990 – 'A Contract With the Devil'.

Equal Treatment

While it is a matter of regret that the three High Court judges found it impossible to include insults to Islam in the present laws on blasphemy (Guardian, May 25), it was pleasing to read that despite the judges expressing their inability to refer this case to the Lords, they have left it open to the Lords to hear the case if they choose to do so. This is surely an indication of the embarrassment they have experienced over this issue.

It is time, in my opinion, that Salman Rushdie and his publishers began to appreciate that they cannot run rough-shod over genuine faith under the very convenient claim for freedom of expression. I would not deny that freedom of expression should be an ideal to aim at, but it is clear that we are as yet a long way from reaching it. The fact that laws of blasphemy exist is proof of that.

If such laws are still found necessary then they should cover all established faiths, especially a faith which is numerically the largest faith in the world today.

(Rev) S. Raymond,
Virgo Fidelis Convent,
London SE19.

Source: ©*The Guardian,* 30th May 1990 – 'Faith and Freedom'.

Defamatory Claims in the Name of Artistic Freedom

by George Chryssides

. . . The debate about the Rushdie affair cannot be separated from what the book itself actually says, and few discussants have actually read it. . . . Indeed I am inclined to believe that the novel is so offensive to Muslims that they are not even prepared to quote the truly offensive material in support of their own case. The angel Gabriel (Gibreel) is portrayed not only as sexually promiscuous: he drinks alcohol, eats pork and commits adultery. Muhammad not only receives 'satanic' verses, but is at one point found drunk in a gutter in between Qur'anic revelations. . . .

Given the degree of respect which Muslims accord both to Gabriel and Muhammad, it is impossible to think of anything which would cause equivalent offence to mainstream Christians, let alone secular materialists. One might speculate as to how Christians would react if Jesus Christ were portrayed as a paedophile or a cannibal, or secular humanists might profitably reflect on how they would react if a novelist used their spouses for artistic subject matter and ficticiously portrayed them as unfaithful, criminally immoral and totally lacking in integrity. . . .

Of course, no such novel could be published in the name of artistic freedom. . . . Since the Buddha, Jesus Christ and Muhammad are no longer alive (at least in the conventional sense), it is possible with impunity, as the Rushdie affair has amply demonstrated, to malign a long deceased religious leader and avoid any legal consequences. . . .

Indeed defamatory claims which bear no claim to literal truth can be more damaging than those that do. If a biblical scholar wishes to advance a particularly shocking theory about Jesus Christ (say, that he was a paedophile), he or she would be obliged to produce some kind of evidence in support of the claim, and the contention would fall into the arena of proper academic debate. But if a novelist writes a work of fiction which makes similar allegations, he is under no such obligation to prove the thesis. The 'truth' of a novel does require the same rigour of defence as the scholarly work. Art is art, not necessarily fact. By writing a work of fiction, Rushdie has thus exonerated himself from the obligations and stringencies which would normally be demanded of a serious scholar. . . .

Source: *Discernment: Focus on the Salman Rushdie Affair* (London), 4/2, 1990, pp. 21–2, 23 – 'Fact and Fiction in the Salman Rushdie Affair'.

Arrogance of Secular Liberalism

by Peter Mullen

. . . It would be unjust and libellous – because false – if I were to sit down and write that the present Archbishop of Canterbury is a child-molester or that the Pope is a practising homosexual. I could legitimately write a novel about a child-molester or a practising homosexual; but I would err greatly if I attached these descriptions to historical characters whose behaviour did not involve those acts.

Moreover, if I were to claim that Rushdie is a pornographer, whose only interest is in making money out of offending the faithful, I would no doubt be criticised by him and his lawyers – because, presumably, I had said something about him which is not true. Well, Rushdie should afford the same liberal courtesy to Muhammad before he is tempted to put words into the Prophet's mouth that are not true.

To say what is not true in print is not an extension of artistic freedom and an enlargement of imaginative consciousness, but a restriction of those qualities. Misrepresentations of the truth are never wholesome. Anyone who creates perverted images in fiction is guilty – perhaps of many things – certainly of creating bad art. That is why Islam mistrusts all art. The canvas as well as the camera can all too easily lie. The same goes for the novel. By these criteria *The Satanic Verses* is an artistic failure and, given its author's preconceptions, it could never have been anything else.

. . . His error, for which he is now paying through monstrous privations – was not to take religion seriously enough. So Rushdie has become the focus – one might say the personal incarnation – of secular liberalism's low estimate of the truth-value of religious belief. Such 'liberals' need to be reminded that it is not liberal to say or write things which are not true; it is the censorship of the lie: it is restrictive of human understanding and necessarily so because it perverts the truth. . . .

. . . Freedom of speech does not mean that anyone can say just what he likes. It means that the rational use of language must, because language itself is rational, involve truth-value. No one is allowed to tell lies in the interests of free speech. For the lie is not, properly, formally (in Wittgenstein's sense) speech at all: it is babel. It is the representation of reality *as it is not.* It is therefore a misuse of language, and that must, at the very lowest level, be bad craftsmanship on the part of the wordsmith. Untruths and inaccuracies do not liberate people, but they enslave. It is always a disservice to give someone a false picture. If one misperceives reality, one pays for the misperception – as surely as missing the bottom step and spraining one's ankle. Rushdie is, in his way, paying for his misrepresentation of truth. . . .

And so, when Harold Pinter stood up and read cowering Rushdie's lecture at the ICA, it was evident that he was holding the Koran in one hand and *The Satanic Verses* in the other and, if he were forced to choose between them, he would prefer *The Satanic Verses.* This shows many things: above all it shows the bankruptcy of Western 'liberal' thought. For what is there in Rushdie's mediocre satire which can compare with the spiritual and moral authority of the Holy Koran? But the fashionable, avant-garde writers – literary peacocks – are actually not much good even at their own job: for they undervalue the weight and seriousness of language. They do not understand that the word is truly made flesh: that when you *say* something, you *do* something; that the great religious texts, the scriptures, are an index to humankind's commitment to what is deepest in us. . . .

Rushdie has done a disservice to us all. By his clever derogatory remarks in *The Satanic Verses,* he has undermined our evaluation of what is supremely valuable in the religious tradition in which whole peoples have found their identity, in which some still seek to educate their children. . . .

Source: Dan Cohn-Sherbok (ed.), *The Salman Rushdie Controversy in Interreligious Perspective,* Lampeter, UK, The Edwin Mellen Press, 1990, pp. 30–1, 33–5 – 'Satanic Asides'.

The Tale of Instant Experts on Islam

by Bhikhu Parekh

. . . In retrospect what strikes one about the Muslim protests since October is not so much their intolerance as their timidity, not their feeling of rage but a sense of hurt, not their anger but their distress. . . . They quietly pursued the matter with the publishers, Members of Parliament, the Attorney-General and the Prime Minister. . . . Neither its author nor its publishers seem to have taken them seriously enough to engage in a dialogue with them. According to Muslim leaders, the publishers either did not reply to their letters and telegrams or did so without any sense of urgency and seriousness. As for Rushdie himself, he tended to dismiss the protesters as illiterate fanatics who had neither read nor understood the book and were only bent on suppressing a critical scrutiny of their cherished dogmas.

The British press was just as dismissive. Neither the quality nor the quantity papers published the offending passages, or invited Muslim spokesmen to state their case, or themselves made an attempt to read the book with their eyes. Instead they mocked the Muslims, accused them of 'intolerance', and wondered if a tolerant society should tolerate the intolerant. Although Muslims were intensely frustrated and angry, and although isolated individuals spoke of violence, no Muslims, to my knowledge, threatened Rushdie's or his wife's life, or even threw a stone at him or his house, something any one of the thousands of hotheads could have easily done at a time when he was unguarded and vulnerable.

. . . the book-burning incident led to a torrent of denunciation. Muslims were called 'barbarians', 'uncivilised', 'fanatics', and compared to the Nazis. Many a writer, some of impeccable liberal credentials, openly wondered how Britain could 'civilise' them and protect their innocent progeny against their parent's 'medieval fundamentalism'. Hardly anyone appreciated that the burning of *The Satanic Verses* was more an act of impatience than of intolerance, and that it bore no resemblance to the Nazi burning of libraries and persecution of intellectuals. No one cared to point out either that only a few months earlier, several Labour Members of Parliament had burnt a copy of the new immigration rules outside the House of Commons without raising so much as a murmur of protest. . . .

The British press's reaction to the Muslim reaction, which it had done much to engineer, albeit unintentionally, followed a sad and predictable pattern. . . . Not surprisingly, almost the entire British press got emotionally unhinged and lost its balance.

. . . Most concentrated not on the book, the source of the controversy, but on the Muslim threat to Rushdie's life.

Anthony Burgess (*The Independent,* 16 February 1989) compared Muslims to Nazis who 'shame' Britain 'through the vindictive agency of bonfires'. Since they wanted a 'theocratic state' and did not like a secular society, they should 'fly to the arms of the Ayatollah or some self-righteous guardian of strict morality'. Their protest was mindless, 'unjustified by argument, thought or anything more intellectual than the throwing of stones [*sic*] or the striking of matches'. Even the otherwise sane and perceptive Peter Jenkins (*The Independent,* 1 March 1989) thundered against the 'Bradford *auto-da-fé*', that 'barbaric act of intolerance', and congratulated Mrs. Thatcher for standing up, like a good Christian, for a writer who had been rude to her. . . .

All the newspapers, including the liberal, debated whether British society had an obligation to tolerate the intolerant and whether multi-culturalism was not a dangerous doctrine. An otherwise perceptive editorial in *The Independent* (18 February 1989) thundered against the evils of something called fundamentalism. A *Guardian* editorial asked Muslims to recognise that they were living in a secular society and that they must change their ways of thought and life. Several newspapers wondered if Britain had not made a 'mistake' in 'letting in' too many Muslims. Even Roy Jenkins, father of the Race Relations Act 1976, lamented that 'we might have been more cautious about allowing the creation in the 1950s [*sic*] of a substantial Muslim community here'. He went further and reached the most bizarre conclusion that the Muslim behaviour has strengthened 'my reluctance to have Turkey in the European community' (*The Independent,* 4 March 1989). Apparently all Muslims, like the proverbial Chinese, looked the same to him, and one threatened misdeed by a section of them was enough to damn the lot.

It was depressing to note . . . a wholly mindless anger first against all *Bradford* Muslims, then against all *British* Muslims, then against all *Muslims,* and ultimately against *Islam* itself. . . . Some 'liberal' commentators, a few of them with a leftist past, such as Fay Weldon, became instant experts on the Koran. They attacked its alleged inhumanity and 'bloodthirsty' conception of Allah, unfavourably compared them to the Bible and its 'loving' God, and gave us most valuable insights into the psychology of the medieval crusaders. The neutral observers were left wondering on which side of the debate lay 'fundamentalism', 'medievalism' and 'intolerance'. The history of the last one thousand years with its crusades, the white man's – and latterly woman's – burden, and the 'civilising' empire, was tragicomically re-enacted before our eyes, and its white and brown *dramatis personae* parroted well-worn lines of their banal roles in all too familiar accents.

The conservative press fully shared these rather ugly feelings and was less inhibited about expressing them . . . .

Source: Dan Cohn-Sherbok (ed.), *The Salman Rushdie Controversy in Interreligious Perspective,* Lampeter, UK, The Edwin Mellen Press, 1990, pp. 74–80 – 'The Rushdie Affair and the British Press'.

Liberalism's Holy War

by W. Webster

. . . Where, then, is our much vaunted freedom of speech? Where is the freedom to publish which we prize so much? The answer is that the freedom of expression we enjoy is very narrowly constrained indeed. This is one reason why the arguments about freedom of expression, which liberals frequently advance in order to defend *The Satanic Verses,* are both ill-considered and, ultimately, dangerous. For these arguments are calmly advanced in a society where practically every medium of expression other than the novel is subject to the most complex and elaborate restrictions; where every programme that we watch on television has been vetted by guardians of public decency; where every film we see has been censored, and where the licence we extend to 'art' encourages us to forget that every 'non-artistic' picture ever published or displayed is subject to rigorous obscenity laws. These laws express, in their selective prohibitions and permissions, a seemingly profound antipathy to sexual love and a deep and almost insane horror of some of the most ordinary parts of the human body, particularly when these are conjoined in some of the most ordinary ways. Not only this, but in this same 'free' society, a law has recently been passed in which civil servants have been deprived of one of the most important freedoms which they had previously enjoyed under the law – the freedom to place the demands of conscience above the demands of their government. . . .

On Not Burning Your Enemy's Flag

The noose of anti-Islamic prejudice was tied long ago. But the events which took place in Britain during 1989 have succeeded in putting the heads of hundreds of thousands of British Muslims inside that noose. That is why we must now begin to untie it. We should not underestimate how difficult this task will be, nor how long it will take. At the same time, however, we should be wary of replacing the West's irrational intolerance of Islam and all its works with an equally irrational and indiscriminate love of Islam. The consequences of inverting prejudice in this way can be seen all too clearly in the history of European and American attitudes towards Jews in this century. For what has happened in many quarters is that a profound and irrational anti-semitism has been replaced by an attitude which amounts to philo-semitism; in both Britain and America there has sometimes been a reluctance to criticise any Jewish or Israeli act and a tendency to release both Israeli politicians and Israeli soldiers from the normal constraints of political morality. . . .

If we insult religious believers in this way, we are not demonstrating intellectual independence or proving that we have emancipated ourselves from our religious heritage. For, as I have already argued, one of the most distinctive characteristics of Judaeo-Christian monotheism is the contempt in which it holds other people's religious faith. If we secularise such religious intolerance and present it as a form of rationalist humanism we are in effect perpetrating one of the worst features of our religious tradition. If, marching under the banner of crusading humanism, we not only insult religious believers, but compound the insult with obscenity, we are doing something which is profoundly repressive and profoundly destructive. For most religions do not disintegrate when they are insulted. They almost invariably internalise the hurt which is inflicted on them and grow more rigid and more cruel.

If we really want to make Islam into the most cruel and tyrannical religion there has ever been, we should go on insulting it as the West has been doing for very many centuries, and as Salman Rushdie is now doing on our behalf. If, however, we are at all interested in the future and vitality of our own culture, in respecting the dignity of Muslims, and in preserving ordinary human sensitivity, we should decide that we can do without a paperback of *The Satanic Verses*. We should also start to face up to our own responsibilities and recognise that Salman Rushdie has been betrayed into his terrible ordeal not primarily by *his* insensitivity but by *ours*. . . .

In Good Faith

It is such extreme language, which is potentially the most violent and the most insulting of all the registers available to Western writers, which, in the pages of *The Satanic Verses,* is brought into conjunction with some of the most sacred traditions of Islam. Although there are other perceived insults in the book, this in itself would be enough to create a sense of outrage among the Muslim faithful. When it is joined to the brothel scenes where the whores take the names of the Prophet's wives, to the knowing use the book makes of the street obscenities of Bombay and to the use of the ancient Christian term of abuse, Mahound, for Muhammad, it is little wonder that many Muslims have come to regard Rushdie not simply as an opponent of Islam, but as a cultural traitor who has sold some of their most sensitive secrets into the hands of the enemy. . . .

A Brief History of Blasphemy

It must be said, however, that Muslims have very good reasons to be especially sensitive to such treatment of their own sacred figures. For both Christian polemicists and Western orientalists sought for centuries to denigrate Islam by attributing to it a fantastic, disreputable or demonic sexuality. And what almost all Muslims know, from their intuitive grasp of their own history, is that there is nothing remotely liberating in this kind of Western fantasy. For in the past such fantasies have always tended to belong to the propaganda which has preceded the sword, the bullet and the bomb. What Muslims see in Rushdie's fictional adaptations of ancient stereotypes is not simply hatred, but the long, terrible, triumphalist hatred which the West has had for Islam almost since its beginnings.

To find such hateful stereotypes revived not by one of their traditional enemies, but by a writer who was himself born to a Muslim family in Bombay, is especially hurtful. When ordinary Muslims in this country see that writer richly repaid for his irreverence, feted and celebrated both by intellectuals and by the Western media, while they are rewarded for their faith with ill-disguised contempt, it is little wonder that they feel betrayed in the most intimate and cruel manner, and feel at the same time that their own future existence, security and safety in the West is threatened. Given all this, it should not be surprising that Muslims in this country reacted to the publication of Rushdie's book in the way that they did, and that a number of them wrote in passionate terms to Penguin Books pleading for the book's withdrawal. It is not surprising either that, when these passionate pleas failed to produce any real response, these Muslims should have resorted to more dramatic methods, burning the book in public in an attempt to interest the media in their campaign. . . .

Source: Webster, W., *A Brief History of Blasphemy,* Orwell Press, Suffolk, 1990.

RESPONSE FROM DIFFERENT FAITHS

Letter from the Chief Rabbi

Sir, The appalling Rushdie affair has released, like Newton's Law, equal and opposite forces of elemental magnitude. It has incited religious passions on the one hand and freedom crusades on the other on a scale and of an intensity probably unmatched in modern times.

In a search for legislative controls to defuse the current supertensions and to promote inter-religious co-existence, it has been suggested that the existing laws of blasphemy be extended beyond their strictly Christian confines. Some Christian and Muslim leaders have supported this idea. But I believe the solution lies elsewhere.

When the Chairman of the Islamic Society for the Promotion of Religious Tolerance in the UK asked me last October to support the protest against the publication of *The Satanic Verses,* I readily agreed, and he was informed that I deprecate not only the falsification of established historical records but the offence caused to the religious conviction and susceptibilities of countless citizens. In a civilised society we should generate respect for other people's religious beliefs and not tolerate a form of denigration and ridicule which can only breed resentment to the point of hatred and strife.

While I fully share the world-wide outrage at the murderous threat against the book's author, publishers and distributors, I stand by my view that the book should not have been published for the reasons I gave, now reinforced by subsequent events which have already cost many lives and may yet erupt into more sinister national and international upheavals.

In my view Jews should not seek an extension of the blasphemy laws. In any event, the Jewish definition of blasphemy is confined to "cursing God" and does not include an affront to any prophet (not even Moses, in our case). Living in a predominantly Christian society, with an established Church, we should be quite content to leave the legislation on blasphemy as it stands enshrining the national respect for the majority faith.

What should concern us are not *religious* offences but *socially* intolerable conduct calculated or likely to incite revulsion or violence, by holding up religious beliefs to scurrilous contempt, or by encouraging murder.

Both Mr Rushdie and the Ayatollah have abused freedom of speech, the one by provocatively offending the genuine faith of many millions of devout believers, and the other by a public call to murder, compounded by offering a rich material reward for an ostensibly spiritual deed. It should be illegal to allow either provocation to be published or broadcast.

We already have legislation proscribing by common consent many excesses in the freedom of expression precious as this is. There are laws not only on blasphemy, but on pornography, libel, incitement of race hatred, subversion and breaches of national security. There may be arguments on the precise definition of these offences, but the principle is universally accepted.

Likewise there should be widespread agreement on prohibiting the publication of anything likely to inflame, through obscene defamation, the feelings or beliefs or any section of society, or liable to provoke public disorder and violence. It must obviously be left to public and parliamentary debate to determine where the lines of what is to be illegal are to be drawn.

If Britain were to pioneer such legislation, other nations would no doubt follow suit, perhaps even leading to an international agreement among all civilised people to protect the supreme values of innocent human life and freedom by outlawing the amplification of words which, as experience has now shown, by poisoning the atmosphere can be as lethal a threat to mankind as any physical pollution.

Yours sincerely,
Jakobovits,
Office of the Chief Rabbi

Permission to reproduce this letter, published in *The Times* (4th February, 1989), granted by the Chief Rabbi.

Runcie Calls for Broader Legislation

by Sandra Barwick

The Archbishop of Canterbury, Dr Robert Runcie, yesterday implicitly called for strengthening of the law against blasphemy to cover religions other than Christianity, in a statement which condemned incitement to murder.

Dr Runcie said that only the utterly insensitive could fail to see that the publication of Mr Rushdie's book, *The Satanic Verses,* had deeply offended Muslims both here and throughout the world. "I understand their feelings and I firmly believe that offence to the religious beliefs of the followers of Islam or any other faith is quite as wrong as offence to the religious beliefs of Christians."

Source: ©*The Independent,* 21st February 1989 – 'Runcie Calls for Broader Legislation'.

BCC, 'Grave Concern' at Impact of Rushdie Controversy

'The British Council of Churches expresses grave concern at the damaging effect on inter-faith and community relations of the controversy surrounding Salman Rushdie's novel *The Satanic Verses*. We recognize something of the deep pain and hurt experienced in the British Muslim community because it believes that the Prophet of Islam has been dishonoured. . . .

' . . . A Pre-Renaissance Habit of Mind?'

' . . . Here is a book that can be read as attacking, however cloudily and symbolically, the probity of Islam's founder and the authenticity of the revelation he recorded. A comparable offence to Christianity would be held by many believers to be blasphemy. Leviticus declared blasphemy to deserve death by stoning; . . . – Editorial, *Church Times*, 24th February 1989.

' . . . Limits to the Right of Free Expression?'

'The row over Salman Rushdie's book *The Satanic Verses* raises important questions for us all. What are the limits to the right of free expression? What are the rights of religious communities to protection from insult? What are our duties as Christians to our Moslem neighbours? Christians must make special efforts to reach out humbly and lovingly to a community that feels rejected. And the Government, while protecting all citizens from violence, must look again at the law of blasphemy. If Christianity merits protection from insult, what about the other ancient religions with many followers in the land?' – Editorial, *The Universe*.

'Bishop Urges Publishers to Withdraw The Satanic Verses'

The Bishop of St Albans, the Rt Rev. John Taylor, yesterday called on Viking Penguin, publishers of *The Satanic Verses,* to withdraw the book and so defuse the row over the Ayatollah Khomeini's death threats against its author, Mr Salman Rushdie.

Bishop Taylor said Viking Penguin had succeeded commercially with the book 'beyond their wildest dreams' but had done so 'at the expense of the hurt feelings of the Moslem community.'

The Bishop said: 'By deciding to withdraw the book they would not only be making a wise commercial decision but also be showing moral responsibility for the havoc they have perhaps unwittingly caused'. . . .

'They could make a responsible decision because of the social harm that has been caused to the people of Britain and the diplomatic row it triggered.' – *The Daily Telegraph,* 22nd March 1989.

The Inter-Faith Network UK

'*The Satanic Verses* contains passages which were bound to cause deep offence to Muslims. There have been peaceful protests from them about the book for many months and inevitably a sense of frustration has developed as time has passed. In this country the Muslim community is a minority. They are naturally concerned about attacks upon the integrity of their faith and its misrepresentation. Like others, they are also concerned at attitudes in a society which does not always appear sympathetic to religious values in the community or in family life.' – Interfaith Network (UK).

World Conference on Religion and Peace

Dear Sir,

Now that the media discussion on *The Satanic Verses* is drawing to a close, it may be well to attempt a healing of the wounds which still afflict our society.

Long before the publication of this book, Muslims in Britain were trying to gain the same rights and protection accorded to other religious communities in our multi-cultural society. The Rushdie book, which Muslims regard as blasphemous, is only one aspect of a society showing itself to be insensitive to the needs and pain in which Muslims find themselves. The courts have now ruled that the law of blasphemy is inapplicable, but the need to discuss this problem with inter-faith dialogue is even more urgent.

We deplore all calls to violence which contravene the highest aspirations of all religious traditions. Muslims in Britain have shown themselves to be peace-loving and law-abiding citizens, and responsible Muslim leaders are resolved to approach this problem within the framework of law. It is our hope that inequalities in that law will be redressed and that all minority religions will be fully protected.

The World Conference on Religion and Peace associates itself with our Muslim friends, and would like to move from the present debate to a more sympathetic appraisal of Islamic life in our society. It is our hope that writers and publishers will now exercise more self-discipline in dealing with the most sacred beliefs of their religious neighbours.

We are deeply concerned that the end result of the affair could lead to persecution of the Muslims in the Western world. If any act of terrorism were to take place this would be a tragedy, and we can only affirm our belief that non-violent protest is a more effective and religious response.

Everyone must join together in challenging extremism and in creating a climate of free discussion.

Yours faithfully,

Canon Gordon Wilson (Christian), Rabbi Albert H. Friedlander (Jewish), Mr. B. Konnur (Hindu), Dr. Syed Aziz Pasha (Muslim), Professor Harmindar Singh (Sikh), Mr. Pankay Vora (Jain).

World Conference on Religion and Peace, London E1. – *The Independent,* 16th March 1989.

Source: *Focus on Christian-Muslim Relations: The Rushdie Affair – Responses and Reactions* (Leicester), 3 (1989), pp. 3, 4, 5, 9, 10.

Cardinals Speak on Rushdie but Pope is Silent

by Brian Dooley

. . . In France, Cardinal Albert Decourtray of Lyon slammed the work as "an offence against religious faith". In a public statement the president of the French bishops' conference . . . complained; "Once again the faith of believers is insulted. Yesterday it was Christians who were offended by a film which disfigured the face of Christ. Today it is the Moslems by this book about the Prophet . . . ".

In America, Cardinal John O'Connor of New York expressed solidarity with local Moslems upset about *The Satanic Verses.* "We deplore the belittling or ridiculing of anyone's religion" . . .

One Vatican historian, Fr Robert Graham, has urged the Pope to speak out against the criticisms of Islam in the book. "It constitutes a severe, lacerating criticism of Islam, and in particular of the prophet Mohammad himself." . . .

Source: *Catholic Herald,* 3rd March 1989 – 'Cardinals Speak on Rushdie but Pope is Silent'.

Rushdie Denounced as a Blasphemer by Vatican Paper

by Michael Sheridan and Tim Kelsey

The Vatican newspaper, *L'Osservatore Romano,* condemned Salman Rushdie's novel, *The Satanic Verses,* as blasphemous at the weekend, and implied that there was no right to free speech for blasphemers. . . .

L'Osservatore Romano said that free speech was no defence for Mr Rushdie. "It is not the first time that, by invoking artistic motives or the principle of free expression, people have sought to justify the improper use of sacred texts or religious elements, which thereby become blasphemous." . . .

Source: ©*The Independent,* 6th March 1989 – 'Rushdie Denounced as a Blasphemer by Vatican Paper'.

Graham Backs Muslims on Verses

The evangelist Billy Graham said yesterday that he sympathised with Muslims protesting against Salman Rushdie's book, The Satanic Verses.

At a press conference to launch his Mission 89 crusade to London he compared demonstrations against the book with Christian protests in the US against the film, The Last Temptation of Christ, which many thought was blasphemous. . . .

Source: ©*The Guardian,* 2nd June 1989 – 'Graham Backs Muslims on Verses'.

Church Leaders Unite to Condemn BBC

The BBC programme The Blasphemers' Banquet, which trenchantly defended Mr Salman Rushdie and heaped scorn on religious fundamentalism, was condemned in Bradford yesterday, . . .

The Bishop of Bradford, the Rt Rev Robert Williamson, called the programme distressing and insulting to a Muslim community which already felt humiliated. . . .

He regretted that instead of showing the sort of smiling, cheerful Muslim children he was familiar with in Bradford schools, the programme repeatedly showed "revolting scenes of Muslim fanatics teaching their children to hit their heads until they bled". . . .

Source: ©*The Guardian,* 2nd August 1989 – 'Church Leaders Unite to Condemn BBC'.

For further reading:

- Roald Dahl, 'Letter to the Editor', *The Times,* 28th February, 1989.
- John Vincent, 'Outrage We Cannot Ignore', *The Times,* 2nd March, 1989.
- Robert Harris, 'Satanic Whiff of Money and Vitriol Takes the Air', *The Times,* 11th February, 1990.
- Edward de Bono, 'The Satanic Verses', *The Times,* 16th February, 1990.
- Jack Mahoney, 'Bounds of Blasphemy', *The Times,* 11th April, 1990.
- Rustom Bharucha, 'The Rushdie Affair: Secular Bigotry and the Ambivalence of Faith', *Third Text,* 11 (Summer 1990), pp. 62–8.
- 'Faith Moves a Mountain', *The Times,* 26th December, 1990.

CHAPTER 5

The Muslim Argument

*The 'Satanic' Verses and the Orientalists**

(A note on the authenticity of the so-called Satanic verses)

by M.M. Ahsan

A number of leading Orientalists have made special studies of the Qur'ān and some of them have translated it into European languages. On the whole the attitude of such scholars of the Occident has been unsympathetic and sometimes hostile. There are a few who still regard the Qur'ān as the writing of the Prophet, *ṣallā Allāhu 'alayhi wa sallam*, and not, as the Muslims regard it, the word of God revealed through the angel Gabriel. Many take pains to point out the alleged borrowing of the Qur'ān from Judaeo-Christian sources. Such erroneous assertions have taken on a formulaic significance and echoes of it are too often heard even after new researches have shown otherwise.[1]

A reader of secondary writings of Islam becomes puzzled when he finds two diametrically opposed conclusions reached by Orientalist and Muslim writers using the same sources and materials. It seems that Muslims are not far wrong when they allege that the Orientalists build their edifice on the foundations of so-called objectivity, using the tools of analytical research and critical examination which leads to interpretations not necessarily based on facts but pure speculation, hypothetical assumption and that

*This is a revised version of the article that appeared in *Hamdard Islamicus,* Vol. 5, No. 1, Spring 1982, pp. 27–36.

sometimes a deliberate attempt has been made by many Orientalists to cast doubt on the teachings of Islam by challenging the authenticity of the Qur'ān and the *Sunnah*. Christian, Marxist and Jewish Orientalists have quite often tried to prove, directly or indirectly, that at least some portions of the Qur'ān and *Ḥadīth* are fabricated or inconsistent and are, therefore, unreliable sources for the Islamic way of life. However, such Orientalists have based their attack on the flimsiest of intellectual grounds. In this paper, an attempt has been made to analyse the Orientalists' allegations about the incorporation of the so-called Satanic verses[2] in the Qur'ān – a theme discussed with relish by almost all Western writers on the life of the Prophet.

Before proceeding further, let us look at the story of the so-called 'Satanic' verses[3] which Orientalists like William Muir, Theodor Nöldeke, among earlier writers, and W. Montgomery Watt among contemporary 'biographers' of the Prophet, narrate with their usual 'masterly' comments.[4] These writers apparently base the story on some historical sources which, at first sight, seem quite weighty but on critical investigation fail to satisfy the criteria of historical criticism.[5] Muslim writers in the past such as Ibn Isḥāq, Ibn Hishām, al-Suhaylī (the commentator of Ibn Hishām and the author of *Rawḍ al-Unuf*), Ibn Kathīr, al-Bayhaqī, Qāḍī 'Iyāḍ, Ibn Khuzaymah, ar-Rāzī, al-Qurṭubī, al-'Aynī, al-Shawkānī, etc., as well as contemporary and near contemporary writers like Abul A'lā Mawdūdī, Sayyid Quṭb, Muḥammad Ḥusayn Haykal, etc., have all rejected the story as preposterous and without foundation.[6]

Aṭ-Ṭabarī, Ibn Sa'd and some other Muslim writers have mentioned (though they vary considerably in matters of detail) that the Prophet Muḥammad, *ṣallā Allāhu 'alayhi wa sallam*, under Satanic inspiration added two verses to *Sūrah an-Najm* (53), which are as follows:[7]

تِلْكَ الغَرَانِيقُ العُلَى ۔ وإنّ شفاعتهنّ لَتُرتجى ۔

[These are the high-soaring ones (deities), whose intercession is to be hoped for!]

The Prophet, it is alleged, recited these along with other verses of *Sūrah an-Najm* in the prayer. The idolaters of Makkah who were present in the Ka'bah at that time joined him in the prayer because he praised their deities and thus won their hearts. The story afterwards reached Abyssinia where the Muslims persecuted by the Makkan infidels had earlier migrated and many of them returned to Makkah under the impression that the disbelievers no longer opposed the Prophet and the Islamic movement. The story also says that the angel Gabriel came to the Prophet the same evening and told him about the mistake he had committed by reciting verses which were never revealed to him. This naturally worried the Prophet and made him apprehensive. Then, 'admonishing' the Prophet, God revealed the following verses of *Sūrah Banī Isrā'īl,* which read:

وَإِن كَادُوا لَيَفْتِنُونَكَ عَنِ الَّذِي أَوْحَيْنَا إِلَيْكَ لِتَفْتَرِيَ عَلَيْنَا غَيْرَهُ۔
وَإِذًا لَّاتَّخَذُوكَ خَلِيلًا۔ وَلَوْلَا أَن ثَبَّتْنَاكَ لَقَدْ كِدتَّ تَرْكَنُ إِلَيْهِمْ
شَيْئًا قَلِيلًا۔ إِذًا لَّأَذَقْنَاكَ ضِعْفَ الْحَيٰوةِ وَضِعْفَ الْمَمَاتِ ثُمَّ
لَا تَجِدُ لَكَ عَلَيْنَا نَصِيرًا۔ (بنی اسرائیل - ۷۳ - ۷۵)۔

They were constantly trying to tempt you away from that which We have revealed to you, so that you may substitute in its place something of your own, in which case they would have actively taken you as a friend. And if We had not made you firm, you might have indeed inclined to them a little. Then We would have made you taste a double punishment in this life and a double punishment after death and then you would not have found any helper against Us. (17: 73–5)

This made the Prophet feel very guilty until God revealed the following consoling verse of *Sūrah al-Ḥajj*:

وَمَا أَرْسَلْنَا مِن قَبْلِكَ مِن رَّسُولٍ وَلَا نَبِيٍّ إِلَّا إِذَا تَمَنَّىٰ أَلْقَى
الشَّيْطَانُ فِي أُمْنِيَّتِهِ۔ فَيَنسَخُ اللَّهُ مَا يُلْقِي الشَّيْطَانُ ثُمَّ يُحْكِمُ
اللَّهُ آيَاتِهِ۔ (الحج - ۵۲)۔

Whenever We sent a Messenger or a Prophet before you and he framed a desire, Satan put obstacles in it. Then Allāh

> removes the obstacles placed by Satan and He firmly establishes His signs. (22: 52)

This is the gist of the story mentioned by aṭ-Ṭabarī and some other writers which has been used by the Orientalists to reinforce their views on the Qur'ān. The story would, among other things, imply that the Prophet and his Companions took the 'Satanic' verses as a true revelation from God, otherwise nobody would have accepted them.

Let us now examine the story and its contents in the light of internal and external evidence and evaluate it on the basis of criteria of historical criticism. In doing so, first of all one has to find out the chronological sequence in the story and establish whether or not all its details relate to one period and are interconnected. Special attention should also be devoted to determining the periods of revelation of the three verses mentioned in the report which will validate or falsify the episode.

It can be easily gleaned from the story that the incident of reciting the 'Satanic' verses and the consequent prostration of the disbelievers in the Ka'bah happened after the first batch of Muslims had migrated to Abyssinia. This migration, according to all reliable historical sources, occurred in the month of Rajab of the fifth year of the Prophetic call or about eight years before the *Hijrah* to Madinah. Therefore, the incident must have happened close to this date and not long after the migration to Abyssinia.

The verses of *Sūrah Banī Isrā'īl* (17: 73–5) which were revealed, according to the story, to 'admonish' the Prophet for allegedly reciting the 'Satanic verses', in fact were not revealed until after the event of the *Mi'rāj*. The *Mi'rāj* or the Ascent of the Prophet, according to historical sources, occurred in the tenth or eleventh year of the Prophetic call, i.e. about two or three years before the *Hijrah* to Madinah. If this is so, then it implies that the 'Satanic' verses were not detected or for some reason no mention was made about the alleged interpolation of the verses for five or six years and only afterwards was the Prophet admonished for it. Can any sensible person, asks Abul A'lā Mawdūdī, believe that the interpolation occurs today, while the admonition takes place six years later and the abrogation of the interpolated verses is publicly announced after nine years (cf. *Sīrat-i Sarwar-i 'Ālam,* Vol. 2, p.

574). The relevant verse of *Sūrah al-Ḥajj* (22: 52) according to the commentators of the Qur'ān was revealed in the first year of the *Hijrah,* i.e. about eight to nine years after the incident and about two and a half years after the so-called admonition of the Prophet (17: 73–5).[8] Could anybody who knows about the Qur'ān, its history and revelation, understand and explain how the incident of interpolation was allowed to be tolerated for six years and also why the offensive 'verses' were not abrogated until after nine years? Watt's theory is that 'the earliest versions do not specify how long afterwards this (abrogation) happened; the probability is that it was weeks or even months'[9] is nothing but a hypothesis. Had he investigated the chronology of the three revelations relative to the story, he could not possibly have missed the facts related above.

Let us now turn to some internal evidence. It has been said in the story that the 'Satanic' interpolation occurred in *Sūrah an-Najm* (53: 19f.) which delighted the idolaters present in the Ka'bah and as a gesture of friendship and good-will, they all bowed down with the Prophet. In order to comment on the story it would seem necessary to read the verses in the Qur'ān, adding the two alleged 'Satanic' verses, and find out what is actually meant to be conveyed here. It would read as follows:

أَفَرَءَيْتُمُ اللّٰتَ وَالْعُزّٰى ـ وَمَنٰوةَ الثَّالِثَةَ الْأُخْرٰى ـ أَلَكُمُ
الذَّكَرُ وَلَهُ الْأُنْثٰى ـ تِلْكَ إِذًا قِسْمَةٌ ضِيزٰى ـ إِنْ هِيَ إِلَّآ أَسْمَآءٌ
سَمَّيْتُمُوهَآ أَنْتُمْ وَآبَآؤُكُم مَّآ أَنْزَلَ اللّٰهُ بِهَا مِنْ سُلْطٰنٍ إِنْ
يَتَّبِعُونَ إِلَّا الظَّنَّ وَمَا تَهْوَى الْأَنْفُسُ ـ وَلَقَدْ جَآءَهُم مِّن
رَّبِّهِمُ الْهُدٰى ـ (النجم ـ ١٩ ـ ٢٣) ـ

Have you considered al-Lāt and al-'Uzzā and Manāt, the third, the other! *These are the high-soaring ones (deities) whose intercession is to be hoped for!* Are the males for you and for Him (God) the females? This indeed is an unjust division. They are but names which you have named, you and your fathers, for which God has revealed no authority. They follow but conjecture and what (their) souls desire. And now the guidance has come to them from their Lord. (53: 19–23)

If one reads the italicized part of the alleged Satanic verses quoted above, one fails to understand how God on the one hand is praising the deities and on the other discrediting them by using the subsequent phrases quoted above. It is also difficult to see how the Quraysh leaders drew the conclusion from this chapter that Muḥammad, *ṣallā Allāhu 'alayhi wa sallam*, was making a conciliatory move and was adopting a policy of give and take.

Drawing conclusions from various reports connected with the story, Watt suggests that 'at one time Muḥammad must have publicly recited the Satanic verses as part of the Qur'ān; it is unthinkable that the story could have been invented later by Muslims or foisted upon them by non-Muslims. Secondly, at some later time Muḥammad announced that these verses were not really part of the Qur'ān and should be replaced by others of a vastly different import'.[10] Watt's suggestion that Muḥammad replaced the 'Satanic' verses with some others of a vastly different import is pure speculation. If one takes the 'Satanic verses' to be true, it would imply that the verses to be found in 53: 19f. were not revealed in the same period. Watt's suggestion also implies that Muḥammad and his followers read the 'Satanic' verses in place of or in addition to the verses found in the Qur'ān for 'weeks and even months' and that when Muḥammad later realized that these verses could not be correct, then the true version and continuation of the passage was revealed to him. This supposition is again pure speculation and is not based on any historical data. The story which we have summarized in the beginning suggests that Muḥammad did not realize his fault until God admonished him *six years later* and that the matter was rectified perhaps *another two and a half years* after.

It is obvious that Watt and other Orientalists accept part of the story and reject the other parts apparently because they are unable to find any link or sequence. Had there been any element of truth in the story, it could have caused a scandal against Islam and the Prophet and every detail must have found its place in the *Ḥadīth* literature. Why is the authentic *Ḥadīth* collection (namely the *Ṣiḥāḥ Sittah*) conspicuously silent about the *scandalous* part of the story? Does it not lead to the conclusion, contrary to the established fact, that *Ḥadīth* literature itself is very defective as it failed to record such an important event which led the Prophet and his Companions to read 'Satanic' verses for weeks, months or perhaps even years without realizing their error? In fact, al-Bukhārī, Muslim, Abū Dāwūd, Nasā'ī and Aḥmad b. Ḥanbal all record the story but only to the extent that was true. They all mention that the Prophet did recite *Sūrah an-Najm* and, at the end when he prostrated, the idolaters present were so overawed that they also joined him in prostration. These leading *Muḥaddithūn* do not mention the blasphemous story which other sources have recorded. The fact that the idolaters became overawed and joined Muḥammad in prostration is not difficult to believe as they all knew what magical effect the Qur'ān exercised on the listeners which was one of the reasons why they called the Qur'ān a *magic* قَالُوٓا إِنَّ هَٰذَا لَسِحْرٌ مُّبِينٌ (يونس - ٧٦)- and the Prophet a *magician* قَالَ الْكَٰفِرُونَ إِنَّ هَٰذَا لَسَٰحِرٌ مُّبِينٌ - (يونس - ٢)- There is much historical data to substantiate the validity of this statement. It will suffice to retell the story of the acceptance of Islam by 'Umar I and the listening to the Qur'ān by the *jinns* ... أَنَّهُ اسْتَمَعَ نَفَرٌ مِّنَ الْجِنِّ فَقَالُوٓا إِنَّا سَمِعْنَا قُرْءَانًا عَجَبًا (الجن - ١)- (72: 1). It is quite likely that after their prostration the Quraysh were very ashamed and tried to hide their shame by inventing the story that they heard Muḥammad praising their deities which made them join him in prostration. The news of the idolaters and Muslims prostrating together spread quickly and it even reached Abyssinia with the additional rumour that Muḥammad had reconciled with the Quraysh and that hostility no longer existed between them.

Apart from the absurd nature of the story and the external and internal criticism which it cannot stand, there is another criterion of evaluation which one should not lose sight of. The Muslim traditionists quite often evaluate *Ḥadīth* on the basis of *riwāyah* (the statement or the news based on the chain of narrators and the text of the *Ḥadīth*) as well as *dirāyah* (credibility of the statement). It means that if something has been attributed to the Prophet of Islam through apparently sound *Ḥadīth*, it will not automatically be accepted if it goes against the Qur'ān and other established traditions and cannot be justified by reasoning.[11] It is here that even if one regards the story of the 'Satanic verses' to be sound on the ground that it has been narrated by a number of Muslim scholars or because it conforms to the requirements of a true narration (which it lacks), no Muslim traditionist will accept this story because it stands in clear contradiction to the established beliefs of the Muslims. The first few verses of *Sūrah an-Najm* themselves very clearly say:

وَالنَّجْمِ إِذَا هَوَىٰ ـ مَا ضَلَّ صَاحِبُكُمْ وَمَا غَوَىٰ ـ وَمَا يَنْطِقُ
عَنِ الْهَوَىٰ ـ إِنْ هُوَ إِلَّا وَحْيٌ يُوحَىٰ ـ عَلَّمَهُ شَدِيدُ الْقُوَىٰ.
(النجم ـ ١ ـ ٥)ـ

> By the star when it sets; your companion errs not, nor does he deviate; nor does he speak out of desire. It is nothing but revelation that is revealed – One Mighty in power has taught him. (53: 1–5)

In *Sūrah al-Jinn* (72: 26–8), it is further declared:

... فَلَا يُظْهِرُ عَلَىٰ غَيْبِهِ أَحَدًا ـ إِلَّا مَنِ ارْتَضَىٰ مِنْ
رَسُولٍ فَإِنَّهُ يَسْلُكُ مِنْ بَيْنِ يَدَيْهِ وَمِنْ خَلْفِهِ رَصَدًا ـ
لِيَعْلَمَ أَنْ قَدْ أَبْلَغُوا رِسَالَاتِ رَبِّهِمْ ـ (الجن ٢٦ ـ ٢٨)ـ

> He reveals not His secrets to any, except to him whom He chooses as a Messenger; for surely He makes a guard to march before him and after him, so that He may know that they have truly delivered the Message of their Lord.

These and other verses make it clear that it is not possible for the Prophet to accept anything in the Qur'ān from any external source. If this is so, then how can one take seriously, let alone believe in the so-called story of the 'Satanic revelation'? This is why the leading traditionists and exegetists in Islam have regarded the story as malicious and without foundation. It is unfortunate that an eminent historian like aṭ-Ṭabarī mentioned this story in his *Ta'rīkh* and did not make any comment on it. It is to be noted that early Muslim historians although meticulous in their *isnād* sometimes acted like a 'tape-recorder', recording anything that came to their knowledge from a sound and apparently reliable source. In a bid to remain objective and convey the message in pure form they seldom gave their own opinion and refrained from analysing the events thereby guiding the reader to their authenticity or otherwise. Aṭ-Ṭabarī was no exception. This he makes very clear at the outset in the following words: 'This book of mine may [be found] to contain some information, mentioned by us on the authority of certain men of the past, which the reader may disapprove of and the listener may find detestable, because he can find nothing sound and no real meaning in it. In such cases, he should know that it is not our fault that such information comes to him, but the fault of someone who transmitted it to us. We have merely reported it as it was reported to us'.[12] Although there is great advantage in such a methodology there are also risks. Unscrupulous people may take advantage of this and try to concoct something as they did indeed in the fabrication of the malicious story of the so-called 'Satanic Verses'. This is why more cautious historians of a later period such as Ibn al-Athīr criticized aṭ-Ṭabarī for his bad historical and literary judgement with regard to some of the material contained in his book. The fact that aṭ-Ṭabarī, Ibn Sa'd and some other historians and scholars recorded this story in their works does not prove that the story itself is true. Modern researchers know that there are a number of reports and events which have been proved incorrect in the light of historical criticism and other available facts. One may refer, for instance, to the article *'Abbāsa* in the new edition of the *Encyclopaedia of Islam,* where aṭ-Ṭabarī's report that Hārūn ar-Rashīd's sister 'Abbāsah was secretly in love with Hārūn's vizier, has been proved incorrect and misleading.[13]

Notes and References

1. There have been very few scholarly writings by Muslims in the English language about Orientalists' views on Islam in general and on the Qur'ān in particular. For a survey of literature on Orientalism, see my bibliography entitled 'Orientalism and the Study of Islam in the West – A Select Bibliography' published in the *Muslim World Book Review,* Vol. 1, No. 4, 1981, pp. 51–60. To this list, *Orientalism, Islam and Islamists* edited by A. Hussain, R. Olson and J. Qureshi (Amana Books, 1984) may be added.
2. In Muslim sources the whole saga is known as *Ḥadīth al-Gharānīq* or the tradition of *Gharānīq,* the high-soaring ones. William Muir was perhaps the first Orientalist to name them 'Satanic verses'. A recent Jewish researcher of Islam regards the episode as 'one of the most striking instances of "abrogation" and "substitutions" ' and suggests that it is called 'Satanic' because of its pagan connotation. Cf. Ilse Lichtenstadter, 'A Note on the

Gharānīq and Related Qur'ānic Problems', *Israel Oriental Studies,* 5 (1975), pp. 54–61.

3. This article has been inspired by the writings of Mawlānā Abul A'lā Mawdūdī and is based, among other sources, on his monumental Qur'ānic exegesis, *Tafhīm al-Qur'ān* and his study on the life of the Prophet entitled *Sīrat-i Sarwar-i 'Ālam,* both in Urdu. It is unfortunate that, due to his death in September, 1979, Mawlānā Mawdūdī could not complete his critique of the Orientalists' writings on the *Sīrah* of the Prophet – a desire which his predecessor, 'Allāmah Shiblī Nu'mānī (1857–1914) the celebrated author of the *Sīrat an-Nabī,* also took to the grave and was not able to accomplish during his lifetime for various reasons.
4. Watt devotes more than eight pages in his *Muhammad at Mecca*, Oxford, 1960, pp. 101–9, to narrating and evaluating the story. A summary of this also appears in his 1968 publication *What is Islam?,* Longman and Librairie de Liban, pp. 42–5; the new edition of this book (1979) also retains the story without any change. See also, *The Introduction to the Qur'ān,* originally written by Richard Bell, but revised by him, Edinburgh, 1970, pp. 55–6. For similar far-fetched arguments and analysis of the story see Michael M.J. Fischer and Mehdi Abedi, 'Bombay Talkies, the Word and the World: Salman Rushdie's *Satanic Verses*', *Cultural Anthropology,* Washington, Vol. 5, No. 2, 1990, pp. 107–59, in particular pp. 124–30. Note their curious argument. 'The story that Muḥammad could have used the Satanic suggestion is rejected by almost all exegetes, but the fact that the story persists as a subject of exegetes' discussions is testimony to the reality of the temptation both for Muḥammad and for later Muslims in their own struggles with such 'Babylons' as London, New York, Paris, or Hamburg' (p. 127).
5. This is why some of the more discerning scholars in the West such as the Italian L. Caetani and the Briton John Burton have rejected the story as baseless and suggested different motives for the concoction of the outrageous tale (cf. L. Caetani, *Annali, dell' Islam* (Milan, 1906), No. 1, pp. 279–81; J. Burton, 'Those are the High-Flying Cranes', *Journal of Semitic Studies*, Vol. 15, No. 2, 1970, pp. 246–65).
6. Abul A'lā Mawdūdī in his Urdu Qur'ānic exegesis, *Tafhīm al-Qur'ān,* Lahore, 1972, Vol. 3, pp. 238–45, and *Sīrat-i Sarwar-i 'Ālam,* Lahore, 1979, Vol. 2, pp. 572–8, critically examines all the aspects of the story and evaluates the writings of early Muslim scholars on the subject quite thoroughly. See also, among others, Sayyid Quṭb, *Fī Ẓilāl al-Qur'ān,* Beirut, 1974, Vol. 4, pp. 2431–3; M.H. Haykal, *The Life of Muḥammad,* translated into English by Ismā'īl R. al-Fārūqī, North American Trust Publications, 1976, pp. 105–14, and Zakaria Bashier, *The Meccan Crucible*, London, 1978, pp. 180–6.
7. Several variants of these two spurious verses have been quoted which are as follows:

الغَرانِقَةُ العُلى - إنّ شَفاعتَهُنّ تُرتَجى -
إنّهَا لَهِيَ الغَرانيقُ العُلى -
وإنّ هُنّ لَهُنّ الغَرانيقُ العُلى وإنّ شَفاعتَهُنّ لَهِيَ الّتي تُرتَجى -
..... إنّ شَفاعَتَهُنّ تُرتَجى - (بِدُونِ الأجنِحَةِ الأولى الغَرانيقُ أوالغَرانِقَةُ -)
(- الرئيس التحرير -)

8. For a fuller discussion of this argument see the Urdu biography (incomplete) of the Prophet by Abul A'lā Mawdūdī entitled *Sīrat-i Sarwar-i 'Ālam,* Lahore, 1979, Vol. 2, pp. 573–7.
9. W. Montgomery Watt, *Muhammad at Mecca,* Oxford University Press, 1960, p. 103.
10. *Ibid.*
11. *The History of aṭ-Ṭabarī (Ta'rīkh al-Rusul wal-Mulūk),* Vol. I, *General Introduction and from the Creation to the Flood,* translation and annotation by Franz Rosenthal, New York, 1989, pp. 170–1.
12. Cf. *Encyclopaedia of Islam,* s.v. *'Abbāsa* (by J. Horovitz).

Publishing Sacrilege is Not Acceptable

by M.H. Faruqi

. . . Living in London, the cultural capital of the English language and exposed to all media distortion and denigration of Islam and Muslims (nothing is ever right about them), one must confess, one has got used to the thing. It is not unconcern or insensitivity, as far as we in *Impact* are concerned. Our attitude to the problem, painful as it is, is based on the recognition of our own limitations and of the reality that the problem is large and long-term and can only be tackled over a period of time. It concerns the place and value of Islam in our own lives and in Muslim societies which claim to be sovereign. The outsider cannot respect us more than we respect ourselves.

The factors of prejudice are historical and political. Challenged by the rise of a superior social, economic and political culture based on unadulterated Abrahamic Faith, the then 'Christian' West had to 'fantasticate' and invent a 'Mahound', a devil god, in order to prevent its flock from being influenced by the pure Message and clean life of Muhammad, peace and blessing of God be upon him. A whole corps of missionary orientalists was raised but in order not to understand Islam and then criticise and counter it. The purpose was to confuse and distort lest their own people were attracted to Islam which was not a new faith: It was a continuation, confirmation and completion of the faith of Jesus and Moses (may God's peace be upon them).

As long as the Muslim world had political and intellectual vigour and Muslim society presented itself as an open book on Islam, it was possible for the non-Muslim to compare the orientalist version with this 'open book' and decide for himself, and people went on deciding and accepting the Truth, Islam. That situation has vastly changed. The earlier corps of missionary orientalists has since been fortified by a later arrival of Zionist orientalists and now we are beginning to have Hindu 'experts of Islam'.

The Muslim response to this intellectual development has less to do with setting their own house in order, protecting their own political and intellectual sovereignty and building and strengthening their institution of learning.

On popular level we have declarations and denunciations: declarations which betray lack of seriousness and denunciations which are patently hollow. On official plane Muslim institutions and authorities bend over backwards to appease the very same experts. Not long ago these 'experts' used to be invited even to help draft their family law and advise on 'reforming' Islam. Today a whole set of similar experts are busy writing laws and blue-prints for social, economic and educational policy for the entire Muslim world.

The Western media is sought to be appeased by expensive public relations exercises and offering them huge advertising largesse. In the end, the regimes end up with losing both their money and their throne. Although one feels immediately affected by whatever is done by the electronic or the print media because it is an ongoing affair and more often than not the slights and abuses are very hurtful, yet the media can be regarded as quite innocent of them all. Firstly, most of the journalists, columnists and editorial writers, in reporting or commenting about Islam and Muslim world are – presumably quite honestly – only drawing from the perceptions and resource file of their experts, orientalist and Islamologists. Secondly, how can a non-Muslim journalist or writer be expected to respect Islam or Muslim sensitivities when he or she finds Muslims themselves showing a great lack of self-respect.

In a situation characterised by both insult and lack of self-respect, one needs a great store of patience and composure, to ignore the negatives and to concentrate on the positives. Rather than try to worry and shout what the Western media should or should not do, one could more usefully think and do 'whatever one can to present our own fact file, the Muslim world view and a Muslim interpretation of ideas and events. Not to say that nothing more cannot be done, but it is more practical to do whatever can be done within the given parameters.

So when last month someone rang to ask, 'What are you going to do about *The Satanic Verses*?', we said, 'Nothing'. *The Satanic Verses* would be what they say they are and can be left for their devotees to recite and enjoy.

Salman Rushdie or 'Simon Rushton', as some of his friends like to call him, is a known character, who, until recently, made no apology about whatever he is: A self-hating Indo-Anglian, totally alienated from his culture, who has also learnt that it is possible to make money by selling self-hate. One had heard about the book mid 1986 when Rushdie was still going through his dirty word processor. It was said to be a social novel about India and Pakistan, the usual subject of the author's sado-masochism, but one had no clue as to what filth he was going to come up with this time. The book was published in Britain last month and we are waiting for the review copy to arrive – which did not – and, if interesting, to do a piece on this latest tome from this growingly interesting author – in the light of the advance publicity lavished by the media.

Two things arrived nearly about the same time. One, a letter from The Islamic Foundation, Leicester, along with a copy of some extracts from *The Satanic Verses*; and two, the news that responding to strong protest by the Muslim leadership in India, Prime Minister Rajiv Gandhi had promptly acted to ban the entry of the title under the Customs Act (though by then some 300 copies had reached Delhi and obviously many had gone under the counter). The extracts read here were utterly shocking and outrageous. Both the writer and the publisher, Viking (an imprint of the more well known Penguin), had gone over the top. The advance reviews of this book and interviews with Rushdie published in Indian magazines made it absolutely clear that the sacrilege was deliberate.

We concede the freedom of an individual even to fantasise filth and to put down his outpouring on a piece of paper if it gave him any enjoyment. The vermin too has its own culture, but as the Indian Muslim MP, Syed Shahabuddin said, no civilised society should allow the *publication* of filth and pollute the human environment.

Faced with the rising anger of the Muslim community, Rushdie was now saying: 'How could I be anti-Muslim when my whole family is Muslim?' Absolute rubbish. To be a traitor, one has to belong to the community one intends to betray. Moreover few of the reviewers or interviewers who have written about him in adulating terms were in any doubt that he was anything but a lapsed believer, nor did he claim otherwise. 'I was religious in quite an unthinking way. Now, I am not', he told Mark Lawson of *The Independent Magazine* (10th September 1988). He was 'someone who would no longer describe himself as religious' Rushdie told *The Observer,* (25th September 1988).

Rushdie also said that pages from the book were 'being taken out of context by groups trying to grab attention' and, as if to balance sacrilege, 'there is another scene which contrasts profane living with the puritanism of the new religion'. He has also written an angry letter to Mr Rajiv Gandhi.

One – 'The book isn't about Islam, but about migration, metamorphosis, divided selves, love, death, London and Bombay'.

Two – 'It deals with a prophet (who is not called Muhammad)'.

Three – Moreover, 'this entire sequence happens in a dream, fictional dream, of a fictional character'.

Four – 'In this dream sequence, I have tried to offer my view of the phenomenon of revelation, the birth of a great world religion: and that view is that of a secular man for whom Islamic culture has been of central importance all his life'.

But Rushdie's defence is hedging around the truth. . . .

The statement that 'actually' the book is not about Islam is falsehood. Six of the nine 'Chapters' deal with an Islamic theme, Islamic symbolism, and with real Islamic characters only thinly disguised by a mix of fantasy and absurd. The 'prophet' Rushdie deals with is not called Muhammad, but he compounds the blasphemy by using the derogatory European Middle Ages synonym of 'Mahound'.

It matters little if 'this entire sequence happens in a dream, fictional dream, of a fictional character', because here we are dealing with the creator of that so-called fiction. Fiction and fantasy are no license for insult and profanity. A deranged mind can dream any dream but the moment he begins to insult and provoke then he enters the no go area. If he has true friends around him, they will ask him to shut up.

Fact of the matter is that not having the courage or the ability of a scholar, Rushdie has simply tried to hide behind the thin veneer of dream and fiction, but his fantasy is very much part of his psyche. . . .

He claims the book is not 'actually' about Islam, yet he also wants to take credit for offering 'my view of the phenomenon of revelation, and the birth of a great world religion'. He also claims that 'Islamic culture has been of central importance all his life', albeit in a secular way. If that is so then probably many of his friends and girl-friends must be itching to convert to this Islam. The fact is that apart from making money out of sacrilege, Rushdie would also like to subvert Islamic values so that no one can point a finger at his 'secular' way of life.

However, Rushdie was more forthcoming and truthful when he was speaking to *India Today,* (15th September 1988). He was not trying to equivocate. He was speaking with a sense of coming triumph.

'Parts of the novel have been in my head since I first began to study Islamic history at the University 20 years ago . . . Actually, one of my major themes is religion and fanaticism. I have talked about the Islamic religion because that is what I know most about . . .

'I have changed names. I have given the name of an Egyptian temple, Abu Simbel, to the leader of Mecca. I have not called the cities by their names. After all this is a visionary thing (sic) . . .

'The book is really about the fact that an idea or a new thing in the world must decide whether to compromise or not. Beyond that, the image out of which the book grew was of the prophet going to the mountain and not being able to tell the difference between the angel and the devil.'

This amply illustrates Rushdie's 'vision', sick or altruistic, as it may be. As long as such fantasy is confined to one's private thoughts or even writings, there would be little cause for anyone to concern himself with it, except the person's own psychiatrist. But to publish illiterate sacrilege and to try to make money out of it on the excuse that it is a work of great literary merit, is not acceptable.

The Muslim community in Britain – and so would be others as information reaches them in course of time – is shocked and outraged beyond any describable measure by the unprecedented enormity of this sacrilege and by the fact that so far a respectable publisher, Penguin, has been insensitive enough to lend its name to this extreme profanity.

Muslim organisations in Britain are, therefore, asking Penguin:

One – To withdraw and pulp all the copies of *The Satanic Verses* and to undertake not to reprint it in the future.

Two – To offer unqualified public apology to the World Muslim community.

Three – To pay damages equal to the returns received from the copies already sold in Britain and abroad.

Failing which they are asking Muslim authorities to freeze all Penguin and Viking business in their jurisdictions and to exempt from copyright law such titles as may be needed for educational purposes. The book should be banned in any case, but banning is meaningless unless it is accompanied by deterrent measures.

These demands have been supported by the Secretary General of the 46-nation Organisation of the Islamic Conference (OIC), Syed Sharifuddin Pirzada, who has called upon member states to 'take strong measures to ensure that this book is withdrawn from circulation by its publisher immediately and its copies destroyed' and 'the blasphemous book and its author must be banned from entry into all Islamic countries'.

Perhaps it would be more salutory if the author is allowed to enter into Islamic jurisdiction and prosecuted under relevant law.

Penguin have so far tried to maintain masterly indifference, telling people writing to them that they 'don't recognise Salman Rushdie's novel in your description', that it has 'been widely praised by critics' and that 'we have no intention of withdrawing the book.'

Surely they are counting on the legal security of the British law against blasphemy which applied only to Christianity. Probably they are hoping that few Muslim authorities would have the will or courage to take on this powerful publishing house and PR network. Definitely they do not seem to be willing to think much of the deeply hurt feelings within the Muslim community.

The demands listed are neither unreasonable, nor unattainable. But it is time now for the Ummah to stand up for the honour and dignity of its Faith, of its Beloved Messenger of God (peace and blessings of God be upon him) and of his family and his companions (may God be pleased with them all). If they do not, then they should be prepared to receive more Rushdies and more Penguins.

We have never ever made an editorial appeal like this, but we are asking readers to pursue these demands both with the publishers and Muslim authorities through telegrams, letters, telephone, personal representation and through all civilised and legitimate means. But please leave Mr Salman Rushdie all to himself and to his charmed circle of 'literary critics'. We have to say this because we also sense a milling anger about the outrage committed by him.

The point Muslims want to make is that while they recognise that people behave according to their level of culture, they do not accept that it is right for anyone to publish and spread obscene sacrilege and make a business out of it.

Penguin cannot argue that they had not been advised. Their Indian editorial adviser Khushwant Singh, is on record having advised them against publishing the book. He had told them 'that the Prophet had been made to be small time impostor in the novel and that if the author could not see that the work would cause trouble he was out of touch with the Indian reality.' Khushwant is himself a distinguished writer. He is not a Muslim, much less a 'fundamentalist'. His advice was, however, over-ruled by a Rushdie friend in Penguin, Peter Mayer.

After Penguin have made amends with the Muslim world, they may also have to do a little house-cleaning . . . , but that's their business.

Source: *Impact International,* 18/20, 28th October–10th November 1988, pp. 12–14.

Dear Mr Rushdie . . .

I have read with interest your open letter to our Prime Minister Mr Rajiv Gandhi, in which you have pleaded for a review of the ban of your book *The Satanic Verses.*

You have made fun of the fact that the order was issued by the finance ministry. Well, you information is half-baked. It was reported in the press that the decision was taken by the entire Cabinet; but as the ban is to be executed by the Customs, which falls under the finance ministry, no other ministry could have issued it.

This aside, it is for Rajiv Gandhi to reply to your letter: he may ignore it as most heads of government do.

I am not one of those, who has not read your book. I have, and am interested to know from you the replies to some questions, as I feel they may help me to understand you better and also for you to plead your case more effectively. We, in India, are ever so worried about communal violence, which erupts on the slightest pretext, we cannot allow a writer, whatever be his motive, to provoke it.

You say in your letter to Mr Gandhi that you 'strongly deny' that your book is 'a direct attack on Islam'. Further, that 'the section of the book in question . . . . deals with a prophet who is not called Muhammad'.

I have read your book. Like you, I have also been a student of Islam. Your statements, therefore, surprise me. I feel you are going back on your own objective just to get the ban lifted. Maybe I am wrong. I will, therefore, appreciate if you would clarify your position by replying openly to the following questions:

1 What is the significance of the title of your book *The Satanic Verses*? Has it not some historical connection? Do not the verses which refer to the three goddesses, condemned as Satanic and repudiated by Allah, the same as your reference to them in your novel? Your words are so clear that no other inference seems possible: "These verses are banished from the true recitation, *al-qur'an.* New verses are thundered in their place." . . .

2 Is Jahilia not the same word as used in Muslim annals for "the era of ignorance" – Jahilia means ignorance – the era before the advent of Islam? Your description is so apt: "The city of Jahilia is built entirely of sand, its structures formed of the desert whence it rises. It is a sight to wonder at . . .

3 Whom had you in mind when you delineated the character of Mahound? Do your descriptions of his various activities not fit those of the Prophet Muhammad? I can quote passage after passage to show the coincidence, but it will be too lengthy; moreover most of them are so offensive that I shudder to reproduce them.

4 From where have you drawn the names of the three goddesses: Lat, Uzza and Manat? They are certainly not the products of your imagination? No one reading about them in you book can think otherwise.

5 Is Hamza not the same as Prophet Muhammad's uncle of the same name? And are his encounters with Hind, as depicted by you, not representative of what happened in the early annals of Islam?

6 Is Abu Simbel in your novel not a reflection of Abu Sufiyan, the inveterate enemy of the Prophet? And Hind, whom you characterise so graphically, not his wife?

7 Is Salman – your namesake – called Persian in your book, not the same as Salman Farsi, a companion of the Prophet?

8 Is Bilal not the first Muezzin of Islam, whom you describe as "the slave Bilal, the one Mahound freed, an enormous black monster, this one, with voice to match his voice"?

9 Is Zamzam, referred to in your novel, not the well held sacred by Muslims? Here is your description: "The city's water comes from underground streams and springs . . . . next to the House of the Black Stone."

10 Does the description of the "Black Stone" in your novel not fit that of Ka'aba? Here are your words: "The graves of Ismail and his mother Hagar the Egyptian lie by the north-west face of the House of the Black Stone, in an enclosure surrounded by a low wall."

These are some of the coincidences; there are many others. You, unlike most authors, have not mentioned that the characters in your novels do not bear any resemblance to persons living or dead. Can you, with your hand on your heart, say that they really don't resemble the characters and situations in the life of the Prophet of Islam. And if they do, what should the authorities do to control a likely occurrence which you as well as I know may disturb the tranquillity of the land.

I have not referred to your section on Ayesha; I found it rather confusing, where you have cleverly mixed fact with fiction. This does not apply, I feel, to your section on Mahound, which represents, to use your own words "the result of five years of work on Islam which has been central to my life". Apart from the Muslim politicians, whom you mention in your open letter to Mr Gandhi, you will be surprised that some of our best intellectuals – both writers and poets – have come out against you: they are J P Dixit, Nissim Ezekiel, Jean Kalgutkar, Vrinda Nabar, Vaskar Nandy, V Raman and Ashim Roy. In a letter to *The Indian Post* they refer to your statement that you knew Islam best and that was why you had talked about it and observed: 'How does he "talk" about this religion? Its founder is named Mahound. Rushdie has not invented this name. This was the name given to the Prophet Mahomed by his European detractors as a term of abuse ('Ma' from 'Mahomet' added to 'hound') and used frequently in various European eschatologies as a creature belonging to the lowest depths of Hell, as the Devil himself.'

After analysing your treatment further, they summarise your approach thus:

How has Rushdie treated the other pillars of Islamic faith? Ayesha, the youngest wife of the Prophet and the one who is regarded as one of the highest authorities of the Traditions is shown as "clad only in butterflies, leading an entire village, lemming-like into the Arabian Sea". The Ka'aba, regarded by the Muslims as the only consecrated spot on earth, is treated no better. Disguised as the "Tent of Black Stone called The Curtain", it has twelve prostitutes with names of the twelve wives of Mahound to add "the tempting spices of profanity". These "tempting spices" were apparently necessary to increase the number of pilgrims. Then what else remains of the basic core of the Islamic faith? The prophet is the Devil, the law-givers are sexual perverts, and the Ka'aba and the Haj examples of depravity and greed. The Koran is of course only a collection of satanic verses.'

The signatories conclude:

'We, the undersigned, are all non-Muslims. We are, therefore, obviously not subscribers to the Islamic faith. We believe that any critique of that faith has to be restrained, reasoned and full of the spirit of respecting diverse cultures and faiths. India's unity and harmony demands it. It is for such harmony and unity that we demand that the ban on this book be not lifted.'

What have you to say, Mr Rushdie, to these friends who are no friends of Mr Rajiv Gandhi and are known upholders of freedom of expression?

Lastly, as one born to Muslim parents and brought up, I think, under Islamic traditions, may I ask you whether you honestly believe that your book will not upset Muslims. Mr Khushwant Singh, who holds you in high esteem, advised your publisher, Penguin, against its publication as he felt that it would injure the religious feelings of Muslims and may disturb the law and order situation. Mr Zamir Ansari, Penguins's representative in India, confirmed this to me though he said a confidential advice sought by Penguin should not have been publicised by Mr Singh. But that is another matter. The fact remains that Mr Singh is no friend of the Government of India – in fact he is one of its most bitter critics – and his opinion has been unequivocal. So is that of Mr M V Kamath, an eminent journalist, who never finds anything right with Mr Rajiv Gandhi. He said that Mr Rushdie's book is full of 'despicable ideas'. If Nehru was alive he would have banned it.

I ask you in the same manner as you have asked Mr Gandhi, our prime minister, whether you consider this ban as really uncalled for, in view of the danger that many persons in public life feel it poses to communal harmony and peace in India. Is democracy a licence to do or undo anything by anyone or everyone?

Some idealists in the past might have dreamt of it; but is it really practical?

May I also remind you that it was Lord Macaulay who incorporated the need for such a ban in our legal system to prevent disorder; it is not Mr Rajiv Gandhi's invention. Mr Soli Sorabjee, whose legal eminence is undisputed, has argued against the ban; but he is a poor judge of public reaction. That is why, like his mentor Mr Nani Palkhivala, he wanted to be in politics but gave up the idea. *The Times of India,* in its editorial, has answered both you and him effectively:

'No, dear Rushdie, we do not wish to build a repressive India. On the contrary we are trying our best to build a liberal India where we can all breathe freely. But in order to build such an India, we have to preserve the India that exists. That may not be a pretty India. But this is the only India we possess.'

Do not pontificate, Mr Rushdie; be logical and face the facts. Answer your critics if you can.

Yours truly,

Rafiq Zakaria

The Illustrated Weekly of India (Bombay), 23rd–29th October, 1988.

Yes, Mr Rushdie,
We Shall Not Permit Literary Colonialism,
Nor Religious Pornography

by Syed Shahabuddin

. . . Yes, Mr Rushdie, we are a religious people and we do not like our religious personalities to be abused and vilified, directly or indirectly. Call us primitive, call us fundamentalists, call us superstitious barbarians, call us what you like, but your book only serves to define what has gone wrong with the Western civilisation – it has lost all sense of distinction between the sacred and the profane.

Life is not all you live and what you can purchase with your royalty paid by a fatigued culture in exchange for your performance as a master of literary gimmicks and as a provider of cultural shock. It is something deeper. You have lost your sense of the super-natural. We have not. Why should you presume we have?

Civilisation is nothing but voluntary acceptance of restraints. You may hold whatever private opinion you like but you do not enjoy an absolute right to express them in public. As for a serious intellectual discussion, there is always a time a place. But a logical argument cannot be on the basis of a piece of historical fiction.

In any case, you cannot claim to be the repository of absolute truths. Rest assured, Rushdies will come and go but the names of Muhammad, Christ or Buddha will last till the end of time. And soon your Satanic Verses will be laid aside, having served its literary purpose of generating excitement and forgotten, even by your champions (many of whom have not, I believe, seen or read it). But the Qur'an, the Bible and the Gita shall continue to be read by millions and not only read but revered and acted upon.

You are aggrieved that some of us have condemned you without a hearing and asked for the ban without reading your book. Yes, I have not read it, nor do I intend to. I do not have to wade through a filthy drain to know what filth is. My first inadvertent step would tell me what I have stepped into. For the synopsis, the review, the excerpts, the opinions of those gloatings were enough. Rushdie, 'the Islamic scholar, the man who studied Islam at the university' has to brag about his Islamic credentials, so that he can convincingly vend his Islamic wares in the West, which has not yet laid the ghost of the crusades to rest, but given it a new cultural trapping which explains why writers like you are so wanted and pampered.

Is any more evidence required in the face of your frank admission: 'I have talked about the Islamic religion subjects which are off limits and that includes God, includes prophets?' That is what you have said. The very title of your book is suggestively derogatory. In the eyes of the believer the Qur'an is the Word of God, and you plead innocence of the possible Muslim reaction. You depict the Prophet whose name the practising Muslim recites five times a day, whom he loves, whom he considers the model for mankind, as an impostor, and you expect us to applaud you?

You have had the nerve to situate the wives of the Prophet, whom we Muslims regard as the mothers of the community, in a brothel and you expect the Muslims to praise your power of imagination? You cannot take shelter behind the plea that after all it is a dream sequence in a piece of fiction. But tell us what compulsion you had to name the Prophet of your novel as Mahound (you are really too clever by half, not just naughty). Anyone conversant with the English language knows that Mahound is an archaic form for Mohammad, the name of the Prophet.

No, your act is not unintentional or a careless slip of the pen. It was deliberate and consciously planned with devilish forethought, with an eye to your market. Here in India, our laws are very clear. Though ignorance of law is no excuse, let me instruct you so that you are more careful if you wish to sell in India. Article 295 A of the Indian Penal Code says: "Whoever, with deliberate and malicious intention of outraging the religious feelings of any class of citizens of India, by words either spoken or written or otherwise, insults or attempts to insult the religion or the religious beliefs of that class, shall be punished with imprisonment – or with fine – or with both. I wish you were in India, Mr Rushdie, to face the music. And then there are other sections like 153 A, 153 B, 292, 293, 295 and 298 of the same Code which may be cited against you.

This is the legal system of a civilised society. We respect each other's religious beliefs. We do not intentionally outrage the religious feelings of others or insult their religion or ridicule the personalities to whom we are emotionally attached or mock our religious susceptibility. I would like to request the liberals on your side – the knights of freedom arrayed behind you in their shining armour – to launch a crusade to have the laws repealed before rushing to defend you, including the Customs Act under which our government banned the entry of your obnoxious product.

And take my word for it, Article 19 of the Constitution of India cannot come to your rescue either, because 'freedom of speech and expression' is subject to 'reasonable restriction' in the interest of inter alia, 'public order, decency or morality or in relation to defamation or incitement to an offence.' Incidentally, only citizens and not aliens can invoke Article 19. In any case, freedom to create is not the licence to abuse.

To sum up, your 'magnum opus' is objectionable on three grounds: It is a crime against human decency; it is an insult to Islam; it is an offence under the Indian law.

And tell your British champions and advisors that India shall not permit 'literary colonialism' nor what may be called religious pornography. Not even in the name of freedom and democracy, not even under the deafening and superb orchestration of your liberal band.

And also tell them not to have sleepless nights over our image abroad. Our image is not so fragile as not to survive this ban nor founded on the acceptance of the mores of your permissive society, but on what we can do as a nation to give a better life, a life of dignity to our people and how we can live with each other in peace, mutual respect and harmony.

Source: *Impact International,* 18/21, 11th–24th November 1988, pp. 17–18.

UK Muslims Act Against Infamous Book

Dr. M.M. Ahsan's Interview in the *Saudi Gazette*

Jeddah, Wed.

One of the Muslim world's leading institutions has appealed to the Ummah to black-list Penguin and its subsidiary Viking, the publisher of Salman Rushdie's sacrilegious book *Satanic Verses.*

Dr M. Manazir Ahsan, the Director General of the Leicester-based Islamic Foundation, told the *Gazette* that a decisive action by Saudi Arabia for banning all books of the two publishers will be in line with the resolution of OIC's Information Ministers meeting held recently in Jeddah.

Dr Ahsan arrived in Jeddah on Monday to perform Umra and pray at the Prophet's Mosque in Madina, and also to brief the Kingdom's Islamic bodies about the action being taken against the publishers. He would call on the Muslim World League's Secretary General Dr Abdullah Omar Nasseef and also others to apprise them of the success achieved in that respect.

The Islamic Foundation was the first to notice the blasphemous chapter of the filthy book and India and South Africa were the first countries to ban the book, Dr Ahsan said.

Soon after its publication the Foundation in co-operation with the UK's other Islamic bodies formed an action committee to proceed against the book and the publishers. The immediate action was to contact the executive chief of Penguin, who, Dr Ahsan said, refused to talk with the action committee.

Both the Penguin and Viking took the plea that the infamous book was favourably reviewed in the UK and nominated for award and found no reason to withdraw it or apologise for its publication.

The publishers' attitude demonstrated that they simply wanted the case to be dismissed outright, Dr Ahsan said. "Not only did the efforts to meet Penguin's chief fail, but he even did not like to talk to us on phone and answer letters from the UK's Islamic missions," he added. A signature campaign to move the publishers was initiated and over 60,000 signatures were obtained from all over the Kingdom, which testified to the Muslims' demand that the book be immediately withdrawn, the misguided author and the publishers make a public apology, and the two should pay damages to a Muslim charity for causing offence and distress to the Muslim Ummah. Even this demonstration of protest did not work on the publishers, Dr Ahsan said.

As developments later revealed the publishers were reported to be only sorry if the publication of the book had caused any offence to Muslims but were not prepared for a public apology and withdrawing the book from the market, Dr Ahsan said.

Dr Ahsan disclosed that Rushdie went into hiding and house-arrested by his own conscience at a place with changed phones and under a cover of security by men and dogs.

The book is scheduled for publication and marketing in the US by February 1989. But the Islamic Foundation in collaboration with other Islamic agencies there is already preoccupied with a campaign not to let the book in.

The infamous book, Dr Ahsan disclosed, was marked to India's noted writer and journalist Khushwant Singh for pre-publication comments and he promptly recommended to the publishers not to print such a baseless book. Singh's comments as referee on South East Asian subjects were not heeded by the publishers, who later sent the manuscript to a Jewish referee who favoured the publication, all to cause fury and anger among the world's Muslims.

London-based Muslim ambassadors have formed a three-member committee, comprising those of Kuwait, Pakistan and Somalia, to look into the legal aspects of the case and make representation with the governments of the UK and EEC countries.

Source: *The Saudi Gazette* (Jeddah), 15th December, 1988.

Carry on Salman Rushdie

. . . The ugly saga of Viking-Penguin's 'Satanic Verses' continues to roll on. Much to the delight of its publishers and their literary and not so literary connoisseurs of this 'rich novel' and to equal bewilderment on the part of the Muslim community as to why some people can be so innocently callous in asserting their 'right' to insult and injure the sanctities of other people.

Last week the Muslim community in Britain was administered some gratuitous advice, part patronising, part intimidating by the British media, both the national and the sensation-seeking tabloid press. Apparently, they had been switched on by the weekend's demonstration by Muslims in Bradford and the reported decision by the W.H. Smith book stores to withdraw the *The Satanic Verses* from its shelves in view of receding sales and growing protest by Muslims up and down the country. Like in other Midland and West Yorkshire towns, Muslims in Bradford had been expressing their anguish at the continued refusal of the publisher to withdraw this filthy and sacrilegious title and tender unqualified apology to the community for this gross insult to its religious sanctities and as a token of their disgust they had also burnt a copy of the book.

'*The Independent*' (16th January) wrote a first editorial entitled, 'Dangers of a Muslim campaign'. This was followed by a lead article in the *Evening Standard,* and everyone joined in next morning – *The Times, The Sun, The Daily Mail* and *The Daily Telegraph. The Guardian* (18th January) followed suit inevitably, but instead of writing a leader, it asked W. L. Webb to do a 'Judgment on Salman'.

The Independent mixed its counsel with words of praise for the Muslim Community. It said: 'The Muslim minority has contributed much to the nation's commerce and entrepreneurial spirit. Its members have been notably law-abiding, and their devotion to family values, hard work and personal integrity are rightly admired'. It seemed to accept that 'It is important that their spiritual values should be respected and that they should be spared (sic) from racial discrimination in all its forms'.

But what should Muslims do if a publisher or publication commits filthy sacrilege against their basic religious sanctities and insists on continuing to do so?

They may feel sad and anguished. They may cry out in protest and helplessness. However, *The Independent* was certain that the book could not be 'overtly blasphemous'.

'It is hardly likely', it argued 'that a worthy and liberal-minded *literati* who sat on the panels awarding these prizes (sic) would have thought so highly of a book which was 'overtly blasphemous', even of another faith' and '*The Satanic Verses* was written as a moral parable, and that is how they interpreted it'. So Muslims should accept Penguin's 'moral parable' on the authority of the '*literati*' and the 'hardly likely' probability of their agreeing to award a prize to any 'overtly blasphemous' work. If they demur and they don't, then 'their leaders should examine the implications of their war against the Rushdie novel' because they 'must not seek to impose their values either on their fellow Britons of other faiths or on the majority who acknowledge no faith at all'.

Although Muslims are seeking to *impose* nothing on nobody, thinly veiled hints are dropped about the implications of their alleged attempt 'to impose their values . . . on the majority'. They are also asked to ponder over a couple of related questions.

Do Muslim leaders 'really feel this book poses a serious threat to their followers?'

'Is their campaign not doubly counter-productive, first in giving the book much publicity, and second, in reminding Britons of the intolerant face which Islam has all too often shown abroad?' And 'It may indeed be thought that Muslims are furnishing material for further moral parables about Islam by attacking Rushdie's fictional creation . . . Their crusade not just against the book but against Rushdie personally does them no credit'. In fact the editorial had started off with attributing another 'discredit' to Bradford Muslims that in burning 'some copies of the book' they had followed 'the example of the Inquisition and Hitler's National Socialists'.

Sadly for the respectability of the newspaper, the whole editorial is based on unjustified assumptions and therefore confused dialectics but it goes on to offer patronising counsels nevertheless. One doubts very much if the leader-writer had even scanned through the 'thick' novel because otherwise (s)he would not have based the whole 'danger' call on one single determinant: the 'hardly likely' fallibility of the *literati.* No need was felt to be precise even about such a small fact as the number of books burnt in Bradford (not 'some', just 'one') yet the jibe of Muslims acting like 'Hitler's National Socialists' is so carelessly hurled at them, for the sake of effect no doubt, but in the style of the tabloid press.

However, Muslims are not at all concerned about 'Rushdie personally', nor about any increase in the sale of the book presumably because some people might rush to buy it when they hear that it blasphemes Islam. If they do, they are sure to regret throwing away £12.95 when they discover that they now belong to 'The Page 15 Club . . . of literary editors, journalists, academics, novelists who have got no further than page 15 with Rushdie's books'.

The Muslims cannot also be deterred from exercising their Fundamental Right to reject insult to their religious sanctities for the fear that some Britons may feel reminded 'of the intolerant face which Islam has all too often shown abroad' or that by doing so they will be 'furnishing material for further moral parables about Islam'. Their objective is simple: that is to make known their sense of outrage and to reject insult with all the moral force at their command.

The Islamic assumption about human nature is based on its innate goodness, its rejection of filth and profanity and its respect for other people's religious sanctities and accordingly the 'Muslim campaign' has received support from across all faith and non-faith communities. So the efforts of the publicists notwithstanding, Muslims have no negative views about the vast majority of Britons and they do not believe that there would be many Britons who derived any pleasure or satisfaction if someone blasphemed Islam, overtly or covertly. As for the tiny tribe of 'parable writers', they did not need any reminder because it already possessed sufficient material about 'the intolerant face of Islam . . . abroad'.

The Independent does not, however, say what Muslims can do if a tiny minority of blinkered *literati* seeks 'to impose' its 'values' on them though it admits that 'the Islamic campaign would be more understandable if Rushdie's novel were in any way trashy', but as the *literati* have decreed its literary merit, no one can dare to admit the possibility that it could still be 'trashy'.

The Daily Telegraph which had only until recently so vehemently backed the official campaign to keep *The Spycatcher* away from these shores was now proclaiming the 'Right to be read'. It believed that should Muslims choose to burn a copy of the book 'in the privacy of their homes [so burning a book was not by itself objectionable, it only mattered where it was burned] . . . Many Christians who have struggled with Mr Rushdie's impenetrable novels will warm their hands at the fireside' and even agreed that 'We may not be able to follow all that Mr Rushdie writes', yet the newspaper was concerned about defending 'absolutely his right to be read'. It was not at all bothered about the contents of the book, literary or trashy, blasphemous or scholarly, thick or readable. Its sole concern seemed to be to defend the interests of the publisher and bookseller.

A warning to the Muslim community was therefore considered to be in order, albeit prefaced by taking note of 'the hard work and enterprising spirit of the Moslem minority, their piety and devotion to family values'. Like *The Independent* which had also lavished similar praise, *The Daily Telegraph* too did not care to reflect on the main cause of this hard work, law-abidingness and devotion. If it did it would have been obvious to it that whatever moral and social values the Muslim community reflected was only because of its faith, its sense of dignity and appreciation of fundamental human values. It has reacted so clearly against sacrilege because it does not suffer from any crisis of values and it does not want to become a flotsam in any pool of relative values.

However, *The Telegraph* said 'the scenes in Bradford over the weekend presented an image of Moslem sentiment in Britain of the most unhelpful possible kind to race relations'. The 'Islamic religious leaders' were, therefore, told that they 'have two obligations' first to maintain a sense of proportion about any perceived threat to their religion posed by Mr Rushdie; and second, to recall that, as citizens or residents of this country, they have a responsibility to respect the British tradition of free speech and not react in the fashion of the ayatollahs.

Presumably it has not been able to go through Mr Rushdie's 'impenetrable' novel, nor does it seem to have cared to find out why Muslims have felt so 'atypically' offended, yet *The Telegraph* chooses to tell Muslims of their 'obligations'. There are no 'ayatollahs' here among Muslims in Britain, nor do they intend to produce them in the future, but it was a little out of character for a Tory newspaper to propound the otherwise 'subversive' doctrine of unfettered 'free speech'. Muslims are exercising their freedom only to express their feelings of disgust that some people should be abusing freedom of expression in order to blaspheme their sanctities and were insistent on doing so.

Like both *The Independent* and *The Daily Telegraph, The Times* as well has tried to make a big fuss about the incident of the token burning of a copy of *The Satanic Verses* in Bradford and used it to judge on 'Islamic intolerance'. Naturally it goes on to offer some lessons in British democracy to 'the newcomers in Britain'.

The Muslim community has been asking the publisher to withdraw and pulp the book . . . because that way instead of polluting the atmosphere by burning the book, it would be possible to recycle the paper and to put it to better use. So despite the isolated case of Bradford burning the book was really a non-issue, but it would be interesting to find out how many similar editorials our national dailies have been written over political demonstrations burning documents or national flags as a token of democratic expression of some protest or disapproval. Though Muslims should better try not to imitate the practice uncritically, the fact remains that such kind of protests are very much a part of the 'free world' democratic culture.

However, while unlike the two other dailies *The Times* admits that many of the allegorical references in the book are 'derogatory' to Muhammad (peace be upon him), 'to his family and to the foundation of Islam', yet it tells them to do nothing except 'neither buy nor read the novel'. Why?

One, anything otherwise would amount to 'intolerance'.

Two, it would not be 'in the interest of community harmony'.

And three, 'Britain is a democracy in which Parliament elected by the majority, makes law applicable to all'.

The argument amounts to saying that Muslims should quietly put up with sacrilege and insult, for to do otherwise would be construed as 'intolerance', affecting, 'community harmony' that a law having been made by a 'Parliament elected by majority' and 'applicable to all' there should be no call for its amendment or improvement if it was found to be wanting in any respect.

The British law happens to be silent on the question of blasphemy against non-Anglican faiths and is in evident need of amendment in that respect as Lord Scarman and others have said in their minority report on Offences against Religion and Public Worship. However, until that happens it would be naive to assume that the spirit of the law as it stood now was to condone blasphemy against Judaism, Hinduism, Islam and other faiths and it would be wrong to demand or expect that people should not express their disapproval of blasphemy nor seek an amendment of the law because doing so would be undemocratic and impair community harmony. It is a very poor view of the community and definitely not true that non-Muslims would be pleased if someone blasphemed Islam and would be angry if Muslims said they protested against it.

The Guardian's 'Judgement of Salman' by W. L. Webb is, however, quite frank because 'For the first time, a very intelligent novelist with a sophisticated and intelligent audience all over the world has brought to bear on Islam, its culture and its history, all subtly and powerfully expressive techniques of modernism.' He is pleased that 'The real struggle will be in that (i.e. Islamic) culture and that the brunt of it would be born (sic) by its own writers and intellectuals' but he would like to see how 'a no longer very brave or liberal (British) culture responds to the local manifestations of the struggle'. Webb's own sympathies are clear and categorical. The Muslim response, however, reminds him of Stalinism, receding from one land and surfacing in 'another militant ideology'.

What is so plain and obvious is that Muslims, 'being newcomers to Britain', have to go a long way before they will be able to win respect for their dignity and their religious sanctities and it would largely depend on their own positive and unilateral attitude towards the good of the society, no matter the distractions caused by the so-called 'parable writers', *literati* or other ethno-centric elements on the social fringe. However, for now the only point Muslims are trying to make is that it is not civilised to insult religious sanctities of any people irrespective of whether it was done in a literary style or a trashy style and that insult only diminishes the insulter. There is no threat to Islam for Islam is protected by God Almighty.

Source: *Impact International,* 19/2, 27th January–9th February 1989, pp. 7–8.

Why Selectively Defend the Freedom of Expression?

Those who are screaming *foul* at the top of their voices on Salman Rushdie's plight did not raise even a finger in protest on scores of other violations of freedom of expression. Here are a few items recently in the news.

- Mr. Englestad of Nevada was fined $1.5 million because he held two birthday parties of Hitler in 1986 and 1988 in a secret room of the casino and hotel he owns. (New York Times, April 3, 1989).
- April 1989 issue of *Playboy* appeared on newsstands in England with two pages torn out (containing Gerry Adam M.P.'s interview, the leader of the Sinn Fein Party, the political wing of IRA).
- Naom Chomsky's *Fateful Triangle* was banned in Canada for quite some time and so was M.A. Hoffman's *The Great Holocaust Trial*.
- In March 1989 Denise de Kalafa, a Brazilian pop singer, was banned from performing at the Cuban-American Festival as she went to Cuba in 1981.
- A southern California radio broadcaster, Tom Leykis, used a steamroller to crush a stack of Cat Stevens records to protest the pop singer's support of Khomeini edict.
- Switzerland's biggest media consultant, the Ringier, fired Huber, a well-known Swiss journalist for supporting the action against Rushdie.
- A Napa County judge halted a weekend concert of *Neo-Nazi* bands from around the country in March 1989.
- A Holocaust survivor's Hebrew translation of *Mein Kampf* has touched off a heated debate in Israel and no publisher is willing to take the heat.
- When Kissinger urged Israel to ban T.V. reporters from Gaza and the Occupied territories in March 1988, no editorial appeared condemning the absolute outrage.

Is the *Freedom of Expression* and the First Amendment for some but not for all? Those who live by the First Amendment have an obligation not to defend it selectively.

Source: ICNA Booklet, p. 6.

Canadian Muslims on Satanic Verses

by Qasim Syed

In Canada we have great respect for the freedom of expression. So when one group of people wants the book Satanic Verses withdrawn by its publisher (Penguin) we feel that this group wants to violate the freedom of expression, and we ought to stand for freedom of expression even though we may not agree with the material in the book. This is a natural reaction and is expected of all freedom loving people. However, every inquiring mind would ask that why in the world this group, also living in Canada, wants this book withdrawn. Recent media coverage does not provide a satisfactory answer to this question. Therefore, in this article a sincere attempt has been made to approach this issue in a systematic and logical fashion in a question answer format.

Q. *Is Islam an intolerant religion which cannot stand any criticism?*
A. Islam is neither an intolerant religion nor afraid of any criticism. Islam in fact is such a peace loving religion that one of the meanings of the word Islam is peace itself. Day in and day out anti-Islamic material is produced. Muslims do not take to the streets and say that this material or that material be withdrawn. So tolerant, reasonable and peaceful are the Islamic principles that, despite all the bad publicity, Islam is earning adherents right in the west.

Q. *Then why Muslims cannot tolerate Satanic Verses?*
A. This book is not based on any civilized criticism of Islam. This sacrilege is based on fabrication, slander, and extreme insult toward Prophet Mohammad, his family and other Islamic personalities, and pristine principles of Islam. And in turn it insults one billion Muslims of the world . . .

Q. *But this a work of fiction, some names have been distorted or changed and the events occur in a sequence of a dream. What is the comment on that?*
A. Everybody would agree that fiction and fantasy are no license for insult, slander and profanity. Anybody can dream or fantasize as he pleases but insulting others is the no go region.

Q. *Did the publisher Penguin have any knowledge about the insulting nature of the book before its publication?*
A. Yes, their own Indian editorial advisor Khushwant Singh (not a Muslim) advised them not to publish the book. He told them, "The Prophet had been made to be a small time impostor in the novel and that if the author could not see that the work would cause trouble he was out of touch with the Indian reality."

Q. *But what about an author's right to freedom of expression?*
A. All environmentally conscious people resist abuse of the environment. All energy conscious people oppose abuse of energy. Similarly, all freedom loving people should stand against abuse of freedom of expression. Freedom of expression should not violate the right of one billion people to religious dignity. Even in Canada freedom of expression has not been absolute. Keegstra and Zundel cases have been recent example of that . . .

Q. *Does Islam believe in freedom of expression?*
A. Yes. In fact, Islam has a complete system of basic human rights (for example, rights to: live, equality, personal liberty, religious freedom, economic protection, freedom from religious distress, justice, etc.). And the history of these human rights does not start with the Magna Carta or U.N.O.'s treaties and covenants. These rights were given fourteen centuries ago. According to Islam, freedom of expression is not only a right but exercising it for the good of mankind is a duty incumbent on all believers.

Furthermore, Islam accords all religions and their followers freedom of religious dignity and the right of protection from religious distress. Qur'an commands, "Do not revile the deities which they invoke beside Allah" (6:108). That means to talk about various religions with reasons and criticizing them with respect or disagreeing with them is a part of freedom of expression. But ridiculing any religion for the purpose of insult is denial of the right to protection from religious distress and religious dignity.

Q. *Has the author inflicted insult on somebody else before?*
A. Yes. Regarding his novel *Midnight Children* both the author and his publisher had to give public apology to the late Prime Minister of India, Mrs. Indira Gandhi, in answer to her libel action. They also paid costs and gave an undertaking to remove from all future editions under their control the passages objected to by her. The author had suggested that Mrs. Gandhi was responsible for the death of her husband through neglect.

Q. *Wouldn't withdrawal of the book make other authors and writers feel insecure?*
A. No. All sensible authors and writers do not use insulting, abusive, and obscene language toward religions of the world and their revered figures. The issue is not the freedom of expression. The issue is the right to religious dignity. In fact authors and writers should be the first to denounce this book because it is a scar on their profession. Disciplinary action against abusers exists in all professions. And this does not weaken the profession but strengthens it.

Q. *If the book is not withdrawn would it enhance the credibility of western freedom of expression around the world?*
A. No. In fact it would be a set back for the credibility, at least in the eyes of one billion Muslims. It will imply that under the pretext freedom of expression the right to religious dignity of any minority can be violated in the West any time.

Q. *Is the demand that the publisher (Penguin) withdraw the book made only by a small number of Muslims?*
A. No. All Muslims around the world want this book withdrawn. The Secretary General of the 46-nation Organization of

the Islamic Conference (OIC), Syed Sharifuddin Pirzada supported this demand. Muslims need help from all Canadians in this peaceful campaign.

Islamic Circle of North America.

List of the Books

Banned

in

CANADA

List of Books Banned in Canada

1) The Battle of Truth
2) Controversy of Zion
3) Hoax of the 20th Century
4) Know Your Enemies
5) The Real Holocaust
6) Rulers of Russia
7) Secret Societies and Suppressive Movements
8) The Talmud Unmasked
9) The Ultimate World Order
10) World Revolution
11) Zionist Factor

There were reasons to ban these books and we want to know:

- What about freedom of the press?
- What about freedom of speech?
- Where was the writers association at that time?

We invite the attention of all the people with no prejudice and ask them:

- Why now there is such an uproar on our demand of banning the book "Satanic Verses" which is another example of hate material, racism and distortion of real history and slander in the 1st degree?

- Why, all of a sudden, are we blamed to be against the freedom of speech and freedom of the press?
- Why now is the Canadian Government, especially the Prime Minister, saying that the board of a few people should not decide what Canadians should read and should not read (Statement of Prime Minister in London, England, visit March 1989)
- Why the elected leaders are not concerned for one specific group . . .

We want to see:

- Canadian Government take a lead in all matters of truth, fairness and justice.
- Canadian Government to be honest and sincere to its people within Canada in particular and everybody in the world in general.
- Canadian Government give priority to decent moral values over unnecessary and meaningless cooperation with indecency.

We are outraged, we are hurt and we are ignored. We feel that:

- You can help us in knowing the truth.
- You can help us in joining the truth.
- You can help in making this beautiful country even a better place to live.

We are determined to:

- Continue our protest until, our demands are met.
- Stand firm on our objectives.
- Solve our problems through democratic and peaceful process.
- Convey and propagate the message of truth through our patience and we will get through to the Political Leaders.

All We Want Now:

- The book "Satanic Verses", the insult to common intellect, be banned in Canada, the book which is based on racism, profanity, slander and distortion of real history.
- An unqualified apology from the Writer, the Publisher and the Distributor.
- No publication in any other language.

Is it . . .

"UNFAIR"

to ask for . . .

"FAIRNESS"

You let us Know

Islamic Circle of North America.

The American Muslims on "The Satanic Verses"

Islamic Circle of North America

Words have power and therefore they have to be used carefully. Words can wound and they can heal. It is naive to say that freedom to use words of hate and destruction can be unlimited. No civilized society allows this. That is why Penguin, or any other mainstream publisher does not publish Ku Klux Klan or the neo Nazi literature.

We Muslims believe that it is highly imprudent and inconsiderate for an individual to completely ignore the religious sensitivities of his fellow citizens while exercising his first amendment rights.

Rights of individuals are undoubtedly guaranteed by the state but it is the spirit of harmony, goodwill, and mutual respect among the members of society that ensures the full enjoyment of these rights by all.

The recent media attention to Mr. Rushdie's book, *The Satanic Verses* and worldwide condemnation of the book by Muslims have given rise to talks on such issues as freedom of expression, decency, and intolerance. We feel truth and honesty have been the real casualties in the nightly drama of the evening news. We draw attention to these facts here so that you may also hear Muslim side of the debate and form your own opinion.

What is in the "The Satanic Verses"

Nearly everyone agrees on one thing about the book; it contains offensive material. But to say this is to put it very mildly. The facts are much harsher. Let's have a brief review of the book:

a) Blasphemous: – Six out of nine chapters deal with Islamic theme, Islamic symbolism and with real Islamic characters. The whole chapter two is about the life and mission of last Prophet of Islam, Muhammad (peace be upon him). Prophet Muhammad is depicted as "Mahound" which means devil. Great companions of Prophet Muhammad (peace be upon him) were described as "those goons" and "those F--- clowns" (page 101) and they also were called "bum" and "scum," (page 101). Wives of Prophet were called "whores" (page 381) and Islamic rituals and terminologies were ridiculed (page 104, 381 and others). The sanctity of Muslims' Holy book the Qur'an was damaged (pages 363 & 364).

b) Racist: – The book contains many racist remarks. For example, one of Prophet Muhammad's companions from Africa was painted as "an enormous black monster" (page 101). There were many negative remarks about Malcolm X, who was Muslim leader of the U.S. (page 413).

c) Anti-Semitic: – Abraham (peace be upon him), the great Prophet, common to Judaism, Christianity and Islam was called "the bastard" (p. 95).

(May Allah forgive us even in quoting these offensive excerpts).

No, Mr. Rushdie's case is not all "intellectual," nor are the Muslims trying to counter his "scholarship" with "a box of matches." Thousands of "intellectual" works which take a less than favorable view of Islam are being published all over the world. We Muslims do not throw such works into the incinerator. We buy them for our libraries and universities and often invite their authors to give a lecture or seminar on their "studies".

Islamic civilization and Muslims cherish scholarship whether it favors them religiously or not. But *The Satanic Verses* does not indulge itself in the intellectual criticism of Islam, it scandalizes and maligns.

The Rushdie Tradition of Getting Attention

Slander and libel are nothing new to Mr. Rushdie. In a previous novel, *Midnight's Children,* he tried his hand at the late Indian prime minister Mrs. Indira Gandhi. She had to be given a public apology by both the author and the publishers in answer to her libel action. They also paid costs and gave an undertaking to remove from all future editions the passages objected to by her.

In *The Satanic Verses,* Rushdie is not libelling an individual, he insults and libels a whole community. It is obscene. It has self-hating racist undertones. And it incites racial as well as religious passions against the Muslim community.

Arrogance or the Commercial Interests of Penguin

Penguin's own Editorial Advisor, Khushwant Singh, an eminent writer (not a Muslim) had told the Penguin, "The Prophet had been made to be small time impostor in the novel." He strongly advised against the publication of the book.

Once the book was published in England, it was strongly criticized by Muslims and non-Muslims alike. It failed to win the Booker's award. In the British parliament the number of members backing a motion condemning the Rushdie book swelled to 33.

For the last four months, tens of thousands of Muslims from all over the U.S. and Canada wrote and called to the Penguin/Viking requesting that the book be withdrawn from Britain, and not be published in the U.S. Muslim leaders made every effort to arrange a meeting with the publisher so that this potentially explosive situation be defused before it reached crisis proportions.

But the publisher had declined even to receive a representative delegation of the Muslim community in the USA.

Are Muslims Intolerant?

The above points establish that Muslims in this country have politely sought to defuse the situation. Yet ironically, it is the Muslims who are now blamed for intolerance.

Yes, we are intolerant of hypocrisy and hate. If that is a crime, we admit to being guilty. Muslims are exercising their freedom only to express their feelings of disgust that some should abuse freedom of expression in order to blaspheme their sacred beliefs and were insistent on doing so. We have rights to protest.

Muslims in America are an eight million strong community. We are here to stay and prosper. A vast majority of us are taxpaying professionals, scientists and educators. We trust that Penguin would not publish any slanderous material condemning Dr. Martin Luther King Jr. because it will be against the sensitivities of the racial relations. Penguin should have exercised better judgment in selecting and printing a book which has offended one fifth of the human race, a billion Muslims.

It is not unusual in the Western democratic societies for the media and the publishing industry to exercise self restraint in the interest of social order as well as in consideration of moral and ethical norms and racial and religious sensitivities of the society. The Muslims would like the people in media and the publishing industry to extend to them the courtesy which had generally been extended to other ethnic, racial and religious groups threatened by stereo-typical portrayal, innuendoes and false characterization.

In raising their objections to *The Satanic Verses,* Muslims are only trying to underscore the difference between the sacred and the profane, and between liberty and license. We see it basically as a moral issue, one about decency and civilization across all religious or ethnic lines. It is not civilized to insult the sanctities of any people. And that is why Muslims were in the protest march against the movie "The Last Temptation of Christ." . . .

Islamic Circle of North America (ICNA), New York.

Muslims Are Not Arsonists: A Reply to Mr. Kenneth Baker

by M.H. Faruqi

The Rt Hon Mr Kenneth Baker, MP
Secretary of State for Education and Science
Elizabeth House
York Road
London SE1 7PH

Dear Mr Baker,
I must confess that my first reaction to your 'Argument before arson' (*The Times,* 30th January 1989) was of a momentary disbelief: disbelief over the by-line.

For the past three weeks, Muslims have been subjected to some quite rough and orchestrated belabouring by the media for no reason other than that they were expressing lawfully and legitimately their deep sense of outrage and hurt over the publication of *The Satanic Verses.* There has been absolutely little factual mention of their cause of concern. Large and peaceful demonstrations in several provincial towns have gone unreported by the national media. They were *censored,* in other words. Then came the Bradford demonstration and the symbolic burning of a copy of the book. Now Muslims became 'arsonists' (as *The Times'* heading of your article clearly suggests), enemies of freedom and followers of Hitler and Stalin.

Muslims were accused of trying 'to impose their values' on fellow Britons and warned that by seeking to do that they would injure 'community harmony'.

They were lectured on British democracy in which 'Parliament elected by the majority' made law 'applicable to all' – as if *The Satanic Verses* were to be treated by Muslims as sanctioned by law; as if the Muslim community was not represented in Parliament by the MPs 'elected by majority'; as if no law (e.g. the Blasphemy law) once enacted can be amended and improved!

Islam was *per se* 'intolerant', it was assumed, and Muslims were told that what they were objecting to as 'filthy sacrilege' was a 'moral parable' thought very highly of by 'a worthy and liberal-minded *literati*' and the message was that by taking exception to this 'great work' of religion and literature, Muslims were showing their own lack of culture and inability to appreciate scholarship.

Muslims were warned that if they did not desist from pressing their objection, then they should be ready for other 'parable' writers to swoop upon them.

In any case, it was argued, that even if the Muslim felt offended, the larger society had the 'right' to read Penguin's *Verses* and it was the duty of the media to uphold and defend that 'right'.

Muslims were in fact reminded that they were 'newcomers' and the clear message was that being 'newcomers', they must not think of their Fundamental Human Rights.

This is an objective and unemotional abstract of the firm counsel administered by responsible sections of the media who had, it seems, assumed that Muslims were just vandals out to destroy culture, scholarship, freedom and social harmony. Now you too Mr Baker have more or less repeated the same things without checking your facts and relying entirely and uncritically on these very sources. You have assumed and presumed and come up with opinions and judgement which bear little relation to facts. However, your entry into the debate is to be welcomed, because at last there is a responsible level at which one can reason with. Unlike the newspapers who generally file your letters in the wastepaper basket, if you try to contradict notions and prejudices held dear by them, one can, at least, expect to be listened to.

So if you bear with me, I would like to go over your 'Argument before arson'.

Sadly for the objectivity of what you have tried to conclude with – Heinrich Heine's supposedly 'prophetic' words that 'Whenever books are burned men also, in the end, are burned' – you too seem to have been taken in by the media's over-exaggerated blow up of the isolated incident when someone chose to draw attention to his feelings to an otherwise insensitive and censorious media by, in our view, unnecessarily, burning his own hard-earned £12.95.

No-one had done it before, nor anyone else is going to adopt it as a standard method of demonstrating protest. Over 15,000 Muslims had marched in London 14 days after the Bradford 'arson' and two days before your article was written in order to express their pain and agony. It was a dignified and peaceful demonstration *sans* arson and it would have been very constructive to have based your counsels on something much more wider and general than having to pick on a single instance and predicate all your judgements and premonitions on unconnected 17th century events. The result is clearly unjust because in order to raise your objection to what you have yourself described as 'symbolic' burning – of just one copy of a blasphemous book – you end up by grilling an entire community of people.

Burning was a non-issue insofar as *The Satanic Verses* was concerned, though it may be observed, in parenthesis, that those who had chosen to burn their £12.95 as a means to draw attention to their deep hurt had only followed the contemporary political culture of freedom and dissent in which it is common practice to burn some controversial publication, report or even flag in order to underline the intensity of opposition. So let us put the issues in their right perspective. But first your assumptions.

I am glad you 'appreciate the intensity of' Muslims' 'feelings' and acknowledge that the 'book has given real and heartfelt offence to many Muslims', but you assume that the offence is felt because 'it portrays a character taken to be the Prophet Muhammad (peace be upon him) in a less than favourable light'.

You assume that 'Mr Rushdie's case is intellectual' 'yet instead of the 'Koran' (The Qur'an), his critics were 'reaching for a box of matches'.

You also assume that the issue was between Muslims and the author, and, therefore, 'those who oppose Mr Rushdie's views must answer and overcome them with counter-views and counter-arguments'.

You say you 'cannot judge the issues in Mr Rushdie's book since I am not an Islamic scholar', yet, you assume that the Muslim concern most probably reflected on their fear 'that Islam is so insecurely based that its walls will fall from the single note sounded by Mr Rushdie's trumpet'.

Therefrom, you go on to infer that Muslim reaction was tantamount to 'censor', 'intolerance' and even undermining of 'the basic freedoms' and you, therefore, feel justified in uttering the warning that 'we cannot allow intolerance to undermine the basic freedoms which so many have found so attractive'.

You have condemned and sentenced a whole community

without giving it a hearing or without informing yourself of its case.

No, Mr Rushdie's case is not at all 'intellectual' (it's 'mental'), nor are the Muslims trying to counter his 'scholarship' with 'a box of matches'. Thousands of 'intellectual' works which take a 'less-than-favourable' view of Islam and more are being published all over the world. However, we never had any *libra prohibitorum,* nor intend to have now. We do not throw such works into the incinerator. We buy them for our libraries and universities and not unoften invite their authors to give a lecture or seminar on their 'studies'.

No, the Muslims are not suffering from any sense of insecurity either for themselves or Islam. Islam stands on its own merit and authenticity, and like, as you mention, our blessed Messiah, Jesus and his teachings, it is not tarnished or diminished by any amount of muck hurled at it.

The Muslims have felt deeply pained and outraged not because the Blessed Prophet has been portrayed 'in a less than favourable light'. They do not seek any 'favour', less or more, for his person or for the Divine Message conveyed through him (peace be upon him). They are simply rejecting the filth and insults hurled upon their deeply held sanctities. Won't you Mr Baker?

You might say that you have come to put up with 'utterly repugnant' portrayals of Jesus, Mary and even of God, but would you accept to be libelled or simply insulted in your personal or public capacity irrespective of the fact whether it was couched within a prized literary cover or it was issued by a trashy publisher?

Ah, there is difference between libelling a person and libelling a past and gone religious figure, you might argue. Yes there is a great difference between the two: one is libelling an individual and the other is libelling a whole community.

The Satanic Verses has not only insulted and libelled a whole community, it is also obscene, it has self-hating racist undertones and – if you follow the highly charged treatment of the subject in the media – it has also incited racial as well as religious passions against the Muslim community. It mattered little if the book was thick and unreadable as you yourself observe, though naturally its dense prose and grasshopper style must make it rather difficult for many non-Muslims to cursorily spot its filthy and profane droppings.

It is very painful and abhorring to repeat or reproduce the

insulting and obscene phrases or sentences from the book. But let me quote very briefly as I assume you would not have had the time to go through all its 546 pages.

Very early in the book, the Prophet Abraham (peace be upon him), the patriarch prophet common to the three main religions of the world, Judaism, Christianity and Islam, is described as 'the bastard'. But more filth is reserved for Muhammad (peace be upon him).

Firstly he is depicted as 'Mahound', the Middle Ages synonym for the Blessed Prophet meaning 'devil' and 'false prophet'. 'What kind of idea are you?' a 'voice is whispering in his ear' and asking . . . 'Man-or-mouse?'. And more.

He is a person without 'qualms' or 'scruples'. 'After his wife's death Mahound was no angel'. 'You understand my meaning', one of his Companions, Salman is said to have 'confided' while 'drunk'.

Khalid, Salman and Bilal, are 'bums' and 'scums' and the latter who came from Abyssinia is further painted as 'an enormous black monster'. The remark is both racist and monstrous.

The wives of the Prophet (peace be upon him) whom Muslims regard as their Mothers are sited in a whore-house and the House of God, The Holy Kabah, in Makkah is turned into a brothel . . .

It is most difficult and painful to reproduce such and many other 'intellectual' vituperations of a diseased and dirty mind, but you do not have to be an 'Islamic scholar' in order to understand the nature of 'the views' which you wanted to be answered and 'overcome . . . with counter-views and counter-arguments'.

But I must admit, Muslims are unable to counter such 'views' and 'arguments'. The Qur'an forbids them from abusing or insulting others whatever the provocation. We have nothing to offer in kind.

There is a great variety of individuals created by God; in fact every person is an individual, and Muslims have, therefore, never challenged Mr Rushdie's freedom of conscience to imagine according to his fantasies and enjoy it within his private domains and circle of fans, critics and *literati.*

No offence is ever caused as long as someone keeps his dirty thoughts to himself or within his charm circle except perhaps when it may be found to have infringed a law. But no-one expects a 'responsible publisher' to peddle insult and sacrilege and insist on publishing it far and wide and translating it into as many languages as possible.

Muslims had expected that as soon as they had explained their 'heartfelt offence' to the publisher, it would take the civilised step to withdraw the unintended offence. Muslim representations were cool and intellectual, but much to the community's disappointment the publisher has chosen to stay adamant. It was sheltering behind pithy and fallacious arguments concerning 'freedom of expression', the praises and prizes won by the book, its own status as a 'serious publisher' etc – and that the sacrilegious and offensive passages constituted only a small part of this large book.

It was later that Muslims came to know that Penguin had been strongly advised against publishing *The Satanic Verses* by a person no less than their own Editorial Adviser in India, Mr Khushwant Singh. Mr Singh is an eminent Indian writer, a member of the upper house, Rajya Sabha, and he is not a Muslim. Which suggested that the sacrilege was very much premeditated and intended to be so.

What can Muslims do?

You say 'one set of laws covers hardcore pornography' and defend 'British laws' which in your view quite rightly, forbid the sale of material which could be held to deprave or corrupt those who read or see it'. You admit that it amounted to imposing censorship but explain you 'believe that there is a line to be drawn between liberty and licence and that is why we have a degree of censorship in Britain today'.

You then refer to 'laws against the incitement of racial hatred', to 'laws against libel and slander' and to what you call 'an infrequently used law against blasphemy' but you then move over to 'the second issue' about 'the degree of tolerance for controversial views'.

As I explained earlier *The Satanic Verses* is obscene, libellous and blasphemous with clear undertones of racism and racial incitement, but evidently they do not seem to come under the mischief of any of the relevant laws – that at least is the expert legal opinion. Muslims have, therefore, approached the problem from a position of legal helplessness. But even if there had been a legal recourse, I see it basically as a 'moral issue', an issue about decency and civilisation across all religious or party political differentiations.

However, the media treatment of the subject has completely overlooked the basically moral nature of the issue. On the other hand those who are themselves victims of powerful censorship are being accused of trying to impose censorship! Had this not been so, I am sure, you would not have formulated your 'Argument' in the way, you felt, you had to on the basis of the 'information' available.

You said 'British Muslims must not hesitate to state their case' and having gone to such lengths to state and explain clearly and unhesitatingly 'their case', I hope I do not have to reiterate that we too firmly believe in tolerance and in basic freedoms. In raising their objections to *The Satanic Verses,* Muslims are only trying to underscore the difference between the sacred and the profane, between tolerance and imposition and, to use your own words, between 'liberty and licence'.

I, therefore, look forward to your personal sympathy and moral support in this matter of great distress and hurt felt by the Muslim community in Britain and all over the world.

Yours sincerely,

M.H. Faruqi
Chief Editor

Source: *Impact International,* 19/3, 10th–23rd February 1989, pp. 7–8.

Mr Baker Replies

Dear Mr Faruqi,

Thank you for your long and thoughtful letter of 6th February concerning my article which *The Times* printed on 30th January.

First let me say how much I do appreciate, as I made clear in the article, the concern the Muslim community must feel not only in this country but across the world about the content of *The Satanic Verses.* This comes across in your letter.

Many of the things which you say in your letter cannot be derived from my article but from the reactions of many people over the course of the last few weeks. Since you wrote, of course, the whole situation has moved on to the international scene – the riots in Pakistan and, now, the statement by the Ayatollah. I must say this statement is quite unacceptable. It is simply wrong for anyone to condemn a person to death in this way and by this statement implicitly encourage people across the world to carry out that sentence. I simply do not believe that this represents the fine and noble strands of the Muslim faith to which you quite rightly referred in your letter – tolerance, a rejection of violence and a love of peace.

Yours sincerely,

Kenneth Baker

Faruqi's Rejoinder

Dear Mr Baker,

Thank you very much for your letter of the 17th instant and for the understanding shown by you for the deep and genuine concern felt in the Muslim community with respect to the continued publication of *The Satanic Verses* and the total insensitivity of its publishers.

Unfortunately, as you rightly point out the issue has been politicised and more unfortunately the almost total black-out of Muslim statements in the national media is having the effect of portraying the Muslim community as an 'outlaw' community raring to execute a 'sentence' passed in a foreign country.

Over the past two weeks the media have been eliciting the views of the community leaders at various levels and although they were fully informed of the clear position of the Muslim community, they chose to focus on a couple of individual expressions of provoked anger (which the police did not find indictable). One radio network was so frank as to ask his Muslim respondent to suggest anyone who would say something 'outrageous' (sic).

Mr Kilroy Silk's programme 'Kilroy' (BBC1, 13th February) was another example of manipulation of anger with a view to obtaining material for his anti-immigrant ideas which he has ventilated in his column in *The Times*.

We have been told that the participants in the programme were carefully selected. A Muslim community leader who was invited on the programme was asked to go back after he had reported at the studio. Probably there was a delayed realisation that he was not 'suitable' material as he did not hold any outrageous views.

Not surprisingly the programme was successful in coaxing and provoking one young girl, one lady and one gentleman into answering a wrong question in 'yes' (say 'Yes' or 'No', 'Yes' or 'No' – Mr Silk will take nothing else for an answer). One person who observed that this was sheer incitement was shoved off the camera. I am afraid Muslims find themselves already tried and convicted by the media.

However, let me state clearly and categorically the Muslim position with respect to the crime of blasphemy against the person of the Blessed Prophet (peace be upon him).*

> The crime when committed by a *Muslim* is punishable with death, if the accused is found guilty after a judicial trial, *but a non-Muslim citizen of a Muslim state, if found guilty of blasphemy is liable only to 'imprisonment'*.
> The law is applicable and enforceable *only within the jurisdiction of the Islamic state.*
> There is no provision in Islamic law for enforcement of its verdict and sentences in countries outside its jurisdiction much less by (Muslim or non-Muslim) citizens of those countries. Even within an Islamic state no citizen is expected to or is allowed to take law into his own hands.

So you are very right in believing that Islam represents 'tolerance, a rejection of violence and a love of peace.' We only wish this knowledge was also reflected by our media.

As Muslims see it, the whole thing revolves around the serious problems of understanding for their feelings and concerns.

When Muslims put forward their objection to the publishers way back in October last year they were not raising any religious or political issues much less an issue of anti-freedom and censorship. They saw it – and still do so – as a purely moral issue of civility and decency in human communications and had expected little difficulty in being understood at the simple human level. In the event they now find all the guns aimed at them as 'enemies of civilisation.'

Finally I would like to draw your attention to the fact that, according to information received by us, some overzealous teachers have been asking their Muslim pupils to study *The Satanic Verses* or to do a project on it. They are told it will improve their proficiency of the English language. You will appreciate that this amounted to intellectual oppression of young and helpless children and I am sure that your department will look into the matter and take appropriate steps in this respect.

I must apologise yet again for writing a long letter but I do so in the encouragement that you regard yourself as a Christian and because the Qur'an tells us that 'you will find most affectionate of them towards those who believe, are those who say: We are Christians.'

This is the reason why Muslims take no satisfaction from the progressive de-Christianisation of this country and, if you recall, they did not support efforts to remove religious education from the National Curriculum.

Yours sincerely,

M.H. Faruqi
Chief Editor

*A friend has drawn attention to some different juristic views on the application of the apostasy law. The above is written from a broad Hanafi position.

Source: *Impact International* (London), 19/3 (1989), pp. 7–8.

Salman Rushdie Did Wrong

by S. Nomanul Haq

Dear Salman Rushdie: A few years ago, when I read your "Midnight's Children," I was overwhelmed. It was not the exuberance of your narrative and stylistic craft, nor the threads of your rich imagination woven with such effective intellectual control that engulfed me. Rather it was your formidable grasp of history and, through that, of the psyche of a complex culture in all its variations that formed the substratum of your style.

And yet it is this question of your knowledge of history that I shall raise in connection with your seriously and alarmingly controversial "The Satanic Verses."

Let me say at once that I do hold you as an artist, not as a historian or a psychologist – nor as theologian. But at the same time you do make use of what are facts of history and psychology, giving them your own distinct treatment.

No writer, you will agree, writes in a historical vacuum. But then, a responsible artist does not, without powerful grounds, mutilate history. Nor, unless there exists a mammoth justification, does he disregard the sensibilities and sensitivities of his own milieu, especially when it forms both the subject matter and the bulk of his or her audience.

Strangely, what I am saying is something that I learned from none other than yourself. You might recall your telling criticism of Sir Richard Attenborough's celebrated film "Gandhi." You enraged Sir Richard, but in the controversy I remained your passionate supporter.

You censured the film for disregarding or minimizing certain important historical facts. And you said that in a work of an artistic nature, one cannot say everything, that there has to be a choice – but that there has to be a rationale of choice. One selects not to mislead but to make the story more meaningful. Ironically, this has precisely been your lapse in "The Satanic Verses."

Most of your western readers are unable to gauge the acuteness of your blow to the very core of the Indian subcontinental culture. They cannot estimate the seriousness of the injury because they do not know the history of the aggrieved.

You do know it and therefore one feels that you foresaw, at least to some extent, the consequences.

There is in your book, for example, the phantasmagoria of your own namesake Salman's corruption of the revealed word by his erroneous rendering of the words of Mahound.

Here the veil is too thin to cover the identity of Mahound: He can be understood in no other way than as a caricature of the Muslim Prophet. You do know that Islam is consistently, acutely and uniquely sensitive to its scripture. Ordinarily, Arabic is written without short vowels, but no copy of the Qur'an today is vowelless: Muslims insist that it should and can be read only in one way. The Muslim view is that even incorrectly reading the Qur'an is a cardinal sin. The Qur'an is neither read nor recited in translation for the very reason that translation might introduce alteration.

This matter is deadly serious, and to make it a subject of insensitive fantasy is equally serious.

There is a further issue that your western reader does not sense; that your corrupt Salman is the namesake not only of you in your book but of a historical personage who was a Persian companion of the Prophet, a companion who has been accorded a particularly elevated status by the Shiites. Given the militancy of the Shiites, when you made Salman the polluter of the revelation, you knew that you were planting your hand in the cluster of bees!

Your response to the uproar has been wavering and inconsistent, and your defense has the odor of self-righteousness. You say that people who have not read your book have no right to criticize it. But do you really think that reading the book will drastically alter their opinions? Then you talk about freedom of expression. Free speech is a tricky issue and cannot be taken too literally.

What do you think the response of black Americans would be if you were to mock Martin Luther King Jr.? Or the reaction of the Jewish community if you eulogized Hitler? Or the anger of a pious Hindu if you were to present a graphic description of the slaughtering of a cow?

As for your waverings, you started out by expressing regret over the fact that you did not write even a more controversial book. You accused the leaders of the angry demonstration in Islamabad of exploiting a religious slogan for secular and political ends. They may have done so, but what about the innocent and ignorant people who died in the violence? You expressed no sympathy for them. And now you issue a three-sentence statement that, at best, has the semblance of regret. Quite honestly, Mr. Rushdie, you heart does not beat in this statement, your expression is glaringly perfunctory.

I am saddened that a bounty has been placed on your head and that a great writer like you, rather than presenting himself to the public, is in hiding. You have elicited the rage of entire nations. This is a pity. But, Mr. Rushdie, you have cut them and they are bleeding: Do something quickly to heal the wound.

Source: *IHT,* 24th February, 1989 in *The Kiss of Judas,* pp. 35–7.

The Devil Incarnate

A sudden outburst of the Western support for Salman Rushdie, the Indian-born British author of *The Satanic Verses,* shows the low regard the West has for Muslims and their religion. The British and the EEC move to protect someone who is a blot on the Western civilisation and the favourable American response to the European behaviour appear as much uncivilised as the fiction weaved by Rushdie. What the civilised people had expected from the West was that it would have made a bonfire of *The Satanic Verses* because it is not only filth thrown at the sensibilities of the Muslims but at the face of everyone who believes in God and the message of love He sent through His messengers.

To see the Western world get riled over the universal condemnations Rushdie is getting is to realise that the Western world doesn't have respect for Islam. The West had committed a number of books into the fire in its long history, because these books either said something uncaring about Christianity or even something that was considered to be obscene. There can be nothing more obscene than a book that vilifies a heavenly religion and all those who believe in God should have condemned it.

In this troubled world of ours, there are two forces fighting for dominance: God's message and atheism. All those who believe in God should be, by necessity, a unified force that fights atheism, which in the garb of Communism is the spearhead of evil and one of its aims is to obscure religions by every means possible, because atheists know that once belief in God wanes they can triumph eventually. That is their dream since time immemorial.

This book is not only a slur on Islam but something that Christians should see as an attack on the belief in God. When the people who believe in one religion condone the slurs against the people of other religions, it might follow that people of different faiths in this world would find it very hard to live and deal with each other on amiable terms.

The Satanic Verses is an insult to decency. Respecting other people's beliefs is the basis of decent human relationship, and Rushdie's insult to all the Muslims of the world should not have deserved the defence the Western governments are providing it. When that kind of thing happens the message the Muslims get from the West does not respect them or their Islamic faith. Receiving that kind of message could very easily spark hatred which is just the opposite of the belief of Christians.

There is a long history of Western distortions of the tenets of Islam and there have been long campaigns mounted by Western people to undermine Islam. Despite the onslaught of attacks on Islam by the Western world, the Muslim people have never attacked Christianity or any other religion or their leaders. Why? Muslims know that it is totally against civilised behaviour and that civilised people do not indulge in using filthy language about someone held in respect.

Christians believe that there had been many prophets. They should not have had any problem in regarding Muhammad as a prophet, like the other prophets who came before him. An attack on God's one messenger is an attack on all His messengers and on His message; it is but a total disbelief in all revelations through the prophets. In short *The Satanic Verses* is a blasphemy of all religions and an insult to all those who believe in God and claim to be civilised. It is the work of the devil incarnate, and all those who are supporting its continued distribution and promotion of it through controversy which will make a market for it through curiosity are aiding the devil in his work!

Source: *The Saudi Gazette* (Jeddah), 24th February, 1989.

A Call for Fairness

Birmingham Central Mosque's Advertisement in *The Times* (3rd March 1989)

THE RUSHDIE AFFAIR

IS IT FAIR that the entire British Nation should pay for one man's greed?

IS IT RIGHT that the fate of British hostages and British commercial interests be jeopardised for a publisher's profit?

Let us be honest and not confuse issues.

No one, repeat, NO ONE, questions Rushdie's right to express himself . . .

BUT – to be vulgar, abusive and obscene is a misuse of this right.

We believe it is wrong and dishonest to insult founders of religion under the pretext of a dream.

It would be dishonest and wrong to portray . . .

> Christ using four letter words
>
> Matthew and Mark indulging in indecencies and molesting children
>
> Moses as a racist and lecherous person

Surely, this would not be considered as criticism – it would be the imagination of a confused mind.

Rushdie has portrayed the Prophet of Islam as a brothel keeper.

Again, this is not criticism, but the imagination of a confused mind.

If Moses, Christ and Mohammed can be allowed to be portrayed as racist, con men and living on immoral earnings, then may we ask what basis would be left for teaching our children a concept of moral behaviour?

Let us think calmly and not be guided by propaganda.

There is much more at stake than the licentious liberty of an insensitive publisher.

We urge the Penguin Group to withdraw this book unreservedly and accept the related demands of the community. It is a small price to pay for the moral interests of the nation.

We appeal to all patriotic, fair minded British Citizens to join us in our protest and write to us so that a joint action can be planned.

Act Against Rushdie Today Before it is Too Late

Britain's move to appease the world-wide Moslems was too little, too late. The Moslems still are expecting that the British leaders will try to realize the depth of injuries to Moslems across the world through The Satanic Verses.

Both Prime Minister Margaret Thatcher and Secretary of State Sir Geoffrey Howe admitted that the book offended the Moslems. Naturally this alone is simply not enough to heal the wounds of enraged Moslems who have protested everywhere they were to be found. Several people have given their lives and hundreds were injured during these demonstrations which are still continuing.

The protests reached a peak after the Leader of the Islamic Republic issued a Divine Decree on February 14 in which the Imam Khomeini ordered the execution of the author, Salman Rushdie who clearly blasphemed Islam and the Islamic sanctities.

The Moslems clearly expect that the British government should openly condemn the book and stop its further sale and publication. They also expect that the author should be tried as he 'offended Moslems' . . .

Banning of the book will not be the first or the last in Britain. Very recently the Thatcher Administration has banned a book, 'Spycatcher' for the simple reason that the book will put the lives of some people in danger as well as that it had offended some.

If Spycatcher can be banned and condemned then why not 'The Satanic Verses' which has hurt one billion Moslems and others who believe that the beliefs of others should be respected even while they exercised their rights to expression.

We would like to remind Mrs. Thatcher of an elementary principle of 'civics', that rights and duties go together. If one of these is ignored it results in a tragedy such as 'The Satanic Verses'. The author while using the rights of expression should have felt responsibility on his part for the feelings of the Moslems, a faith to which he belongs by birth even if not by conviction. And we cannot imagine that he could have been as a novelist so crassly insensitive to the feelings of Moslems who believe with a direct and simple faith and love and trust their Prophet Mohammad (S) beyond anyone living or dead in the world now, or in any future.

We hope that Mrs. Thatcher will take appropriate action against the author and the book today if only to defuse the situation. Tomorrow may be too late.

Source: *Tehran Times,* 7th March 1989.

An Affront to Civility

by Khurshid Ahmad

Mr. Chairman . . .

The struggle of the Islamic *Umma* the world over, whether in the political field or otherwise, is for one supreme objective: the establishment of the Islamic social order and the unity and solidarity of the *Umma* on the basis of the Qur'an and *Sunnah. Alhamdulillah,* the waves of Islamic resurgence are mounting in all parts of the world and while the struggle is long and arduous, the silver lining on the horizon is widening and expanding to herald the dawn of a new and bright era for Islam.

Mr. Chairman, in this context the problems of the Muslim communities living under non-Muslim governments deserve to be constantly reviewed by the leaders of the Islamic *Umma.* Islam, today is the second largest religion in Europe. According to conservative estimates there are over 8 million Muslims in Western Europe and around 10 million in Eastern Europe and European Russia. In almost every European country there is a distinct Muslim Community. These Communities are part of the galaxy of the Islamic *Umma* and they are making every effort to protect and strengthen their ideological identity and to lend their support and co-operation to the issues and problems faced by the Islamic *Umma.* They represent the voice of Islam in the Western world and through them the frontiers of Islam have been extended to lands not directly under the control of the Muslims. They also constitute a bridge between the Islamic and the Western worlds. I hope the Organization of Islamic Countries (OIC) will take greater interest in the problems and prospects of this Islamic hinterland.

Mr. Chairman, I want to take this opportunity to invite the attention of this Conference to the gruesome challenge that Muslim Communities in the West, nay the entire world of Islam, faces today because of the vicious intellectual and literary assaults on Islam that are assuming menacing proportions in the West. Contemporary Islamic awakening is being grossly misrepresented as the rise of fundamentalism and fanaticism. These efforts have been on the increase, but all limits of decency and toleration have been broken by a scandalous novel *The Satanic Verses* by one Salman Rushdie, published by Penguin/Viking in the UK and USA. This vicious book, which has been, on pure literary criteria, rated as low by a number of top literary critics, even as unreadable, has been chosen to be promoted on a vast scale and translated in twenty languages of the world. Even before the book appeared in print in September 1988, a calculated effort was made by the Western media to project this book which contains vicious attacks, abominable falsifications and calumnious and slanderous statements against the Prophet Abraham (a Prophet in whom all adherents of Judaism, Christianity and Islam believe) and the Prophet Muhammad (peace be upon him), his respected and revered wives (who are more sacred and respected in the eyes of all Muslims than their own mothers) and a number of close companions of the Prophet, who represent for the Muslims the noblest specimens of humanity. The authenticity of the Qur'an and of the prophetic Traditions has been blatantly denigrated. The whole book is an exercise in scandalous vilifications and blasphemous statements causing gross provocation to all the followers of Islam and polluting the minds of Western readers and the younger generations against Islam, its Book, its Prophet and its religious leaders and sources of guidance.

The fact that this vicious and slanderous book has been published and is being wantonly projected by the Western media is an affront not only to the Muslim faith and conscience, but to the good sense of the entire civilized world. To defend this book in the name of freedom of conscience and expression amounts to adding insult to injury. Vilification of any person is a crime against humanity and has always been so treated in the civilized society. But vilification of a Prophet, his family and his companions is a far more heinous crime. Circulation of such slanders through instruments of mass media under the false cover of freedom of expression can never be condoned. That is why every society has some kind of a law of libel and some safeguards to protect the honour of the living and the dead.

While we respect the values of freedom of opinion, belief and expression and we welcome honest dissent and critical discussion, not only in respect of political issues but also in matters relating to ideology, religion and culture, no one has a right to publicize in the name of artistic freedom outright lies, calculated distortions and blasphemous allegations. There are certain values that must be respected by all and there are certain limits beyond which no civilized society can allow corrupt minds to deprave the minds and morals of the innocent and uninformed humans. Commitment to freedom is fundamental, but commitment to truth is more fundamental. Muslims have always stood for freedom, but we have never and shall never tolerate vilification of our religion and obscene and blasphemous attacks on our Prophet. That is why Muslims the world over have risen to protest against these slanderous attacks on their values and will not rest until this mischief is undone. I assure this Conference that the Muslims in the UK and Europe are aware of their responsibilities, both to the law of the land and to the demands of their faith and honour.

We are happy that some Muslim Governments have taken a firm stand on this issue. We hope this Conference will express the Muslim position on this international challenge in clear and unequivocal terms. We expect not only a forthright condemnation of this vicious attack on Islam and the shamefaced efforts to condone it, but use of all instruments of economic, diplomatic, cultural and political leverage to see that the book and its translations are withdrawn, all printed copies pulped, an unqualified apology rendered by the publishers, and a commitment not to allow the repetition of such slanderous episodes in the future. A resolution along the above lines is the minimum this Conference can do to join its voice and influence to the universal protest of the Islamic *Umma* against this blasphemy. The Conference should make the following eight demands:

1. The blasphemous novel *The Satanic Verses* by Salman Rushdie be immediately banned in all those Muslim countries where it has not yet been banned;
2. The publishers forthwith:
   (i) withdraw this novel from the market, and pulp the same;
   (ii) offer an unconditional public apology to all Muslims; and
   (iii) commit not to publish or promote it in any other form or language in the future;
3. If the publishers fail to comply with the above forthwith, such publishers and their holding companies be blacklisted and import of all their publications banned in all Muslim countries;
4. Economic sanctions be used against all those who extend protection to this blasphemous book against Islam;
5. The author of this novel be banned from entry into any Muslim State;
6. Wide publicity be given to the measures taken by the Muslim States so that it serves as a deterrent and in future no one dares to degrade Islam in this manner;
7. Embassies in non-Muslim States be directed to contact the Governments of their countries to take effective action in banning this book and seeking its withdrawal from the market.
8. Finally, positive efforts be made at all levels to project the true message of Islam through the latest technology available.

Mr. Chairman, I hope and pray that the leaders of the Muslim countries and organizations gathered here will rise to the occasion and fulfil their duty.

Source: From the speech by Khurshid Ahmad, Leader, Delegation of the Islamic Council of Europe, at the 18th Islamic Foreign Ministers' Conference, held in Riyadh on 12th March 1989.

Muslims and Britain

by M.H. Faruqi

. . . We now live in a world supposed to be enlightened and guided by such holier texts as the Universal Declaration of Human Rights and more recently by the 'Declaration on the Elimination of All Forms of Intolerance and of Discrimination Based on Religion and Belief'. The very first article of the Universal Declaration begins by underscoring the fundamental principles governing the whole concept of human rights: of all human beings being 'born free and equal in dignity and rights'. But even if there was no such declaration, respect for human dignity has always been regarded as a fundamental basis in human relationship in all civilised societies. The opposite has never been true and no one has ever tried to assert his absolute 'right to insult or to abuse' others. There are, from time to time, slips and failures in maintaining the dignity of expression, but such unintended insults are always withdrawn the moment it is discovered or pointed out that a transgression has been committed.

Examples galore, but three would suffice.

Not long ago the Midland Bank axed its television campaign following complaints by members of the British Jewish community who said the advertisement perpetuated 'the myth of the stereotype Jew'. The advertisement had featured a Jewish-looking character as an example of a small businessman achieving success with the help of the bank. A few dozen protests and the Midland Bank lost little time in withdrawing the £1.5m advertising campaign. They said they had 'not foreseen that it would arouse so much concern within the Jewish community', admitted 'that it was offensive and should not have been shown', expressed their 'regret' and axed the advert. Neither the bank, nor anyone else on their behalf tried to argue that the programme had been created by a Jewish director and played by Jewish actors and rather than being insulting it was in fact highlighting 'the quality of enterprise and success' in the community. Nor did they try to take shelter behind the doctrine of artistic freedom, freedom to lampoon and freedom to outrage. No one tried to accuse the Jewish community that it was seeking to impose its values over British society. Rightly so.

Mr Hayim Pinner secretary of the Board of Jewish Deputies also revealed that 'We already have an informal arrangement with publishing companies to show us works of Jewish interest first' and the Board 'would be happy if anything on television could also come to us first'. Again no one accused the community of operating its own censorship over publishing and now trying to extend it over the electronic media. That would have been dodging the central issue: that of civility in human communications, because stripped of civility communication ceases to be what it is intended for and becomes an instrument of oppression.

More recently, barely two weeks ago, the microphone of the Speaker of the House of Commons happened to utter some word described as 'expletive', but even the inanimate voice system refused to transmit the word. No one complained of the system stifling his right to 'free' expression. It was simply treated as a 'Satanic' non word. No fuss, no crisis! That was civility and dignity and it should have been so.

The other day the most senior judge at the Old Bailey, Sir James Miskin, 64, happened to refer to Black people as 'nig nogs'. It was an after dinner speech and he used the words 'nig nog', and 'murderous Sikhs' in order to illustrate his point with respect to many defects in the criminal justice system. These remarks were noted by a Leicester magistrate, Michael Prickett, who wrote to Sir James objecting to his choice of words, and copied his letter to the Lord Chancellor, the Home Secretary and the Commission for Racial Equality. And Sir James quickly apologised admitting that it was a 'silly expression' and he 'regretted' having used it.

Compare the Midland Bank advert, the 'expletive' coming out of the Speaker's microphone and Sir James' 'nig nog' with the filth and abuse heaped on Abraham, and Muhammad (peace be upon them) and on very many sanctities of Islam in *The Satanic Verses*.

When last autumn Muslims took exception to what is now generally admitted to be most foul and filthy book, the so-called *Satanic Verses* (Viking Penguin, September 1988), they believed that they were raising the most ordinary point about decency and dignity. They were not concerned with the literary faults or merits of the 'novel' (it were other critics who said the book was 'dense', 'impenetrable' and in fact 'unreadable' and called for punishing its author for its 'atrocious English'). They were not objecting to its 'theological' or 'scholarly' criticism even if it had any such elements. They had no wish or intention to challenge anyone's freedom of expression or to impose their 'mediaeval' or 'censorious' values over 'the civilised' world.

What they were talking about was not even exclusively Islamic, it was the universal value common to all people – of all faiths or no faith – that it is not civilised to abuse and insult whatever the context or form of expression. They did not assume any malice on the part of the publishers.

Even though it had come out that Penguin had been advised by their editorial consultant in India, Mr Khushwant Singh, a Sikh and not a 'Muslim fundamentalist', that publishing the book would be 'lethal', because 'there are several derogatory references to the Prophet and the Koran' and 'Muhammad is made out to be a small-time impostor'. Khushwant Singh said he had 'read the manuscript and I was positive it would cause a lot of trouble'. His warning was disregarded by the Penguin chairman Peter Mayer. One assumed it was just the commercial objective to make money out of outrage and nothing more.

It would be interesting to read the correspondence between Khushwant Singh and Peter Mayer or to look into the notes if any of the telephonic conversation between them. The Penguin have, however, maintained a studied silence over the matter taking cover behind the author. The powerful media have, on the other hand, adopted the cause to distort the issue and launch a one-sided campaign of more insults against Muslims. Insofar as Muslims are concerned they are no doubt angry with the author, but they were quite clear that the problem lay with the publishers, their insensitivity and arrogance in refusing to withdraw their insult. It seems they want to turn a bad editorial judgement into a war of civilisation between a 'backward and uncultured' Muslim community and an 'enlightened' world community and by recklessly flaunting Salman Rushdie as the brown knight of their crusade, they have only served to worsen things for him.

Last week Penguin did send out some indirect signals to test whether the Muslim community would call off its campaign if they inserted a 'Muslim statement' in the book, paid some money to an Islamic charity and agreed to discuss the question of the paperback edition of the book. It was a non-starter insofar as Muslims were concerned. The publishers had however tried to approach Muslim organisations separately in order possibly to try to sell separate formulae but without having to make any agreement. They failed to discover any differences of position among Muslims who have since agreed to refer all overtures to the U.K. Action Committee on Islamic Affairs at the Islamic Cultural Centre, London. The Action Committee has since been able to bring together some major Islamic groups who had so far been working regionally.

Britain can rightly boast of having the largest number of experts on Islam and Muslim world, but, it appears, that when it came to the crunch, they all failed their country and their tax-payers. They have allowed themselves to lose sight of the real issue and got distracted by the deafening cacophony surrounding the battle to defend *The Satanic Verses*. The subject is deserving of a serious study, after all the noise and dust has settled down, but there is little doubt that the uninformed output about Islam and Muslims that has come up during the past three or four months far surpasses all the bitter polemics produced during the crusading centuries.

Instead of showing any understanding, the Muslim feeling of hurt was variously seen as the rise of Islamic militantism orchestrated by Libya, Saudi Arabia and Iran, as a reaction of insecurity by people caught in a climate of modernity and change, as a melancholy desire to escape into the dark ages and as a refusal to integrate with the British way of life. Neither was true.

Some condescending words have been said no doubt about their respect for their Faith, their devotion to family values, their law-abidingness and their contribution to the nation's commerce and entrepreneurial spirit etc. but they have been warned that if they continued to object to the highly praised *Satanic Verses* they risked inviting a backlash from the host community and even losing the cultural rights they have so far enjoyed.

There was never an attempt to understand Muslim feelings of deep hurt caused by the book, yet they were condemned *ex parte* as vandals and enemies of freedom!

Four months after, enter Ayatollah Khomeini with his sentence of death for the author and that provided an occasion for everyone to run riot. The Ayatollah is the supreme religious and political leader of a sovereign country and well within his rights to issue any decree in accordance with the laws of his country. But no one tried to take an objective look at the situation and to weigh the probability of that 'sentence' being actually executed in Britain.

There is no doubt that and not uncharacteristically the Ayatollah had articulated in the most forceful way that great outrage felt all over the Muslim world over the unremitting offence of sacrilege against the person of the blessed Prophet. Any orientalist would have confirmed to the Foreign Office the relevant Islamic law in this regard. But then was it applicable in Britain? Were members of the Muslim community in Britain, earlier praised for their law-abidingness, going to execute a decree passed in another country howso angry they might have been?

The job of finding an answer to the serious question was left to the media whose primary interest lies in finding or imagining the abnormal because what was normal was not 'news'. No attempt was made to establish contact with Muslim leaders – individually or collectively – and to get an answer to their overplayed anxieties. On the other hand total reliance seems to have been placed on media reports which had sought to manipulate the genuine anger of Muslims.

The climax of incomprehension came when the Home Secretary armed with such sensational appreciation of the situation travelled to Birmingham to lecture the community to abide by the laws of the country or else – to get out. Obviously on the basis of advice he had received, the Home Secretary had assumed *a priori* that Muslims had become outlaws and needed to be lectured in a firm and stern language. Part of the preliminary smothering work was done by the tabloid press who seem to have been able to obtain a copy of the minister's speech and to headline his words of warning to Muslims.

In its now five-month long moral campaign for the withdrawal of *The Satanic Verses,* the Muslim community had been quite clear in its mind that given the laws of the country, the government had no direct responsibility in the matter.

Under the normal course of the law the book could not be banned and there was no law to stop or punish sacrilege against Islam. They of course expected the national leadership to show an understanding of their anguish and hurt and think of ways and means of mitigating it and ensuring that such grievous transgression did not happen in the future.

Their expression within the laws and etiquette of their country of citizenship was in fact an act of integration but surprisingly they are construed as refusal or unwillingness to integrate.

Mr Hurd's dialogue with Muslim community leaders in Birmingham did not seem to be very helpful either. The passionate plea by the chairman of the Birmingham Central Mosque Dr Nasim that 'those who support Mr Rushdie's right to express himself', the way he has expressed himself, should 'realise what they are defending' elicited not only incomprehension but also a little irritation. The Home Secretary acknowledged that 'shocked', 'angry', and yet he said, it is not the job of the ministers in this country 'to go about condemning the books'. Raising his voice above the noisy reaction (*The Times,* 25th February) Mr Hurd said: 'I tell you very strongly. Once you start on that, I promise you it is a slope you would regret having pushed us down'. There was no intention to reform the blasphemy law to extend its protection to non-Anglican faiths, the Muslims may protest lawfully and as loudly as they may, but the government could do little in the matter. The Home Secretary was quite clear.

Muslims are not seeking any particular form of legislation, whether reforming the blasphemy law, extending the scope of criminal libel to slandering named religious personalities or any other piece of law. They, however, believe that their right to 'equal dignity' as against the duty to receive unequal indignity is a Fundamental Right and needs to be provided for within the broader context of human rights in Britain.

It is not all helpful to go on repeating the admitted virtues of freedom of expression and of tolerance when that 'freedom' is used as license to abuse and when preaching of tolerance becomes tantamount to intolerance of contrary views. The specifics and details of a legal redress can always be settled provided there is a political will; however, even before there is will there has to be an understanding. The situation was well summed up by Edward Taylor Conservative MP for Southend when he pointed out that while Muslims were being asked to observe law, there was no law to answer their primary concern.

On the contrary things are being said and hinted that if they did not withdraw their objection to *The Satanic Verses,* the Muslims might as well disqualify themselves from enjoying other rights. It seems that when Muslims were subjects of the British Empire they were considered more deserving of rights and dignity than what some people would like them to be entitled to as British Citizens . . .

Source: *Impact International,* 10th–23rd March 1989, pp. 5–8.

Now Can You Beat That, Rushdie

by Mazlan Nordin

Dear Mr. Salman (Rushdie),

I wonder whether you are sleeping soundly nowadays. A recent news report from London quoted the National Union of Teachers as saying that racist abuse and harassment have risen in British schools following controversy over your book *The Satanic Verses.* White pupils have been taunting Asian classmates for religious beliefs. This is apart from the deaths of some 12 people in Pakistan and India after clashes with police and others. How very apt is the title of your book.

The book has been stoutly defended in a New York rally attended by several hundred writers, including Norman Mailer. Mr. Mailer was reported to have made a ringing declaration, "It is our duty to state to the world that if he (meaning you) is ever assassinated it will then become our obligation to stand in his place."

Suffice for me to repeat here the somewhat mocking comments of Bernard Levin, a famous Jewish writer, in a special article in the *Times* titled "Humbugs of the world unite." He said, I quote:

"What, if anything is that supposed to mean? It can hardly mean that if Mr. Rushdie is killed, Mr. Mailer and his fellow writers will be willing to be buried along with him like Catewayo's wives. Nor, surely, that they would at once all start writing books calculated to give moral affront to Muslims and thus put themselves into the same danger as Mr. Rushdie is now in.

" . . . I am not just jeering at Mr. Mailer and his hollow bombast. I suspect that his words were meant to echo Voltaire's celebrated dictum, 'I detest what you say but I will defend to the death you right to say it', but, if so, there are two serious flaws in his point.

The first is that Voltaire never said it; it was invented and attached to him in a modern biography. The second is that although he might well have defended the unfettered expression of a view he abhorred, it is very unlikely that he would have been willing to die for it. Nor, I am pretty sure, would Mr. Mailer. And another thing, if Mr. Mailer were willing to give his life for fellow writer Rushdie's, would he do so for me? Come to think of it, would Rushdie?"

You'll note that I have spoken of Bernard Levin as a Jewish writer, but this is simply to indicate his different stance from that of another Jew, and I quote here from the London *Sunday Times* profile on you: "In print he (meaning you) was accused of being a deracinated Indian who denied his own background, of being published by a Jew (Peter Mayer, head of Viking)."

Incidentally, the article mentioned your experience at Rugby where you encountered "the wog-baiting of English public schoolboys" but that you were "shielded from its uglier manifestations by being pale-skinned and well-educated with impeccable English voice."

I have read your book *Midnight's Children* about India which won the prestigious Booker Prize. I read that you had to apologise to the family of Indira Gandhi because a teeny-weeny part indicated that she neglected her husband. Wasn't there something about a Miss Ironpants there? It has been suggested that the character so named is the present Prime Minister of Pakistan, Benazir Bhutto. What, no apology?

But what saddens us most is your portrayal of our Prophet Muhammad . . .

May I commend to you the following story of Prophet Muhammad as related by Dr. Ali Shariati, one of the ideologues of the Islamic revolution in Iran.

"A Jewish woman pours down filth on him from the roof of the house while he is on his way and he says nothing. One day, as usual, he passes along his everyday route and did not see the dirt being poured. He asks, 'Where is my friend today? She hasn't come to see me.' When told that she is sick he pays her a visit."

I understand that you wrote a paper on Islam for part of your history tripos. You might, therefore, know that the first Iranian to accept Islam was one by the name of Salman (repeat Salman) Farsi, who later became a part of the Prophet's family. I am mentioning this because you have been "sentenced" to death by Ayatullah Khomeini, and much has been written about it in the media. I cannot, however, recall what the western press made out of a news despatch about hundreds of people in San Diego, California welcoming back as "heroes" Captain Will Rogers and his crew of the *USS Vincennes* which "mistakenly shot down an Iran Airbus in the Persian Gulf on July 3, 1988, killing all 290 aboard."

Now can you beat that.

Source: *New Straits Times* and *New Sunday Times* (Kuala Lumpur) 24th March 1989 in *The Kiss of Judas,* pp. 54–6.

Intellectual Prostitution

What deepens the anguish of Muslims and leads to the death of many innocents is the feeling of betrayal. Proud of their honorary white status, brown sahibs like Salman Rushdie take every opportunity to heap ridicule and contempt on the beliefs, culture and civilisations of the people they left behind.

Rushdie is guilty of not only intellectual prostitution but culpable homicide, for as a nominal Muslim he should have foreseen that *The Satanic Verses* would provoke reaction of such magnitude that it would lead to violence and death. In the scale of human worth, are the lives of Muslims still not equal to that of a white man?

No one has the right to denigrate the prophets of the great religions, including Moses, Jesus or Buddha. Having defamed the Holy Prophet, Rushdie cannot claim the protection of "free speech" even in a liberal-decadent society that allows its own prophet, Jesus, whom we hold in reverence, to be ridiculed and blasphemed against in plays, books, musicals and films.

Rushdie's pandering to the west in the hope of raking in royalties and prizes should be repudiated by all – especially the west. What allowed this insult to Islam to be published in the first place was the duplicity of Britain, where blasphemy against Christianity is an offence and blasphemy against other great religions isn't. The British, having felt the anger of Muslims world-wide, belatedly came up with a statement condemning Rushdie for likening Britain and Nazi Germany – but still did not condemn the blasphemy. *The Economist* describes the publishers and distributors of Rushdie's book as "those who have suddenly found themselves in the front line of the defence of western values." Do western values include the right to blaspheme and cause innocent deaths of Muslims?

It is unfortunate that President Bush should disregard the sentiments of a billion Muslims and find it important to support Rushdie. He says that inciting murder and offering rewards for its perpetration are deeply offensive to norms of civilised behaviour. As a former director of the CIA, Mr. Bush should know better than to make such statement. The West German foreign minister states that the recall of western Europe's ambassadors from Iran is a signal to Iran for the "maintenance of human dignity and free speech." Free speech doesn't include blasphemy – and the signal in not only to Iran but to 46 Muslim nations from Indonesia to Morocco. Yugoslavia's decision to publish the book at this juncture will embitter the Muslims of that country and ultimately lead to its own balkanisation. And Russia, in contemplating publication, would be unwise to forget that over 40 million Muslims live in the soft underbelly of the Soviet empire.

There seems to be a deliberate attempt to disrupt the recent feeling of grudging respect for Islam in the west. The Mujahideen's defeat of a superpower, Russia, in the name of Islam, is an event unparalleled in history. The courage of Palestinians braving Israeli bullets in the Occupied Territories comes from their deep faith in Islam.

Who would benefit most from a rupture between Islam and Christianity? Western states say that when governments urge terrorism, compromise is not possible. Does only Muslim Iran come under this category? Why such outrage over a sentence of death on a nominally Muslim heretic when every day the death sentence is carried out against defenceless Muslims in Palestine? Why does the west not react?

These double standards must end or the world will enter another age, of a new crusade of Islam against the west. The rift between us is still small, but any further aggravation will inflame Muslims everywhere. We are witnessing the casting of a mosaic of events.

Muslims are appalled and pained that the west has not only made no attempt to stop this blatant blasphemy but has supported the outrage at the highest levels.

Rushdie's own words in *The Satanic Verses* are self-fulfilling – the blasphemy cannot be forgiven. But his real punishment will be a personal one, when he finally realises the enormity of his sin.

S.K. Islamabadi
Chittagong, Bangladesh

Source: *Asia Week* (Hong Kong), 31st March 1989 in *The Kiss of Judas,* pp. 56–7.

Between Fairness and Freedom: The Motives Behind the Controversy

by Ahmad Zaki Hammad

Greed and hate lie at the heart of the controversy inflamed by Salman Rushdie's *Satanic Verses.* The author (and Allah knows who else) strove night and day to create the dramatic image of an embattled intellectual persecuted by a band of Medieval, narrow-minded, fanatic fundamentalists.

The trick is clearer than ever. It should not mask the ugly reality of a deliberate exploitation of religion for commercial purposes. An insightful psychiatrist will tell us that a man who has spent his entire adult life expressing public contempt for his homeland, hatred for his native culture, and now slandering the beautiful model of morality and spirituality the Prophet of Islam represents can only be in deep disgust of himself.

If the facts are too glaring, then let me borrow the garb of fiction and imagine the following.

Once upon a time, a young man was forced to live in Bombay and grew up to hate his religion, his culture, his people, the world, and then himself. So he decided to pursue a career as a preacher of hate. His name was Fasdan Kufri.

Fasdan sat thinking to himself one brooding afternoon of ways to fool the believers of religion. A dark sleep overcame him, and he began to dream. In the blackness of his room, he saw a glittering crystal ball on a table and began to stroke it. Strange names that he had never before heard came to his tongue, and he invoked them.

To his surprise a shadow appeared. His name, he declared, was Wasswass, if you want. He had many names.

"Good! Good! Very Good!" came the low, vile, throaty breath of stale air from Wasswass in a deafening whisper. He was after all chief of the Lot.

"I know what you want from me, Fasdan. And this is what you shall do. In the name of fiction and free expression, slander the Prophet with obscenity and abuse. Say what you will against Ibrahim, and, yes, say much, much about Muhammad, his family, and the Companions. The more filthy you speak the more filthy rich you will become. Imagine the wealth, the fame, Fasdan, the glory! And think of the cash to come when you write about Jesus and Moses.

"Yes . . . the believers will burst with anger. A few will die. But worry not. The mighty press will come quickly to defend your right to free expression, and they will magnify your voice even louder. No one will ever see that you are crying 'FIRE' in the world theater. No one will dare speak ill of you for offending and inciting others.

"Remember this. Your name will be mentioned in every home, in every paper. It will make you person of the week, person of the month, person of the year – and I will make you the person of eternity."

Fasdan, wide-eyed, agreed.

Bored with fiction? Sorry, this is my first attempt.

Islam is not against a person's right to hold contrary views. It is in fact intended to continue the heritage of all the prophets of Allah and to coexist with other religions in the world, as it has very successfully for 14 centuries.

Islam has no problem with individual freedoms, expression or otherwise. But one's freedoms stop where another's begin. For less than this is not freedom, but injury.

As for the constitutional arguments that have been used lately, it is clear that the First Amendment's authors were attempting to provide solutions to a complex of "freedom" problems that had a specific history in Europe; namely, the lack of political, publishing, and religious tolerance.

The five freedoms were originally intended, in fact, to safeguard their practice in the interest of truth and harmony in a pluralistic society. They were never a license to slander, defame, or propagate falsehood, which fosters hate, mistrust, and discord between people, and which remains illegal. And though fiction is protected by this freedom, fictionalization – the distortion of actual events involving real people – should not be.

The issue raised by the *Satanic Verses* is not freedom of expression but "freedom to be insolent," as our Shaykh Muhammad Al-Ghazali told *Time* magazine recently.

It is in the interest of all in America to preserve the intent of these freedoms, which did not allow for blatantly anti-religious hate literature of any kind. Indeed, such freedom is a blessing from Allah, and His revealed truth should not be mocked by those who seek refuge in this very freedom. Obviously, no real freedom can be of the unethical and anarchic type that assault, incite, and divide.

But freedom was not invented in 1776. Islam is all about freedom.

It came to free humanity from the worship of other than Allah, to free the weak from the oppression of the strong, to free some from prejudice and others from inferiority complexes, to free societies of social ills, to free man to be the brother of man, to free people from darkness with light, to free the desperate with hope, the ill with comfort, the destitute with charity, the homeless with acceptance, the addicted with compassion, the downtrodden with dignity, the sinner with forgiveness, the frustrated with fulfilment, the tearful with joy, the disturbed with peace, the lonely with companionship, the tired with relief, the hate filled with love, the tested with patience, the brutalized with mercy, the ignorant with knowledge, the soul from selfishness, the injured with justice, and to free the worldly with Paradise.

Islam is freedom-loving. But, once more, there is a world of difference between the right to express a thought and the right to spit one out like a poison pit viper.

In Chicago right now there is a controversy over this very notion of freedom of expression at the famous Art Institute. One artist has displayed a work which consists of an American flag draped on the floor that people must walk upon to write in a book. He contends it is his right to self-expression.

Many veterans and common Americans hold this to be an intolerable abuse of freedom and are going to court. It turns out that the court will decide between them based on something known as the "flag laws," which restrict how the banner may be displayed and used.

"We believe in freedom of expression," one veteran told a reporter. "But that stops when it comes to the flag."

Then what of the Messenger, peace be upon him? Certainly, he is more than a banner. He is a Prophet of God, a model of moral and spiritual excellence, and a guiding light for Muslims and humanity. Those who believe in him shouldn't be expected to stand by while his message, his image is stepped on by some leftist idealogue.

This Rushdie affair is not about basic freedom of expression. It is about a poisoned soul. This is neither Eastern nor Western, but ethical in nature.

So the "mutual satanization," as it has been called, between some in the West and others who are Muslims, should stop. Rushdie capitalized (literally!) on just this misguided state of relations. By dredging up the ridicule and vilification of Islam and the Prophet from Europe's Medieval, Inquisitional past, he raised the level of mistrust to dangerous heights. This was exacerbated by the media's incessant portrayal of Muslims as fanatics, fundamentalists, and terrorists. A shift, away from this "attack-strike-back" posture to one of bridge-building, needs to occur, though it obviously will not sell as many newspapers.

In this regard, I believe it is fair to say that had the media acted with restraint, rather than fanning the flames of this controversy, it would not have turned into the international fire-storm it has become. And though I am reluctant to criticize Muslims at a time when they have been under such an unfair attack, may I suggest that some Muslims as well could have benefited by more deliberation and less emotion. Yet in the same breath, I am compelled to make *du'a* for the common Muslims, who have in effect drawn a mantle of civility around the body religious of Islam – not selfishly, but in the interest of the rights of man the worshipper. Certainly, the God-fearing have inalienable rights, including the right not to have their beliefs mocked.

We Muslims do not subscribe to spontaneous and emotional violence, but to a due process of law and order. *Let not enmity between you and a people lead you to injustice.* I strongly believe that a reservoir of goodwill and goodness endures in the non-Muslim religious communities of the West. (We have received letters and words of support from non-Muslims here regarding this unfortunate controversy.)

Let us remember, in all things, excess is sin – whether it be a politically timely zeal for religion or the jackpot fanaticism of art, displayed in Rushdie's and Viking Press' hate-inspiring *Satanic Verses.* Neither flimsy freedoms nor rigid dogma comprise the essence, the ethos, the elevation of human beings in civilization, but balance and the middle path in all things. This is Islam.

Then let there be dialogue that entertains alternatives, that stimulates, enlightens, and arouses our mutual passion for moral excellence. *And the final end is unto your Lord. – IH*

The Position Statement of the Islamic Society of North America

We wish to share the following points in regard to the recent controversy over Salman Rushdie's book, The Satanic Verses:

1. By depicting Islam, Prophet Muhammad, peace be upon him, his family, his Companions, his teachings, and the Angels, in a malicious, slanderous, highly defamatory manner, and by making obscene and derogatory references specifically to the Prophet's wives, Rushdie has grievously offended and violated the sanctity of the Muslim community. What makes it more painful is the fact that the author's blatant assault on Islam and the Prophet, besides being clearly unnecessary for his literary purposes, is in reckless disregard of the historical truths and heartfelt beliefs of the one billion-member Muslim community, and deliberately so.

2. We reaffirm our commitment to the freedom of thought and expression guaranteed to all people in this country, and which is at the same time a cherished Islamic value. However, it should also be pointed out that it is highly imprudent and inconsiderate for an individual to completely ignore the religious sensitivities of his fellows in humanity while exercising his freedoms. An individual's rights are undoubtedly guaranteed by the state, but

it is the spirit of harmony, goodwill and mutual respect among the members of society that ensures the full and balanced enjoyment and responsible exercise of these rights by all. The ideal of freedom of expression should not be a refuge for slander with the intent to do malice, nor blatant lies, nor defamatory ridicule. The publishers and booksellers of America, as well as the media, have a responsibility to maintain an acceptable standard of fairness that should exclude works of slander and bigotry.

3. Beyond the issue of freedom of expression, the media and publishing industry has traditionally exercised a sophisticated self-restraint in the interest of social order and harmony, as well as in consideration of moral and ethical norms and the ethno-racial and religious sensitivities of society. Muslims would like the media and publishing industry to accord them the same rights and consideration which have generally been extended to other ethnic, racial, and religious minorities threatened by stereotypical portrayal, innuendo, and false characterization. It is regrettable that Viking-Penguin, Inc., the publishers of *The Satanic Verses* in the U.S., has shown complete insensitivity to our concerns and has declined even to receive a representative delegation of the Muslim American community. It must have become clear to them by now that this book has hurt the feelings of hundreds of millions of Muslims throughout the world. We believe that a public apology is only appropriate and conducive to harmony and goodwill.

4. The purpose of our peaceful expression of dismay with the contents of Rushdie's *Satanic Verses* is to register the depth of our feelings against the author's flagrantly slanderous references to the Prophet and his family; to correct errors and misconceptions about Islam that are likely to be taken as facts by the readers of this book; to impress upon the publishers that they should have exercised better judgement in selecting and printing a book which has injured one-fifth of humanity; and to encourage the dissemination of accurate information about Islam, in North America and elsewhere.

5. Muslim Americans are grateful for statements issued by Cardinal O'Connor of New York, the Archbishop of Canterbury, and the Lord Chief Rabbi of the United Kingdom in condemning

this book. We urge the communities of faith in North America to add their voices of condemnation to ours. In the face of such assault on belief in God, religious consciousness, divine revelation, and the person of the Prophet Abraham, the patriarch of Islam, Christianity, and Judaism.

6. Despite our strong feelings about the contents of this hate-inspiring book, Islam does not condone violence or the incitement to violence directed against its author and those associated with its publication. Equally, we cannot condone the highly incendiary remarks of those who have suggested that violence be taken against Muslims at large.

7. Muslim Americans recognize those individuals in the news media who extended themselves to bring a balance of opinion and commentary to the American public throughout this affair. We anxiously await the day this attitude will become generalized throughout the fourth estate.

8. It is only sensible and in harmony with the American tradition of fairness and tolerance for publishers and booksellers in the United States to refuse to broker hate against Islam and Muslims – or any other religion or people for that matter – and to voluntarily withdraw this slanderous work from their shelves. We condemn the threat or use of violence to secure such withdrawal. It is, however, most inappropriate and in bad taste for American and European novelists to taunt Muslims on both continents and throughout the world with public readings constituting a frontal attack on Islam and its revered principal figures.

9. Muslim Americans affirm their belief in and commitment to the One True God of all humanity; and affirm their utmost respect for all the Prophets and Messengers – including Noah, Abraham, Moses, Jesus, and Muhammad (may the peace and blessings of God be upon them all); and affirm their commitment to human equality and brotherhood. For all this is vital to the moral-social order, and a light unto humanity.

In the words of Allah as revealed to the Prophet Muhammad in the Quran:

Say: My Lord has forbidden indecencies, whether open or veiled, and sin and violence, and that you associate with Allah that for which He sent down no authority, and that you say concerning Allah what you know not (7:33)

O mankind! We have created you male and female, and appointed you peoples and tribes, that you may know one another. Surely the noblest among you in the sight of Allah is the most God-fearing of you (49:13)

Source: *Islamic Horizons,* 18/1–4, March–April 1989, pp. 40–3.

Novelist's Freedom vs Worshipper's Dignity

by Ali Mazrui

In the autumn of 1988 a debate started in Britain. It concerned Salman Rushdie's novel, *The Satanic Verses.* Muslims in Britain exploded in indignation. The novel was declared blasphemous – and copies were ceremonially burnt.

In November 1988 I visited Lahore and Islamabad in Pakistan. Discussions about Rushdie's novel had already started there. One analogy particularly struck me. 'It is as if Rushdie had composed a brilliant poem about the private parts of his parents, and then recited the poem in the market place to the cheers and laughter of strangers! These strangers then paid him money for all the jokes about his parents' genitalia.' This charge that I heard levelled against Rushdie in Pakistan was of pornographic betrayal of ancestry. It was a concept of *treason* in a special sense.

In February 1989 Ayatullah Khomeini passed the death sentence on Salman Rushdie. Other leaders in Teheran offered a reward to anybody who killed Rushdie. Before long the reward had risen beyond $5 million dollars – and diplomatic relations between Britain and Iran rapidly deteriorated. Britain was supported by its partners in the European community, and the President of the United States expressed concern.

The West was bewildered by the depth of Muslim anger. The Muslims were bewildered by western insensitivity. Was this yet another problem of conflict of culture? Westerners had been busy looking for motives behind the reaction of Muslims.

– Was Iran's reaction due to a battle between moderates and hardliners?

– Was Rajiv Gandhi courting the Muslim vote in India?

– Was Benazir Bhutto in Pakistan being undermined through Rushdie?

Motives of writer Salman Rushdie hardly interest western political speculators. On the other hand, Muslims are more mystified by the author's motives than by the motives of the demonstrators in the streets of Dhaka and Karachi. Westerners find it hard to understand the anger of the demonstrators and of the governmental bans. Muslims find it hard to understand what they regard as the author's cultural treachery.

As for the assertion that one cannot be indignant about a book unless one has read it himself or herself, it is a new qualification about having an opinion: that you cannot form an opinion unless you have experienced the thing yourself. There are millions of believing Christians who have read only a few pages of the Bible. There are also Muslims who can read the Qur'an without understanding it. There are also believing Jews who know only a few quotes from the Torah. Many of those who have theories about Ayatullah Khomeini do not speak a word of Farsi. How many know from direct experience that Khomeini has really passed the death sentence on Rushdie? What about those indignant Muslims who *have* read the book? There is the assumption that all Muslim critics of Rushdie must be ignorant of the English language or incapable of understanding great literature.

Treason: Political and Cultural

Central to the crisis of mutual incomprehension was indeed the concept of *treason.* The western world does understand the concept of treason to the state. Indeed, the West understands capital punishment imposed on a traitor to the *state.* What the West does not understand is the idea of treason to what Islam calls the *Umma,* the religious community, treason to the faith.

English law does not always distinguish between the state and the Royal Family. Treason in England has included violating the King's consort, or raping the monarch's eldest unmarried daughter, as well as the sexual violation of the wife of the eldest son and heir. To the present day treason under English law includes 'polluting' the Royal bloodline or obscuring it. In addition, English law does of course regard it as treasonable the act of 'giving aid and comfort to the King's enemies.'

The basic law of the United States defines treason more narrowly in terms of war and military defence. The American founding fathers were aware that the concept of 'treason' could be used by tyrants as an excuse for suppressing liberty, stifling dissent, or preventing legitimate rebellion. The founding fathers' own revolt against King George III of England was 'treason' against the English monarch.

And so the American Constitution defined treason to the United States as consisting 'only in levying war against them, and in adhering to their enemies, giving them aid and comfort.'

In the twentieth century defending the United States came to mean defending its ideology of liberal capitalism against the threat of communism, real or perceived. The hysteria of the McCarthy era soon after the Second World War hit Julius and Ethel Rosenberg in June 1953. Julius had once been an active member of the Communist Party. They were executed as spies at the ages of 35 and 32 respectively.

Britain executed after World War II a Briton who had broadcast propaganda on the radio on behalf of Nazi Germany. And in the Middle of World War I, Sir Roger Casement – an Irish patriot who had served Britain well for a long time and then turned against Britain for the sake of Irish freedom – was executed for treason. Strangely enough, last-minute evidence of Casement's alleged homosexuality sealed his fate. Treason to his King was confused with treason to his gender.

In Islam there is no sharp distinction between church and state. The concept of treason is often indistinguishable from apostasy. The supreme penalty of treason to the *Umma* was indeed often death.

For his novel *The Satanic Verses* Salman Rushdie was perceived by many Muslims as being guilty of *cultural treason*. Rushdie had not merely rejected Islam: nor had he merely disagreed with it. Almost unanimously Muslims who had read the book concluded that Rushdie had *abused* Islam. What is more, he had been lionised, praised and lavishly rewarded and financed by outright enemies and hostile critics of Islam.

Islam is not unique in regarding attack on religion as a threat to the state. Scottish law until the 18th century made blasphemy not only a crime but also a capital offence. The Scottish heritage went back at least to the Mosaic Law on one side and the legacy of Roman Emperor Justinian I, on the other. Mosaic law decreed death by stoning as the penalty for the blasphemer. Emperor Justinian – who reigned from 527 to 565 A.D. – reinforced the death penalty for blasphemy.

In Britain today blasphemy is no longer a capital crime – but it is still both a statutory and common law offence. It has been recognised as an offence under the common law from the 17th century. But blasphemy in Britain is only applicable to the Anglican faith. On February 20, 1989 sections of the British press raised the question of whether it was not time that blasphemy in Britain was also defined in reference to Judaism, Hinduism and Islam, all of which are well represented in the British population.

Perhaps the most fundamental blasphemy in Salman Rushdie's novel concerns the very title of his novel, *The Satanic Verses.* To explain the issues to people in the western world let us first place The Qur'an, the holy book of Islam, in the context of world literature. It is not just Rushdie's book which should concern western historians of literature. It is also The Qur'an itself as a work of art – the book which Rushdie virtually abuses by calling it 'the Satanic Verses.'

The Qur'an as World Literature

The Qur'an is the most widely read book in *its original language* in human history. The Bible is the most widely read book *in translation.* The Bible is also a *multi-authored* work. But the Qur'an is in a class by itself as a book which is recited by millions of believers, five times every day, in the very language in which it was first written.

The Qur'an is also a work of immense learning and versatility – obviously sensitised to the legacies of both the Christian Bible and the Jewish Torah. In addition it shows a capacity for direct legislative change, moral reform, refinement of rules of etiquette, and the power of poetry. Could such a book have been written by a camel herder and travelling salesman (peace be upon him)?

For Muslims the literary and spiritual genius of the Qur'an

could more easily be explained. There is a religious doctrine in Islam to the effect that the Qur'an is impossible to imitate. And yet no book in history has been subjected to more *attempts* at imitation. No other Arab of Muhammad's (peace be upon him) day has been put forward as the 'real' author of the Qur'an. To Muslims, the secret of the miracle is, quite simply, that it is the Word of God.

Salman Rushdie's blasphemy does not lie in his saying that the Qur'an is the work of Muhammad. If Salman Rushdie had simply said that the Qur'an was the work of the Prophet Muhammad and not the word of God, he would have been repeating the normal interpretation of non-Muslims. The blasphemy lies more in Rushdie's suggestion that it is the work of the Devil. By the term 'Satanic Verses' he refers to more than an alleged incident in the history of Islamic revelation. Rushdie suggests that Muhammad (peace be upon him) is incapable of distinguishing between inspiration through an angel and inspiration from a devil. Indeed, Rushdie gives the Prophet a name which Rushdie himself describes as 'the Devil's synonym: *Mahound.*'

Rushdie suggests that Muhammad (peace be upon him) was not only incapable of distinguishing between what had been inspired by the Devil and what had come from the Archangel. Muhammad (peace be upon him) could not even tell between what he himself had dictated to the scribe and what the scriber had mischievously substituted. The Persian scribe in Rushdie's book tells us how he first changed little things in what the Prophet (peace be upon him) had dictated to see if Muhammad (peace be upon him) would notice.

'Little things at first. If Mahound recited a verse in which God was described as *all-hearing, all-knowing,* I would write, *all knowing, all wise.* Here's the point: Mahound did not notice the alterations . . . So the next time I changed a bigger thing. He said *Christian,* I wrote down *Jew.* He'd notice that, surely; how could he not? But when I read him the chapter he nodded and thanked me politely, and I went out of the tent with tears in my eyes . . . ' (p.368)

In the end the scribe carried it too far, and Mahound's suspicion was aroused. But the novelist Rushdie has already done his mischief of creating doubt about the authenticity of the Qur'an even as Muhammad's (peace be upon him) own work, let alone as the word of God.

The Qur'an is also the ultimate constitution of the community of believers. American political morality expects its citizens to be ready to 'uphold, protect and defend the Constitution of the United States.' Muslims expect all believers to be ready to defend the Qur'an as their own ultimate fundamental law.

Rushdie not only casts doubt on the authenticity of the source of that fundamental law. He satirizes its rules and attributes fictitious dicta to it.

' . . . rules about every damn thing, if a man farts let him turn his face to the wind, a rule about which hand to use for the purpose of cleaning one's behind . . . sodomy and the missionary position were approved of by the archangel, whereas the forbidden postures included all those in which the female was on top . . . ' (p.364)

This is more than suggesting that John Milton did not write *Paradise Lost*. It is worse than alleging that what Americans take to be their Constitution consists of bastardized passages inserted by mischievous scribes still loyal to George III of England. If American patriotism consists of upholding, protecting and defending the Constitution of the United States, does not casting doubt on the authenticity of the Constitution come close to being the ultimate treason?

The Defamation of the Dead

Another issue of conflict of cultures at the centre of the Rushdie debate is the question of *comparative defamation*. Western law of libel and slander tends to focus on the *individual,* and seldom on a whole *class* of people. American law is more sensitive to 'class action' than British law is, but on the whole it is individuals rather than groups of people who sue under libel or slander in western societies.

In Salman Rushdie's novel the question arose whether he has libelled whole classes of Muslims – ranging from the Shiites (as symbolized by Rushdie's character 'the Imam') to the wives of the Prophet Muhammad.

A related difficulty concerns the fact that western law provides very little protection against libel for *those who are dead.* If twelve women alive today were portrayed in a novel under their own names – as the *equivalent* of prostitutes, they would have some kind of legal recourse. But Rushdie is libelling women who have been dead some fourteen hundred years – the wives of the Prophet Muhammad (peace be upon him). Reputations of people who have been dead for so long have very little protection under western concepts of libel and slander.

It is true that Rushdie does not say it was the Prophet's real wives who were prostitutes. He creates prostitutes who adopt the names of the Prophet's wives – whores who play at being the spouses of Mahound. Rushdie uses the trick of *a play within a play* – like Hamlet staging a play in order to find out if his uncle killed his father before marrying his mother.

Rushdie suggests that the customers of the prostitutes get additional sexual excitement out of pretending to make love to the Prophet's wives.

> 'the fifteen-year-old whore 'Ayesha' was the most popular with the paying public, just as her namesake was with Mahound . . . The fifteen-year-old whispered something in the grocer's ear. At once a light began to shine in his eyes . . . She told him . . . about her deflowering at the age of twelve . . . and afterwards he paid double the normal fee, because 'it's been the best time of my life.' 'We'll have to be careful about heart conditions,' the Madam said . . . ' (p.380).

Rushdie goes on to say that the prostitutes who were pretending to be Mahound's wives became:

> 'so skillful in their roles that their previous selves began to fade away . . . and the day came when the prostitutes went together to the Madam to announce that now that they had begun to think of themselves as the wives of the prophet they required a better grade of husband than some spurting stone . . . The Madam then married them all off herself, and in that den of degeneracy, that anti-mosque, that labyrinth of profanity, Baal became the husband of the wives of the former businessman, Mahound' (p.383).

In other words all the prostitutes were 'married' to the character called Baal who pretended to be a eunuch at the brothel. Baal, as the 'husband' of twelve whores, pretended to be the Prophet Mahound. He even fell in love with 'Ayesha', the prostitute named after the Prophet's favourite wife.

> 'In short, (Baal) had fallen prey to the seductions of becoming the secret, profane mirror of Mahound . . . ' (p.382).

Rushdie's game of 'the play within the play' is nevertheless a prostitution of the reputations of 12 innocent and respectable women. Had these women been alive western law would have protected their reputations. But being deceased for so long, western law offers no sanctuary.

Is *Satanic Verses* the equivalent of *The Last Temptation of Christ?* In the film Jesus is portrayed as dreaming out his sexual fantasies. The hypothesis is offensive to both Christians and Muslims (since Jesus is a revered Prophet in Islam). But while *The Last Temptation of Christ* is indeed *un-Christian,* it is not *abusive.* Jesus is portrayed as essentially good, even divine. But his goodness is struggling with his humanity as he approaches death. It is almost like the human anguish which made him cry out 'Father, why have you forsaken me?' On the whole, therefore, *The Last Temptation of Christ* is far less abusive of Jesus than Rushdie has been of the Prophet and his wives.

The real equivalent of comparative blasphemy would be in portraying the Virgin Mary as a prostitute, and Jesus as the son of one of her sexual clients. Also comparable would be any novel based on the thesis that the 12 apostles were Jesus's homosexual lovers, and the Last Supper was their last sexual orgy together. It would be interesting to speculate which ones of the leading western writers would march in a procession in defence of the 'rights' of such a novelist.

What is clear is that neither the Virgin Mary in the first hypothesis of prostitution nor Jesus and the Twelve Apostles in the second hypothesis of a homosexual orgy would receive much legal protection under western laws of libel, slander or defamation.

Comparative Censorship

Under English law, on the other hand, there could be some protection under the laws against blasphemy. And throughout the western world there is one medium which would almost certainly censor any artistic work based on the thesis that Mary was a prostitute or Jesus a homosexual. That medium is television – precisely that medium which in the West can reach the largest number of people. All western protestations of freedom of speech *are* contradicted daily by censorship (official and unofficial) on western mass media. It is to this problem of comparative censorship that we must now turn. To a certain extent censorship in the industrialized world has basically moved from the printed word to the electronic media.

In Britain elaborate efforts have been made by the Thatcher government to stop or discourage journalists interviewing so-called Northern Ireland 'terrorists'. Margaret Thatcher has argued that publicity is the oxygen of terrorism. Is that different from saying democracy is the oxygen of terrorism?

In parts of the United Kingdom you can quote a so-called militant of the Irish Republican Army – but you may not let his own *voice* say those words. Nor may you show him visibly on TV making his case.

Sinn Fein as a political arm of the Irish Republican Army is also subject to severe censorship in parts of the United Kingdom – especially on the electronic media. Even elected parliamentarians for that particular political party are subject to those constraints.

Peter Wright's book *Spycatcher* was chased by Margaret Thatcher's government to different parts of the *White Commonwealth* – in a bid by the British government to have the book banned. The Thatcher Government did not always have its way as it traversed the world to get the book suppressed. But the very fact that the Government of Britain had criteria of censorship of its own (however secular) belies the same Government's protestations in defence of Rushdie's 'freedom of expression'. Margaret Thatcher was on firmer moral ground in defending Rushdie's life.

I personally have also been censored in Britain and the United States, as well as in South Africa and my own native Kenya. In program 3 'New Gods' of my BBC/PBS Television series *The Africans: A Triple Heritage* I start with a bust of Karl Marx. The viewer is supposed to hear my voice saying:

'Religion is the sigh of the oppressed creature and the soul of soul-less conditions.' So said Karl Mark, the last of the great Jewish Prophets.

The Public Broadcasting System was afraid of offending Jewish viewers. The potentially offending phrase was 'the last of the great Jewish prophets'.

Viewers in the United States did not hear me say 'the last of the great Jewish prophets'. It was censored, in spite of the fact that it made it difficult for me to make the case about 'the Semitic impact on Africa' (Jesus, Muhammad and Marx).

But since the series had already been shown in Britain, many American journalists knew about the decision. The president of WETA was attacked at the National Press Club in Washington, D.C. for showing a TV series which had *previously* had the statement 'the last of the great Jewish prophets'.

No journalist anywhere in the U.S.A. took up the cudgels on my behalf on the issue of my being able to say that Marx was the last of the great Jewish Prophets. Originally I expected criticism from my Marxist friends. Marxists might not want to concede that Marx was a 'prophet' when he personally saw himself as a 'scientist'. Marx had repudiated his Jewish heritage – so the Marxists might object to my referring to it. But in America it was not my Marxist friends who were offended – it was my Jewish friends.

WETA and the PBS decided to delete the phrase, 'the last of the great Jewish prophets' – the most direct form of censorship exercised on *The Africans.* WETA believed that a hostile alliance of Rightwing gentiles and irate Jewish liberals was more than the series could cope with in the U.S.A. So the phrase was well and truly excised. But even this was not enough to put an end to the 'Jewish question'. The TV critic of the *New York Times,* John Corry, complained that there was not enough reference to the Jews in *The Africans.* He also complained that there was virtually no reference to *Israel.* In reality there were references to Jews in five out of the nine programmes – including the most moving Afro-Jewish comparison of all, made in a slave dungeon in Ghana in Programme 4:

> 'As an African visiting a place like this, seeing all this, I begin to have some kind of idea as to what the Jew might feel if he visits Auschwitz or some other Nazi German concentration camp and sense those powerful emotions of bewilderment, of anger, of infinite sadness.'

Moreover, *The Africans* showed only four non-African countries on the screen as part of the story – Britain (a former colonial power), France (also a former colonial power), the United States (a superpower) and Jerusalem (the Knesset and all). Programme 3 covered Sadat's historic visit to Jerusalem.

It is not clear how much more about Israel and Jews John Corry wanted in a television series about Africa before he would accept the 'balance' was right! It is ironic that in a review of the companion book to the TV series a reviewer in the British Journal, *African Affairs* (January 1987), the Journal of The Royal African Society, complained that I devoted too much space in the book to the Jews. The book-reviewer was convinced that I was exaggerating the relevance of 'the Jewish Question' to the African condition.

What was the reaction of the Jews themselves? Israelis saw *The Africans* when it was shown across the border in Jordan. The *Jerusalem Post* reviewed the companion book and referred to the Jordanian showing of the series. The Post's review was sympathetic and emphasized my treatment of the Jews in the book. An Israeli Fellow of an Oxford College in Britain wrote enthusiastically to me about the TV series. My boss at the University of Michigan at the time, President Harold Shapiro and his wife Vivian, held a major reception in honour of my TV series and also hosted a distinguished dinner in my honour. All this in the midst of the controversy. (Since then Professor Shapiro has left Michigan to become Princeton University's first Jewish President ever). But the fact remains that American gentiles censored me in order to protect the presumed sensitivities of the Jews.

Comparative Incitement to Violence

What about Ayatullah Khomeini's death sentence on Salman Rushdie? Surely that is completely outside western standards of legitimate behaviour? What was new about the Ayatullah Khomeini's death sentence was not the idea of murder by remote control – it was the openness with which it was declared. It was worthy of Agatha Christie's famous title *A Murder is Announced.* If western countries want to kill somebody in some other country, it becomes part of a covert operation. The Central Intelligence Agency or MI5 may take the initiative. The Israelis may fly all the way to Tunis and kill somebody in his bed. Western cinemagoers enjoy *James Bond 007.* He is simply an exaggeration of something utterly believable. As for *Mission Impossible* for

American TV viewers, it emphasizes the principle of deniability.

> 'Should you or your associates ever get caught, the Secretary will totally disavow any link with you. This tape will self-destruct in five seconds. Good Luck, Jim.'

As for attempted assassination by bombing, there seems little doubt that the Reagan Administration wanted to kill Mu'ammar Qadhafi from the air in the course of the bombing in Tripoli in 1986. The planes had instructions to bomb what they thought was his residence. In a bid to kill Qadhafi, the Americans killed a lot of other people – and missed their primary target. They did kill Qadhafi's adopted child, though. Was that a consolation prize? In the 1960s the Americans also conspired to kill Fidel Castro. Then there was President Reagan's declaration to alleged terrorists 'You can run, but you cannot hide.' This was a declaration that the sovereignty of other countries was no asylum for enemies of America. The United States skyjacked an Egyptian civilian airplane in international skies because there was a suspect on board. The United States also deliberately violated Italian sovereignty in the course of the same operation.

A dual way in which the West contrives to catch suspects is either by direct kidnapping or by enticing the victim just beyond a particular country's territorial waters. A particularly interesting illustration is that of the Israeli nuclear scientist, Vanunu. To many Israelis Mordechai Vanunu was guilty of double-treason. He was a traitor to his own state of Israel because he published intimate nuclear secrets in a *British* newspaper (September 1986). He was also a traitor to his Jewish faith because he became a Christian at about the same time. (*Time,* April 11, 1988 and *Newsweek,* September 7, 1987).

The Israeli Secret Service kidnapped him abroad – and then subjected him to a secret trial for *treason.* He was enticed to Rome by a woman calling herself Cindy. He was sentenced to 18 years for treason, espionage and revealing state secrets. If the Iranians had been as sophisticated as the Israelis, they would have enticed Salman Rushdie to international waters – and then kidnapped him for a secret trial to Teheran.

The United States has also invoked the legalistic strategy of enticing a possible kidnap victim outside a friendly country's territorial waters – before seizing him. The fate of the Lebanese called Yunis, accused of hijacking a plane in 1985, is a case in point. *Yunis* has already spent 17 months in relative isolation before being tried in the U.S.A.

Sometimes countries are ambivalent about cultural treason. Jewish opinion is ambivalent about Sister Teresa Benedicta of the Cross of the Carmelite Convent. (*Time,* May 4, 1987 'Religion'). She was born as Edith Stein, a Jew, in 1891. In 1922 – after reading a biography of St. Teresa of Avila, Edith Stein was baptized a Catholic. *Cultural Treason?* In 1942 the Gestapo picked her up in Echt, the Netherlands. She died in the gas chamber within a week. Did she die because she was born a Jew? Or did she die as punishment to the Catholic Church? In May 1987 Pope John Paul II beatified Sister Teresa Benedicta – to the indignation of many Jews.

On Literature and Anarchy

In sentencing Rushdie to death in absentia, the Ayatullah has understandably been seen as inciting violence against a citizen of another country. And yet Mr Rushdie is still alive – while twenty other people in the sub-continent in which he was born are dead. Who is inciting whom to violence? Did Mr Rushdie really fail to see that what he had written was the sort of stuff which could provoke violent demonstrations in the Indian sub-continent? Or did he not care? When India prudently decided to ban the book, Rushdie appealed to Rajiv Gandhi to lift the ban.

But Mr Rushdie and his publishers had been warned about the explosive nature of *The Satanic Verses* by Indian advisors *before* the book was published. *Mr Khushwant Singh,* a non-Muslim advisor to Penguin publishers, warned Penguin about the book before publication. He warned that the book could disturb law and order in India. As for Rushdie himself, he was born an Indian and wrote about the partition of the sub-continent. In a previous book he has shown sensitivity to how easily ordinary folks in India can kill each other for religious reasons. Mr Rushdie was probably perfectly aware that an article published in *The Deccan Herald* portraying the Prophet Muhammad (peace be upon him) as an idiot, resulted in riots and the death of 50 people.

Even without being published in India, *The Satanic Verses* has already killed more than a dozen people in Mr Rushdie's country of birth. It has also resulted in deaths in Pakistan. Had it been actually published in India, casualty numbers would have gone up ten times.

Part of the price of having the world transformed into a Global Village is that incitement can become trans-territorial. The West is quite used to *destabilization by remote control* – incitement to collective violence. The U.S. could destabilize Salvador Allende's Chile – and have the incitement confirmed by President Ford and Secretary Henry Kissinger.

Iran's nationalist revolution under Musaddeq in 1950s was sabotaged by the Central Intelligence Agency of the U.S.A. – with its own brand of incitement to violence. Musaddeq fell and the Shah was restored. Both South Africa and Israel incite violence among some of their neighbours.

On Religion and Race

Is the Satanic Verses the most divisive book in world politics since Hitler's *Mein Kampf*? Of course Hitler's book was *anti-Jewish* while *The Satanic Verses* is *anti-Muslim*. Hitler had political aspirations – while Rushdie's ambitions seem to be basically financial and mercenary. But fundamentally the two books are works of alienation and fundamentally divisive in intent and in impact.

Alan Bullock in his book *Hitler, A Study in Tyranny* (New York: Harper and Row, 1964) said:

' . . . *Mein Kampf* is a remarkably interesting book for anyone trying to understand Hitler . . . '

Is *Satanic Verses* also remarkably interesting for anyone trying to understand Salman Rushdie? But *Mein Kampf* did not become a political best-seller until after Hitler came to power. Hitler's original title was *Four and a Half Years of Struggle Against Lies, Stupidity and Cowardice.* I am not sure if Rushdie sees himself as engaged in many years of struggle against Muslim 'Lies, Stupidity and Cowardice'. The publisher summarized the title to *Mein Kampf – My Struggle.* Rushdie and his publishers compressed their title to *The Satanic Verses.*

If Hitler hurt the Jews, and Rushdie hurt the Muslims, did both dislike the *Blacks* as well? There is no doubt about Hitler's Negrophobia. But are there elements of *Negrophobia* in Salman Rushdie's *Satanic Verses* as well?

Here we need to deal with the point of convergence between religion and racism. In Medieval Europe the ultimate *religious symbol* of the devil on earth was Muhammad (peace be upon him). The ultimate *racial symbol* of the devil on earth was the black man. Islam was the ultimate religious distance away from *godliness*. Blackness was the ultimate racial distance away from *humanness*.

Much later Rudyard Kipling portrayed the black colonial as 'half devil, half child'. For a long time Muhammad (peace be upon him) was regarded as full devil. The white man later had a name of scorn for the Black man. The name was 'Nigger'. The white man in medieval times also had a scornful name for the Prophet of Islam – the name was 'Mahound'.

Rushdie claims that just as 'Blacks all chose to wear with pride the names they were given in scorn, likewise, our mountain-climbing, prophet-motivated solitary is to be the medieval baby-frightener the Devil's synonym: Mahound'. Rushdie adds:

> 'That's him. Mahound the businessman, climbing his hot mountain in the Hijaz. The mirage of a city shines below him in the sun'. (p. 93)

Rushdie also turns his torch-light on Bilal – the first Black Muslim in history. Rushdie reminds us that the Prophet (peace be upon him) had seen Bilal being punished for believing in one God. It was like Kunta Kinte being whipped to give up his African name, Toby Vs. Kunta Kinte.

Bilal was asked outside the pagan Temple of Lat to enumerate the Gods. ' "One" he answered in that huge musical voice. Blasphemy, punishable by death. They stretched him out in the fairground with a boulder on his chest. How many did you say? One, he repeated, one. A second boulder was added to the first. One on one. Mahound paid his owner a large price and set him free.' Bilal became the first great voice of Islam. *Black Vocal Power in World History began with Seyyidna Bilal.*

Rushdie seems to give Bilal credit for his uncompromising monotheism – allegedly more uncompromising than even Mahound himself. After all, according to Rushdie, Mahound temporarily accepted a Pagan Trinity (three pre-Islamic goddesses – below the Supreme God.) Bilal was dismayed. He exclaimed 'God cannot be four'. (p. 107) Mahound later reneged on this compromise – regarding these verses as Satanic. Rushdie does not either give Bilal or Islam the explicit credit of being a multi-racial religion from so early a stage. Bilal set the grand precedent of Islamic multi-racialism – fourteen centuries before President Carter tried to persuade his own church in Georgia to go multi-racial. Rushdie cannot resist certain epithets against the Black man, Bilal. Rushdie makes a character think of the Black man, Bilal, as

> 'scum . . . the slave Bilal, the one Mahound freed, an enormous black monster, this one, with a voice to match his size'. (p. 101)

Baal in the novel is the poet and satirist. Probably Rushdie sees himself in the character Baal (not to be confused with Bilal). And what does the poet Baal say to the black man Bilal? 'If Mahound's ideas were worth anything, do you think they'd be popular with trash like you?'. (p. 104) Bilal reacts but the Persian Salman restrains him. Salman says to the Black man 'We should be honoured that the mighty Baal has chosen to attack us,' he smiles, and Bilal relaxes, subsides. (p. 104)

Rushdie gives Bilal a re-incarnation as a Black American convert to Islam. This time Bilal is called *Bilal X* – like *Malcolm X*. Bilal seems to follow the leadership of a Shi'ite Imam in rebellion against a reincarnation of the Prophet's wife Ayesha – this time Empress Ayesha. *Bilal X* has the same old vocal power of the original Bilal. Under the influence of the Imam the Black American not only wants to re-write history. He has been taught to rebel against history – to regard as 'the intoxicant, the creation and possession of the Devil, of the great Shaitan, the greatest of the lies – progress, science, right'.

The Black American's beautiful voice is mobilized against history. Bilal X declaims to the listening night (on the radio):

'We will unmake history, and when it is unravelled, we will see Paradise standing there, in all its glory and light'. (p. 210)

The Imam has taught the Black American that 'history is a deviation from the Path, knowledge is a delusion . . . ' Rushdie tells us 'The Imam chose Bilal for this (propaganda) task on account of the beauty of his voice, which in its previous incarnation succeeded in climbing the Everest of the hit parade, not once but a dozen times, to the very top. The voice is rich and authoritative, a voice in the habit of being listened to; well nourished, highly trained, the voice of American confidence, a weapon of the West turned against its makers, whose might upholds the Empress and her tyranny'. When Bilal X, the Black American protested at such a description of his voice, and insisted that it was unjust to equate him with Yankee imperialism, Rushdie puts the following words in the mouth of the Imam:

> 'Bilal, your suffering is ours as well. But to be raised in the house of power is to learn its ways, to soak them up, through that very skin that is the cause of your oppression. The habit of power, its timbre, its posture, its way of being with others. It is a disease, Bilal, infecting all who come too near it. If the powerful trample over you, you are infected by the soles of their feet'. (p. 211).

Is Rushdie making fun of African Americans generally? Or is he satirizing Afroamerican Muslims? Or is he ridiculing the significance of Malcolm X? But since many Afroamerican Muslims regard Islam as one route back towards re-Africanization, and therefore a point of return to Roots, is Salman Rushdie simply continuing his basic contempt for his own roots?

Kunta Kinte – if Alex Haley is right – was a Muslim. Alex Haley went looking for his own roots. Salman Rushdie turned his back on his own. To the question whether *The Satanic Verses is racist as Mein Kampf* was, the answer is definitely *not.* But there is an undercurrent of *Negrophobia* in both books. The two books are also both *anti-Semitic* – but directed at different sections of the Semitic peoples. While Hitler was primarily anti-Jewish, there is an undercurrent of *anti-Arabism* in Rushdie. Rushdie cannot believe that Muslim Pakistanis can be pro-Palestinian without prostituting themselves to Arab governments.

In his earlier book, *Shame,* Salman Rushdie says:

> ' . . . about anti-Semitism, an interesting phenomenon, under whose influence people who have never met a Jew vilify all Jews for the sake of maintaining solidarity with the Arab states which offer Pakistani workers, these days, employment and much-needed foreign exchange . . . ' (p. 72)

There is a school of thought on the Cornell campus which says that the case for banning *The Satanic Verses* is implicitly a case for banning the *Qur'an* also. It is like telling Israelis that if they banned *Mein Kampf* they might as well ban the Bible and the Torah. *Mein Kampf* and *The Satanic Verses* are hate literature – the Qur'an and the Torah are not.

Conclusion

Mr Rushdie should have known that no great culture can be reformed by abusing it. The best approach towards reform is a re-ordering of values within the existing paradigm. In order to get Americans to vote for equal rights for women, it would be counterproductive to tell them that their founding fathers – from Washington to Jefferson – were just male chauvinist pigs (even if they were). It is better to tell Americans that equal rights for women is the logical conclusion of the wisdom and heritage of the founding fathers ('All *men* are created equal').

Mr Rushdie says that his novel is not about Islam but about migration. But Islam is partly about migration and asylum. The Muslim calendar does not begin with the *birth* of Muhammad. It does not begin with the *death* of Muhammad. It does not begin with the first revelation of the Qur'an – the day he became a Prophet. The Islamic calendar begins with the day Muhammad *migrated* from Makkah to Madinah. The principle of Asylum is celebrated in the concept of the Hijra. Is Islam against writers?

Rushdie makes his prophet Mahound say that there is no difference between writers and whores. It is true that some writers prostitute themselves. Rushdie himself has been accused of that, as he enriches himself at the expense of the dignity of others. Could Rushdie have written a novel more respectful of Islam while still critical of that heritage? Of course he could. But it would have amused Westerners less. Rushdie himself says in another book, *Shame:*

> ' . . . every story one chooses to tell is a kind of censorship, it prevents the telling of other tales'. (p. 72)

Yet Rushdie makes fun of the Hijra. He makes his poet Baal compose a valedictory ode after Mahound's departure from Jahiliya (i.e. Makkah).

What kind of idea does Submission (Islam) seem today? One full of fear. An idea that runs away. (p.126)

Of course Rushdie did not know that within a few months of publishing those lines, Rushdie himself would go into hiding – and issue a Satanic verse of apology from his hiding place.

Source: *Impact International,* 19/7, 28th April–11th May 1989, pp. 10–15.

Secularism at Bay

by Yaqub Zaki

To a fanfare of trumpets the British daily *The Guardian* announced that today (March 2) the national press carries a statement signed by about 1,000 writers in support of Salman Rushdie and 'freedom and speech.' The 'national press' here appears to be a synonym for *The Guardian,* for the statement appeared nowhere else. *The Guardian* in its self-appointed role of advocate for the defence (of Rushdie), for several days ran articles by Peter Jenkins containing jibes against religion in general and Islam in particular.

At first sight, the formidable array of names appears impressive, but even a momentary perusal reveals that the 1,000 listed are practically without exception lightweight figures. One's amazement grows as one's eye traces each column; the 'writers' turn out to be journalists and MPs, like Roy Hattersley, Dr. David Owen, Denis Healey, John Silkins and, inevitably, Roy Jenkins. The presence in the list of the father of the permissive society should raise few eyebrows, but the 'writers' also turn out to be journalists like Catherine Whitehorn or Polly Toynbee, who wrote a hostile article on Malika Salihbegovic, one of the Sarajevo Twelve, when she sought political asylum in Britain.

Many too are showbiz personalities who probably never wrote a line in their lives but are household names because they host chat shows on television, like Denis Norden or Frank Muir. Where they are famous they also happen to be Jewish, like Arthur Miller, probably better known as the husband of Marilyn Monroe than as author of *The Crucible,* Eugene Ionesco, Asa Briggs, the vice-chancellor of Sussex University, and the economist John Kenneth Galbraith, the darling of the establishment. Others proud to have their names alongside Rushdie's are Richard Hoggart, the academic who attacked the UN when it passed a resolution to the effect that zionism was a form of racism and, also inevitably, Auberon Waugh, who distinguished himself in *The Times* 20 years ago by an article in which he stated that in the Middle East, 'it is believed that Allah will be born of a man,' which is why Muslim males wear a *shalwar.*

Katherine Cookson whose paperback novels about working-class life crowd the pop shelves of every bookshop is here as is Alan Sillitoe, a Jewish novelist of similar themes, but writers of stature have obviously declined to compromise their reputation by upholding Rushdie's turgid prose as literature. Practically the only well-known writers to figure in the list are Alberto Moravia (Italy), Iris Murdoch (US) and Shusaku Endo (Japan). Japan figures in the form of one other writer, Ishiguro, who having lived in Britain all his life is not recognized in Japan as Japanese, while Endo is a Christian.

Perhaps it is hardly necessary to add that the list reads like the roll-call of a synagogue: practically the entire zionist establishment is there, including French minister Regis Debray and Elie Weisel, whose writings on the holocaust (the term is his own invention) secured him the Nobel Prize, besides Jewish playwrights like Arnold Wesker and Harold Pinter, and even the latter's mistress-turned-wife, Lady Antonia Fraser. (When Pinter left his wife and moved in with Antonia, Mrs. Pinter was interviewed by the press and said: 'I don't even know what he'll do for clothes: he has left everything here. But he's ok for shoes. Antonia has big feet, you know.')

Among names like Mordechai Richter, Jill Hyem and Allen Ginsberg (the beatnick poet), Muslim names may seem a little odd. There is not a single Turkish, Malaysian or Indonesian name, but Muslim names do figure: all the Pakistani Communists are there as is the large Egyptian secularist establishment that flourished under president Anwar Sadat, together with colourful feminist personalities like the Egyptian (not Tunisian, as stated here) secular journalist who worked in Dar al-Hilal, Amina Said, a militant feminist. Equally militant, there figures here too Nawal as-Sadawi, who authored a book on the sexology of women. Nawal is too ugly to attract men, but here too is Dabiyya Khamis of the United Arab Emirates, notorious in the Middle East for her numerous liaisons. Dabiyya is a poet of sorts, and writes self-indulgent prose poetry replete with sexual implications.

On the male side, there is Anis Mansur, married to a Copt, one of the pillars of the secular establishment under Sadat, and who accompanied the Egyptian leader on his famous flight to Jerusalem. Praised by the Israeli literary establishment, most of his work consists of plagiarisms from the writing of Louis Awad, the Coptic writer. Among expatriates there is Fuad Ajami, a mercenary who works for the American political establishment. Said Aburish, another enemy of the Islamic movement, is near the top of the list. None of these Arab writers seems to feel any embarrassment at being juxtaposed with Israeli writers like Yeheida Amichal. All are without exception journalists; there is not a single literary figure among them.

Most of the Pakistanis like Mazhar Tirmidhi and Amin Mughal are totally unknown, even to Pakistanis. The sole exception is Hanif Kureishi, author of the pornographic film *Sammy and Rosie Get Laid* and the no less charming *My Beautiful Launderette* (about homosexual life). The sole Bangladeshi to appear on the list, Safir Ahmad, has to his credit a 30-page booklet on astronomy. However, the entire Iranian court in exile is here, complete even down to Amir Taheri (of *The Times* fame).

Names of writers would seem to be a very flexible category, since publishers figure on the list. The entire Calder family (all Jewish) is here as is Collins and Co, who somehow managed to figure twice. Collins are well-known for their Israeli business connections, while Liz Calder is a former mistress of Salman Rushdie. The reviewers are, of course, out in force.

Since three-quarters of the names have never been heard of, this prompts the question: who are these people and what induced them to sign? Perhaps the inclusion of the Rationalist Press supplies a clue. This publisher, which publishes exclusively works on atheism, is a bulwark of the secular establishment. Rushdie has become, overnight, a hero of the secularists. Strength is lent to this view not only by the inclusion of an anti-Catholic novelist like Edna O'Brien, or of the numerous Jewish atheists and the

Marxists who crowd these columns, but by reference to the tone of the articles appearing almost daily in the press, with their barely concealed contempt for religious beliefs of any kind.

Obviously the secularists must be aghast at the progress of Islam over these last 15 years, specially since the Islamic revolution in Iran. The fact that secularism is on the defensive in the East has given the secularists in the west a siege mentality. Never before have secularist publications evinced quite this note of near panic. Till about 10 years ago these people had inhabited a world of illusion: that 'progress' (dialectically conceived) would eventually put to flight all forms of 'superstition,' religion in the East would dwindle and die and the fruits of the (European) Enlightenment would spread through (western) education. Muslims were just a bunch of superstitious bigots, but even they would see the light.

At one stroke, Imam Khomeini has turned the tables on them, and in the easiest and most effective manner, by simply stating what the penalty for apostasy is in Islamic law and holding up to all Muslims worldwide the vision of a State untainted by such pollutions as Salman Rushdie.

Source: M.A. Anees, *The Kiss of Judas,* pp. 142–5.

Anatomy of the Rushdie Affair: Blasphemy Vs. Moral Choices

by Ekramul Haque

Despite Muslim furor over "The Satanic Verses," the book seems to be selling briskly in the United States. It is on the New York Times best seller list for the last several weeks. Some have argued that a vulgar and malicious book such as this one could not have broken even, least made a big profit, had it not been for the publicity. From any angle, it was a catch-22. If Muslims did not protest, the book would have sold less, but the distortions will have gone unanswered. If they did, something both Salman Rushdie and Viking-Penguin must have prayed for, it would have become a mega hit. The collective wisdom of Muslims opted for the latter.

"The Satanic Verses" is one of the most sacrilegious books ever written about any religion. And, perhaps, it is the only book written about a religion with a pornographic approach. Muslim outrage against Mr. Rushdie is not only justified, it was inevitable.

Conspiring to Defame

Besides the indecency factor, there is a conspiracy aspect of the book that is hard to overlook. And Mr. Rushdie, who played a greedy pawn in the West's dirty campaign against Islam, knew from the very beginning why and for whom he was writing his latest book, which is insolvent on both facts and artistic values. The Penguin (UK) is said to have paid Mr. Rushdie $850,000 (another report puts the figure in pounds) as advance money, perhaps considering the risk the one-time Muslim would be facing in the days ahead. This is perhaps more money than Mr. Rushdie had been advanced for all of his earlier books combined. It is learnt that the publishers had two other "Muslim writers" lined up for similar onslaughts on Islam. Soon after the book became a "prime-time news" in the United States and other Western countries, Haneef Qureishi, another UK-based "Muslim writer," defended Mr. Rushdie. I have read Mr. Qureishi, and I know that his writings smack of the same opportunism that Mr. Rushdie has made the mainstay of his literary career.

Book at Any Price

Controversy comes easy for Mr. Rushdie, and of his own volition. His so-called fictions have always relied on some distorted facts about his childhood society and religion, to provide a greater kick to the Western readers. After all, Britain, whose nationality laws discriminate against its foreign-born citizens, would not have welcomed him for anything less than the cultural treason. Mr. Rushdie's penchant for Third World-bashing got him in trouble when the late Indian Prime Minister Indira Gandhi sued him in a British court for his remarks in "Midnight's Children" that she was responsible for her husband's death through negligence. Mr. Rushdie, who had no facts to back him up, pleaded guilty and both he and his publisher apologized to Mrs. Gandhi. But this time it was Muslims, a safe target for ridicule, or at least that's what Mr. Rushdie and his publishers must have thought.

Enemy's Enemy is Friend

The episode over "The Satanic Verses" has also exposed the uneasy alliance between Mr. Rushdie and his defenders in the British Government. Mr. Rushdie has compared the British society with Hitler's Third Reich, indirectly hinting at the institutionalized discrimination in that country. The fact is that Britain not only not treats its citizens equally, it also discriminates against other religions. The country's unwritten constitution protects only the Queen's religion against blasphemy. Their mutual disdain notwithstanding Mr. Rushdie and the British Government found a commonality of interest in defending the author's right to blaspheme Islam.

Getting Our Acts Together

As we agonize over a lack of concrete results of our crusade against "The Satanic Verses," Muslim countries must share most of the blame for the debacle. Countries like Pakistan, Egypt and Saudi Arabia could have easily made an impact by boycotting Viking-Penguin. If deeds matter, then these and other countries have essentially paid only lip service to Islam. They apparently justified their capitulation to the West in the national interest. Which in no case should take precedence over the defense of Islam.

As I write this, I cannot but recall the Saudi outrage at the film "Death of a Princess" only a few years ago. The Saudi royal family mobilized its resources and spent hundreds of millions of dollars to save the family honor. As the self-appointed "*Guardians of Harmain-e-Sharifain*", it does not behove them to keep silent when the Qur'an's authenticity is challenged, and the Holy Prophet's and his family's honor is trampled.

The cowardice of Muslim countries was evident during a recent gathering of the Organization of Islamic Conference (OIC). Despite loss of Muslim lives in Pakistan and Bangladesh over the book, the OIC initially dumped the matter on its cultural committee, only to bring it on the political committee after some members objected. While the Iranians took a hard-line, others were divided between those seeking moderation and those favoring ignoring the book and its author. The final declaration called for banning the book and its author from entry into member countries. The absence of a call for boycotting all Viking-Penguin publications and strong condemnation of Mr. Rushdie clearly showed the conferees' fear of retribution from the Western countries.

Source: *The Message,* June 1989, pp. 7–8.

The Long March Against Sacrilege

by M.H. Faruqi

. . . Time is the best healer and human memory being short, most personal wounds heal with the passage of time, but obviously this has not been the case with regard to 'The Satanic Verses'. The book, said to be a piece of prized fiction, was published last September, and seven months after its publication British Muslims were as determined as ever to get the book withdrawn and to obtain a redress in law against such mischief. On 27th May more than 50,000 Muslims from all over Britain converged in London, in the Parliament Square, to demonstrate their unhappiness and their outrage at the continued publication of this rag book of filth, profanity, racism and sacrilege. The clear message of the march was that the problem cannot be wished away. The reason is simple: it's a matter of principle.

Muslims in Britain are not up against the book, because they are intolerant of criticism or they feel that it threatens the validity of Islam. Islam has been criticised from the very beginning of its revelation and there shall always be people who will criticise it from various angles and with various motives. That is how the human intellect is meant to work. That is how people come to Truth if they want to – by subjecting it to debate and criticism.

Islam is a faith of reasoned and rational conviction and not a belief into self-imagined totems or fetish, dramas or mysteries. Criticism also helps those who are already Muslims to test, from time to time, the eternal validity of their faith in face of new ideas and dialectics. Unfortunately 'The Satanic Verses' is not a book of criticism, much as some people want to see it in that light. Fortunately the Truth of Islam is time-tested and protected by

God Himself and Muslims have no worry or responsibility about protecting it against any 'threat' posed by this writer or that publisher.

'The Satanic Verses' neither threatens Islam, nor is it a book of criticism. It is incapable of being either. The point Muslims are trying to make is that it is pure and simple filth, motivated by no purpose other than to outrage and, surely, make money out of this. It is an insult to human dignity and it abuses and prostitutes the noble and cherished principles of freedom. The human society, despite all its differences and negatives, is held together by the transcending principle of civility and respect for mutual dignity. It is this principle of civility and dignity that Muslims are so keen to uphold and have it recognised in a practical sense.

The form and specifics are less important than the recognition of the principle that it is not civilised to insult people's religious sanctities and that if someone wanted to make money out of sacrilege then he/she should pay for it. Whether it is done by extending the scope of the law against blasphemy to cover non-Anglican faiths as well, by amending the public order or criminal libel acts, or for that matter through any other suitable piece of enactment, is a matter of detail rather than of objectives. The measures can be tailored to the objective of deterring sacrilege – and saving social commotion and public disorder – provided the objective is recognised. For want of better articulation perhaps, some Muslims have narrowed down their demand to the extension of blasphemy law but perhaps there is sense in the argument that the law has become archaic and even if it were to be extended to cover Islam as well, given the complicated nature of the legal procedure and the largely secular climate of opinion, it will not be easy to obtain conviction of the blasphemer. Which would be counterproductive, as the ITV's Hypothetical 'Satanic Scenario' seemed to suggest, though much to the unhappiness of many Muslim viewers of the programme. . . . The exact form of legal redress against sacrilege and blasphemy will, therefore, have to be worked out in consultation with the law-making bodies, once the principle has been recognised.

There is no doubt that Muslim community has made its point, clearly and convincingly, that the book is really and truly offensive and the point has begun to be recognised and appreciated by important section of national opinion; religious and political, official and non-official. Even the media which had allowed itself to be unnecessarily outraged and become intimidatory without listening to the Muslim point of view is becoming appreciative of Muslim concern. The Prime Minister Mrs Margaret Thatcher recognises that the book is deeply offensive. 'There is no doubt about the genuine sense of outrage and injury felt by Muslims over this book'. The Home Secretary Mr Douglas Hurd told this the other day to the Tory Reform Group. He also paid tribute to the 'passion and dignity' with which 'almost all British Muslim leaders have expressed 'their indignation' and said that 'every Minister and every member of Parliament who has talked to local Muslim leaders in recent months has come away with a greater understanding of their case and an enhanced respect for the priority which they give to the defence of their faith'.

On the other side of the political spectrum the Deputy Leader of the Labour Party and Shadow Home Secretary Mr Roy Hattersley has come out in a forceful condemnation of what 'is no doubt . . . both offensive and an insult to the Muslim community'. 'Indeed passages within it are a blasphemy against the Islamic religion', he told an 'Id reception in Birmingham and said: 'I very much regret the publication of this book and look forward to the day when it is no longer on sale.'

Mr Hattersley's words were a clear departure from the earlier derisory and dismissive tone of quite a few of his colleagues in the Labour Party. From Mrs Thatcher to Douglas Hurd to Roy Hattersley is indeed a great progress in the understanding of the Muslim objection to the publication of 'The Satanic Verses' since they first registered it seven months ago. Clearly the views of Mr Hurd and Mr Hattersley are shared by many of their party and parliamentary colleagues, but this convergence of views about the book stops here and there remains a still unbridged gap between what the Muslims seek and where 'the Government does not agree with the particular remedies sought by British Muslims'. To quote Mr Hurd.

Somehow Mr Hurd – in other words the Government – seems to see the problem in terms simply of race and racial harmony and sees its solution in 'equality of opportunity and uncompromising opposition to racial discrimination in whatever form it comes'. Where, it is obvious, Muslims have been unable to make their case fully understood is that Muslims in Britain – who range from black to fair, yellow and white – are not 'a' race in any sense of the word and the problem of 'The Satanic Verses' is not at all a racial problem, though parts of the book are also racist and anti-black. Equality is no doubt central to social and communal harmony but what is central to equality itself is equality in dignity.

Equality is fundamentally a qualitative value because quantitative equality is a concept that can be used as a goal, but can neither be imposed nor fully achieved. And those who are talking of removing inequality by abolishing the blasphemy law are propounding a funny if not a morbid idea: of equal indignity. If it is not possible to give equal protection in law to Islam, as indeed to all other religions so defined, then it is not the Muslims who are saying that abolish the blasphemy law and allow us equal freedom to insult Christianity. This cannot be the Muslim position because respect for the person of Jesus Christ and Virgin Mary (peace be upon them) is equally an Islamic value. Muslims do not believe that if they cannot be protected from insult, their neighbours too should be exposed to indignity.

Unlike many other libertarians, Mr Hattersley does 'not share the view that it ('The Satanic Verses') is a novel of great literary distinction' but that is of little practical consequence to Muslims because like the Home Secretary he too does not go beyond appreciating the Muslim 'feeling of outrage'. He is correct when he says that (given the existing legal and social framework) 'there is no way in which "Satanic Verses" could be banned', but he is not right when he rejects introduction of corrective legislation, though the words he uses to say this ('to introduce legislation which made the banning of books possible') are clearly inapplicable to the situation of 'outrage' which he admits and 'shares' with the Muslim Community.

So there is a bridge ahead to be crossed or a gap to be bridged by both Muslims and the country's political leadership.

The Muslims can only do this by trying to understand and to relate to the larger society they are living in. Understanding is always a two-way thing. Those who seek understanding owe it more and owe to themselves to also try to understand those who they think are misunderstanding them. In order to do this they do not have to go any far except to look nearer – into the clear teachings of Islam.

Islam is premised on the innate goodness of human nature which means that howso indifferent or even hostile the other person may be, he/she is in nature a 'good' person. A minority may choose to remain blind and malicious to the end, but this can never be true of society as a whole. Islam, in the words of the Blessed Prophet, is also *'Nasiha'*, an attitude of good counsel and good will towards mankind and above all it is more about deeds than words.

'The Satanic Verses' has not been withdrawn (there are other than British reasons for this as well) and there is no imminent programme to introduce any bill against sacrilege, yet the Muslim campaign has come a long way in winning genuine and 'enhanced respect' for the sincerity and seriousness with which they take Islam.

Also very importantly the book stands totally 'absurdised', like a hyper-bloated pipe devoid of any tune. That would not have been the case if it had had an unchallenged print run of 20 or 50 thousand and a subsequent run of quiet selling paperbacks. Its filthy message would have been taken seriously in that event, but now almost every Muslim school child in Britain knows full well what the book is about and is intellectually equipped to deal with the muck that it is. School teachers may not have been really fair when earlier they began to ask their young and vulnerable pupils – both Muslim and non-Muslim – to do projects on 'The Satanic Verses'. However, having been forced to read it, Muslim youngsters are much more capable of dealing with the 'electric' filth of the book. They are more confident and strengthened in their faith.

Naturally there are two ways of dealing with a 'pathogen': to nip it before it becomes an epidemic or if that is not possible then build one's immunity system and let the epidemic burn itself out. The writer and publisher of the book may have won a place in the Guinness Book of Records and even made some money out of the enterprise, but in their arrant rejection of sane counsels to withdraw their 'Satanic Verses', they have clearly overpublished themselves to the point of absurdity. People may still buy it out of curiosity or malice, but few if any will not regret having thrown away their money on a thick tome of 'dense' and 'unreadable' 'novel' they understood little of it except that it was regarded as vulgar and offensive by Muslims. The Muslim demand for the withdrawal and pulping of the book is a demand of civility and decency, a demand of principle, though the publishers can still go on absurdising themselves over and again – until they come to realise that it is not respectable to publish insult and go on publishing it. As *Impact* said earlier insult only diminishes the insulter. Muslims have not been diminished. . . .

Source: *Impact International,* 19/11, 9th–22nd June 1989, pp. 10–12.

Loss and Gain in the British Muslim Campaign So far . . . An Assessment

For the first time, Muslims throughout Britain have come together on a common cause, to protect what they hold to be most dear and precious to them and indeed to humanity. Now, almost one year on, it is useful and necessary for us to review the campaign against "The Satanic Verses" and the forces that have banded together to defend and promote this grossly offensive, sacrilegious and malicious book.

To many it would seem that the Muslims have been quite unsuccessful in the campaign so far. All requests, petitions, demonstrations against the publishers have left them unmoved. Viking Penguin remain intransigent. On the legal front, apart from a brief judgement allowing an appeal, it does not look as if there will be any extension of the Blasphemy Law which many Muslims have been calling for. The government is also unmoved and prefers to champion freedom of speech under the existing law, a law that at present gives no protection against abuse and insult, or incitement to religious hatred, and which allows all sorts of obscenities in the name of freedom of artistic expression. There has also been a lot of negative effect on the Muslim community which some individuals in their pronouncements and in their behaviour at demonstrations, the placards they carry and the slogans they shout – acting in a manner which is totally unIslamic and destructive of the very aims for which we are campaigning – for truth and decency and civilized values, and doing great harm to the image of the Muslim community. And there does not seem to be any desire or capability on the part of the community to educate or control these elements.

A few voices have been heard asking: Why not call off the whole thing? We are wasting our precious time which could better be spent on more constructive things. We are not properly equipped and are being constantly bruised and shown up by the powerful anti-Islamic forces in this country and in the west as a whole who maintain a powerful political and communication stranglehold as they fight tooth and nail to protect their perceived interests and intellectual space.

While some of this is true, it is important to recognize that the Muslim community in Britain is a relatively young community. It is not a homogeneous community. It is not yet a united community. It is an inexperienced community. It still has a lot to learn. Compared to other communities it has as yet no effective clout in the seats of power, in the media or in economic circles.

The campaign has exposed the community but at the same time it has given it strength and shown it ways of working and interacting. The campaign undoubtedly has achieved a lot that is positive.

For the first time, as we stated at the outset, Muslims in many parts of the country have come together on a common cause, to protect what they hold to be most dear and precious to them and indeed to humanity. A few years ago the threat to deny Muslims the right to prepare animals for food the Islamic way provided one platform to bring the community together. For the first time Muslims from many parts of the country from Bristol in the southwest to Glasgow in the north and beyond have come to know one another, have been travelling up and down the country at their own expense and on their own time and have made enormous sacrifices to protect what is dearest to them, their love of God and His noble Prophet, peace be upon him. People whose work was localised or limited to members of their own particular school of thought have now got to know, meet and appreciate others. They are now able to see their local work as important in itself and in the wider national context. It has brought about the beginnings of closer association and understanding, though there is still a long way to go.

Through the spontaneous initiative that led to the formation of the UK Action Committee on Islamic Affairs (UKACIAF), the framework is now there for fairly rapid and close consultation and action on this and on many other issues. The UK Action

Committee on Islamic Affairs is concerned to consolidate this framework.

Most of the major organisations and mosques are represented on the UKACIAF and the door is always wide open for others to join in and work with others upholding the values of Islam and the interests of the community at large. There are also now regional action communities in the Southwest, the Midlands, the North and in Scotland and these provide the impetus for immediate, far-reaching and effective action at the grassroots level.

Ordinary Muslims have taken up this issue. The campaign has politicised the Muslim community. Ordinary Muslims now realise that they have a role and importance in their own right in this society. In many cases they hold the balance of power in local and national elections and have a decisive role to play in this democratic society. Politicians and political parties can no longer afford to ignore the feelings and views of Muslims. The message has gone abroad in the land that MPs and others who do not show an understanding and support of just Muslim positions cannot expect to get their support in national and local elections.

Muslims as a result of this campaign are beginning to learn more about the political processes of the country. Channels of communication have been opened with MPs, government ministers, political parties. The message now is that Muslims have both responsibilities and rights in a democratic society, and will work not only to carry out their duties but to secure their rights and interests.

Muslims are also beginning to learn about the legal processes of this country. There is much that they are not happy with in the state of the existing law, its processes and those who dispense it but it is a dynamic situation and open to change to reflect the legitimate rights and concerns of Muslims. This is an area which we will continue to explore.

People are beginning to be more conscious of the media and its power. In many, if not the majority of cases, they have come out bruised in the encounters and exposure. They realise that they are often dealing with a sophisticated, but often crude and unscrupulous media. There is the realisation that a new range of skills and outlook has got be to developed and cultivated. People have begun to see the importance of the local and national press, radio and television. They are now beginning to read and watch and respond. They have also begun to set some of the pace and determine the agenda. This is a battle for hearts and minds; it is not a platform for hurling insults, for issuing provocative calls, or for personal and self aggrandizement. It is a battle for decency and honour.

The UK Action Committee has also been concerned to campaign for this cause at the level of the Ummah and at an international level. It has pursued this matter vigorously with individual Muslim governments and with the Organisation of the Islamic Conference providing them with information and lobbying them to take a united stand. It has been instrumental in getting adopted the OIC Declaration Against Blasphemy and has continued to work to get the declaration implemented. There is of course much that still remains to be done in this regard. There has been a tendency on the part of many, to discount or even pour scorn on the efforts made by the UK Action Committee to pursue the matter at the OIC level and to make representations to Muslim ambassadors on the grounds that the governments concerned do not have the interests of the Muslims at heart, to put it mildly. These governments however do have a major role to play and the opportunity should be given to them to show effective concern for protecting Muslim honour and Islamic sanctities.

The campaign against this deeply offensive book, its publishers and all those who support it and similar publications and material, will go on. We call upon all – Muslims and non-Muslims alike – to work for the upholding of civilized values and the creation of a society where anti-religious and immoral forces are not given the freedom to wreak havoc. In this respect, it is heartening to note the support for the Muslim position from some MPs, leading members of the Church, the Jewish and other religious communities, from literary and professional circles, and from many individuals throughout the country.

We would like to emphasize that the UKACIAF has not used the language of abuse and threats in its campaign and will not support or condone any abusive or illegal actions. We have sought to achieve our ends through argument and persuasion, and through consultation. We realise that the Rushdie affair has pitted us in a veritable war with virulently anti-Islamic and indeed anti-religious and immoral forces but we do not at the outset assume that individuals or institutions automatically, inherently and perpetually are against us and the values we cherish.

With God is success and guidance.

Source: UK Action Committee on Islamic Affairs *Bulletin,* July 1989.

When Fools Rushed In

by Fazlun Khalid

Muslims may ignore other Muslims being harassed, vilified or even killed by others, they may even do these things to fellow Muslims themselves, but attack the very essence of Islam and they close ranks. Young Muslims who had been worrying the older generation with their indulgent ways – pool, pop and pepsi – are now returning to the mosques in droves. The degree of activism is unprecedented as 'The Satanic Verses' episode has at a stroke politicised the mass of pliant Muslims. Awaking from their docility they have begun to realise that all talks of multi-culturalism had been hollow. The secular liberal milieu has not been as open and as receptive to the feelings of others as they have been propagandized to believe, particularly when it comes to allowing them, as Muslims, to air their views.

Symbolic burning and marching were all they had in reply to snide headlines and malevolent copy. Not for them the privilege of the editorial columns, centre page spreads, feature articles, the TV screen and radio. One gets the measure of it when Kilroy Silk is given the unprecedented opportunity to write twenty four vicious column inches in The Times (10 March) and paid for it, in reply to an advertisement inserted by the Birmingham Mosque for which they had to pay over £5,000. Then we were treated to a solid half hour of vituperation from Fay Weldon on Channel Four (30 March), subsequently reprinted in the Listener (18 May). We have had 'Iranian Nights' at the Royal Court and Shalom Salaam on BBC 2 and lately the 'Blasphemers Banquet' on prime time BBC 1.

The result of this has been Muslim children harassed in schools, Muslim adults under pressure at work and abused in the streets. Xenophobia runs deep. The secular liberal anti-racist mask has indeed slipped.

The joker in the pack has been Tariq Ali, super brat of the sixties. One time burner of effigies, leader of demos, hurler of abuse, he has now joined the Establishment. Comfortably ensconced in Channel 4, he patronises, like Rushdie, the people to whom he once belonged. These cultural mutants are the product of a sustained campaign which has lasted for four centuries. First territory, then labour, then the mind have been progressively colonised and exploited. We have 'third world' politicians and technocrats destroying the ecologies of their own countries, in pursuit of dollars and development, as agents of western aid donors. We also have 'third world' writers and intellectuals who defecate upon the inner ecology of their own people as the agents of secular bigots who recognise no moral limits.

When Muslims are told to go back to the 'east' or wherever they came from, they in fact have nowhere to go – not even to so called Muslim countries. Most of the cultures of the world it seems have already been reprocessed in the image of liberal secularism. One goes 'west' wherever one goes. People who resist this new imperialism are branded as fundamentalists. Muslims it seems are the only people left who are willing to meet this challenge.

Two very experienced psychiatrists, both Muslim, told me independently that Rushdie's writings exhibited quite patent schizophrenic tendencies. One of them had read all three of his latest books and the other only 'The Satanic Verses'. The obvious manifestation of this is that Rushdie had written an alleged masterpiece in English for an audience whose language it was not, but who was very angry about its content. Furthermore, the very same literati who accused Muslims of not reading the work, actually did not understand it themselves. One is forced to this conclusion by Bhikhu Parekh's incisive analysis in his article in the 'New Statesman and Society' (28 March). It was also apparent from the 'review of reviewers' (Independent 16 February) that 'The Satanic Verses' for many people was an indigestible 'collection of rented spare parts'. It made sense that the reviewers could not make any sense of the book. No wonder then that the average reader could not make sense of it either. What emerges is that this man by writing an incomprehensible book has made himself very rich, got more than 20 people killed, created an international incident and put back community relations in Britain by 20 years.

Does all this not bring into question the integrity of Michael Foot who keeps on insisting that the book is brilliant, and others in the Booker Prize Committee? Does this not bring into question the Booker Prize itself and all the awards that purport to shower recognition on works of 'good literary merit'? Did the Booker Committee and the literati understand the nuances of the gutter language of Bombay? Were they familiar with the names of people and places Muslims hold in reverence?

There is of course no question that Muslims have behaved impeccably and have broken no laws in spite of being intimidated by vicious attacks.

Michael Foot in 'Historical Rushdie' (Guardian 10 March) epitomised the views of those who support Rushdie. What becomes apparent from this article, is that he and his fellow travellers have their gods and fundamentalisms too. And if his piece did not personify 'militant wrath', it is difficult to imagine what did. He has taken the easy option and resorted to the use of well worn cliches and prejudices about religion in general, and Islam in particular. He forgets the two hideous global wars originating in the west which took place not in the name of religion, but nationalism. Is this not a good case for dismantling all nation states? The Iran/Iraq war was not a religious war. Atheistic states since the 1917 Bolshevik revolution have caused untold misery to millions with the opium of totalitarian stateism. Not a word about the courageous, suffering Afghans. Not a word about the most destructive modern day fundamentalism of all, Zionism. No tears for the Palestinians.

Some luminaries have said that as Islam is the youngest of the semitic religions it has some 'catching up' to do. This patronizing attitude has caused some wry smiles amongst the Muslims. As secularists gain control they invent and define 'fundamentalism' to suit their own purposes, put believers on the defensive and eventually suck people into their own ranks who, like Rushdie, they use as proxies. Muslims will not be drawn into this trap.

When the dust eventually settles over this most unfortunate business, or perhaps before it, there will be a need for a meeting of minds such as existed under Muslims, in Islamic Spain, until they were driven out or forced to convert to Christianity.

When the time comes to get down to real business, Muslims would propose two main themes for the agenda of the new millennium. Firstly, a fundamental re-evaluation of nation state ideology and an examination of the merits of bio-regional communities who will have control of their own destinies – something far beyond the manipulative mechanism we call democracy. Secondly, the dismantling of the national and international banking systems which is again an instrument of control and exploitation and its replacement with an 'interest free' economic system. This will come to be seen in time as the only solution to curb the concentration of wealth and the drug of over-consumption which saps the soul and ravages the environment.

Source: *Impact International,* 19/7, 8th–21st September 1989, p. 15.

Looking at Rushdie Affair in Hindsight: Censorship in the U.S. Abounds, But Do We Know?

by Omer Bin Abdullah

Not very long ago Salman Rushdie's book "The Satanic Verses" enraged the Muslim world and threw many Muslims in a quandary. The intensity of Muslim anguish can be understood by only those who endear their religion the way the Muslims do.

The West and the American media were quick to portray Muslim reaction in a negative light and suppress arguments that pointed to the real issue behind the controversy. They instead talked endlessly about Ayatollah Khomeini's death sentence against the blasphemer Mr. Rushdie. This campaign was a copybook effort from Goebbels's well-known method of unleashing untruth with such intensity that it not only obscures the truth but also assumes respectability.

On the other hand, the West projected itself as the bastion of intellectual, journalistic and cultural freedom.

In tackling the Rushdie affair, Muslims unwillingly played into the hands of the media, which manoeuvred them into being defensive. Many Muslims also ended up criticizing Imam Khomeini or distancing themselves from him, lest they be branded "terrorists" or "fundamentalists." Instead of battling Penguin-Viking, they often fought amongst themselves. This gave the West a chance to exploit the Shiite-Sunni differences.

The media was successful in conveying the impression that Americans make no compromise on the issue of freedom of expression. Americans in particular boasted about free speech being enshrined in their Constitution.

If Muslims had the real facts about the freedom of expression and media practice of self-censorship, they would have met the challenge with greater confidence and poise.

A knowledge of the following would have tremendously helped.

The Washington Post's Richard Harwood writes in his Ombudsman column (April 1989) that, "The Censorship of speech is even enjoying a certain popularity among students of various universities including Stanford, Michigan, Wisconsin and Emory." He wrote that according to *The New York Times* the students wish to banish "racist, sexist and anti-homosexual epithets, jokes and other kinds of harassment that occur in small-group settings, when one student intends to make others uncomfortable." Thus we see that a certain sensitivity to the feelings of others is re-emerging after the tumultuous 1960s when the students at the University of California at Berkeley demanded 'free speech' including the right to say things that the authorities considered obscene.

Mr. Harwood says that the universities, however, are not the principal focus of anti-First Amendment sentiment. The Supreme Court, along with legislatures and other courts throughout the U.S., plays a significant role. Himself a media man, he says that the media's treatment of the *intifada* is a recent case in point where reports of Zionist brutalities against Palestinians have been relegated to inner pages and the television news has stopped providing film footage.

The censorship of "commercial speech" is a commonplace throughout the U.S. According to a *Los Angeles Times* study, at least 300 American newspapers have formal guidelines stipulating the kinds of advertisements that are not fit to print.

Arguing against the First Amendment protection of speeches such as paid advertising, Mr. Harwood says "there is nothing in the law or logic to require a newspaper to publish whatever garbage comes over the transom, or a network to put on air every foot of film, or recorded bite of sound available to it."

He further says: "The idea of selection is a central idea and a necessity of the news business, the idea that human intelligence is at work in deciding what is and what is not to be published or broadcast . . . If we do not discriminate, if we have no values and render no judgments, it is a game for idiots."

The Surgeon General of the United States, C. Everett Koop, told a meeting of Roman Catholic doctors in Chicago, Illinois in September 1986 that:

"The issue we take with pornography has nothing to do with the First Amendment. It seems to me that our country has never permitted or condoned speech that endangers the lives of others."

The First Amendment, adopted in 1791, states that "Congress shall make no laws respecting an establishment of religion, or prohibiting the free exercise thereof, or abridging the freedom of speech, or of the press; or the right of the people peaceably to assemble, and to petition the Government for a redress of grievances."

In "Historical Dictionary of Censorship in the United States" (Greenwood Press, Westport, Ct.), Leon Hurwitz says that the rights granted by this Amendment are not absolute. The U.S. Supreme Court has upheld the interests of the community peace, for example in affirming the conviction of a Syracuse speaker (*Feiner vs New York State:* 1951) whose speech was considered offensive by some people in the audience.

In "The Law of Mass Communications: Freedom and Control of Print and Broadcast Media" (The Foundation Press, Mineola, NY: 1986; p. 345), Harold Nelson and Dwight Teeter Jr. tell us: "The statutes and court decisions say only that writings, pictures, statues and substances which are obscene, lewd, immoral, lascivious, lecherous, libidinous, and so forth, may not be circulated in or imported into this nation."

A judge declaring a book obscene in a 1955 decision (*The State of California vs David S. Alberts*), said it was not necessary for him to read a book cover to cover in order to form an opinion. He said he had read it only to the point which was deemed obscene. This contrasts with the call of Mr. Rushdie and his supporters that "The Satanic Verses" should be read in its entirety before an opinion is formed about it.

In 1983, the Florida Court of Appeals ruling in the case involving Cox Broadcasting and *Doe vs Sarasota-Bradenton Television Company* said:

"We deplore the lack of sensitivity to the rights of others that is sometimes displayed by such an unfettered exercise of First Amendment rights. While we shall remain ever attentive to protect inviolate these First Amendment rights, we do so with the admonition that these rights should not be arbitrarily exercised when unnecessary and detrimental to the right of others." "The Law of Mass Communications," (p. 243)

Reverend Kenneth L. Dean, pastor of the First Baptist Church in Rochester, New York, commenting on Salman Rushdie's book, said: "In recent years it has been suggested that what is obscene should be defined by the local community. In the international community, Rushdie's book ought to be declared obscene. It is obscene because it is offensive to the human spirit and serves no good purpose."

Mr. Dean continued: "Freedom of expression does not permit exhibitionism in public for individuals. Somewhere in the world of writing books there is a line that gets crossed and an author's expression becomes exhibitionist . . . Rushdie crosses the line. He has a right to his thoughts and inner feelings, but it is not acceptable for all this to be strewn before the international community as legitimate debate. Sickness ought to be handled in the hospital, in the confession sitting or in the psychiatrist's office."

Has speech really been "free" in the West?

The Western hypocrisy over the situation in occupied Palestine is apparent to us all. The U.S. is ready to send forces to invade powerless nations in South America to restore democracy but it cannot do the same when Israel brutalizes more than a million people under its occupation.

There are other examples. We see the outward manifestation of pristine morality to defend democracy in Panama and a cruel unconcern when it involves Zionist barbarism in the occupied land or the racist inhumanity in South Africa. This phenomenon is not much different than what we find in some developing countries where the opposition is invariably anti-national. In the case of U.S., democracy is only 'threatened' when this country's economic or perceived strategic interests seem under stress.

The University of Chicago and Temple University covertly suppressed Dr. Ismail al Faruqi's translation of a book on Prophet Muhammad (peace be upon him). The book was finally published by a Muslim organization.

When a literary arts magazine, the *Red Cross,* published articles on Palestinians in 1989, Jews protested through the Anti-Defamation League of B'nai B'rith and the National Endowment of Arts, an agency of the U.S. government quickly acted by withdrawing a grant for the magazine.

The *Washington Report on the Middle East Affairs* (Nov. 1989) says that Cornell University was pressured into refusing D. Alfred M. Lilienthal's collection of papers on the Middle East. His alma mater also refused a bequest that would have established the Lilienthal Lecture Series, in which the common heritage of Islam, Christianity and non-Zionist Judaism would be emphasized.

Dan Yaron, who has translated Hitler's "Mein Kampf" into Hebrew cannot find a publisher. Some have warned that if it is ever published there will be battles in the street. When it came to "The Satanic Verses," publishers in 19 languages, including Hebrew, were ready to offer their services.

The Impact of Muslim Outrage

Although the Western social scientists and media barons may not like to admit it, but the echoes of the forceful Muslim response to Rushdie/Viking blasphemy are certainly being heard. People are becoming sensitive to blasphemy and use of abusive language under the garb of "freedom of speech."

During the first half of 1989 alone, we have seen some moves toward redefining the American concept of "free speech."

On July 12, 1989, the House of Representatives voted to cut the proposed $171 million budget for the National Endowment for the Arts (NEA) by $45,000. The amount deducted had been spent on two controversial photography exhibits.

The budget cut inspired the incoming president of NEA, John Frohnmayer, to remark: " . . . I recognize that the $45,000 cut is a very clear signal from the House of Representatives and one that the NEA and myself personally would be ill-advised to ignore." (*The Washington Post,* July 13, 1989).

The controversial exhibits included an Andres Serrano photograph of a Christ-like figure in a container of urine, and the Robert Maplethorpe show, which included a series of homoerotic and sadomasochistic pictures. The Corcoran Gallery of Arts in Washington, D.C. refused to hang these pictures and cancelled the show. There were protests against NEA, but they soon died down. And in this case, the custodians of the First Amendment were quick to react to Mr. Serrano's blasphemy.

The U.S. Senate, on March 16, 1989, passed a bill 97-0 that would make it a crime to knowingly display the American flag on the floor or the ground. This was a follow-up on the furore caused in Chicago where some people stepped on the American flag. Now that Supreme Court has de-sanctified the flag, everyone from President Bush downwards is trying to re-sanctify it.

On April 4, 1989 Pepsi Cola announced that it had dropped its TV commercial featuring Madonna, following boycott threats from church members who had objected to one of her songs, even though the company had no connection with this production.

The Washington Post, (April 13, 1989) reported that the superintendent of U.S. Naval Academy ordered the destruction of 5,000 copies of a satirical student magazine designed as a parody of the notorious *Playboy* magazine. It was argued that the satire could be offensive to some on the campus. The next day, the newspaper carried a news-item that Liberty University, a Christian educational institution, had expelled two of its students for airing a program on the campus radio satirizing the chancellor.

The list goes on. On the basis of the forgoing examples it is doubtful how any informed and unbiased American would support "The Satanic Verses."

The freedom is never absolute; it should not be. The First Amendment also puts some restrictions in the exercise of the freedom of speech. Muslims in the West and the United States have to know the facts and make their protests in a manner that convinces the authorities that "The Satanic Verses" has been supported not because of its merits but because it is inimical to Islam.

Source: *The Message International,* January 1990, pp. 9–10.

Holy Freedom and the 'Liberals'

by Shabbir Akhtar

Law does not change the heart
– but it does restrain the heartless.

– Martin Luther King.

Every great tragedy teaches a truism; and *The Satanic Verses* affair is no exception. 'Law does not change the heart – but it does restrain the heartless'. Martin Luther King's maxim may well serve to introduce our theme. The freedom to express opinions on political and religious matters has to be restrained in the interests of social harmony. There are limits to freedom of speech even in liberal democracies; and there ought to be. For it is dangerous to allow motives of profit and sensationalism alone to determine the boundaries of public taste. We need the firm yoke of the law to ensure that the interests of weaker individuals and groups are not substantially harmed by the irresponsible attitudes or actions of the more powerful individuals and groups in the same society. Accordingly, there are many legislative procedures for curtailing freedom of speech. For example, the Press Council and the laws of libel protect individuals' reputations from the extravagant claims of journalists and writers. Any juridical system that allows Jeffrey Archer and Elton John – and most recently Andrew Neil of 'The Sunday Times' and Pamella Bordes fame – to seek redress for libel cannot boast absolute freedom of speech.

In the United Kingdom we have laws restricting by common consent many excesses in the freedom of expression. No-one should deny the value of freedom of expression; and one of the problems we must recognise in a multi-cultural society is the possibility of being routinely outraged. But the question here is about the *limits* of this outrage. According to English law, what is not prohibited is permitted; but many things are explicitly prohibited – blasphemy, obscenity, sedition, treason, incitement to racial hatred, breaches of national security, subversion, contempt of court and of Parliament, and libel. To be sure, there are disputes, sometimes intractable, about the precise definition of the offences involved – but the underlying principles are universally accepted. It is unreasonable to extend this concern to the prohibition of the publication of books like *The Satanic Verses* which are likely to inflame, through defamation, the feelings of a given section of society and, in doing so, to provoke disorder? To be sure, prolonged public and parliamentary debate would together serve to establish the precise content of the law. But surely the moral concern behind the proposed legal enactment can readily be discerned and registered.

It is ironic that many in the present Conservative government should give lectures to their Muslim citizens about the virtues of freedom of speech. For we are living at a time of increased press censorship and routine political interference. We have for example the Official Secrets Act, the recent legal battle over *Spycatcher* and the continuing broadcasting difficulties over *Death on the Rock*. And who can ignore the formation of external watchdogs to police the media industry? The appointment of Lord Rees-Mogg as head of the British Standards Council is itself a sufficient indication of the government's desire to control certain freedoms.

During the *Satanic Verses* affair, countless writers both in the West and elsewhere have been busy praising the virtues of freedom of speech and condemning the Muslim predilection towards censorship. Yet many professional writers would no doubt accept that one can abuse the privilege of freedom. In the international PEN charter of the world association of writers, the final sentence of the concluding paragraph reads: 'And since freedom implies voluntary restraint, members pledge themselves to oppose such evils of a free press as mendacious publication, deliberate falsehood and distortion of facts for political and personal ends'. Why can't Muslims appeal to this principle in their attempt to make a case against the publication of *The Satanic Verses*?

The liberal thinker Michael Ignatieff ('The Observer', 2 April 1989) has misleadingly argued that, at root, the disagreement between Muslims and their opponents is over 'incompatible conceptions of freedom, one in which freedom's limit is the sacred, one in which it is not'. Now, liberals certainly place the limit elsewhere – which is natural – since they reject the sacred. But the contrast, as Ignatieff wishes to interpret it, would be meaningful only if the opposite of the Islamic notion of freedom was virtual anarchy. And of course it isn't. Liberals do recognise the limits of freedom of speech; it would be odd if they drew the line at the sacred given that they reject the sacred. But, to men of faith, it may well seem arbitrary that the limits are drawn at the parameters of race and gender.

Ignatieff argues – an argument he repeats in 'The Observer', 11 February 1990 – mistakenly, that behind this disagreement of principle lies another radical disagreement – namely, whether 'offence can be given to beliefs as such or merely to individuals'.

Now, as it stands, this formulation of the issue seems incoherent. Can one attach any sense to Ignatieff's claim about offence being given to beliefs as such? Beliefs are not sentient creatures; consequently they are not capable of taking offence. Only people are offended in the required sense. Among the beliefs these people hold are beliefs about themselves and their universe – beliefs about race, gender and religious conviction. Laws never protect doctrines or beliefs as such against outrage. They protect the people who hold these beliefs against offence.

The point is not a quibble. Ignatieff tries to argue that, in a 'theocratic' state like Iran, the law protects certain doctrines while in allegedly free societies, like the United Kingdom, the law does not protect doctrines as such but rather protects individuals. It protects individuals through the application of laws of libel or laws against incitement to racial hatred. If so, Ignatieff has to reckon with the fact that the law of blasphemy remains on the statute books. This seems, on his understanding, an attempt to protect a doctrine rather than an individual. He dismisses it as a dead relic from a dead Christian past.

A Christian believer may wish to disagree. In any case, the issue remains. Ignatieff can dismiss it because he misidentifies it. The issue is not whether one should protect individuals rather than beliefs. For it is incoherent to protect beliefs as such unless there are people who hold them and who might be offended by an attack on them. In one sense, one has no choice but to protect people, as opposed to their beliefs. It is both possible and necessary to protect beliefs because people's sensibilities are at stake. The real reason for Ignatieff's rejection of the blasphemy law is not that it protects doctrines as opposed to individuals but because it recognises that religious conviction can be as relevant a consideration as race and gender in the formulation of legal restraint.

Religion is, for Muslims, as much a part of their essential self-definition as race or gender. There is a sense in which one cannot escape one's race or, arguably, gender. But for the overwhelming majority of Muslims, religion is also an inescapable fact of one's nature. So, the stock liberal argument fails. It is not as though one could simply discard one's religious conviction for another or even for none at all. For many Muslims, Islam is a part of their being from the cradle to the grave. Such a feature cannot reasonably be seen as being peripheral or incidental to one's self-image.

This is not an argument primarily for protecting ideas against abuse – in any case, as I have shown, an incoherent proposal. It is an argument for protecting the collective dignity of those groups – such as Muslims, Sikhs and others – whose members, rightly or wrongly, do define their own ideals of the worth of their lives in terms of irreducible religious notions.

II

'That Muslims are denied equal treatment under the law is,' said Roy Hattersley in a speech on 2 April 1989 at the Birmingham Central Mosque, 'a matter of indisputable fact.' He is, of course, right. Settlers from Canada, New Zealand and Australia are welcome while those from India and Pakistan are merely immigrants who need to go through potentially racist testing procedures. Catholics and Jews have their own voluntary-aided schools reflecting their respective religious convictions while applications from Muslims are refused on the grounds that such schools are too 'separatist' in ethos. We need not extend this list in order to show that all races and religions do not receive equality of treatment in contemporary Britain.

There is, however, one particularly obvious inequality within the law which has been the subject of intense controversy during this affair. Christian, or rather Anglican, sensibilities alone are officially protected. Anachronistic as it may appear in a largely secular society, blasphemy remains both a statutory and a common law offence in modern Britain. As the established church, the Church of England has since the 17th Century uniquely enjoyed a legally enforceable protection against blasphemy (where the offence is orally published) and blasphemous libel (where it is published in a written form). Originally at least, any attack on the Anglican creed was necessarily an attack on the state. Blasphemy was therefore an indictable offence (triable by jury) of common law. It consisted of any publication of words attacking the Anglican denomination of the Christian faith or its scriptures in a manner so scurrilous as to pass beyond the limits of decent debate or controversy and tend to lead to a breach of the peace. The offence is punishable by fine and imprisonment at the discretion of the court.'

Britain is one of the few European countries in which the offence of blasphemy is still recognised in the legal system. Despite persistent campaigns for its abolition for many decades – notably by The National Secular Society – the law of blasphemy remains on the statute books. As late as 1979, Mary Whitehouse was able to take *Gay News* to task, under the blasphemy provisions, for publishing a poem in which Christ is shown experiencing temptation to homosexuality. She won. The House of Lords' decision in the case contained a slight redefinition of the scope of the offence such that blasphemous libel is committed in any published writing concerning God or Christ, the Christian religion, the Bible, or some sacred subject, employing language that is scurrilous and abusive and tending to vilify the Christian religion and hence having a tendency to lead to a breach of the peace. In the case of Whitehouse –v– Lemon and Gay News Limited, Lord Scarman took the view that protection under the present legislation does not extend beyond the Christian religion.

In 1981, the Law Commission published its Working Paper No 79. The Commission provisionally proposed the abolition without replacement of the common law offence of blasphemy and blasphemous libel on grounds of various shortcomings, including unclarity of offence and restriction to Christianity. The Commission refused to propose a new offence to deal with blasphemous conduct. To date, however, the criminal law of blasphemy remains on the books; the Law Commission's attempt to abolish it is one of several attempts that have failed.

Muslim sensibilities are not protected in the United Kingdom under the current blasphemy law or indeed under any contemporary enactment. *The Satanic Verses* does not seem to contravene any contemporary British laws on race relations or libel. To

Muslims the fact that Rushdie has written vilely enough to provoke anger but, as it happens, in a context that enables him to avoid the normal penalty of law, is a sufficient reason to suspect an inadequacy in the existing legislation. Were Muhammad, peace be upon him, alive, he could of course successfully take to court Rushdie and his publishers for blasphemous libel. But there are no provisions for protecting the sensibilities of individuals (or communities) whose self-esteem is linked to their respect for Muhammad, peace be upon him, and his ideals.

The issue here is not merely of equality under the law. For one way, popular with secularists, of attaining equality of treatment would be simply to abolish the law of blasphemy. That would, however, be cold comfort to Muslims: while removing the privileged position afforded to a Christian denomination, it would leave Muslims as unprotected as ever. Such a solution would rely on a drastic principle parallel in motivation to the impractical view that one way to solve all human problems is by exterminating the human race!

There are no doubt difficulties in extending the blasphemy law to protect the God of the Jews and Muslims as well as the Christians.

Neither inability to define blasphemy nor the presence of agreed difficulties in application of the proposed law is a sufficient reason for refusal to legislate in this area of sensibility. Virtually all areas of profound human concern are the subject of keen disagreement but that fact alone does not deter us from making laws to regulate behaviour. There are arguments, sometimes intractable, about the precise definition of many offences; public and parliamentary debate can, however, jointly sort out the details once the underlying principles have been accepted. The fact that we cannot provide an uncontroversial definition of an offence can never be an adequate ground for abandoning the search for formulating proper legal restraint and the corresponding punishment.

It is important to know the purpose of law. Legislation cannot make us fully tolerant of one another. Those who hate Islam will, even under a tighter law, seek other means of abusing it. But the ability of human beings to evade even the most precise legal regulation is no reason for refusing to impose legal constraint. Law does not change the heart – but it does restrain the heartless. And that is already a great achievement.

Nor will it do to entrust matters to the discretion of individuals in the hope that men and women can never be utterly insensitive to each other's feelings. Arguments in favour of self-censorship are, in political and ideological contexts, weak and implausible. It is unsurprising that we do not merely request racists to self-censor their literature. The law does it for them since the issue is too public in its consequences to be left purely to private decision and discretion. There is no evidence, historically or contemporaneously, for the view that human beings will cease to harm the interests of others once the fetters of law are removed to make room for voluntary charity.

The law may be a blunt instrument but we cannot do without it. In the context of the *Satanic Verses* affair there is an urgent need for an enactment to protect Muslim sensibilities against gratuitous provocation. Whether or not the enactment involves an extension of the existing blasphemy regulations is really a matter of detail. It may well be that, in a secular society like Britain, the Muslim's best bet is to campaign for a law making certain kinds of conduct or publication socially unacceptable as opposed to religiously offensive. Lord Jakobovits, the Chief Rabbi, has wisely counselled Muslims along these lines arguing that some enactment should prohibit socially intolerable conduct calculated or likely to incite revulsion or violence by holding up religious beliefs to scurrilous contempt . . . (The Times, 4 March 1989). Thus, for example, Muslims may contend that while insulting a revered but dead religious leader like Muhammad, peace be upon him, need not be an indictable offence in a secular society, such polemic could excite the anger of those citizens whose self-image is created by reference to his ideals and lifestyle – and hence may lead to a breach of the peace.

The Commission for Racial Equality has now established that Muslims are a distinct group of people bound together by a common faith. The Race Relations Act does not, except in Ulster, identify religion as a ground for discrimination; accordingly the equal opportunities policies of local authorities do not normally interpret it as a relevant determinant in service delivery. Yet, in the case of Muslims, the *Satanic Verses* saga has strongly indicated that religious affiliation is far more central than colour and ethnic origin in determining the needs and aspirations of Muslims. Indeed, for Muslims, faith takes on a significance at least as great as race and gender in any proper interpretation of their self-identity. Unsurprisingly, the demands of Muslim communities cannot always be subsumed under the geographical category of Asian. In fact, Asians often see themselves as religious groups – ie as Sikhs, Hindus, and Muslims. It is entirely reasonable to identify Muslims as a distinct group of people on grounds of their self-professed Islamic identity.

The Race Relations Act, therefore, needs amendment. Ethnicity cannot be the sole factor in identifying a group as a community with shared convictions. The Commission for Racial Equality has rightly viewed with sympathy attempts to classify Jews and Travellers as distinct groups. Why not Muslims?

III

'Freedom is not a holy belief, nor even a supreme value.' So wrote Michael Ignatieff in 'The Observer' of 2 April 1989. It is, he tells us, a contestable concept. Is it? To be sure, liberal thinkers would argue that all the central concepts of modern secular political theory are essentially contestable. Freedom, rights, power, democracy itself. Yet the behaviour of apologists for liberalism during the Rushdie affair gives the lie to the claim that they interpret freedom to be a negotiable value.

It is an axiom of democratic thought that the truth about the political world is not ascertainable in a final or absolute way – and that all men and women are fallible, not least those in positions of power and influence. Accordingly, individuals and groups with conflicting interests should properly discuss and negotiate solutions on the basis of enlightened self-interest. But there has been little evidence of any such reasoning in this affair. The notion of negotiating with these 'uncivilised' Muslims has been dogmatically rejected. It has indeed been a case of our 'light and sagacity' versus their 'darkness and obscurantism'.

It is the Muslims who have wished to remind liberals that freedom is indeed a contestable concept. The Muslims have plausibly argued that the issue is not the right to censure Islam for that right exists and is routinely exercised. The issue is whether or not any civilised society should tolerate, let alone encourage, writers to mock and insult the convictions of a major world constituency. Does the secular clergy have the right to canonise freedom of speech as an absolute value overriding all other relevant considerations?

The liberal fundamentalists have betrayed themselves. For the central principle of secular liberalism is that difference in ideological posture, among groups and individuals should rarely if ever, entail a restriction of human sympathies. Yet the powerless Muslims were burnt at the stake for defending their dignity as believers.

It is significant that the British Muslims' protest, with all its powerlessness – only the rightless burn books and demonstrate on the streets – has elicited anger rather than sympathy. Could it be that Islam challenges the moral absolutism of the liberal establishment setting itself up as the sole cultural overseer and arbiter of public taste and value? Even a purely rhetorical protest by the British Muslims has galvanised the opposition; everyone has gathered together to warm themselves by the fire of Western passion. Where is the negotiated compromise, the judicious pragmatism of a liberal democratic culture committed to rejecting authoritarian dictate and the passionate arrogance that allegedly engenders? After the *Satanic Verses* episode, it is even harder to endorse a faith in the humility of secular liberal postures of power.

The point is hugely significant. Islam is a salutary reminder of the need for political humility in secular statecraft. It is always a routine assumption of Western political theory that the possibilities of political humility are exhausted by purely secular postures of power, yet the assumption is questionable. For it is secular statecraft, not theocracy, that gave us Hiroshima and two 'World' (or rather European) wars. Some of the most incisive critiques of the abuse of power have come from the pen of those troubled by the hubris of secularity when it rejects any liability to forces greater than itself. With so much talk of The Thought Police and 'Muslim Fundamentalists' in the same breath, it is well to remember that Orwell's political masterpiece *1984* is a critique of totalitarianism in secular dress. Big Brother was not an Ayatollah, not even an ordinary Muslim. The Liberal Inquisition has its Thought Police too.

IV

Freedom is more holy to liberals than Michael Ignatieff would have us believe. In fact, liberal society too holds certain shibboleths beyond rational debate. Some things do matter; and principles cannot be weighed in the scales of pragmatism or diplomacy. Yet if freedom of speech be a sacred or otherwise unnegotiable value for the liberal West, why shouldn't the question of Muhammad's, peace be upon him, honour have a similar status for the Muslim believers?

The Archbishop of York wrote in a letter to 'The Times' (1 March, 1989) that abolishing the law of blasphemy would indicate that in the last resort our society holds nothing sacred, apart from the freedom of writers to write what they like. This is, for obvious reasons, attractive to writers . . . (but) . . . why should it have absolute priority over all other claims to sacredness? Fair question, surely; and one not to be answered by evasive liberal rhetoric about religious intolerance being particularly oppressive. Intolerance, no matter what its source, leads to oppression and denial of human rights. It is a prejudice, if a pardonable one, to think that the intolerance of those who make particularly loud professions of tolerance is to be preferred to the intolerance of those who don't.

Source: *Impact International,* 20/4, 23rd February–8th March 1990, pp. 9–11.

The Rushdie Affair: A Muslim's Perspective

by Mushahid Hussain

Given the ferment among Muslims from Kosovo (in the Balkans) to Kashmir (in the South Asian subcontinent), there is a new drawing of battle lines, with the West fearful of a resurgent Islam. The Rushdie Affair remains an important element in the West versus Islam conflict. The uproar over what is seen by an overwhelming majority of Muslims as Rushdie's wilful act of blasphemy needs to be examined from three aspects so that the current conflict over *The Satanic Verses* is better understood. First, the issue of freedom of expression; second, what Muslims perceive as Western double standards; and, third, the political context which defines the debate. A key component of this is antagonism between Islam and the West rooted in history, culture and religion.

First, freedom to speak or write or any freedom for that matter is never absolute, just as the freedom to use firearms is not absolute. It is limited by law, in the case of the pen by libel, and by special constraints and other generally accepted norms of behaviour, and in the case of Muslim societies, by religion as well. Islam, for Muslims who profess to be its followers – of which Salman Rushdie presumably was one, at least by birth – is not just a religion requiring observance of rituals on special occasions, it is also a way of life. Islamic consciousness is in the marrow of Muslims. It shapes their worldview, outlook and cultural patterns of behaviour. For Muslims, the centrality of their beliefs revolves around an unquestioned faith in the Koran, as a book of God and of the Prophet Muhammad as His Messenger, believed by Muslims to be the only human being who is perfection personified.

Every society has certain values which are sacrosanct. Western societies, since they are secular, accord less of a priority to religion than is accorded to Islam by Muslims. The reaction, therefore, to what Rushdie wrote was predictable, more so given the fact that he came from a Muslim background, was apparently aware of the vitals of the religion he was born into, and could thus not be unaware of the possible consequences of the use of his pen among his fellow Muslims. As far back as 1929, Ghazi Ilam Din, a Muslim from Lahore during the days of the Raj, killed a Hindu writer Raj Pal, who had ridiculed the Prophet Mohammad in a book titled *Rangeela Rasool* (The Colourful Prophet). And who was the first to volunteer to be Ghazi Ilam Din's lawyer, despite the killer's proud public confession that he had killed 'for the cause of Islam'? The man was Mohammad Ali Jinnah, then the most eminent of barristers in India, who was later to found the State of Pakistan. It needs to be noted that Jinnah was a liberal constitutionalist in the Western political tradition and represented an outlook and lifestyle perhaps even more secular than his Hindu counterparts. Ghazi Ilam Din later went to the gallows, an unrepentant but popular Muslim folk hero still remembered now as a *shaheed* (martyr). Even mainstream American newspapers seemed shocked at Rushdie's malicious attack on all that is sacred to Muslims. *The New York Times* book review, in its issue of 29 January 1989 wrote: 'How are we to understand the adoption – by a writer born Muslim – of so defamatory a name for the Prophet of Islam?' *The Washington Times* review, published in its 13 February 1989 issue, was even more explicit: 'But having discovered no literary reason why Rushdie chose to portray Mohammad's wives as prostitutes, the Koran as the work of Satan and the founders of the faith as roughnecks and cheats, I had to admit to a certain sympathy with the Islamic leaders' complaints.'

The second aspect emerged from the edict of Imam Khomeini. The Western response to this *fatwa* narrowed down to an expression of apparent shock and horror as if an apparently appalled West had never sponsored assassinations on foreign soil of selected political targets. Additionally, Imam Khomeini was represented as being alone or Iran-isolated within Islam on the question of this edict. Both these aspects are factually incorrect. On 16 March 1989 the Islamic Foreign Ministers Conference convened in Riyadh, Saudi Arabia, endorsed the view earlier expressed by Imam Khomeini that Salman Rushdie is 'an apostate', the only difference being that it stopped short of imposing a punishment for his apostasy. Regarding the death sentence which Imam Khomeini had imposed on Rushdie, the Saudi Arabian Foreign Minister, Prince Saud al Faisal, said that the Islamic Foreign Ministers were not competent to do this since their conference was 'a political body and not an assembly of jurisprudents', adding that such a sentence was 'the job of theologians'. The Chief Saudi religious leader, Sheikh Abdul Aziz bin Abdullah bin Baz, for instance, recommended that Salman Rushdie be put on trial *in absentia* in a Muslim country for committing heresy.

Muslims are agreed that Rushdie has committed heresy; the only difference is on the most appropriate method to deal with this. One Muslim writer said: 'To Muslims, the integrity of their beliefs is more important than the national or territorial integrity of a modern state; the violation of this integrity represents an act of high treason deserving the harshest punishment. It is only against this background that the indignation of Muslims at this libellous book can be understood.'

What was galling to Muslims was the Western response to Imam Khomeini's edict, as if the West had never condoned the taking of life in pursuit of its own interests and for issues which are seen as being vital to the West. The table below lists the West's track record in pursuit of 'higher' goals like 'national security' and 'anti-terrorism'. This effectively debunks the attempt by the West to take the moral high ground on this issue vis-a-vis Islam by making the Rushdie Affair seem like a question of superior values, civilisation and way of life.

The third aspect is the political context which has deeply influenced the Western view on this debate. The Palestinian-American Professor Edward Said remarked in his 1980 study *Covering Islam:* 'I have not been able to discover any period in European or American history since the Middle Ages in which Islam was generally discussed or thought about outside a framework created by passion, prejudice and political interests'. Since the Islamic Revolution in Iran in 1979, a new Islamic identity and consciousness has emerged among Muslims, which is both highly politicised and radicalised. The West feels threatened by this new political expression of Islam. It is thus no accident that 'responsible, liberal' newspapers like *The* (London) *Guardian* can take the liberty of dismissing Imam Khomeini as a 'bearded bastard', which it did in a November 1979 editorial. Rushdie is only one manifestation of the conflict between the West and Islam; it ranges from resistance to the scarf for Muslim women in Europe, to opposition to Turkey's entry into the 'European family' come 1992, or support for Gorbachev's use of force against Muslims in Azerbaijan as opposed to his peaceful pleading with the Christian secessionists in Lithuania. Attitudes, in large measure, are shaped by recent religious history, and the Western response to Rushdie is no exception. In 1683 when the armies of Christian Austria stopped the military might of Muslim Turkey at the gates of Vienna, Viennese bakers celebrated the defeat of the 'Infidels' by baking the *croissant* – shaped like a crescent, the Islamic symbol which was also the Turkish emblem. Today, the *croissant* is staple menu at every Western breakfast table.

There is little doubt that Muslims, too, are guilty of hypocrisy and double standards, particularly the majority of regimes and rulers in Muslim countries. The Saudis, for instance, who raised such a hullabaloo over the 1980 film *The Death of a Princess,* which was only a critique of the medieval despotism of the House of Saud, were content to remain silent on an issue central to the beliefs of all Muslims, since they saw the Rushdie Affair as yet another opportunity tailor-made for the West to indulge in the popular pastime of Iran-bashing. Muslim rulers and regimes, mostly occupying high office either through *coups d'etat* or courtesy of family inheritance, are as scared as the West of this new radicalised Islamic ethos.

A recent episode during a meeting between Yasser Arafat and a Muslim ruler is instructive in this regard. While Arafat was visiting a Muslim country, he noticed that local television was dishing up government propaganda, particularly promoting the personality cult of the corrupt autocrat. When Arafat complained to the ruler, asking why there was no mention of the *Intifada* of the Palestinians on their television, the ruler smilingly replied: 'Do you want me to give ideas to my people on how to resist a regime and throw stones at the police?' More than anything else, this comment sums up the problem of Muslim countries: most have minority regimes, which do not reflect the aspirations of their own people. This is also one reason why some Western writers erroneously viewed the Rushdie Affair as a 'subcontinental issue'. No Arab country allows demonstrations by its people for fear that these may turn into rallies against the regime or the ruler, akin to what happened with the rally called by Ceausescu, which led to popular revolt.

Rushdie's writing *The Satanic Verses* is like a Jew who tries to justify the Holocaust, who defends Hitler's extermination of millions of Jews and dismisses his crime in light hearted humour at the expense of the victims of Auschwitz. No serious Western publisher would think such trash worthy of publication and certainly not worth a million dollar advance. Freedom of expression is not at issue in this case and it is time that Western intellectuals stopped pandering to the ego of a man who is callous enough to let more people suffer, even perhaps die, so that he continues to make money out of insulting a personality revered by a billion Muslims. John Le Carré summed up the issue in *The Guardian*: 'Nobody has a God-given right to insult a great religion and be published with impunity.'

Western countries' officially-sponsored violence, on foreign soil, of selected targets

Date	*Country*	*Target*	*Ostensible reason*	*Western response*
1960	Israel	Ex-Nazi Adolph Eichmann is kidnapped in Argentina.	War crimes against Jews.	Action hailed for bringing criminal to justice.
1985	USA	CIA-planted bomb fails to kill Syed Muhammad Hussein Fazlullah, Lebanon's *Hizbullah* chief.	Alleged role in terrorism.	'Much ado about nothing'; 'part of the game'.
1985	France	French secret service agents sink *Rainbow Warrior,* ship of the anti-nuclear Green-peace movement.	Interference in French nuclear tests in South Pacific.	Condemnation by New Zealand, but no international outrage.
1986	USA	US planes bomb Colonel Qaddafi's residence in Tripoli, killing his daughter.	Qaddafi's alleged role in fermenting terrorism.	'Disappointment' at not killing Qaddafi.
1988	Israel	Israeli squad kills PLO military chief Abu Jihad.	Masterminding Palestinian uprising.	Israeli efficiency acclaimed; act of murder and violation of International Law ignored.

Continued

1988 UK	British commandos gun down IRA members in Gibraltar.	Alleged 'terrorists'.	No reaction.

Source: *Index on Censorship,* 4/90, pp. 12–13.

Your Satanic Majesty, Not Again!

by Syed Zafarudin Sayeed

In what seems to be Salman Rushdie's attempt at fence-mending with Muslims, the author of the infamous *The Satanic Verses* has actually hurled more offenses at his former co-religionists. The technique he has used is to arouse and exploit the moral sensibilities of his readers to promote his brand of morality. Mr. Rushdie's article in Newsweek (February 12) headlined "A Pen Against the Sword" makes one think of him as a saintly writer who is under brutal attack for writing a most ennobling work. The fact, however, is that through his morally depraved and perverted nature he has abused a pen and caused the death of at least 40 innocent Muslims around the world.

Anyone with some basic knowledge of human history would know that Muslims of the world are second to none in their appreciation of the pen and its role in history. But Muslims will never use that pen to unleash invectives on others. Islam inspires such a deep love and passion for the noble contributions of pen that the swords have become ineffective in frightening the Muslims. Throughout history, Muslims have preserved the integrity of the pen even at the cost of their lives. In protesting the publication of *Satanic Verses,* the Muslims had a dual objective: to defend the honor of the Prophet and his household and to express displeasure at the disgrace that Mr. Rushdie has brought on the pen.

It is Not an Issue of Freedom of Expression

Muslims have consistently stated that the writing or publishing *The Satanic Verses* has nothing to do with the rights of individuals to express themselves freely. In fact freedom of conscience and freedom of expression are among the most important and fundamental rights unconditionally guaranteed under Islam. And certainly when it comes to societies where Muslims are in minority they can never advocate suppression of such freedoms. Thus the attempts to project Muslims as opponents of freedom of expression are a grave misrepresentation. While Islam promotes freedom of expression, it does not give any protection to acts of defamation, character assassination and blasphemy. The author of *Satanic Verses* does not distinguish between what is normally understood as the freedom of conscience and freedom of expression and the actions that are offensive and insulting. In fact he asserts that freedom of expression is of no value without the freedom to offend and satirize. He says, "What is freedom of expression? Without the freedom to offend it ceases to exist. Without the freedom to challenge, even to satirize all orthodoxies, including religious orthodoxies, it ceases to exist."

As a free man, Mr. Rushdie may interpret and exercise freedom of expression the way he wants, but it is ridiculous on his part to expect Muslims not to respond to his satires and offenses.

It is an Issue of Moral Responsibility

Censorship is practiced all over the world including Britain and the United States. And it is practiced by governments and private organizations. Any claims to contrary are simply absurd. Prof. Ali Mazrui, for example, has cited numerous examples of such acts of censorship while addressing the issues related to the *Satanic Verses* last year. What Muslims have been asking for, and have been successful to some extent in getting is recognition and understanding that writers and artists also have a moral and social responsibility for their work. We have to continue our efforts along these lines. Muslims have never been afraid of critics and have not shied away from challenges. History of Islam and Muslims is filled with many examples in this regard. However, Muslims will not allow anyone to engage in acts of insults and abuse against Islam. Those who disregard these natural sensitivities of Muslims, are being unfair.

It is a Satanic Work

The entire debate about *The Satanic Verses* is very simple and straightforward. The author and his allies have claimed that *The Satanic Verses* is a sort of "masterpiece," "an excellent piece of literature," and "the work of an artist." What they have disregarded is the Muslim position that no one, including the writers and the artists, has the right to abuse Islam.

It should be understood by everyone that Muslims have a very special relationship with Islam. They live for it and they give their lives for it. The author is so arrogant that he refuses to listen to any voice except to his own. His irrationality is very persistent. For Mr. Rushdie and his likes the issues of morality, ethics, and social responsibility are of no value. Instead, they nurture elements of obscenity, pornography, vulgarity, and filth and present them as art and literature. Muslims on the other hand consider all such literature and art a satanic work.

Mr. Rushdie has shown us how irrational he is. On the one hand he uses the most sacred names in the history of Islam in a profane, filthy and obscene manner to amuse himself and his kind, and on the other, complains about "bigots and racists" who have tried to exploit his case by using his name to taunt Muslim and non-Muslim Asian children and adults in a manner that he finds "repulsive, defiling and humiliating." He does not seem to recognize that different people respond to such situations differently. There are some who ignore such things, others get upset and angry. There are those who react to it in the manner of an eye for an eye and a tooth for a tooth. Also, there are those who return a stone for a brick.

Facilitating Profanity

For the West's predominantly Christian, societies, the events of Reformation and Renaissance, the advent of industrial and technological revolutions, urbanization and freedom from monarchies and church domination have ushered in a drastically different socio-cultural era. Everything has changed to the extent that it will never again be the same. Several generations have been raised under the motto that God is "dead." Ethics and morality have no definite meanings. In politics, economics, culture, and society what counts and matters is power. One reflection of these changes in the post-enlightenment era is the fact that profanity, obscenity, and vulgarity have become impossible to define. What might be most profane, obscene and vulgar to one might very strangely be profound, adorable, and ennobling to others. *The Satanic Verses* is recognizably and admittedly a manifestation of this confusion. Realizing this full well, Mr. Rushdie and his supporters are telling Muslims that profane and chaste, good and evil, and sacred and violent are relative. This is unacceptable to Muslims.

Mr. Rushdie and his publishers, Viking-Penguin, have to understand that by making new charges against Islam and continuing to promote the book, they are making a reconciliation with Muslims even more improbable.

Source: *The Message International,* March 1990, pp. 9–10.

The Author as the Stooge

by M.H. Faruqi

. . . After having inflicted gratuitous insult to over 1,000 million Muslims of the world (even the liberal mouthpiece 'The Guardian' confessed roundly to this fact the other day in its 14 February 1990 'Fatwa Anniversary' editorial), the 'celebrity' author of Penguin Viking's classic sacrilege, 'The Satanic Verses', returned earlier this month to offer a gratuitous explanation of his 'Good Faith' ('The Independent', 4 February 1990), that is gratuitous insofar as the Muslims were concerned, otherwise everything has been fully charged for. This particular essay, 'In Good Faith' was 'sold' to the newspaper 'for close to £100,000'. There have been other interviews and paid-for excerpts and he has already made 'well over £1m' from his 'magnum profanicus'. Therefore whether or not 'The Satanic Verses' went into the paperback, there is little doubt that in a world dominated by a so-called Liberal minority, there isn't going to be a shortage of money for writing sacrilege, more so if it concerned Islam and Muslims.

Right from the days of its pre-launch publicity to the latest protestation of 'Good Faith', Salman Rushdie, the former advertising agency jingle-writer has written his ad lib several times over, generally gleeful and 'naughty', but sometimes also pretending to be 'nice', depending upon who he was speaking to. Everyone knew the author of 'Grimus', 'Midnight's Children' and 'Shame' to be a writer of fiction, a novelist, but the story-teller now wanted to promote himself as a 'social reformer'. Thus we find him telling the Indian magazine 'India Today' (15 September 1988) that '*Actually* one of my *major themes* (emphasis ours) is religion and fanaticism' and that he had 'talked about the Islamic religion because that is what I know the most about'. (Did he not then know how seriously 'the Islamic religion' took offence to abusing or insulting Muhammad, peace be upon him? It was apostasy and apostasy was punishable with death. One assumes he knew that, despite the 'God-shaped hole' in his hollow cardiac machine. Instead he had chosen deliberately to seek 'reform' through outrage.)

Rushdie was yet more eloquent when he spoke to another Indian magazine. He told 'Sunday' weekly (18–24 September 1988) that the book 'is a serious attempt to write about religion and revelation from the point of view of a secular person.' Why pick on Muhammad (peace be upon him) alone to insult and ridicule him, when the professed aim is 'serious' and the supposed canvas broad and universal, not confined to Islam and Muslims alone! Because 'Muhammad (peace be upon him) is a very interesting figure. He's the only Prophet (peace be upon him) who exists even remotely inside history', Rushdie went on to explain his choice. Totally oblivious of the possibility that his secular crusade could turn out to be a non-starter even in a secular India, he was then priming the world's largest English-reading market after North America. India was the first country to ban 'The Satanic Verses', but Rushdie went on with his actor-slogan-writer-novelist and 'Islamic reformer' act in the British radio and television programmes produced for the 'Indo-Pakistanis'. He wanted to be taken more seriously than a mere Highbury yarn-weaver, *Jolaha* in his Indo-Anglian tongue. It was only later when faced with worldwide condemnation that he had to think of a new line that the book wasn't actually about Islam, but rather about 'migration, metamorphosis, divided selves, love, death'. Rather than meaning to outrage Muslims he was trying to empathise with their lot as immigrants, he was now saying, a point he turned to in his 15 January interview in 'The Guardian'.

Empathy? Even Malise Ruthven's passionate defence of Salman Rushdie (*A Satanic Affair: Salman Rushdie & The Rage of Islam,* Chatto & Windus, London, 1990) could not fail to state that 'Several critics have sensed a lack of empathy in Rushdie's treatment of traditionally disadvantaged groups.' He quotes Timothy Brenan: 'The book's characterisation of West Indians (like its characterisation of women) are often embarrassing and offensive'. (*Salman Rushdie and the Third World: Myths of the Nation,* London, 1989.) Ruthven refers further to Feroza Jussawalla's comment ('Resurrecting the Prophet: The Case of Salman, the Otherwise' in *Public Culture,* Vol 2, No 1, Fall 1989, p.107) 'that Rushdie's British education makes him "condescending to all things Indian", ' yet Ruthven, tries to show understanding: 'Empathy in fiction, however, comes more readily with the creation of 'rounded' characters' and 'since Rushdie's thesis appears to be that the migrant's experience leads to the discarding and assuming of identities, to create "rounded" characters would surely be false to method . . . ' What Ruthven is saying is that given his 'method', it was difficult for Rushdie to create 'rounded' characters. But the 'difficulty' was of his own making and, the fact remained that Rushdie looked to all 'traditionally disadvantaged groups', including women, with condescension, if not exactly contempt. That much about his empathy with Muslims and immigrants.

Rushdie accuses his critics of not reading his book. He is lucky that only the Muslims happen to have, of necessity, read his 'Satanic Verses'. Not the Chinese, the 'West Indians', the Sikhs, the Hindus, nor the English! . . . Given the media hype and the fact that it was regarded as offensive by Muslims, for sure great many people have bought the book but were unable to read through its dense pages of 'magic realism', making 'The Satanic Verses' probably 'one of the least read best-sellers in literary history', to quote Ruthven yet again (The Daily Telegraph, 3 February 1990). If they had read it, unlike Muslims, they would have acted long ago on the advice of Lord Dacre, the historian,

Professor Hugh Trevor-Roper, 'to waylay him in a dark street and seek to improve . . . Rushdie's manners.'

Salman Rushdie's long 7,000-words, £100,000 price-tag 'essay', is an interesting study material about the person and psychological condition of its author, though the material must be read and interpreted very carefully, in view of the fact that its writer was not a free person: He was hostage of his benefactors and beneficiaries. Not surprisingly, he has said little new and one doubts that even if he were to repent sincerely, in the Islamic sense of 'Tawba', he would have the freedom to make it known.

Most of the points Rushdie makes by way of explanation are mere elaborations on his previous polemic, and these were dealt with in *Impact* 18:20, 28 October–10 November 1988. Only that, he now combines the argument about his empathy for migrants with the more profound social and ideological objectives. He still does not want to say that 'The Satanic Verses' is 'only a novel' and thus need not be taken seriously'. That would be too humiliating for his ego, perhaps. He wants it to be taken as 'a work of radical dissent.'

The problem is he wants to have it both ways. He did not want to nor was he capable of writing a serious and scholarly work of radical critique of the 'Islamic religion'. Had he done so, criticisms or disputations about the book would not have been known outside the pages of Islamic or Orientalist journals. But he would have also not received all that fabulous 'auction' money that he got otherwise. He would not have entered the pages of history. So he chose the medium of fiction, the garb of dream and fantasy, but the language of filth and profanity. The device was clever and disarming as none of its potential critics could answer back its filth and profanity in the same language. It also won the acclaim of the large and powerful worldwide constituency of Islam haters, the so-called liberals and the alienated literati included.

The book was welcomed as a Devil-sent gift capable of destabilising the nascent Muslim communities in the West as well as the English-reading young generation in the Muslim countries. Whatever may be Rushdie's own explanation – and he has yet to offer a logical and consistent explanation – the point came out in almost all the major reviews of the book: That here was a 'brilliant' son of Islam who had come up with such a 'devastating' ridicule of the 'Islamic religion' and its two unassailable authenticities,

The Qur'an and Muhammad (peace be upon him) – something which no Islamologist (as the former Orientalists have christened themselves lately) could hope or dare to do.

Malise Ruthven approvingly describes 'The Satanic Verses' as a brilliant, playful, transgressive work that explores and parodies the very ingredients of Indo-British Muslim identity, mixing fact with fiction, history with myth' that 'trod on most of the sensitive spots in this brittle collective ego: the integrity of the Qur'an, the sexuality of the Prophet Muhammad (peace be upon him) and his wives, the Mothers of the Believers (may God be pleased with them) op. cit., p.9). There are therefore no two opinions about the nature of the book: offensive to Muslims and pleasing to the secular and alienated liberals and all those who were motivated by malice towards Islam and Muslims.

Rushdie's protestation of 'Good Faith' was, however, irrelevant to Muslim concerns. They were neither asking nor expecting any explanation from him. Their demands were addressed to Penguin Books who they assumed were a respectable and responsible multinational publishing house. The author was just an individual given to his fantasies and frailties, but for the publishers to spread filth and sacrilege was not acceptable.

The Muslim demands were, therefore, addressed in the first place to Penguin Books and these were:

One, to withdraw and pulp all the copies of 'The Satanic Verses' and to undertake not to reprint it in the future.

Two, to offer unqualified public apology to the World Muslim community.

Three, to pay damages to a Muslim charity equal to the returns received from the copies already sold in Britain and abroad.

There being no law to seek proscription of the book or any other legal redress against this gross sacrilege, the British Muslim community has been pursuing its painful and acute concerns from a position of total rightlessness, but in absolute confidence about the moral justness of its cause and in the well-placed hope that eventually the publishers, the government and the general public will be able to understand and appreciate their sense of hurt and provide the needful redress and recompense.

That this has not happened so far is understandable. Being a newly arrived – or more exactly 'brought over' – community to help meet the manpower shortage in the lower and unpopular scale of economic activity, it has yet to find its place in the life of its new country. It also faces a great degree of ignorance about its culture and way of life, an ignorance which is compounded as much by factors of historical prejudice as by the post-modernist phenomenon of what has best been described by Shabbir Akhtar as 'Liberal Inquisition'.

Then there is the media which is, more often than not, more interested in making up a 'good story', than in fair reporting be it through a little 'editing', distortion or through provocation or a complete blackout of the Muslim point of view. All this has been happening while the whole debate is alleged to have been in defence of the doctrine of freedom of expression. The Muslims in Bradford were little aware that while choosing to symbolically burn a copy of 'The Satanic Verses' in January last year to draw attention to their deep hurt they were also being manipulated by a national newspaper. Burning books, flags or effigies are very much part of popular and lawful methods of protest in Western 'liberal' tradition. As Keith Vaz, Labour MP for Leicester East has pointed out ('The Guardian', 14 February 1990), an effigy of Nicholas Ridley was burned in Hampshire by those opposing its over-development, and poll tax notices were burned in Scotland. A copy of the 1988 Immigration Act was burned outside the Home Office in August 1988, a month before the publication of 'The Satanic Verses'. There was no fuss about any of that, but the 'book-burning' in Bradford was turned into a 'cardinal sin' and used as an excuse to bash Bradfordian and all other Muslim communities as if it were they who had committed blasphemy, albeit against the liberal secular 'religion'.

So the Muslims have still to go a long way towards winning a recognition of their human rights and the right to equal dignity. Maybe they will not, but nothing diminishes their right to object to being abused and insulted. In the end bad manners only diminish the insulter.

In standing up to more than one year of strident and incessant campaign of abuse and intimidation, the Muslim community in Britain has made enormous gains in self-esteem and in its consciousness of the dignity of Islam and Muhammad (peace be upon him). Its young generation, its school boys and girls, who were the primary target of 'The Satanic Verses' for secularisation and de-Islamisation have acquired great confidence and competence to deal with all the distortions and falsifications of Islam and Islamic teachings. As far as the book is concerned it may have sold a million copies 'because' of the strong protests by Muslims worldwide, and it might even go on to touch another million mark, but it stands thoroughly *absurdised.* Muslims were initially shocked and hurt because they assumed they were citizens of a civilised Christian society and not because they felt the book was going to damage their faith. In the event they have learnt that while the society at large may be Christian in its feelings and ethos, the affairs of the country were dominated by a secular (read 'irreligious') liberal minority. It is not assumed though that attacks and provocations against Islam and Islamic sensitivities shall cease in the immediate future, but then you are insulted only once.

The problem, including Rushdie's occultation, is unresolved because the publishers have remained dismissive of the demand to withdraw the book. They seem to enjoy the notoriety achieved by the book. They feel confident that their liberal and secular friends in the establishments in the Muslim countries would ensure that the 'Declaration on Joint Islamic Action to Combat Blasphemy Against Islam' adopted by the 18th Islamic Conference of Foreign Ministers held in Riyadh in March 1989, which called for sanctions against the Penguin publishing and holding companies remained just dots of ink on paper and was not implemented.

Penguin have also been quite smart in choosing for themselves a low profile and flaunting the naive author to take all the flak and even risk losing his neck. Salman Rushdie should thank Khomeini for issuing his Fatwa and helping him to slip away from the public eye. Although Muslim leaders in Britain had made it clear at the very start of the campaign that their demands were addressed to the publishers and publishers alone and told the community not to try to touch the author of 'The Satanic Verses' even with a pair of tongs, the way Rushdie and his book were flaunted and used to bash and beat the Muslim community, to add more insult to injury, it was not improbable that someone felt provoked enough to try to take the law into his own hands. Rather than trying to understand the true import of the Fatwa – to state the Islamic law about abusing the Prophet (peace be upon him) and the law against apostasy and to underscore the enormity of the offence caused by the publication of the book – the publishers' lobby chose to use the statement as a peg for further publicity for the book as well as a stick to beat and intimidate Muslims. This was in spite of the fact that Muslim leaders had made it amply clear that although apostasy was punishable with death, but like all laws it applied only within its own (Islamic) jurisdiction. In other words it was not applicable in Britain. No one, including even those who were spiritually or politically committed to Iran, took the position that he would personally carry out the 'death sentence'. Yet so great was the brouhaha that the British government was forced to sever diplomatic relations with Tehran and lose the large and expanding Iranian market for British goods and services.

Of late a new element appears to have entered the situation. With Mrs Margaret Thatcher running into trouble with the country's liberal and money lobby, 'The Satanic Verses' affair seems to have come handy to serve as a useful whip to flog 'Mrs Torture' and to destabilise her. Also because, of late, the government had appeared to be trying to distance itself gradually from its earlier uncritical support of Rushdie and Penguin – to write as they like and to publish as they like. Yet so powerful is the pressure exerted by the 'Friends of Penguin' that Mrs Thatcher had to assure the Commons last week that she defended the freedom of speech and the freedom to write in a democracy although the dispute here was not about the freedom of speech, it was about the abuse of this freedom to inflict insult and sacrilege upon a whole community of people.

The Penguin lobby is powerful and unassailable and as the publishers continue to bask in their intransigence, there is little hope of the deadlock being broken early, unless Rushdie tries to take his affairs into his own hands and refuses to act as a shield for Penguin Books. He has already stated that he is 'not a Muslim' and this might help him escape the charge of apostasy, even if he were to come under the jurisdiction of Islamic law. All he needed now was to show repentance, ask his publishers to cease further publication of 'The Satanic Verses' and to pay to an Islamic charity all the gains of his sacrilege. After all he did admit in his last month's review of Thomas Pynchon's new novel, 'Vineland', in 'The New York Times Book Review' that there were things which 'are unfortunately, unprintable here.' He was referring to 'Billy Barf's "Three-Note-Blues" called "I'm a Cop" with lyrics that' were unprintable. So instead of insisting that the NYTBR also publish the 'unprintable part of the lyrics, he refrained from reproducing them in his review. Why can't he use the same common sense about 'The Satanic Verses'?

Source: *Impact International,* 20/4, 23rd February–8th March 1990, pp. 16–18.

The Rushdie Malaise: A Critique of Some Writings on the Rushdie Affair

by Ziauddin Sardar

I

We are the truth, all else is falsehood. This is the basic premise of the civilization that dominates the world – the Western civilization. It is the driving force of its history, its organizing principle, secularism, and all its literary products. What it actually means is that Western perception is used as a yardstick to measure reality: Western culture becomes *the* culture into which all other cultures must be subsumed; Western history becomes *the* history, the histories of all other people, cultures and civilizations are only a pre-modern version of European history and therefore only a small segment of the Grand History of Western Civilization; secularism becomes *the* value of society to which all other values must refer; and Western art and literature present the apex of human experience in front of which all else pales into insignificance. Kenneth Clarke's book and the television series based on it summed up the logic of this enterprise: *Civilization.* It began with the Greeks and ended with modern Britain: nothing else happened in the middle, there has been and is nothing of significance in the world since it began except the European and his Self.

A Post-Modernist Novel With a Specific Purpose

Salman Rushdie's *The Satanic Verses* is a postmodernist novel. It is therefore cast in a specific mould and is designed to serve a very specific purpose. Ridicule of Islam, abuse of the Prophet Muhammad and accompanying blasphemy are only surface offences – a residue of the Orientalist tradition. The novel has a deeper significance which has been meticulously worked out over five years. The postmodern genre of magical realism, of which Rushdie is an exponent, aims at turning history into amnesia: it deliberately and systematically blurs the boundaries of fact and fiction. This is done with the aim of proving and showing that reality is often imagined and imagination often becomes real. In a reductionist sense, the novel can be seen as the fictional form of Marxist theorist Jean Baudrillard's theory of semulacurum (the word actually appears in the novel a couple of times): television is not what you see in a box at one corner in the living room, *that* is reality; you, the viewer, are the image. The world turned upside down where 'Dynasty' and 'Dallas' are the real thing and our imitative behaviour of the soap opera the celluloid image. Rushdie painstakingly rewrites every aspect of the *Sīrah,* the life of the Prophet Muhammad, the paradigm of Muslim behaviour and identity, and seals it in his own, postmodernist, dogmatic secularist, image. The hope is that his image of the *Sīrah* will become the actual reality, and our perception, however historically accurate, the image. If his readers accept his picture, then Rushdie accomplishes the following goals: he makes the foundations of Islam a secularist enterprise and therefore part of the Grand History of secularism; he wipes out the deep and intrinsic connection between Muslim cultural and religious identity and the Prophetic paradigm, therefore making Islamic culture and Muslim identity an appendage to Western culture; and finally, as a result of these, he succeeds in writing Islamic history and Muslim identity – at least in the minds of his Western readers at whom the book is largely aimed – out of existence. This is the real purpose of *The Satanic Verses.*

Rushdie's novel is meant for people who, like him, have a God-shaped hole in their heart. It is aimed at a postmodern world where doubt and confusion, dark pessimism, loneliness, and absolute meaninglessness is the norm. In the best tradition of post-modernist literature it is a panic book, a product of panic internal void, panic ideology, panic sex, and panic culture. All his characters are desperate people living desperate lives – an echo of the author's own desperation! Rushdie aims to produce empathy between him and his reader and thus show that Islam, its Prophet and its scripture too suffer from the same malaise. As one of his characters in the novel asks, in a state of desperate doubt and confusion: 'Does a firm persuasion that a thing is so, make it so?' What the Muslims say is the historical reality of the origins of their world-view does not make it so; what I, Rushdie, am saying, with my doubts and panics so similar to yours, my readers, must surely be of much more significance!

. . . Rushdie 'plays the role of court satirist too well'. However, for him his assumed burden of writing Islam out of history and projecting a 'linear progress of history' which ends with Western civilization is no joke. Indeed, he even takes his role as a prophet of postmodernism very seriously and systematically gives clues in his novels to show that he considers himself to be on a par with the Prophet Muhammad: 'thus, as history records, Muhammad was about forty years old when his revelations began; so now is Rushdie, and so is his character, Gibreel Farishta. Like Rushdie, Muhammad was not only a seer, but a social agitator, substituting religious brotherhood for the tribal identities of the Arab peoples; and his attack on pagan worship was a direct threat to the commercial enterprise set up around the pilgrimage to the pagan Ka'ba, just as Rushdie in the novel continues the critique developed in *Midnight's Children* where religion is portrayed as "a good business arrangement".'

The kind of goals that Rushdie sets himself could only be accomplished in a work of fiction. Muslims, of all people, as their history demonstrates so vividly, are aware of the power of ideas. Faith may or may not move mountains; but ideas certainly do, particularly when they are transformed into literature or technology. For then they can be turned into ideologies, bulldozers, tools of suppression, physical and psychological torture and used to justify the eradication of entire cultures and histories. There is no vehicle more powerful for a direct onslaught on a peoples' cultural and religious identity than a work of fiction. It has an international audience, and when backed by a powerful publisher like Penguin, it can totally saturate the global market-place. Moreover, it gives no recourse to the victims to shoot it down.

The 'Brown Sahib'

That Rushdie is an Indian/Pakistani Muslim is also significant. It gives his voice certain authenticity and eager listeners waiting to have their perceptions confirmed become even more ready to be convinced: he is one of them, surely he must know what he is talking about! Indeed, Rushdie takes considerable care to provide his readers with flavours of 'authentic culture' – the names of his characters, the predominance of local lingo, generous use of Urdu/Hindi terms. All this makes his narrative appear authentic. . . . The paradox returns again and again: Rushdie's work is in 'an aesthetic double-bind: an encyclopaedic frenzy, a narrative canvas packed with the colours and gestures of human "stuff", and yet set within a horrifying narrative closure'; 'despite the fresh thinking about national form, about a new homelessness that is also a wordliness, about a double-edged post-colonial responsibility, *The Satanic Verses* shows how strangely detached and insensitive the logic of cosmopolitan "universality" can be'; and why, oh why, is there so much 'real history in Rushdie's work?' . . .

However, for most Muslims there is nothing paradoxical here. Rushdie is an instantly recognizable historic type, the 'brown sahib' who is at once an insider and a total, alien, outsider. The history of the Indian subcontinent is punctuated with the activities of so many brown sahibs who, in exchange for recognition and acceptance, always tried to out-do the sahib at his own game. After all, would the East India Company have succeeded in taking over the Mughal Empire with such ease if it had not had at its disposal a network of brown sahibs ever ready to sell their people short for this or that favour? . . . The brown sahib has an acute inferiority complex about his original identity: he hates his Indian/Muslim self. Yet, on the other hand, he knows he can never be accepted as a *pukkah* sahib. Thus a distance grows between himself and his identities and he experiences a loss of meaning and reality which manifests itself in desolution, desperation and internal panic. The belief that one's personality can always undergo fundamental change can only produce an epidemic of self-blame. And just like that postmodern manifestation of an old disease, herpes, which no matter how hard you scratch irritates more and more, this self-blame takes the brown sahib to his logical end: in a final suicidal attempt to become what he can never become he eradicates the one thing that can save him from the brink of insanity, his original identity. He thus fulfils the ultimate desire of the sahib by going the distance that even the sahib would be reluctant to go. In more ways than one, *The Satanic Verses* is also a long and tortuous suicide note.

Given the fact that postmodern pathological symptoms of nihilism are so strongly ingrained in Rushdie, it was natural for him to become a brown sahib spokesperson for the Left. In modern times, just as knowledge is largely manufactured, in its manifestation as science, technology, disciplines (economics, sociology, anthropology, Orientalism), so is literature. Novelists are made, processed and manufactured; gone are the days when novelists were *born* as novelists and wrote from life experience to enrich the lives of others: Cervantes, Flaubert, Henry James. Nowadays they are nursed, produced, packaged as commodities and when necessary presented as spokespersons for this or that cause. But not everyone can queue up to be manufactured. Only the select few with the right Oxbridge background who totally identify with Europe and its culture and promote the cause of European civilization in their work – you must totally conform to the dictates of militant dogmatic secularism. Under these circumstances it is not pursuit of literature as a tool for moral and poetic uplift of people that persuades writers to become professional novelists, but the oldest motives of all: power and money.

But once you have entered the Star Chamber there are a number of privileges to be had. In these postmodernist times, literature occupies the same place as God in traditional worldviews, and the novelist is the high-priest of society. When Rushdie said that 'it is to literature that I turn to fill the God-shaped hole within me' he was not just describing his own mental condition, but also stating an accepted 'truth' of postmodernism. As demigods the members of the Star Chamber yield tremendous power and they defend their role as guardians of public morality ruthlessly. Rushdie wrote *The Satanic Verses* in the full knowledge that his Star Chamber status will ensure that the secularist establishment will rush to protect and defend him. Indeed, the defence of Rushdie is the defence of the privileged status of the postmodernist novelist in society: if the group of omnipotent/helpless children with weak egos and socially distorted superegos who are generally acknowledged to be the *literati* are seen to surrender one inch of their territory, then the position of every one of them will be compromised. Rushdie therefore had to be defended with all the might at their disposal – even if it meant sinking into unadulterated racism.

Documentation of the Affair

Both *The Rushdie File* (edited by Lisa Appignanesi and Sara Maitland, Fourth Estate, London, 1989) and *The Kiss of Judas* (edited by Munawar Ahmad Anees, Quill, Kuala Lumpur, 1989) provide us with a good sample of writings of Rushdie's defenders. While the *File* gives more weight to his defenders, not surprisingly, *Judas* contains more from the Islamic perspective. The *File* contains no editorial comments, it simply allows the weighted bias towards the defenders and Rushdie's own interviews and comments, to make its case. Munawar Anees gives his editorial perspectives in *Judas* and thus plays his subjectivity up front. The *File* was designed to have a limited life – which it has now outlived. *Judas* will last much longer not least because it contains Ali Mazrui's brilliant defence and Manazir Ahsan's scholarly examination of the origins and validity of the satanic verses incident.

A Defender of Rushdie

Neither of the anthologies contain Fay Weldon. Her pamphlet 'Sacred Cows' started life as an 'Opinion' on Channel Four entitled 'Sackcloth and Ashes' (March 1989) and was later printed in *The Listener* (18 May 1989), *New Statesman and Society, The Observer* and a slightly modified form as a Chatto CounterBlast (Chatto & Windus, London, 1989) – it is certainly good to see that certain individuals have a more than equal opportunity to exercise their freedom of expression. Here I have used the text of her 'Opinion' piece delivered direct to camera; it brings out her true personality and well illustrates the nature of postmodernist fiction. Weldon begins by announcing that 'we [have] failed to take relevant facts on board, we were frightened of rethinking'. What are the facts that she wants to take on board, and what rethinking is she asking for? Here is the first 'fact': 'Muslims believe that words are dangerous things in themselves, able to insult and by insulting destroying the God.' For a novelist to suggest that words do not have any power is daft; but then to go on and suggest further that Muslims are so stupid that they think that certain words will destroy God is to reveal a dumbfounding arrogance. Weldon wants Christian Churches to rethink their position on Islam; they are far too tolerant, as their history no doubt shows: ' . . . put up your mosques next to our churches, scorn us as unbelievers all you like, we are too frightened by the past, too intimidated by history . . . to stand up and dominate like you, like we used to. 'I want our Church back', she declares, 'in the vigour of its belief that it's the one and only Church, and prepared to say so. Then I can choose not to believe its far-fetchedness.'

'Have the Christians', she asks, 'not read the Koran? Do they not know how the believer in Mohammad regards the unbeliever?' And she then produces this 'verse' from the Qur'ān: 'When the unbeliever holds out his hand, take it. But when he turns his back, slay him. You have my authority'. This 'verse', of course, is total fabrication; an indication of the level to which postmodernist defenders of Rushdie will sink to promote hatred. We continue:

> I recommend a thorough reading of the Koran to everyone. Allah the all-seeing, all-knowing, I am glad to see, is compassionate as well as vengeful; that is to say, he does sometimes turn a blind eye, knowing people are weak; he sometimes even rescues people from the abysmal fires of Gehenna. I just want to know what Allah has to be merciful about, what there is to forgive. It is, from the Western view, an entirely circular argument. Muhammad invents the sin in order for Allah to be seen forgiving it. To punish and chastise is the norm: compassion is when it doesn't happen.

Even from the perspective of the undoubtedly superior Western logic, there is no contradiction between being compassionate and vengeful – if Allah is indeed vengeful; Allah, if He chooses, can be compassionate in His vengeance and forgive. By any logic, if God exists He is a *de facto* God. He exists because He exists; not because we have willed Him into existence. The argument is circular only in the sense that Allah should have instituted a consultation process, with Weldon as the chief advisor and goddess, before He takes revenge on anyone. But what is this:

Muhammad invented sin? Is one to understand Christianity, Judaism, Hinduism, Zoroastrianism and other religions before Islam did not have the concept of sin?

The Qur'ān that Weldon read 'comes in a very nice Penguin edition. Arthur Arberry did this translation'. The Penguin edition of the Qur'ān, if Weldon actually read it, is translated by N.J. Dawood, and it is one of the most inaccurate, misleading and distorted versions on the market (and the preferred choice of Salman Rushdie). The Arthur Arberry translation comes in a nice Oxford University Press (who hold the copyright; the American edition is published by Macmillan, 1979) edition: it looks so different from the Penguin edition that one would have to be virtually blind to confuse the two. Arberry's translation, Weldon tells us, 'moved him. So it should; it is a great poem'. But Weldon is not willing to allow Arberry, who spent his entire life studying the Qur'ān and Muslim traditions and is considered, both by Muslims and non-Muslims, to be one of the great Orientalists of recent times, the freedom to be influenced by the Qur'ān. *Her* interpretation is far superior; it has to be! So she throws scorn and sarcasm at Arberry's feelings: 'he acknowledges his gratitude to whatever power, or Power, inspired the man and the Prophet who first recited these scriptures – revelations supernaturally received, he explains'. Like all knowledgeable persons, Arberry is far more humble.

After deriding Arberry, Weldon quotes *Sūrah Al-Kāfirūn* ('The Unbelievers' – 109: 1–6):

> Say: O unbelievers,
> I serve not what you serve,
> and you are not serving what I serve,
> nor am I serving what you have served,
> neither are you serving what I serve.
> To you your religion and to me my religion!

And she adds, in the usual scornful manner: 'Oh yes. Except for me, the unbeliever, mine shall be the fire of Gehenna, and its mighty chastisements will never be lightened.' Had Weldon actually read Arberry's interpretation of the Qur'ān, she would have known that the Qur'ān does not promise paradise to the believer without corresponding action. Indeed together with belief *(īmān)* it is righteousness and good action *('amal al-Ṣāliḥ)* that the Qur'ān wants; and the righteous unbelievers, unless they are Fay Weldon, need not worry about Gehenna too much. The word which is translated by Arberry as 'serve' *(mā ta'budūn)* alludes both to positive concepts and false objects of worship and values; amongst the latter is a person's belief in his/her own self-sufficiency and superiority, considering one's ignorance to be superior knowledge, spreading *fitna* or hatred by false accusation and innuendoes about other people, seeking to suppress or dominate others and the attribution of superhuman and divine qualities to human beings. On all these counts, Weldon has something to worry about!

The verses quoted by Weldon (109: 1–6) are a supreme example of the 'live and let live' attitude of the Qur'ān. But Weldon's main concern is to sow the seeds of conflict and distrust and vent her fear and hatred of Muslims:

> . . . this violent frightening poem . . . This divine revelation from Allah to Muhammad in the seventh century, with its Bible tales retold, its rules for desert living, its rejection of monogamy, its despisal for women – yes, I know the Prophet says treat females with kindness and respect, and I dare say it was better than what went before – only chastise them when they're rebellious, and so forth; and the women go to heaven too, but since heaven is a place full of beautiful houris and glasses of wine beneath the bough, what are the women to do? Fetch the wine, I suppose. See how awful one gets, so easily, about another culture's belief structure . . . (Amen!)

Why have billions of Muslims who have lived since the beginning of Islam, including non-Muslims like Arberry, not been frightened by 'this violent and frightening poem'? How come it led to the creation of one of the greatest material and intellectual civilizations on the one hand, and an unparalleled tradition of mysticism on the other? There is fear and there is violence; but it is not in the message of the Qur'ān. The fear is within the heart and mind of Fay Weldon: the fear of her own ignorance, her inner barrenness, the abject darkness that resides within her. The violence is the outcome of her intrinsic fear and hatred, her urge to dominate, her arrogant belief in her own self-righteous, superior position – violence is what she has done to the Qur'ān by misrepresentation, plain falsification, and downright ignorance.

And some poem! At any one single space-time co-ordinate, it is in the hearts, minds and memories, cover to cover, of millions of people who can recite all of it, or any part from anywhere to anywhere. A poem whose segments are recited, and have been recited for fourteen hundred years, five times a day by most devout Muslims. A poem that led Ibn Haytham to lay the foundations of modern optics and Rumi to the apex of mystical ecstasy. A poem that can build or destroy empires. A poem that can shape the social structure of a society, build economic systems and construct political institutions. A poem that is a religion, a civilization, a culture, a world-view. How many poems are there like it? Or perhaps our processed feminist novelist does not know what a poem is?

Dogmatic Secularist

To say that the Qur'ān despises women is like saying that Fay Weldon despises Salman Rushdie. In either case it is a total distortion of fact. Even when the Qur'ān says 'men' it applies equally to women. But it is also a fact that in contemporary Muslim societies, women are discriminated against and suppressed. That discrimination and suppression is not due to the teachings of the Qur'ān, but the chauvinism and arrogance of Muslim men. It is an appalling state of affairs that cannot and should not be tolerated, and that has to be fought at every juncture by all right-minded people. First Weldon states, with a sense of original discovery, that Muslim women are harassed and suppressed; then she argues that rates of divorce, wife-beating etc. among Muslims in Britain are somehow way ahead of the more 'liberated' host community:

> Muslim women in our midst, with their arranged marriages, their children in care, their high divorce rate, the wife beatings, the intimidation, the penalties for recalcitrance . . . their unregulated work in Dickensian sweatshops, abandoned and betrayed, as they try to keep house and home together, the impossibly exploitative piece-work at home . . .

Why did Weldon leave out child abuse, rape, homicide, alcoholism, and drug addiction? One hopes that Muslims are not being favoured! If the champion of dogmatic secularism had checked her facts, she would have discovered that in purely percentage terms, there is simply no comparison between the divorce rate, children in care, wife-beating and so on in the Muslim community and the host community. In Britain, one in three marriages ends in divorce; and second marriages are as likely to fall apart as the first time around (Social and Community Planning Research, *British Social Attitudes,* Gower, 1989). And 'arranged marriages' are not always arranged, in the sense of being forced; even when the parties involved choose their own partners, the marriages are still 'arranged' by their parents; they are often willingly entered into (as in the case of Benazir Bhutto), and surprise, surprise, they seldom end in divorce.

'The mosque', Weldon announces, 'where the Muslim children go every day after school – often frightened of going, I am told by social workers, but there is no escape for them – to be taught the Koran'. But who are these 'social workers'? Are they the same Penguin who published Arberry? If Muslim children do go to the mosque every day – a luxury many Muslim communities do not have because there are not enough mosques, enough schools, enough teachers – they may be upset about missing *Neighbours* or *East Enders* or playing football, but why should they be afraid? And if they are afraid, are they more afraid than any child going to school every morning? Most Muslim children go to Sunday schools, which are organized sometimes in mosques and sometimes in other community centres, where they learn not just the Qur'ān, Islamic history and Muslim culture, but also get involved in debates and discussions, sports and learn such things as karate which may come in handy when dealing with those who insist on shoving their self-righteous superiority down their throats.

As Weldon's attack on Islam continues, she says she would be frightened if she were a child being taught the Qur'ān, because the Qur'ān stipulates that only a believer can escape hell-fire. She attributed this pressurized fear as the reason 'why, when we in the West try to engage even the most intelligent and sophisticated Muslim in conversation about these matters, we find a blank wall of non-comprehension. Terror intervenes'.

So there are intelligent and sophisticated Muslims after all, even though they have been frightened out of their wits by the Qur'ān! Has it not occurred to her that the 'blank wall of non-comprehension' may be a reaction to the lethal fusion of sheer arrogance and ignorance on her part, that it is not the Muslims' minds that are closed but hers? They can comprehend people who do not believe, but can she comprehend people who do believe? A closed mind perceives all other minds to be closed, it can do nothing else. And that 'frightened child' who 'looks out of the adult's eyes'. Muslims are really like children: slap them and tell them to shut up and sit down.

Demigod of Public Morality

While the Muslims are child-like and immoral, evil and hateful, indeed totally black, Salman Rushdie himself is an adult, moral, good, full of love and totally white. Islam 'is not a religion of kindness but of terror'; and the Qur'ān, in another of her vicious fabrications, 'gives the believer permission to hate the unbeliever'. *The Satanic Verses* on the other hand, is a novel of love and goodness, is extraordinary poetry, which does not give permission to hate and is the stuff of revelation. The author, an 'ex-colleague of mine in an advertising agency, is too human, too modern, too witty, too intelligent, to lay down rules for the human race . . .'. Too human? Surely, a slip of the tongue? He soars high above ordinary mortals. He is, surely, God incarnate, not the child-like son but the Father himself: 'as a piece of writing, *The Satanic Verses* reads pretty much like the works of St. John the Divine at the end of our own Bible . . . St. Salman the Divine'. 'I'm joking', she adds with a smirk. A joke? Surely not, Ms. Weldon? Do you not have the conviction of your belief? Let us pray: Our Father who art in hiding, forgive us our sins that we are upset and angry by your ridicule and abuse and postmodernist attempts to write us out of history . . .

Weldon – who is an archetype of intellectually sterile and barren, emotionally panic-stricken and infantile, postmodernist novelists who see themselves as demi-gods of public morality – and other defenders of Rushdie (who are examined in some detail in my book, co-authored with Merryl Wyn Davies, *Distorted Imagination: Postmodern Lessons from the Rushdie Affair,* Grey Seal, London, 1990) operate in the firm conviction that Muslims are fair game. If, for example, she had said the same things about Jews or Blacks or even homosexuals, she would be, in no uncertain terms, drawn and quartered, taken to court, and hounded out of the Star Chamber. But this assumption is partly valid: Muslims are fair game insofar as they are powerless; but intellectually they can take on anyone that postmodernists can throw at them and reduce them to pulp.

. . . One thing that is totally irrelevant in the Rushdie affair . . . is Salman Rushdie himself. What is of concern is the postmodern enterprise of secularizing the world and subsuming all other cultures, and its latest, most obnoxious, literary product: *The Satanic Verses*. The Muslim protest, in Britain and throughout the world, has shown that this enterprise will face serious resistance from the world of Islam. However, to go beyond resistance we need to understand the nature and goals of dogmatic secularism, particularly in its postmodernist variation; only then can we dismantle it brick by brick and render it harmless. In this war of ideas, with the very survival of Muslims as Muslims at stake, we need to make sure that we do not fall victim to the allures of postmodernist techniques: that we do not react with fright and panic, abuse and ridicule, meaningless violence and terror, self-satisfying slogans and righteous indignation. It is only at the intellectual level that the advance of the postmodern culture of panic and doubt in its new phase of self-glorification can be halted and its exponents persuaded to keep off the territory that provides Muslims, as well as other cultures, with identity and meaning. It is going to be a long, hard, war and we might as well settle down and prepare ourselves for coming battles. Meanwhile, the ghost of the Rushdie affair will become a new permanent feature of the postmodern scene. Ever present, it will haunt the Western *literati* till the final moments of their panic-stricken, meaningless, barren and lonely lives, while keeping Muslim intellectuals on their toes and on the look out for the next intellectual onslaught.

Source: *Muslim World Book Review,* 10/3, 1990, pp. 3–17.

II

. . . In 'Is Nothing Sacred?', his Herbert Read Memorial Lecture (delivered by Harold Pinter at the Institute of Contemporary Arts in London on 6 February 1990; broadcast on BBC 2, printed by

Granta, and by numerous publications in Europe and the US), Salman Rushdie makes a Messianic plea for 'the unimportant-looking little room' of literary fiction 'where we can hear voices talking about everything in every possible way'. But is this space open to all, . . . or is it a more exclusive domain for a select few? It seems, Rushdie admits, that 'for many millions of human beings, these (literary) books are entirely without attraction or value'. So the 'unimportant-looking room is only for those select few who aspire to the condition of literature and their equally elitist readers.

Islam, it would also seem, is against such an enterprise. Why? Because Islam 'has set its face so resolutely against the idea that it, like all ideas, is an event inside history'. Surely, some mistake here! The Prophet of Islam was a real, living person who existed inside history; and insofar as the idea of Islam is based on what he taught, Islam is an event in history. And the Qur'ān, as it was revealed over a period of 23 years, is both a revelatory event and a permanent text inside history; indeed, even its interpretation must take history into account as many of its verses are a commentary on actual, historical events! Rushdie makes this infantile assertion to negate the enterprise of Islam (in *The Satanic Verses* this notion occurs as the 'Untime of the Imam') – to write it off from history and thus make it irrelevant to our times.

Rushdie needs to establish this false premise so that his opening assertion can be driven home. 'We have been witnessing an attack upon a particular work of fiction', he writes, 'that is also an attack upon the very idea of the novel form'. This inductive leap in the dark – from one work of fiction to all 'the novel forms' – is, like all inductive leaps, logically invalid; Muslims are only protesting about *The Satanic Verses,* they are clearly not protesting about other novels, including other works of Rushdie. The trick here is to produce a positive emotion by combining two irrationally negative ideas. If one accepts the false premise that Muslims regard their world-view to be an idea outside history, then it is a small step to believe that an attack on Rushdie is an attack on all literature!

But let us not be too harsh on logical and factual grounds. Rushdie is writing a love letter, answering an attack, 'not by an attack but a declaration of love'. Quite apart from the fact that this 'love' is in sharp contrast to the hatred and contempt he showed towards Muslims a year ago, Rushdie's love has special qualities when compared with faith. 'Love need not be blind', he tells his readers, 'faith must, ultimately, be a leap in the dark'. So the believers are by definition irrational. They 'revere the sacred unquestioningly' and are thus 'paralysed by it'. Moreover, 'the idea of the sacred is quite simply one of the most conservative notions in any culture, because it seeks to turn other ideas – Uncertainty, Progress, Change – into crime'. By this logic, cultures with sacred notions are doomed for having turned 'progress' and 'change' into 'crimes': where else can they go except towards oblivion? It is indeed surprising that Islam, despite its sacred notions, made so much progress that it became a world civilization. It is also surprising that traditional cultures, being paralysed, still seem so much better at making peace with nature and conserving the environment. But the assertion is false on another ground: it assumes that all uncertainty, all progress, all change, is Good. Secular societies have deified progress and change. Societies based on sacred notions make value judgements to ensure that change is progress and that progress is not at the expense of one's physical, social and psychological well-being. If Rushdie has a poor knowledge of Islam, surely one would expect him to know something about traditional cultures as well as contemporary ecological and environmental movements?

But need faith be a leap in the dark? Faith can be reasoned and many conscientious believers base their beliefs on rational grounds. Indeed, faith can be as reasoned as theoretical physics or modern cosmology much of which, after all the calculations and observations, is based on faith, on certain metaphysical assumptions about nature, space, time and so on. Read Khun and Feyerabend. The Cosmological and Design arguments for the existence of a Creator may not convince some; but they are still reasoned arguments just as string theory and the big bang theory of the universe are based on certain arguments. There is no way reason or logic can arbitrate between the axiomatic claims of religion or of science. Indeed, every student of modern history of ideas knows this. Only Rushdie can sell this obsolete, nineteenth-century, view and be hailed as a great thinker. But even a century earlier, Pascal demonstrated in his famous wager that it is more reasonable to believe than not to believe.

Militant Secularism

Unconcerned about the banality of his statements, Rushdie proceeds to state that 'religion seeks to privilege one language above all others' whereas 'the novel has always been about the way in which different languages, values and narratives quarrel'. All ideologies, indeed all discursive thought, seek to privilege one language over another. (Perhaps the sole exception is the kind of mystical discourse that has little cognitive content.) Inasfar as the postmodern novel is a child of militant secularism, it seeks to privilege the language of secularism. It does that by throwing scorn on the notion of the sacred, by writing traditional people and world-views out of history, by dramatizing non-secular alternatives as cul-de-sacs, and by demonstrating, with all the array of literary devices at its disposal, that secularism is the only real experience we have. Indeed Rushdie, paraphrasing Marx without comprehending, tells us that fiction begins with the acceptance that 'all that is solid *has* melted into air, that reality and morality are not givens but imperfect human constructs' – thus by definition Rushdie's kind of fiction starts from a metaphysical stance that writes off all the believers and everything they could hold sacred, with relativism (cognitive as well as moral) as the only truth. This is why in his novel one cannot find a single character with reasoned faith who is a decent human being. Such fiction only privileges one language over all others.

Starting from the point that nothing matters, everything is meaningless, Rushdie's fiction proceeds to claim a rather large territory for itself. It is in 'its origins the schismatic Other of the sacred (and authorless) text, so it is also the art most likely to fill our god-shaped holes.' Since god-shaped holes can only be filled by some kind of god – square pegs do not fit round holes – literature then is god. It is thus both *the* sacred enterprise as well as an authority unto itself. As Richard Webster points out in his truly brilliant study, *A Brief History of Blasphemy* (The Orwell Press, Suffolk, 1990) – and Rushdie himself admits – individuals with 'god-shaped-holes' are not without spiritual yearnings. The 'zealous emptiness yearns to be filled once again with faith'. Into this emptiness, Rushdie has 'poured the art of the novel, so that the novel has become his religion, the faith which he is prepared to defend against all who challenge it'.

However, Rushdie's defence of his creed turned out to be limp, based on naive assertions, and frankly, an insult to the intelligence of thinking people. On 4 February 1990, *The Independent on Sunday* gave Rushdie unprecedented access – an interview, editorial and three full pages; plus a cool £100,000 – to present his case. 'In Good Faith' also appeared in *Newsweek* which is said to have dispensed with $250,000 for the privilege (the left-wing weekly, *The Nation,* which has supported Rushdie with Messianic fervour expected to publish the silence-breaking article; but, as usual, Rushdie threw loyalty to the wind and went for the highest bidder. Greed? Who mentioned the word?)

Burlesquing Religion

Rushdie starts by reminding us that *The Satanic Verses* is a work of fiction. But it has been described 'as a work of bad history, as an anti-religious pamphlet, as the product of an international-capitalist conspiracy, as an act of murder, as the product of a person comparable to Hitler . . . ' To Hitler, who has figured largely in the Rushdie debate, and to the question whether *The Satanic Verses* is or is not 'bad history' we shall come shortly. But, first, can there be any doubt that *The Satanic Verses* is anti-religious? I mean one has to be a dupe of superannuated wishfulness to believe that a novel whose religion is secularism, whose credo doubt, which uses many languages but all of them as comment on the religion it parodies, abuses or ridicules, or in Rushdie's words 'burlesques' and 'satirizes', can be a pro-religious work! Does Rushdie really believe that his (very few) Muslim readers are that stupid?

We have made a category mistake, Rushdie tells us. A category mistake, indeed: but who made that mistake? To read fiction as though it were fact is a category mistake, we are told. But if the novel is totally fiction, why was it necessary to mimic the *Sīra* in so much detail, why was it necessary to ensure that every major event in the *Sīra* is meticulously reproduced, why was it necessary to paraphrase Martin Lings' *Life of Muhammad Based on Early Sources,* (Allen & Unwin, London, 1983) page after page? Why does Mahound's description match word for word the description given for the physical appearance of the Prophet by so many standard texts of the *Sīra*? How is it possible for a deranged character, suffering from delusions, to remember the names (even

I have to look them up, *every time*!) and physical descriptions of every one of the Prophet's wives in a dream sequence? Are the verses of the Qur'ān, even though they may appear in a dream, fact or fiction? Why does the author take great care, even with the minutest of points, to tell his (initiated) readers that he is talking about the *Sīra* – to the extent of being too-clever-by-half? And what are we to make of a text that selectively paraphrases only where it suits the ideological purpose of the author from an extensive historical corpus? And what are we to say when fiction claims the right to overturn 1400 years of devoted striving to make clear the distinction between fact and fable? Yes. A category mistake has been made. For Rushdie to tell us that facts are only tangentially necessary for his fiction is truly adding insult to that category injury.

'I am being enveloped in and described by a language that does not fit me', cries Rushdie. That's exactly what every believing Muslim said after reading his novel. Indeed, while this experience may be new for Rushdie, it is nothing new for Muslims. The culture of modernity, its ruling ideology of secularism, Orientalism – the Western study devoted to explaining Islam – all strive to fit the Muslims with false descriptions, false language, false identity. The pervasiveness of these 'images of ignorance' based upon a 'distorted imagination' are the attitudes that constructed and are confirmed by the whole of *The Satanic Verses*.

Abuse Being a Literary Language

And now to abuse and ridicule. First Rushdie offers his own crude parody of what the Muslims find offensive in the novel. Then he suggests that his critics are unfamiliar with the conventions of literary fiction . . . and quite incapable of distinguishing between the novelist and his characters. Let me state categorically: it is not the bits of the novel that Muslims find offensive: they find the rewriting of the *Sīra* as an insulting parody offensive; they find the attempt at the creation of an anti-Qur'ān ridiculously arrogant and offensive; they find the attempt at writing Muslim culture out of history offensive; they find being given the point-blank choice (even in fiction) of oblivion or total acceptance of triumphant secularism offensive; they find the argument that the only future they have in Britain is without their cultural identity offensive; they find the portrayal of believers, blacks and women offensive; and they find it offensive that religion can only be discussed in terms and conditions of secularism, that it is as secularism says it is, however foreign its portrayal of God and faith is to the believer. In short: Muslims find the whole damn novel offensive, 'not the piece of blubber, but the whole wretched whale'. By isolating the alleged Muslim offensive into a few sentences, Rushdie, as Webster points out, is 'doing precisely of what he alleges his Muslim critics are doing. He discusses a book which simply does not exist'.

The purpose of insulting, obscene and abusive language, argues Rushdie, is 'to create a literary language and literary forms in which the experience of formerly-colonised, still-disadvantaged people might find full expression'. Further explanation is provided from the novel itself: 'to turn insults into strengths, whigs, tories, Blacks all chose to wear with pride the names they were given in scorn'. First, who is Rushdie to undertake such an exercise on behalf of Muslims? Especially, when he tells us: 'I believe in no god, and have not done so since I was a young adolescent.' Thus, to argue, in Webster's words, 'That he is reclaiming language on behalf of all Muslims is an act of quite extraordinary presumption'. Second, do we really want to reclaim these images? Are all nasty historical images, products of ignorant and distorted perceptions as they are, worth reclaiming? Should the Blacks wear the epithet 'niggers' with pride? Should the Muslims go round reclaiming the Western historic legacy that describes them as fanatic, licentious, barbaric and bloodthirsty? Webster again: 'it is difficult to avoid the conclusion that . . . Salman Rushdie is offering to Muslim readers not a renewed sense of pride and dignity but an oblique and unintended invitation to internalise centuries of Christian contempt.'

And so to the central message of the novel. 'What does the novel dissent from?', asks Rushdie. 'Certainly not from people's right to faith, though I have none. It dissents most clearly from imposed orthodoxies of all types, from the view that the world is quite clearly This and not That.' Wrong again. By presenting faith as a cheap con-trick, the novel kills the option of faith for the reader. Moreover, by presenting his Babu world-view as *the* ideology of sweetness and light, worthy of any and all respect, Rushdie's fiction thrusts the undiluted acidic dogma of secularism down the throats of his unsuspecting readers. It offers not dissent but imposes the orthodoxy of doubt, the dogma of moral relativism and the creed of triumphant secularism. It is as liberating as the torture gadgetry of the Spanish Inquisition. When blasphemy is used in the fashion of Rushdie, Webster points out, 'there can be nothing liberating about it. For this is exactly the way in which blasphemy tends to be used by orthodox religious thinkers in order to sustain their own repressive ideologies of purity against the challenges posed by other cultures'.

The Convoluted Sermon

The arguments, if they can be described as such, in 'In Good Faith' are either of truly 'bewildering naivety' or are directed towards soft targets. For example, Rushdie finds it hard to believe that people 'have been willing to judge *The Satanic Verses* and its author, without reading it, without finding out what manner of man this fellow might be . . . ' But since the novel is written for Western audiences, and since for the vast majority of Muslims, as Rushdie tells us right at the beginning, fiction is quite meaningless, this is hardly surprising. Either Rushdie must concede that Muslims are intelligent and can and do read fiction as fiction, or he must concede that being fools they will judge him without reading his unreadable book. And what logic says that one has to read a book to judge its author? How many Marxists have dipped into *Das Kapital* let alone read it from cover to cover? How many of those who fought Hitler (who mentioned him?) for the manner of man he was actually read *Mein Kampft*? Even in British law, one has only to prove that an offence exists, not to prove that one has read the offensive material. But there is another more important point to be made here. Did it occur to the author of *The Satanic Verses* that his Western readers will accept his picture of the Prophet Muḥammad without ever trying to find out what manner of man he was? Did he not know that in his novel history and fable are so merged that knowledge is precluded, the potential for truth obscured, the ability to make reasoned evaluations fundamentally eroded, the possibility of dialogue made a nonsense? Does he really believe that after his long and convoluted sermon, his readers will rush out to find out for themselves what manner of world-view is Islam?

Apart from mute non-statements, Rushdie has no answers to the cogent criticism of Muslim protesters such as Shabbir Akhtar, Ali Mazrui and others. Instead, crude character assassination wins the day: so Rana Kabbani is described as a 'Stalinist' for pointing out that 'writers should be accountable to the community'! As Webster notes, this is a particularly ironic charge since the novelist Martin Amis, an enthusiastic supporter, already subscribes to this view – but, on this point Rushdie follows a clear logic: anyone who dares to criticize him or his sacrosanct art must either be a lunatic or a follower of some nasty authoritarian character of European history.

A Lonely Saint

In the end, Rushdie tries to paint himself as a lonely saint bravely trying to stop the tide of fundamentalist wrath that is coming towards him: 'the solitary figure of a single writer brandishing an "unreadable" book' against 'a religion boasting one billion believers'. He told his friend Blake Morrison, in the *Independent on Sunday* interview (also published in *Granta* 31, Spring 1990, pp.113–25; Penguin, London), 'there was so much of it, a whole tidal wave coming at me, and I just couldn't shout loud enough to be heard'. This from a man who has sold over a million copies in hardback, had his wayward novel translated even into obscure European languages, who can, by simply lifting a phone, be on the front page of any newspaper, anywhere in Europe or the United States, or any television news bulletin, or even turn himself into a lengthy documentary without any effort. Add to this the support of the European and American liberal establishment, that generated pro-Rushdie and anti-Muslim copy and footage greater than Mount Cone, one can safely say that Rushdie has the intellectual and communication resources of the entire Western civilization behind him. And even after all the political, social and cultural havoc he has caused, he still demands his paperback: 'if the paperback doesn't exist, the book has effectively been suppressed.' So freedom of expression now includes the right to be in paperback: if this is the case then there are countless authors, including this one, who are being denied this freedom. Would someone stand up and defend us? The irony is that this 'solitary', egoist writer of fortune is holding a billion believers to ransom!

Pieces of Literary Polemics

Both 'Is Nothing Sacred?' and 'In Good Faith' have been hailed as the 'greatest pieces of literary polemics ever written'. Indeed, it seems that Rushdie cannot write anything that can be described by ordinary, human, superlatives. This is partly because he is championing an ideology, an ideology which is incapable of questioning its own assumptions, which sees all Muslims as 'fanatics' and 'fundamentalists'. And partly because he has the undying support of a group of friends who occupy key positions in the media. The situation is such that if Rushdie coughed a diseased phlegm on the face of one of his novelist friends, it would be captured on film by Tariq Ali and turned into a documentary, which would be commissioned by Farouk Dhondy and shown in the 'Rear Window' slot of Channel Four; Blake Morrison would reprint it as the lead story in *The Independent on Sunday* which would also contain an instant poll of various luminaries (Harold Pinter, Fay Weldon, Margaret Drabble, Ian McEwan, Arnold Wesker, Penelope Lively, Michael Foot: 'it is the most brilliant piece of political writing I've ever read in my life' (what an impoverished life!), et al.) and, Hanif Qureshi would write a lyrical appreciation of it in the *Guardian* as well as make an extensive appearance on 'The Late Show' or 'The South Bank Show' ('The more filthy the better as far as I am concerned, I too have spat a lot of phlegm in my life . . . '), Bill Buford would put it on the cover of *Granta* and Granta would also publish the damn thing as a pamphlet.

The Supremist Malaise

Malise Ruthven too sees Muslims in much the same light with one difference: they are not just enemies of freedom, they are also definitely inferior beings. Unlike Rushdie who keeps his liberal supremacy at a subtle level, Ruthven, who I first met during my days at *Arabia: Islamic World Review* some ten years ago, is unashamedly supremist. In his world, there is a strong, rigid, pecking order with liberal secularists topping the bill. One knows that one is in familiar territory right from page one. Scene: Hyde Park, London. Action: Amongst the French, Spanish and the Dutch, and the 'sophisticated, suave metropolitans like the blacks', all wandering around the park, some 'utterly foreign', 'aliens' are observed. These aliens look 'wild and scraggy with curly, grey-flecked beards' and 'wear white hats and long baggy trousers with flapping shirt tails'. Dialogue: '*I* am writing a book. Have *you* read *The Satanic Verses*? What about Dante?' Commentary: 'Until recent times, women were positively discouraged from praying in mosques, lest they distract men from their devotions.' Source for Commentary: Edward Lane, *An Account of the Manners and Customs of the Modern Egyptians,* London, 1836. Who? Edward Lane, the gentleman-scholar of the colonial times who found the Egyptians to be sexually inflammable and perverted, depraved, violent, obstinate, stupid with a tendency to venerate idiots and, at least some of them, having a strong penchant for eating glass (see Rana Kabbani's analysis in *Europe's Myth of the Orient,* Macmillan, London, 1986). Ruthven is a postmodern reincarnation of Lane, and *A Satanic Affair* (Chatto & Windus, London, 1990) is Victorian paternalism and jingoism at its best.

The 'aliens' in the park are from the Indian subcontinent and are Muslims, inferior to Arabs. They are 'harsh, neurotic and insecure'. Unlike the Arabs who are secure in their identity because the Qur'ān is in Arabic, the 'Indo-Muslim identity . . . is still unsure of itself: it thrives on conflict and persecution, for only through such can it reinforce its sense of distinctiveness.' If the poor sods feel persecuted there may be a strong reason for it; after all they are living in a society that discriminates against them. But what's this about they 'thrive on violence?' Does this reflect the legacy of Edward Lane or is it an observation? Until the Rushdie affair blew up, the subcontinental Muslims were described as model, law-abiding citizens. Indeed, even Ruthven admits that 'If race were taken out of the equation, many, perhaps most, Bradford Muslims, would reveal themselves to be model Tory citizens.' Make up your mind man: either they are model tories or conflict-seeking, bloodthirsty renegades? But consistency and logic are not Ruthven's strong points.

Distorting History

To say that Ruthven is totally confused would be the merest inkling of the true state of affairs. He tells us that the 'doctrine' that the Prophet was merely the recipient of revelation and did not interfere with it was 'canonized' in the ninth century after the debate between the Mutazilis and some group called '*Ḥadīth* Folk'. Does that mean that the Muslims before that period believed that the revelation was interfered with by the Prophet? If so, why does not history – the same history that does not bother to hide the incident of the Satanic verses – tell us so? The debate about the created or uncreated nature of the Qur'ān was between the Mutazilis and the Asharites – and not '*Ḥadīth* Folk' and continued till the tenth century. We have numerous other equally banal statements. He tells us, for example, that death by stoning is a Qur'ānic injunction; it is not in the Qur'ān. In Islam, we are informed, 'to question is to question the rule of God': yet, questioning is *the* methodology of the Qur'ān, the Qur'ān repeatedly asks questions and exhorts believers and unbelievers to ask questions and seek their answers. We are further told that 'the methodology of the *ḥadīth* collectors depended more on *isnāds* than content'. Does that mean that if a *ḥadīth* is contrary to Qur'ānic teachings it was accepted because the *isnād* was foolproof? Why did the Muslim scholars then insist that any valid *ḥadīth* must agree with the Qur'ān and reason before one proceeds to check the *isnād?* Were they really so foolish as to travel for hundreds of miles checking for *isnād* while the content was clearly against the Qur'ān or reason? Something is wrong somewhere – and it is in Ruthven's head. A point made amply clear when we hear Ruthven announce that 'Sunni Islam, lacking in educated priesthood, seemed to have committed the sin of *shirk,* by elevating the Qur'ān to the level of God.' Does that mean that Shī'a Islam does not regard the Qur'ān as the Word of God? The Qur'ān is Islam: to be a Muslim is to (voluntarily) accept that the commands of the Qur'ān are the commands of God. 'Muslim apologists', we read further, 'rationalise the Prophet's twelve wives . . . in terms of his needs to form political and tribal alliances' but 'like Joseph Smith, the Mormon prophet, Muḥammad may have justified his sexual urges by reference to divine revelation.' Ruthven too has his sexual urges as we learn when he encounters a prostitute, in the good company of Shabbir Akhtar, and wants to give her some money to 'listen' (tell us another one!) to her. Would Ruthven, then, be ready to marry elderly widows much past their prime? Would he marry an old woman who was about to die in three months? Can he deny that, even today, marriage plays a great part in bringing warring tribes together and strengthening tribal loyalties in Arabia? Secular apologists have developed a strange knack of imposing their personal, convoluted and irrational theories on data that can easily be explained on the basis of real historical facts.

Ruthven has taken the classical bogey of the Prophet's marriages from Maxime Rodinson. His methodology has three components. First, to give himself scholarly pretensions he uses a number of select, aggressively anti-Islamic Orientalists, old and new, who also help justify his absurd and outlandish theories. Thus Michael Cook, the co-author of *Hagarism,* who argues that Islam is a barbaric conspiracy with Judaic roots (see M.D. Valimamad's review in *MWBR,* Vol.1, No.2 (1981), pp.64–6), is the main source for Ruthven's portrait of the Prophet. Supporting cast includes Sir William Muir, the nineteenth-century Orientalist who painted a picture of the Prophet as an anti-thesis of Jesus (Jesus was chaste, Muḥammad was sensual; Jesus loved peace, Muḥammad was violent; Jesus was sincere, Muḥammad was insincere – in short, Jesus was good and holy, Muḥammad was bad and evil); and John Wansbrough, A. Guillaume and W. Montgomery Watt. To counter the criticism he may receive for using a particular category of jingoist Orientalists, Ruthven states that 'pious Muslims have occasionally taken offence at the treatment' of the Prophet 'by such writers'. I suppose that since they are pious, it automatically excludes them from being intelligent, objective and critical! Drawing freely from these authors, Ruthven tells us that the Prophet behaved with 'utter ruthlessness', that the origins of the Qur'ānic text are obscure, *Zinā* (adultery) strikes at the root of the Islamic cosmic order and historic *Dār al-Islām* was like 'the old pre-Gorbachev Soviet bloc'. The first two suggestions are, of course, a total distortion of history, the second a product of Ruthven's deranged mind, but the reasons for the last comparison are interesting. Apparently, some *fuqahā'* (jurists) forbade Muslims to go to *Dār al-Ḥarb.* It does not occur to Ruthven that such a ruling may have been introduced during the period when Muslim travellers risked their lives by entering non-Muslim lands. After all, the Christians of yore were not all that hospitable towards the 'Saracens'.

Labelling Muslims

The second component of Ruthven's method is labelling; if you label someone, say call them fundamentalist, then obviously you have understood them. We are thus treated to a classification of Muslims in Britain, like the Deobandis, Barelwi and Tablighi Jamaat who get their funding from Saudi Arabia (a little difficult when they are banned from the country). The Islamic movement, we are told, has two mainsprings: the Ahmadiyya which exercises an influence on the 'better educated' despite the fact that its founder Mirza Ghulam Ahmad (1839–1908) 'announced that he was receiving revelations directly from God' and went on to declare himself 'an avatar of Krishna' and claimed that 'he travelled to Kashmir and Afghanistan in order to convert the Ten Lost Tribes of Israel'; and the other *Jamā'at-e-Islāmī,* which is an extreme right-wing fundamentalist organization. Thus enlightened, Ruthven tells his readers that the notion of *izzat,* or honour, dictates everything these groups do and everyone, but everyone, suffers from some kind of sexual hang-up. Most have 'trouble performing with wives they have no feelings for, wives chosen by their relatives in Pakistan'. Local prostitutes thus do brisk business: 'there was no scandal to the faith in the services (they) render the community . . . no threat to *izzat* in the back-to-backs.'

The third aspect of Ruthven's methodology is to ransack unsavoury Muslim fringe groups and use their literature and opinions both to provide evidence for his absurd theories and as a trump card in discussion. Thus, we are told that 'embedded in the generalised anti-Western thrust of fundamentalist discourse there exists a specific anti-semitic thread'. The evidence for this generalization comes from the articles of Yaqub Zaki. Does Mosley provide us with evidence that there is a general anti-semitic trend in Britain? We are further told that 'in the Islamic literary tradition' superhuman myths are attributed to Muḥammad: 'he was born circumcised, the earth swallowed up his excrement (does she not swallow all our excrement?) . . . His shirt was enough to cure a Jew's blindness . . . ' This is at the same level as considering the journalism of the *Sun* as the literary tradition of Britain. (You know, all those stories about vivacious nurses and naughty vicars bonking in the church garden!) In Bradford, Ruthven asks a Muslim scientist called 'Anwar', (who, my friends in Bradford assure me, does not exist): 'Isn't there a conflict between the Qur'ānic view of creation and Darwinian evolution'; and then tells the reader that he did not want to remind Anwar about Shaikh bin Baz, the blind Saudi jurist, who declared that the earth was flat. I would not want to remind Ruthven about the countless liberal secularists who go around looking for UFOs or religiously read such primers as *The Chariots of God* and other similar lunacies. But I would like to invite him to come and ask me the questions he asked 'Anwar': I would take great pleasure in teaching him Darwinism and the Qur'ānic view of science!

Ruthven goes around Bradford cornering various people and engaging them in discussion. 'I went to Bradford to listen', he tells us repeatedly; but the statement is used, every time, to make a condescending point. He meets Sher Azam, President of the Council of Mosques, and presents two arguments: (1) *The Satanic Verses* is a work of fiction, and you have to see the book as a whole, not just offending bits out of context, and (2) no one is compelled to buy a book they do not like. The first argument I have already tackled in my discussion of Rushdie's 'In Good Faith'; let me answer the second question in the way it deserves to be answered. Suppose I write a fictional work based on the life of Malise Ruthven. I change certain details but ensure that he is clearly recognizable as Malise Ruthven, writer and journalist. The details I change make him look like . . . well, lets just say a really nasty piece of work with all manner of evil sidelines. Will Ruthven worry about buying the book or will he take me to court for libel and defamation? When Duncan Campbell, the investigative journalist, recently found himself in a similar situation, as victim of a BBC drama-doc, he did not worry about watching it in his sitting room – he took the BBC to court and won. The idea that an offence only exists if you buy a book is a particularly dumbfounding one. The same can be said of the other question he asks Anwar: 'You have studied Islam and know that what's in the book isn't true. Why does it matter, since you know the truth?' Knowing the truth does not repeal an offence: Ruthven knows the truth about my proposed book about him; it does not mean that the libel and defamation it contains have been sorted out. Ruthven takes great pride in scoring points from people who are not equipped to defend themselves. However, when he meets Shabbir Akhtar the tables are turned. He has no answer to the counter-arguments produced by Akhtar – he thus resorts to character assassination and suggests that Akhtar should consider therapy! The kettle proposing a solution for a black pot!

Eventually, Ruthven wanders into a conference where an impressive account of *The Satanic Verses,* locating it in the context of world literature, is being presented. Ruthven tells us that the Muslim gathering at the conference had serious problems in understanding the beauty of magical realism. 'There is something wrong when a book of this kind is called literature', Muslims kept shouting. This was a strange reaction on their part as magical realism developed by Jorge Borges and Gabreil Garcia Marquez in South America deliberately subverts the dominant mode of narrative realism by introducing surrealistic events. This subversion of narrative forms has a political dimension: 'it involved a deliberate, self-conscious attempt to break with the cultural imperialism of European form.' Since *The Satanic Verses* fiasco, we have had a long line of bearded academics telling us that magical realism is a new and liberating form of literature that benefits Third World folk. First: there is nothing new in magical realism – it is there in Kafka and Beckett. Second: Borges, Garcia, Llosa, Fuentes et al. are more European than South American: as they themselves emphasize and is obvious in their politics and attitudes towards the indigenous people of Latin America. An issue in Mario Vargas Llosa's campaign for the presidency of Peru was his condescending attitude towards the Peruvian Indians. Indeed, more aware South American novelists, like Vlady Kociancich (author of *The Last Days of William Shakespear,* Heinemann, London, 1990), although a student of Borges and still writing in a similar genre, cannot distance themselves further from the magical realists. Third: magical realism gives the appearance of speaking from the perspective that incorporates the Other but in so doing it merely utilizes that conception of the Other that fits within the Orientalist paradigm. The grotesqueries in *Midnights Children* could have sat happily in Kipling; Carlos Fuentes' murdering, looting, obnoxious Mexican revolutionary in *The Old Gringo* would have no problem in finding a place in any conventional, anti-Mexican novel. Those who sing the praises of magical realism as a liberating literary force are in fact promoting a new brand of a favourite Western brew: 'cultural imperialism'.

Islamic Fundamentalism

Throughout the book, Ruthven glibly compares Christian and Islamic fundamentalism and applies the characteristics of one to the other. But Christian fundamentalism and Islamic fundamentalism have merely an 'ism' in common – they are not comparable 'isms'. The distinction is to be found in the adjectives Christian and Islamic. Both 'isms' arise from different roots, are founded on different texts, history of ideas and institutional and philosophic worlds of thought and action. Neither are simplistic movements and both contain many diverse shades of opinion and interpretative stances. The crucial point is that both fundamentalisms are interpretative even though their approach is literal in the sense of self-evident meaning of their founding texts. Christian fundamentalism is incomprehensible without knowing the history of Christianity and the modern disputes of Christian exegesis that have occasioned a variety and diversity of fundamentalist responses. The same is true of 'Islamic fundamentalism', but here a major distinction must be added. The term 'Islamic fundamentalism' has been imposed rather than chosen by the Muslim proponents of a variety of interpretations of the contemporary meaning of being a Muslim. If the definitional points and doctrinal argumentation of Christian fundamentalism were put to such Muslims they would deny, as articles of their very faith, that they could or should or in fact do subscribe to such notions. To analyse Islamic fundamentalism as if it were a Christian response to the Bible is total nonsense.

Ruthven comes up with two insights by studying 'Islamic fundamentalism' in terms of 'Christian fundamentalism': (1) the privatizing of religion is an essential component of what is generally called 'fundamentalism'; and (2) materialism is central to fundamentalism. For Muslims, we are told, this 'privatisation . . . takes the form of internalising the text of the Qur'ān'. This is of course a totally postmodern statement: it is quite meaningless. All believing Muslims try to internalize the text of the Qur'ān – that is the definition of being a Muslim. It is the Sufis who, by common consent, succeed most in internalizing the text of the Qur'ān: but they are generally considered to be at the opposite end of the scale to fundamentalism. And Muslim fundamentalists are no more or less materialists than non-fundamentalists: the vast majority of those dubbed 'fundamentalists' in Pakistan, India,

Bangladesh, Iran, Turkey, Tunisia, Algeria, Nigeria and the Sudan are poor people, existing just above subsistence level. To dub them materialist is the height of secularist folly.

This absurd analysis has a purpose. It labels Muslims with certain characteristics which enables Ruthven to reach his preconceived conclusion: 'Islamic fundamentalism, like fascism, holds out the vision of a "fully integrated" society free from damaging divisions of class and wealth . . . Like fascism, it seeks a psychological foundation in absolute certainty: the only difference being that instead of the Will of the Leader, it relies on the Will of God . . . The fundamentalist mentality – absolutist, anti-democratic and highly authoritarian – is prone to see conspiracies where none exist . . .' So Hitler comes in useful again. But what is this: Ruthven actually likes Muslims: 'I am', he writes, 'well disposed towards religious fundamentalism'. Why? The answer is given a few pages later where Ruthven delivers his *coup de grace*: 'fundamentalism . . . is hard, factualistic and philistine, impervious to the multi-layered nuances of meaning that reside in texts, in fiction, in music and iconographies, in the cell of art and culture where modernity – that universal modernity created by a vibrant, still dynamic "West" – stores its spiritual wealth.' So, fundamentalism may be inferior, but Ruthven is well disposed towards it because he is a supremist: like the fascist, he believes in the purity of his dominating and subjugating culture, that 'universal modernity' that preserves the purity and hegemony of the 'vibrant, still dynamic West'. Ruthven's supremist mediocrity does not allow him to see the naivety of his statement. If the spirituality of Ruthven's culture is only found in texts, fiction, music and iconographies, then it is a very impoverished spirituality for it is not readily accessible; moreover, it is only accessible to a select few since only the elite plough through literary texts and fiction, appreciate classical music, and patronize art galleries. Or, is one to believe that all pop music, pulp fiction, cultish iconography is spiritually uplifting? It is a basic tenet of belief of postmodernist writers that great art and literature is only accessible in the seminar rooms of universities and colleges; that the ordinary mass of people have nothing to do with literature and art – indeed, they should be kept away from such enterprises!

We now move to the climax of Ruthven's hierarchical litany. This time it is that of cultural evolution wherein the Greek alphabet is the fittest not merely to survive but to triumph over the rest with their lingering associations with that most primitive stage of all, the fully oral culture, wherein the residents of his subcontinental imaginings are to be located since they merely know the Qur'ān as a sound form – as a literary text it is incomprehensible to them. Islam is inferior because it is an oral culture. As evidence Ruthven tells us: 'the deep connection with orality is maintained in Islamic law, where oral testimony still predominates and written affidavits are not usually taken in evidence.' Writing things down has been the Muslim custom since the inception of Islam. The Qur'ān says: 'When you contract a debt for a fixed term, record it in writing' (2: 282). Writing was common when the Qur'ān was revealed; the Prophet recorded all his contracts and treaties in writing. In an Islamic court, oral testimony is preferred to written affidavits for a simple reason: affidavits can be obtained under duress; oral testimony allows the person concerned to speak freely in the presence of a judge. The case of the Guildford Four – who were imprisoned on the basis of confessions signed under pressure from the police, and released several years later after their convictions were quashed – illustrates the point well. . . .

Murderous Act

In 'In Good Faith', Rushdie asks: 'How is freedom gained?' And answers: 'It is taken: never given.' In a world where secularist magicians wield the power of description and render invisible and inaudible any information or reasoned argument that challenges their talisman, Muslims have to take their freedom and break out of their authoritarian spell. We must fight to ensure that we have access and freedom to describe ourselves with our own languages and categories. Secularism demands that Muslims answer only as questioned, according to the agenda of relevant issues determined by the secular imagination – whether or not these are relevant to Muslim inquiry. The very act of answering these questions is an act of subjugation and willing cultural annihilation. As Webster reminds us so eloquently, in this 'secularised and agnostic culture the greatest threat to human values seems increasingly likely to come not from murderous faith, as it has done for many centuries, but from murderous art'. Muslims must ensure that they set their own agenda of issues and discussion and not be led by a murderous sect of confused and ignorant, but highly articulate and powerful, secularist *literati*.

. . . The existential anxiety of Rushdie and Ruthven sees its expression in the supremist and authoritarian theology that is postmodern fiction. Their products are like the museum of photography designed by a blind architect. There will always be individuals ready to admire and pay a high price for their 'art'.

Source: *Muslim World Book Review,* 11/1, 1990, pp. 3–19.

Islam and the Return of Rushdie as the Prodigal Son

. . . With reference to Philip J. Stewart's letter (2 January) regarding Salman Rushdie's "offence", it seems that following the author's reported conversion to Islam, not only non-Muslims but some Muslims too, are confused over the issue. That Rushdie is an apostate and has blasphemed against Islam by abusing the Prophet *(Shatm al-Rasul)* in *The Satanic Verses* has not only been maintained by Iran but also by more than 40 member states of the Organisation of Islamic Conference (OIC) at their Foreign Ministers' Conference held in Riyadh in March 1989.

The author cannot be automatically absolved of the offence following his conversion to Islam if the book continues in circulation and the author does not repent of having written it. Indeed, his affirmation of Islam becomes meaningless if the offence he had committed by writing and publishing *The Satanic Verses* continues in circulation in the form of hardback and translations.

This is why the UK Action Committee on Islamic Affairs and other Muslim leaders in Britain and abroad have doubted his sincerity in embracing Islam and regarded it as "an apparent ploy to get him off the hook". Notwithstanding his somersaults regarding the publication of the paperback edition, his crime becomes all the more grave if he claims to be a Muslim and continues to insult the Prophet and Islam through the continued publication and circulation of the sacrilegious book worldwide.

M. Manazir Ahsan
Director General
The Islamic Foundation
Leicester
2 January

Source: ©*The Independent,* 4th January 1991.

Back Into the Fold?

by Shabbir Akhtar

Salman Rushdie, the prodigal son of Islam, wishes to return home. Fair enough. But there is a distant land from which no one returns. Let Rushdie find his way home; and the Muslim father will forgive.

Nor is fear a disreputable motive for conversion. Islam is not Christianity; and fear, no less than love, is a worthy emotion. But while the fear of Allah is a virtue, fear of others around us is cowardice. The suspicion is that Rushdie fears the Iranians, while Allah has a greater claim upon this emotion.

Rushdie is welcome to convert to Islam, if he wishes. He is not doing a favour to anyone; on the contrary, Allah is doing him a favour by guiding him to Islam. But Rushdie must "enter fully into a state of peace and submission" (Qur'an: 2:208). This is, therefore, the fundamental attitude all believers should cultivate.

Actions normally speak louder than words. But actions must at least reflect and be compatible with one's speeches. So his book, *The Satanic Verses,* must go. We have had enough of Rushdie's Faustian nonsense. *The Satanic Verses* is acknowledged, even by many non-Muslims, to be a calculated attempt to vilify and slander Prophet Muhammad (peace be upon him) and his noble spouses and companions. Certain characters, such as the Persian companion of Prophet Muhammad, Salman al-Farsi, are created afresh specifically as mouthpieces through whom Rushdie can parody the principles of Islam.

Again, Mahound is an offensive description that no self-confessing Muslim has ever applied to the noble Prophet of Allah. So conclusive is the case against the continued publication of *The Satanic Verses* at this late hour that no fair-minded observer has any choice in the matter.

Conversions to a faith can be sincere or opportunist. Anyone who publicly declares that "There is no God except Allah, and Muhammad is His last envoy" is a Muslim. Once one sincerely utters that statement, such an individual must then attempt to live according to the laws of Islam. Rushdie would be no exception.

Individuals who genuinely convert to a faith often display a kind of zeal not found in ordinary adherents. If Rushdie is to be the St Paul of Islam, he must immediately stop persecuting his brothers. *The Satanic Verses* must be withdrawn as proof of his sincerity. Otherwise, Muslims are entitled to doubt his motives.

Muslims have suffered grievously during the Rushdie episode. Admittedly, he has also suffered much and has little chance of resuming a normal life in the near future. He is, nevertheless, lucky for there is still a possibility that one day he will. But those Muslims who have died during the affair have no chance of resuming any kind of life. The dependents of those martyrs now live in abject poverty, entirely dependent on our charity. Rushdie should apologise to these people. If they demand retaliation or compensation, they are entitled to it. If they forgive and remit, agreeing to forego their right, Allah will exalt them further.

Muslims in Britain are, naturally, not in a charitable mood. Years of racism and isolation have embittered the most innocent, generous and pure-hearted among us. We may forgive; we won't forget. It is up to Rushdie to create a mood of reconciliation. His continued insistence that his novel is not meant to be offensive does not help matters. If one wishes to enjoy a romantic evening, one does not begin by fighting with one's wife.

Hostile forces to Islam recognise that it is hard to convert Muslims to other faiths. They have therefore been busy trying to encourage Muslims to be unfaithful to their own traditions. Such disloyalty would be a first step towards disbelief. "Subvert, if not convert" is their motto. Muslims will, of course, always remain loyal to Islam; and the more Islam is attacked, the more it grows in strength.

Let us return to our main theme – the withdrawal of the

blasphemous book, *The Satanic Verses.* Throughout this period, Rushdie has frequently been rewriting the commandments and changing his opinions. Clinically and cynically, he exploits every situation to his advantage. Like his friends in the "Liberal Inquisition", he has little respect for the laws of consistency. Once upon a time, *The Satanic Verses* was written in order to "break various orthodox taboos" – to shatter the myth of the Prophet's righteousness and the authenticity of the Qur'an vouchsafed to him. Recently, he asked Muslims to believe that his novel was never intended to be offensive. Can we take him seriously?

In contrast, Muslim protesters have maintained a remarkably consistent stance throughout the last two years or so. What is wrong is wrong and eternally so. Our demands have been simple and modest. Muslims have believed sincerely in the truth of their cause; they have behaved magnanimously and mercifully.

It is now widely recognised that Muslims are the best readers of *The Satanic Verses.* The Liberal Inquisition does not know Islam; it merely pretends to despise it while secretly admiring it. None of Rushdie's literary supporters have the kind of multi-lingual scholarship required for any proper reading of a book written in half a dozen languages. As for the so called experts on Islam who believe – Muslims cannot assess the nature of their own faith – well, their days are numbered. After Rushdie orientalism is not merely irreverent, but irrelevant.

In the current climate of confrontation, there can be no neutral or apolitical uses of any piece of writing on Islam. This is necessarily true of a book that has wounded an entire civilisation. Indeed, deciding precisely how much of the surrounding political context should be read into the text of Rushdie's novel is itself a political, not literary, judgement.

The days of imposed leadership and expertise are over. Our religious scholars are the creators of our past; our thinkers are the creators of our present; our pure-hearted young men and women are the hope of our future. The rest do not count in our battle. They are, as Nietzsche would say, merely mankind.

The Rushdie affair has proved that, to Muslims, books matter and that there is a book around that can still move mountains. "Mahound," Rushdie's character, "wrote a book" that has continued to topple the dynasties for centuries. As the Germans say, one is afraid of the fellow who writes one book in a life-time, not the one who writes one every year. The West, for all its claims to intellectual achievement, does not see scholarship and knowledge as anything more than a means to secular power. Islam, the intellectual religion par excellence, knows the true value of the scholar's ink.

In any case, we Muslims have consistently given a clear message, saying nothing merely out of malice and leaving nothing unsaid merely out of cowardice. For if the trumpet gives an uncertain sound, who shall prepare for battle? It is for us to state our case, not pleading for any help except from Allah – our only Lord and Patron. And victory is near.

Source: *Africa Events,* 7/2, February 1991.

A Testimony: Rushdie's Commercialized Blasphemy

by Ali A. Mazrui

. . . Salman Rushdie has "distanced" himself from some of his characters in *The Satanic Verses.* He has dissociated himself from the blasphemy of the characters he has created. Would you agree that is a major concession to the sensibilities of Muslims?

Verbal distancing from blasphemy is easier than financial "distancing". I assume Salman Rushdie is still collecting royalties from new sales of *The Satanic Verses.* How can that be regarded as "dissociation" from the blasphemy of the novel? Rushdie is still gaining from commercialized blasphemy . . .

Salman Rushdie recently announced that he has converted to Islam and therefore he should automatically be forgiven for the offence he committed against Islam. That is the death *fatwa* should be lifted as well. Some Muslims have doubted his sincerity, arguing that he only announced his conversion in order to save his skin. What are your comments?

It would be difficult to dispute his sincerity if he was indeed to forego millions of earnings from *The Satanic Verses.* If he made such a sacrifice, we would have to give him the benefit of the doubt.

As for the *fatwa,* the Ayatullahs in Iran and other Muslims have taken the position that what is done cannot be undone by saying "I am sorry". Under Western law, remorse is not a reason for not punishing an offender either. What Western traitor or murderer escaped punishment by saying "I am sorry"? . . .

Source: *Africa Events* (London), 7/2, February 1991, p. 39.

APPENDIX I

Correspondence on the Affair

(a) *Letter sent by the Islamic Foundation, Leicester, to Muslim Organizations, Mosques, and Prominent Muslim Leaders in Britain*

3rd October, 1988

Dear Brother in Islam,

As-salamu Alaykum.

May Allah keep you in the best of health and Iman (Ameen).

With deep anguish and distress we are writing this note to draw your attention to the recently published blasphemous novel, *The Satanic Verses* by Salman Rushdie (Penguin 1988). This work, thinly disguised as a piece of literature, not only grossly distorts the Islamic history in general, but also portrays in the worst possible colours the very characters of the Prophet Ibrahim and the Prophet Muhammad (peace be upon them).

It may however be clarified that the Prophet Muhammad (peace be upon him) is referred to in this novel as 'Mahound' – a misnomer used about him in the medieval West. The work also disfigures the characters of the Prophet's Companions (Bilal, Salman, Farsi, Hamza, Abu Sufyan, Hind, Khalid and several others – may Allah be pleased with them) and the Prophet's holy wives; and describes the Islamic creed and rituals in the most foul language. Some of the relevant extracts from the novel, quite painful to read, are enclosed for your perusal and an early action.

Based on the myth of the interpolation of the so-called 'Satanic Verses' into the Qur'an, this novel stands out as the crassest sacrilege of all that is sacred for the Muslims.

In view of the sinister nature of the novel and the irreparable damage it would inflict on the image of Islam, we request you to take a united stand on this issue and demand the authorities/publisher to withdraw this novel immediately and make a public apology for the offence caused to Islam and Muslims.

To begin with, you should kindly make it a point to record immediately your protest with the publisher, either by post or telephone, preferably both.

Postal address:	Penguin Publishers, Ltd., 27 Wrights Lane, LONDON, W.8
By telephone:	01-938 2200 (Publicity Section, Viking, Penguin Books)

May Allah reward you for doing urgently all that is possible in this noble cause.

Wassalam.

Yours in Islam,

Dr. M.M. Ahsan, Director General
Syed Faiyazuddin Ahmad, Director, Public Relations and Administration
Dr. A.R. Kidwai, Research Fellow

P.S. Enclosed please find an article exploding the myth of the 'Satanic Verses'.*

*This article appears on pp. 131–41 of this book.

(b) *Letter sent by the UK Action Committee on Islamic Affairs, London, to Penguin Books*

19th October 1988

Mr. T. Glover,
Penguin Books
27 Wrights Lane,
LONDON, W8

Dear Mr. Glover,

We are an action committee, formed to represent the major Muslim Organisations of the United Kingdom, to respond to the publication by yourselves, of a book by Salman Rushdie, entitled the 'Satanic Verses'.

This book has greatly offended and disgusted the Muslim Community, not only in the United Kingdom, but also worldwide and it is our desire that you should firstly offer us some sort of explanation as to why such a piece of fiction should be published in the first place, completely disregarding the feelings of almost 1 billion Muslims worldwide and secondly, that you should cease publication immediately and withdraw the book forthwith.

We understand that there have already been death threats made against the Author (Daily Telegraph, 12/10/1988) and although we condemn such violent reactions, it must be realised that certain quarters will be so angered by the book that they may well decide to take such drastic steps. We are therefore concerned that the continued sale of this book may incite much unwanted violence, which we all want to avoid and we hope you will take serious consideration of this point.

Also we understand that there are moves afoot to begin a total ban in the Muslim countries of all the publications of Penguin and its subsidiaries or sub-publishers and again we would hope that you would not take such a thing too lightly.

It is also hoped that we may be able to resolve this matter without having to meet in person with yourselves, but if you desire a meeting, please contact us to arrange it.

Yours sincerely,

Iqbal Sacranie,
Joint Convenor

N.B. We are also sending a protest signed within 1/2 hour after Friday congregational prayer at the Central Mosque in London. This is only a specimen of what may follow from the hundreds of other mosques.

(c) *Reply to UK Action Committee on Islamic Affairs from Viking*

24th October 1988

Mr Iqbal Sacranie
Joint Convenor
UK Action Committee
on Islamic Affairs
146 Park Road
London NW8 7RG

Dear Mr Sacranie,

Thank you for your letter of 19th October and the petition of protest included with it. We have noted their contents.

We are sorry for any distress the book has caused you and some of your fellow-Muslims, but we feel your reaction is based on a misreading of the book. We can't put it better than the reviewer in last week's *Listener*: 'the novel doesn't debunk Islam at all but on the contrary endorses it as one of the "grand narratives" we use in order to make sense of our experience.' Furthermore, as a purely literary work the book has received the highest possible praise: in London, the *Sunday Times* called it 'a masterpiece' and in India, the *Indian Post* characterized it as 'wondrous and uplifting' – these are just two of many such reviews that we could quote. We don't expect to be able to change your mind about the novel, but we hope this goes some way towards answering your question as to why we thought it worth publishing. You ask that the book be withdrawn: we don't believe any purpose is ever served in banning books, and certainly not in this case where the book has already been widely circulated and widely praised. We, and Mr Rushdie, do indeed take seriously the threats to which you refer. We can only say as non-Moslems that we find it very distressing that followers of a great religion like Islam can threaten violence in this way, and we pray that nothing comes of them. We hope you are able to use your influence to prevent any further threats being issued: apart from the fact that all such threats are humanly to be abhorred, they surely only add to the notoriety of the book and increase the public's interest in it, which is clearly not the hope of the people who issue them.

Yours sincerely,

Viking Editorial Director

Statement issued by The Penguin Group

We wish to make it clear that, despite a number of requests from Islamic organisations and members of the public to withdraw Salman Rushdie's novel from sale, we cannot do this. To do so would be wholly inconsistent with our position as a serious publisher who believes in freedom of expression.

Opinions may differ about any work, but we never set out to publish with intent to offend. We certainly regret any distress the book may have caused but we believe that calling the book blasphemous and offensive to Islam is the result in many cases of a failure to read in its entirety what is, after all, a work of fiction.

The sequence most commonly cited happens, in the words of its author, "in a dream, the fictional dream of an Indian movie star, and one who is losing his mind, at that."

The Satanic Verses has been enthusiastically received by reviewers and literary critics in the countries in which it has so far appeared, namely in Britain and Canada. It is being published in nine languages around the world. It is perceived as a major and serious literary work by one of the most gifted novelists writing today in English. His earlier books have become standard works of modern literature. The Sunday Times reviewer referred to his new book as 'a masterpiece' and the reviewer in the Indian Post called it 'wondrous and uplifting'.

These are only two of hundreds of examples from newspapers, magazines and literary reviews that could be quoted. In recognition of its qualities, *The Satanic Verses* was shortlisted for the 1988 Booker Prize, Britain's foremost award for literary fiction, an award Rushdie won earlier with his novel *Midnight's Children*. The new work has just won first prize in the fiction category of the Whitbread Award.

We would only add as a general proposition that we do not believe any purpose is served by the banning of books and we vigorously defend that principle.

The Penguin Group

APPENDIX II

Correspondence with the Home Office Minister

Mr Patten's Letter
to Muslim Leaders in Britain

HOME OFFICE
Queen Anne's Gate
London SW1H 9AT

4 July 1989

Dear ....

I am writing to you, and to a number of other influential British Muslims, to set forth in full some of our recent thinking in the light of continuing concern – focusing on, but not exclusively related to the publication of "The Satanic Verses".

The last few months have been difficult ones for British Muslims. The issue of race relations has been thrown into sharp relief and all of us have had to think deeply about our objectives and priorities: about what it means to be British, and particularly what it means to be a British Muslim. These reflections have been the more difficult because of the long-term importance of the consequences that hinge on them.

I would not seek to pretend that the controversy over the book "The Satanic Verses" had ebbed away, and that life could now go on again exactly as before. The Government understands how much hurt and anxiety that book has caused, and we also understand that insults, particularly to a deeply held faith, are not easily forgotten or forgiven.

But we now have an opportunity to take stock.

The single most important guiding principle as we move forward must be the aim of full participation in our society by Muslim and other ethnic minority groups. Modern Britain has plenty of room for diversity and variety. But there cannot be room for separation or segregation. It is to the benefit of all, including the minorities themselves, that they should be part of the mainstream of British life. I can assure all ethnic minority groups, including Muslims, that the Government will do all it can to encourage this and to welcome their full participation.

Since 1945, several million people from the new Commonwealth countries have chosen to settle in Britain or have been born here into ethnic minority communities.

They have brought with them a rich and diverse heritage which has added to Britain's wealth of culture and tradition. Many have come with values that can only be admired such as firm faith; a commitment to family life; a belief in hard work and enterprise; respect for the law and a will to succeed. To their credit, they have kept those values at the core of their life in Britain too.

Of course, the process of adjusting to large numbers of people with different backgrounds has not always been straightforward, nor could one have expected it to be. And similarly, it has not been easy for many people who have had to adjust to a way of life very different from the one they had left behind. There are inevitable stresses and strains.

Putting down new roots in a new community does not mean severing the old. No-one would expect or indeed want British Muslims, or any other group, to lay aside their faith, traditions or heritage. But the new roots must be put down and must go deep, too.

Language is the most obvious example. It is quite natural and reasonable for the parents of an Asian child, born in Britain, to want to bring that child up able to speak their own mother tongue. But they must not forget that for that child to prosper in Britain and to reach his or her full potential, he or she will also have to have a fluent command of English.

As with language, so with knowledge of institutions, history and traditions. Of course, British Muslim children should be brought up faithful in the religion of Islam and well-versed in the Holy Koran according to the wishes of their parents. Nobody could or should suggest otherwise. But if they are also to make the most of their lives and opportunities as British citizens, then they must also have a clear understanding of British democratic processes, of its laws, the system of Government and the history that lies behind them, and indeed of their own rights and responsibilities.

I would emphasise that greater integration in the sense of a fuller participation in British life does not mean forfeiting your faith or forgetting your roots. Muslims cannot and should not be expected to do this, nor Hindus or Sikhs, Catholics or Jews. But between all these groups there should be a shared link – the link of being settled in Britain with all that involves.

Of course we recognise that each group will have its own specific issues which are of importance. But we also recognise that they must be dealt with in their proper context, within the framework of the laws and standards we share, and against the background of our desire to create a society free from racial and sex discrimination, with equality of opportunity for all.

I am glad to be able to say that the particular concerns raised by "The Satanic Verses" have been, for the most part, handled in this responsible way by the great majority of Muslims in this country.

Many people, quite understandably upset and hurt by that book, have exercised their right to protest and to express their grievance openly and freely. The vast majority have remained within the law in doing so, and I commend their restraint and that of their leaders and spokesmen.

I am grateful, too, that Muslim leaders have made public their regret for the behaviour of a very small minority who use the peaceful demonstrations as an excuse for violent disorder. Violence does their cause, and the reputation of Muslim communities generally, no good whatsoever, and I hope that their behaviour will continue not to be exonerated or tolerated by the responsible majority.

This is an appropriate occasion for me to restate the Government's view on "The Satanic Verses". We have throughout the last few months been guided by two principles: the freedom of speech, thought and expression; and the notion of the rule of law.

The same freedom which has enabled Muslims to meet, march and protest against the book, also preserves any author's right to freedom of expression for so long as no law is broken. To rule otherwise would be to chip away at the fundamental freedom on which our democracy is built. That is why we have no power to intervene with publishers or to have "The Satanic Verses" removed from bookshop shelves. Nor would we seek or want such power.

So freedom of expression prevails for as long as no law is broken. It follows that we must consider whether the book is within the law.

Many Muslims have argued that the law of Blasphemy should be amended to take books such as this outside the boundary of what is legally acceptable. We have considered their arguments carefully and reached the conclusion that it would be unwise for a variety of reasons to amend the law of blasphemy, not least the clear lack of agreement over whether the law should be reformed or repealed.

Firstly, the difficulties in re-defining what should or should not be blasphemous would be immense. People hold with great passion diametrically opposing views on the subject. For example, should protection be extended to all faiths, including the very minor or very obscure? Should it extend only to faiths believing in one God? Or to 'major' or 'mainstream' faiths only? I believe there is no equitable, just or right answer to these questions.

Secondly, an alteration in law could lead to a rush of litigation which would damage relations between faiths.

I hope you can appreciate how divisive and how damaging such litigations might be, and how inappropriate our legal mechanisms are for dealing with matters of faith and individual belief. Indeed, the Christian faith, no longer relies on it, preferring to recognise that the strength of their own belief is the best armour against mockers and blasphemers.

The important principle, and the only one which Government and the law can realistically protect, is that individuals should be free to choose their own faith and to worship without interference, in an atmosphere of mutual respect and toleration.

At the heart of our thinking is a Britain where Christians, Muslims, Jews, Hindus, Sikhs and others can all work and live together, each retaining proudly their own faith and identity, but each sharing in common the bond of being by birth or choice, British.

I very much hope this is a message you will be able to share with members of your Community.

Yours sincerely,

John Patten
Minister of State
Home Office

The Muslim Response

THE UK ACTION COMMITTEE ON ISLAMIC AFFAIRS
146 Park Road, London NW8 7RG

19 July 1989

The Rt. Hon. Mr John Patten, M.P.
Minister of State
Home Office
50 Queen Anne's Gate
London SW1H 9AT

Dear Mr Patten,

Thank you very much for your letter dated 4 July 1989 setting forth 'in full' some of your 'recent thinking' concerning the Muslim community in Britain.

The UK Action Committee on Islamic Affairs would like at the outset to assure you that as British Muslims we are concerned about the strength and stability of our country and the common welfare of all. We do share the commitment you set out to the principle that all groups must aim at full participation in our society. Muslims are not and do not seek to be a ghetto community. Ours is, as it must be, an open and outward looking community. Participation, however, cannot mean as you rightly observed forfeiting our faith, the proper practice of which, we are convinced, can only contribute to the well-being of society as a whole. Your remarks on the Muslim community's contribution to Britain's wealth and culture, its firm faith, commitment to family life, belief in hard work and enterprise, its respect for the law and the will to succeed are all apposite in this context.

We do welcome your many encouraging statements and assurances such as those on full participation, the right of people to worship in an atmosphere of mutual respect and toleration, and the recognition that each group in British society will have its own specific issues which are of importance. However, there are a number of assumptions and inferences in your letter which seem to detract from the statement of these fine principles.

There is, I can assure you, no conflict or tension between practising our faith and having a fluent command of English or having a clear understanding of British democratic processes, laws, system of Government and the history that lies behind them. There is no question that Muslims, like others in the society, have rights and responsibilities and being British, have indeed put down roots that must grow deeper. However, the mere fact that you felt the need to refer to these self-evident truths, perhaps calling into question thereby the motives and objectives of the community, reflects on the communication gap between the Government and the Muslim community.

On the issue of race relations, which you highlight at the very beginning of your letter, we believe that it is very unhelpful to look at human relations in Britain on the basis of race and it is most misleading to see the Muslim community as an ethnic community. Such categorizations distort a lot of perspectives and serve to make racism endemic in our society; they also make for bad laws and create major difficulties in the provision of essential services whether it is in employment, education, housing and welfare or in the dispensing of law. We look forward to the time when people in Britain will not be classified according to the colour of their skin or ethnic origin but according to their worth and contribution to the well-being of society.

This will undoubtedly require fundamental changes in the attitude of policy makers and citizens as a whole. The quality of participation of the Muslims, as indeed of others, in British society will depend on the quality of rights and opportunities they are accorded as human beings, and as a religious community. While we acknowledge that we have responsibilities to the society we live in, we feel that these responsibilities will be better discharged if the community's need to preserve its ethos is recognised and if the facilities and where necessary the legal provisions for doing so are accorded, not grudgingly or as a result of a process of attrition, but willingly and in a spirit of goodwill and harmony.

On the question of the sacrilegious and offensive book, "The Satanic Verses", the UK Action Committee on Islamic Affairs has sought to use all peaceful means, reason and persuasion to get the book withdrawn, to seek legal redress and to educate public opinion in Britain on the sacrilegious and mischievous nature of this publication. We will continue to do so. We certainly have not encouraged and will not encourage or condone any act of violent disorder and we condemn any criminal act or act of provocation or incitement to violence from any individual or group whether they be Muslims, agents provocateurs or police. We sincerely hope that the Government and the law enforcement agencies will also condemn and deal vigorously with the acts of provocation and violence which are directed against Muslim individuals and institutions at an increasingly alarming rate in certain parts of the country in the wake of the publication of this book.

We do appreciate your statement that 'the Government understands how much hurt and anxiety that book has caused' but we find it totally incomprehensible that there is no discernible willingness on the part of the Government to take effective action against what is not only sacrilege but a calculated attempt to create public disorder and mischief by giving free rein to insult and abuse.

Instead we are repeatedly told about two guiding principles: the freedom of speech, thought, and expression; and the notion of the rule of law. All of us uphold and cherish these freedoms. But the notion that people have a 'right' to commit sacrilege and insult and abuse the deeply held sanctities of other people is extraordinary. There can be no absolute freedom of expression except in a society where there is complete absence of law or government. The notion of the rule of law and unregulated and undisciplined freedom of speech, thought and action cannot and do not go together.

The crisis over "The Satanic Verses" refuses to go away for the perfectly understandable reason that our legal framework does not envisage a situation in which an offence of sacrilege could be committed against religions other than the Anglican faith. This is why the Muslim community has been seeking the enactment of an appropriate law to correct this legal deficiency. Many have sought to have the blasphemy laws extended to cover other faiths as well for the reasons that (1) such a law already existed; (2) a minority but quite weighty section of the Law Commission report had recommended such an extension of the law and (3) very importantly the Church of England itself had agreed with the need to provide cover against blasphemy to Islam and other non-Anglican faiths as well. However, it is true to say that the Muslim community's demand is objective-specific; it is not concerned with the title of the law.

We strongly feel that there is an urgent and pressing need for legislation to deal with sacrilege and incitement to religious hatred and abuse, a need which has found support among sections of Parliament and other responsible opinion in this country. You mentioned certain assumed difficulties and problems. All law-making involves problems of definition, of scope and of implementation, but they are resolved keeping in view the objectives of the proposed legislation. The real problem in this case is in fact the unwillingness of the Government. It has approached the question from a fixed and negative position *ab initio* and it has been affirming and re-affirming this position without any consultation with the Muslim community. We cannot say that this is satisfactory or reassuring in any way.

Instead, the Muslim community is sometimes offered equality in 'indignity' by the offer to repeal the blasphemy law altogether. We covet no freedom to commit sacrilege against others faiths. It is not our position that if Islamic sanctities are not protected against sacrilege, then the existing protection of the Anglican faith should also be removed. Muslims do not want to be a party to any such move.

You are no doubt aware, as Muslims are acutely aware, that there is an articulate and powerful, and in many respects, unscrupulous body of opinion in this country and in the western world who not only see the desirability but also regard it as a necessity to attack not only Islam and Muslims but indeed religious belief and institutions as such. This does not make for the freedom you rightly champion 'to worship without interference, in an atmosphere of mutual respect and toleration' which is the 'principle which the Government and the law can realistically protect'. Moreover, we firmly believe that the attack on religion will not only produce alienation, but erode the foundations of civilized values and society.

The Action Committee therefore wishes to reiterate its demand for a suitable enactment to criminalise abuse of and insult to religious sanctities and incitement to religious hatred. There already exist laws to deal with criminal libel and incitement to racial hatred and another identical law would not impinge on the principle of the proper exercise of the freedom of expression.

The Action Committee also requests the Government to use its good offices with the publishers to have the sacrilegious and offensive book withdrawn and thereby remove the cause of offence and help normalise community relations.

The British Muslim community greatly looks forward to playing a constructive role in the well-being and stability of the country, in the spirit of mutual respect, dignity and harmony. We therefore expect a helpful response to our acute concerns which have been brought into sharp focus in the wake of the publication of "The Satanic Verses".

We expect the dynamic processes of the law to be used to help create a society that is not only free from racial and sex discrimination but free from religious discrimination and abuse as well. For, quite frankly, there is no joy in being told that there is equal freedom for both the blasphemer and the blasphemed, the abuser and the abused.

With best wishes and kind regards,

Yours sincerely,

Iqbal Sacranie

Joint Convenor
UK ACTION COMMITTEE ON ISLAMIC AFFAIRS

APPENDIX III

Organisation of Islamic Conference Documents

(a) *Letter*

5 November 1988

THE GENERAL SECRETARIAT OF THE ORGANISATION OF THE ISLAMIC CONFERENCE PRESENTS ITS COMPLIMENTS

and has the honour to draw urgent attention to the recent attempt by the enemies of Islam to vilify the essence of our faith by malicious slander against the holy prophet (peace be upon him) and his blessed companions.

Blasphemy has been committed by a so-called Muslim 'Salman Rushdie' of Indian origin residing in London. He has written a slanderous and sacrilegious novel titled 'The Satanic Verses'. The novel published by Penguin, has attempted to disfigure the image of the prophet's (peace be upon him) Sahaba, Ummahat-el-Mominin, and has described the Islamic faith and the religious customs in the most foul language. The enemies of Islam are not content with this step and are planning to acclaim the novel. It is most distressing to note that this novel has been shortlisted for literary awards.

Muslims have been anguished and hurt all over the world and are demanding action. It is imperative for all the Muslim states to take strong measures immediately and the enemies of Islam get the message that their unholy attempts will not be tolerated. The Ummah should react collectively and firmly to this vicious attempt.

ALL THE MEMBER STATES ARE THEREFORE URGED TO TAKE THE FOLLOWING STEPS ON PRIORITY BASIS:

[A] THE NOVEL SHOULD BE BANNED IN ALL MUSLIM STATES.

[B] THE PUBLISHER SHOULD BE MADE TO WITHDRAW THIS NOVEL FROM THE MARKET, AND DESTROY ITS COPIES FOLLOWED BY A PUBLIC APOLOGY.

[C] IF THE PUBLISHERS FAIL TO COMPLY, THE PUBLISHER SHOULD BE BLACKLISTED AND IMPORT OF ALL THEIR PUBLICATIONS BANNED IN THE RESPECTIVE MUSLIM STATES.

[D] THE AUTHOR OF THIS NOVEL BE BANNED FROM ENTRY INTO ANY MUSLIM STATE.

[E] WIDE PUBLICITY TO BE GIVEN TO THE MEASURES TAKEN BY THE MUSLIM STATES SO THAT IT SERVES AS A DETERRENT AND IN FUTURE THE ENEMIES OF ISLAM DO NOT ATTEMPT DENIGRATING ISLAM.

[F] THE EMBASSIES IN NON-MUSLIM STATES BE DIRECTED TO CONTACT THE GOVERNMENTS THERE TO TAKE EFFECTIVE ACTION BANNING THIS NOVEL AND ITS WITHDRAWAL FROM THE MARKETS.

The Secretary General of the Organisation of the Islamic Conference, on his part, had immediately addressed to the situation. In the First Conference of Islamic Information Ministers held in Jeddah 29 Safar – 2 Rabi Al-Awal, 1409H (10–12 October 1988) he expressed indignation and anguish of the Islamic Ummah on this slanderous publication and proposed that strong measures should be taken against the author and the publishers of this malicious attack against the Holy Prophet and the sentiments of Muslims.

The general Secretariat avails itself of this opportunity to express the assurances of its highest consideration.

(b) *Declaration*

DECLARATION BY ISLAMIC CONFERENCE OF FOREIGN MINISTERS

ON

JOINT ISLAMIC ACTION TO COMBAT BLASPHEMY AGAINST ISLAM

The Eighteenth Islamic Conference of Foreign Ministers held in Riyadh, the Kingdom of Saudi Arabia, from 6–9 Sha'ban 1409 (13–16 March 1989) resolved to protect and safeguard the Muqaddasat (the Sacred Book, personalities and places) of the glorious Islamic Ummah, and maintain respect for the noble religion of Islam, declares:

The Almighty Allah, in His infinite mercy which encompasses heavens and earth, has revealed the religion of Islam as a guidance to mankind. Islam is the religion of peace, brotherhood and compassion towards mankind. Tolerance is an article of faith for all Muslims, nothing is dearer to Muslims than their noble religion; nothing more worthy of veneration than the Holy Quran, our Prophet Muhammad, peace be upon him, his family and wives, his companions, the two Holy Mosques, the Al-Aqsa Mosque, and the eminent personalities of Islam as well as all the Islamic holy places. These are Muqaddasat which should never be violated in any way.

There can be no doubt that the right to the freedom of thought and to the freedom of opinion and expression should not be exercised at the expense of other people's rights and cannot be abused to revile Islam and its Muqaddasat.

The Universal Declaration of Human Rights stipulates inter alia that in the exercise of his rights and freedoms, man must abide by certain restrictions aimed at securing due recognition and respect for the rights and freedoms of others and at meeting the legitimate requirements of morality and public order. This principle is also in accord with the concept of human rights in Islam.

Blasphemy against any revealed religion cannot be justified, either morally or legally on the basis of the right to freedom of thought, opinion or expression. It is indeed a most despicable act which deserves universal condemnation.

All Islamic States are resolved to coordinate their efforts in accordance with the Shariah at national, regional and international levels to effectively combat blasphemy against Islam and the slandering of Islamic personalities.

The Islamic countries strongly condemn the blasphemous book "The Satanic Verses", whose author they regard as an apostate. This publication transgresses all norms of civility and decency and is a deliberate attempt to malign Islam and the venerated Islamic personalities. There can be no doubt that the wickedness of the author has broken all rules of ethics, decency and respect for the feelings of more than a billion Muslims throughout the world and that it is a flagrant abuse of the principle of freedom of expression.

The Conference urges all Member States to ban the book "The Satanic Verses", to prevent the entry of its author in all Islamic countries and calls upon publishing houses to immediately withdraw the book from circulation and upon Member States to boycott any publishing house that does not comply.

The Conference appeals to all members of the international community to ban the sale or distribution of this book. It urges them to pass the necessary legislation to protect the religious beliefs of others and also urges publishing houses to ban the publication of any books that insult or ridicule religious sentiments.

The Conference declares that all Islamic countries shall individually and collectively exert effective and coordinated efforts to ensure respect for Islam and its noble values throughout the world and to protect and safeguard the Islamic Muqaddasat.

(c) *Resolution*

Resolution No.21/19–C
on the
Unified Stand on Sacrilegious
Acts Against Islamic Holy Places
and Values

The Nineteenth Islamic Conference of Foreign Ministers (Session of Peace, Interdependence and Development), held in Cairo, Arab Republic of Egypt, from 9 to 14 Muharram, 14H (31st July – 5th August 1990).

Inspired by the heavenly teachings of the Holy Quran and the True Islamic religion, the religion of mercy, brotherhood, selflessness, justice and is an assurance of a good life for the Islamic community and mankind at large;

Emphasizing the profound veneration of the Muslims for the Messenger of Islam, Mohamed (God's prayers and peace be upon him), the Holy Quran, the prophets, the angels, the revered members of the prophet's family, descendants and companions and the three Holy Mosques, the Holy Mosque at Makkah Al-Mukarramah, the Holy Mosque at Madina Al Munawwara and the Holy Mosque of Al Aqsa and all the other Islamic holy places;

Convinced that the teachings of the most venerable Prophet and the ordinances of the Holy Quran as well as the sound Islamic systems provide the best guarantee for the good life, happiness, complementarity and successes of human society on earth and in the hereafter.

Declaring that according to the foundations of the Islamic creed, sacrifice for the sake of preserving the sanctity of Islamic holy places, are dearest and most sublime than any thing else, and stressing its absolute conviction that it is incumbent upon it to fulfil its Islamic duty by adopting a firm attitude towards those who belittle the beliefs of the Muslims religion.

Reaffirming and Recalling the special declaration adopted by the 18th Islamic Conference of Foreign Ministers held in Riyadh on the unified Islamic stand against any insult or blasphemy, and the need to take the necessary measures to combat such acts, as referred to in the above-mentioned declaration;

1. *Condemns* most vehemently, any individual or governmental stand in support of any insult directed against the sanctities of revealed religions; and take exception to disregarding such insults as are directed against moral and human principles, cultural values and the religious beliefs of the majority of people, under the pretext of allowing the freedom of belief, expression and writing and respect for the principles of non-interference in the internal affairs of other states.

2. *Reaffirms* that it is the opinion of all the Ulemas that any insult, show of disrespect or slighting of the great prophets, the holy books and the holy Quran, also of the most revered Prophet, his noble family and his devoted companions, constitutes a most sacrilegious act, and those who commit such acts are definitely apostates.

3. *Pays tribute* to all zealous Muslim and non-Muslim personalities, centres, organizations and governments who, motivated by their Islamic and human obligation and being aware of their cultural message and moral principles, stood up to such violation of the religious sanctities as of divine religions.

4. *Calls on* Member States of the United Nations and all other international organizations to contribute to the preservation of the cultural heritage of all creeds.

5. *Urges* Member States to request its missions throughout the world, to follow up this important issue and to cooperate and coordinate their activities with the OIC Secretary General in this respect.

6. *Requests* the Secretary General of the Organization of

Islamic Conference, through the General Secretariat and through his Assistants to follow up and carefully monitor all suspicious and blasphemous manoeuvers directed against Islamic Holy Places in all parts of the world in collaboration with Member States.

7. *Commends* the efforts of the Ministers of Culture and Information and all affiliated institutions to draw up an Islamic information and cultural strategy aimed at sheltering the Islamic Ummah from enemy propaganda.

8. *Urges* the Member States to take the necessary measures in respect of publishing houses and their holding companies to ban the publishing and sale of any information material or publications prejudicial to Islam.

APPENDIX IV

Statement by the UK Action Committee on Islamic Affairs

POSITION STATEMENT ON THE CONTINUED PUBLICATION OF THE SACRILEGIOUS "SATANIC VERSES"

issued at the Press Conference held on Saturday, 29th December, 1990 at the Islamic Cultural Centre, London, after Rushdie's reported conversion to Islam.

The publication of the *Satanic Verses* in the Autumn of 1988 was certainly one of the most profane and filthy attempts in recent history to abuse, insult and revile the blessed Messenger of God (peace be upon him), his household and companions (may God be pleased with them all) and to ridicule and revile Islamic sanctities.

All Islamic schools of thought are unanimously of the view that attempting to insult the Blessed Prophet (peace be upon him) is the most serious crime in the eyes of Islamic Law. The crime is considered as transgressing the limits *(hudud),* is worse than treason and is a capital offence. However, the sentence is only applicable where Islamic jurisdiction applies.

The British Muslim Community was inflamed by the publication of this sacrilegious book. However, it is to the credit of the Muslim Community that the campaign has been kept within peaceful bounds fully respecting British Law. The author's enforced hiding over the past months has been entirely the result of continuing insult and provocation on his part: At an early stage he said if he had known that his book was going to produce such a reaction by Muslims, he would have penned a stronger and more 'critical' book on Islam. In other words he would have gone even further in his insult and mockery of Islamic sanctities.

The U.K. Action Committee on Islamic Affairs felt that there was no way in which the Muslim World could condone or ignore the conduct of the author or the multinational Viking Penguin publishing group which chose to ignore the pre-publication advice of their own experts that the book was 'lethal' and went ahead to issue the 'Satanic Verses'. The Action Committee, therefore, asked Penguin to:

1) Withdraw and pulp the offensive book.
2) Undertake not to publish in any form or manner any further editions or translations of the book.
3) Tender an unqualified apology to the followers of Islam.
4) Pay damages to an agreed charity.

None of these demands were addressed to the author of the profanity, irrespective of any quibbling whether he was a Muslim, an apostate or a non-Muslim. In any case he was outside the jurisdiction of Islam, and Muslims decided to leave him to his own fate. The author has received the backing of an "assorted group of secular intellectuals" (*The Times* editorial, 26 December 1990) who had come to discover in the writer a 'great reformer' of Islam. As to the Muslim demand that Penguin 'withdraw, pulp and apologise', the publishers have had nothing but an arrogant and contemptuous disdain although what was being required of them was normal, polite and not without precedent. A whole Penguin edition of the French cartoonist Sine's book *Massacre* was literally burnt by Allen Lane, Chief of Penguin, and declared 'out of print' as soon as he was told that the book was regarded as blasphemous and offensive. The Muslim demand to pulp was, therefore, also 'environment-friendly'.

We are now being told that Salman Rushdie has become a Muslim. One would normally rejoice to hear someone entering the fold of Islam and in the case of Mr. Rushdie the beginning of the end of the continuing offence caused by the publication of his book. Sadly, however, he has been as equivocal about his latest 'conversion' as he has been previously in the matter of his 'apologies', just playing with words without any content or meaning.

He says he has 'embraced' Islam as against *accepting* it. He signs a funny statement in the presence of a visiting official from a Muslim country and a few of his subordinates. The statement suggests no genuine repentance and commitment. He later writes in *The Times* that he is 'able now to say that I am Muslim'. Yet he was less than forthcoming when John Humphries asked him on BBC 1 television (News at Nine, December 24th, 1990): 'Now you have actually become a Muslim, have you?' Instead of saying 'Thank God, Yes,' he gave a long-winded answer that he has 'moved closer and closer to an engagement with religious faith' and he has 'no quarrel with the central tenets of Islam'.

But Islam is neither an external entity for someone to 'embrace' it, nor is it 'engagement with religious faith'. There are no 'witnesses', 'insiders' or 'outsiders' in Islam or Muslims with 'observer' status. As the word itself means, Islam is *submission,* to God and His Prophet (peace be upon him). Mr. Rushdie simply claims the 'ability' to say that 'I am Muslim', but he is not able to say clearly and unequivocally that he is now Muslim and willing to *submit* to Islam.

Frances de Souza, chairwoman of the Rushdie Defence Committee therefore, rightly thinks that 'Salman Rushdie feels very strongly that he has not necessarily changed his position'. She points out to *The Times* (December 27th 1990): 'He has talked about embracing the religion. Conversion is not the word he has used.'

While the question of Rushdie's religion can be left as something between him and God, there is little evidence of regret or repentance over his past. Instead of making amends, he is being mischievous.

He does not admit that the *Satanic Verses* is 'offensive' and he does not intend to repudiate, much less withdraw it. He even lies that the 'six Muslim scholars agreed with me that the book was not offensive and was not written to be offensive'. Sheikh Gamal Manna' has said that nothing like this has happened. Rushdie still maintains that the book is 'a serious work of art' and wants Muslims to appreciate it as a 'portrait' of conflict between the material and the spiritual worlds. He belittles Muslim objections to sacrilege as a 'furore'.

Rushdie is less than honest when he says 'that I do not agree with any statement in my novel the *Satanic Verses* uttered by any of the characters who insult the Prophet Muhammad or who cast aspersions upon Islam or upon the authenticity of the Holy Quran, or who reject the divinity of Allah.' It was as if he himself had not put those insulting words into their mouths and the characters were living objects who had spoken for themselves. In any case when John Humphries asked him 'Are you sorry for what you have written?' he replied: 'I am very sorry for the way it (the book) has been taken', adding that the question of the withdrawal of the book does not arise. The fault therefore did not lie with the writer, but with those who feel 'upset'!

Rushdie has, however, undertaken 'not to publish the paperback edition of the *Satanic Verses* or to permit any further agreements for translation into other languages, *while any risk of further offence exists.*'

The paperback edition stands long abandoned by Penguin and what Rushdie claims to be an 'enormous gesture' translates into nothing. He is putting a stop to 'any further agreements for translations into other languages', that is translations that have not yet taken place and lie in the uncertain future and even that too depended on the existence of 'any risk of further offence'. The moment it was felt that this can be done with impunity and without any risk, the author shall feel free to make 'further agreements for translation'. There is no undertaking about filming rights and electronic publishing. Meanwhile the English language hardback and all non-English editions would continue to circulate.

The U.K. Action Committee on Islamic Affairs, therefore, feels that the whole thing is a disingenuous ploy to bail out the unrepentant author of the *Satanic Verses* without meeting any of the concerns of the Muslim Community and indeed dismissing it and mocking it as causing a 'furore' over nothing. The only difference is that what was sought to be achieved previously through the pen of an 'unbeliever' Rushdie is sought to be pursued with the help of a 'Muslim' Rushdie.

The Action Committee, therefore, reiterates its position that it would continue to campaign against the publishers. It will seek full implementation of the resolutions of the Organisation of the Islamic Conference until the British Muslim Community's demands – namely, withdrawal, apology and damages – are met. It also appeals to Muslims in Britain and abroad not to be misled or confused by the new PR campaign designed to rehabilitate Rushdie and his profane and filthy book, the *Satanic Verses*.

The real issue is the continued publication of the book. By refusing to see the problem in its true perspective the writer and his 'friends' are only helping to complicate things for Rushdie.

Given these circumstances the U.K. Action Committee on Islamic Affairs has no alternative but to continue with the campaign until such time as its demands are met.

The U.K. Action Committee on Islamic Affairs (UKACIA), formed in October, 1988 immediately after the publication of Rushdie's sacrilegious and deeply offensive and malicious book, represents major Muslim organisations, institutions and mosques in the United Kingdom. The National Committee consists of representatives from all such organisations and includes individual scholars from various professions (Ulema, doctors, lawyers, accountants, students, etc). The Action Committee has been persistently campaigning for an unconditional and total withdrawal of the sacrilegious book, together with an unqualified apology by the publisher and the author and payment of damages to an agreed charity. It is also campaigning for suitable legislation to criminalise incitement to religious hatred and abuse and deal with sacrilege and insult to religious sanctities, in the hope of attaining safeguards and a consensus against the appearance of similar sacrilege in the future.

Annotated Bibliography

A. Books and Monographs

AKHTAR, Shabbir
Be Careful with Muhammad: The Salman Rushdie Affair
Horsham, UK: Biblios Publishers' Distribution Services Ltd., for Bellew Publishing Co., 1989, 136pp. £6.95 (PB).

A brilliant work describing 'the believer's anguish', exposing 'secular fundamentalism' and 'liberal inquisition' of Muslims and representing the Muslim response to *The Satanic Verses.* Sets out also the challenges to Muslims in a secular, liberal and un-Islamic society and explains the rationale behind the Muslim campaign for the withdrawal of the blasphemous book. Unmasks the anti-Islam forces at work in the Western literary, political and media establishment. Without betraying any apologia, it offers an immensely compelling vindication of the Islamic stance.

ALI, S. Rashadath
The Satanic Conspiracy
Calcutta: Peacock Publications, 1990, 69pp.

Recounts and analyses *The Satanic Verses* controversy. Examines the role of the media and offers the Muslim viewpoint on the controversy and related issues.

ANEES, Munawar Ahmad
The Kiss of Judas: Affairs of a Brown Sahib
Kuala Lumpur: Quill Publishers, 1989, 165pp. $10.00.

Discusses the Rushdie affair with special reference to the Western media's slanderous campaign against Muslims and its abuse of freedom of expression. Along with the Western insensitivity to Muslim sanctities it also documents the Muslim response to the saga.

APPIGANANESI, Lisa and MAITLAND, Sara (eds.)
The Rushdie File
London: Fourth Estate Ltd., 1989, 258pp.

Defends Rushdie's abuse of freedom of expression and warns against the so-called threat of Muslim fundamentalism. Claiming to provide documentation from all sides of the controversy, it is markedly biased in favour of Rushdie. It provides a chronology of events and wide selection of media coverage up to the middle of 1989.

Are You Being Kept in the Dark?: The Satanic Verses – Rushdie Dilemma
Jamaica, NY: Islamic Circle of North America, 1989, 23pp.

Attempts to highlight the nature of and reasons for the American Muslims' campaign against the book. Briefly outlines why the book is so offensive to Muslims.

BRENNAN, Timothy
Salman Rushdie and the Third World: Myths of the Nation
London: Macmillan, 1989, 203pp. £29.50 (PB).

Basically a study of Rushdie as the Third World literary cosmopolitan strongly influenced by post-modernism, Brennan remarks: '*The Satanic Verses* projects itself as a rival Qur'an with Rushdie as its Prophet and the devil as its supernatural voice.' Originally written for a Ph.D. thesis, the work presents a fair critique of Rushdie's writings.

BUCKAS, Hafez Mohamed Yusuf (ed.)
A Factual Response to Salman Rushdie's Concoction: 'The Satanic Verses' Through the Researched Works of Western Scholars
Durban, SA: Islamic Da'wah College International, 1989, 112pp.

Criticizes the Western media and British government for their hostile attitude to the Muslim protest against *The Satanic Verses.* Quotes extensively Western scholars acknowledging the greatness of Islam, the Prophet and the Qur'an.

DEEDAT, Ahmed
How Rushdie Fooled the West: The Satanic Verses Unexpurgated
Birmingham: Islamic Propagation Centre, 1989, 24pp.

Highlights Rushdie's use of four-lettered and other abusive words in the book and holds that it not only abuses Islam and Muslims, but offends the Queen and white women in general.

DOLD, Bernard E.
Salman Rushdie's Britannic Verses: A Bad Case of Culture Shock
Messina, Italy: Istituto di Lingue e Letterature Germaniche e Slave Facolta di Magistero, Universita di Messina, 1989, 109pp.

Explains why the novel is such difficult and bad reading. Analyses how the book is offensive also from the Western perspective.

KABBANI, Rana
Letter to Christendom
London: Virago, 1989, 70pp. £3.99.

Tracing the history of the Western prejudice against Islam, it analyses the fallacies in the Western conception of Islam. *The Satanic Verses,* according to the author, resurrects in the West the whole stock of hatred and bigotry against Islam. Urges for a cordial and meaningful dialogue between Islam and the West.

LEE, Simon
The Cost of Free Speech
London: Faber & Faber, 1990, 149pp. £4.99.

A highly readable and persuasive book that argues for re-examining and redefining the absolute commitment to the freedom of expression in view of the Rushdie controversy. Since one's absolute right to freedom of expression might trample on another's equally genuine rights and lead to hatred and violence, it is proper, the author concludes, to question the sanctity and limit of free speech.

LEE, Simon (et al.)
Law, Blasphemy and the Multi-Faith Society: Report of a Seminar organized by the Commission for Racial Equality and Inter-Faith Network of the United Kingdom
London: Commission for Racial Equality, 1990, 99pp. £1.50.

Contains five contributions from leading Muslim and non-Muslim scholars at a Seminar on the law of blasphemy. The need for some fresh legislative provision for dealing with blasphemy was stressed in the Seminar.

LINSTAD, Trond Ali and MAOULA, Saoud El (eds.)
International Seminar on Islam: Debates on the Rushdie Affair
Oslo, Norway: Muslim Magazine in Association with Jasmin Publishers, 1990, 56pp.

Both Muslim and Norwegian speakers trace out the relationship between

Islam and the West and explore grounds for a new dialogue on mutual acceptance and respect.

MAZRUI, Ali A.
The Satanic Verses or A Satanic Novel? – The Moral Dilemmas of the Rushdie Affair
Greenpoint, NY: The Committee of Muslim Scholars and Leaders of North America, 1989, 34pp.

Apart from being a masterly critique of *The Satanic Verses,* it takes up the issues of censorship, cultural treason, race relations and religious sensitivity.

McFRANCIS, D.H.
Satanic Verses: A Christian Point of View
Herts: Harewood Books, 1989. 75p.

Commends the spirited Muslim response to the scurrilous attack on their faith by *The Satanic Verses.*

MEHDI, Mohammad T.
Islam and Intolerance – A Reply to Salman Rushdie
New York: New World Press, 1990, 96pp. $7.95.

Dispels the widespread notion in the West that Islam is an intolerant religion. Evaluates Rushdie's offence and reaffirms Muslims' reasoned arguments for the withdrawal of the offensive book.

MENDUS, Susan (et al.)
Free Speech: Report of a Seminar Organized by the Commission for Racial Equality and the Policy Studies Institute, September, 1989
London: Commission for Racial Equality, 1990, 118pp. £2.00 (PB).

Discusses free speech, race relations and conflict of values in the context of the Rushdie affair. In his contribution Shabbir Akhtar exposes the Thought Police of the Liberals.

MICHELL, John
Rushdie's Insult
London: Radical Traditionalist Papers No. 7/Blasphemy No. 2, February 1989, 8pp.

A well-written monograph of great value that condemns the absolutism on behalf of free expression and urges that the wretched affair should be resolved without delay.

MUSTAPHA, Muhammad
An Islamic Reply to The Satanic Verses from Western Authors
Trinidad and Tobago: T.K. Industries, 1989, 100pp. + xxxii.

Refutes the assaults on Islamic sanctities in *The Satanic Verses* on the authority of quotations from Western scholars.

OMER, Mutaharunnisa
The Holy Prophet and the Satanic Slander
Madras, India: The Women's Islamic Social and Educational Service Trust, 1989, 152pp.

One of the earliest writings from the Muslim perspective on the Rushdie affair, highlights the origin and development of the Orientalists' campaign of distortion and vilification of Islam and shows how Rushdie surpassed them all in defiling Islam, the Prophet and Muslim sanctities. Four of the nine chapters of this well-written book delineate the Prophet's life and mission.

PIPES, Daniel
The Rushdie Affair: The Ayatollah, the Novelist and the West
Caroll, USA: Birch Lane Press, 1990, 224pp. $18.95.

First published as an article under the same title in *Commentary,* 87/6 (June 1989). Offering a summary of *The Satanic Verses* it tries to explain why Muslims 'found it inconceivably offensive'. In discussing the Muslim campaign, it concentrates on Khomeini's *fatwa* and holds: 'Khomeini succeeded in imposing his will on the West in a temporary and partial way.'

The Position of the Islamic Society for the Promotion of Religious Tolerance in the UK in the Rushdie Affair.
London: The Islamic Society for the Promotion of Religious Tolerance in the UK, n.d., 8pp.

Represents the Society's policy on the Affair, which differs markedly from the mainstream Muslim position. Though it acknowledges the offence caused by 'self-publicist and arrogant Rushdie' in distorting Islamic history, it urges Muslims to exercise restraint and forgiveness. Disagrees on both the concept and execution of the law of apostasy. It, however, maintains that freedom of expression should not be abused for insulting others.

QURESHI, Shoaib and KHAN, Javed
The Politics of the Satanic Verses: Unmasking Western Attitudes
Leicester: Muslim Community Studies Institute, 1989, 48pp.

Describes the reasons for the Muslim campaign against cultural imperialism and looks at issues of relevance to British Muslims: secularism, sacrilege and the British government standpoint.

RUTHVEN, Malise
Satanic Affair: Salman Rushdie and the Rage of Islam
London: Chatto & Windus, 1989, 224pp. £12.95.

Brands the British Muslims as ignorant faithful incapable of appreciating literature and art and discovers Muslim fundamentalism at work behind the campaign against *The Satanic Verses.* Abounds in the Orientalists' prejudices against Islam and Muslims.

SAMBHLI, M. Atiqur-Rahman
Our Campaign Against 'The Satanic Verses' and the Death Edict
London: Islamic Defence Council, 1990, 45pp. £1.00.

Written by a leading activist in the British Muslim campaign against *The Satanic Verses* it censures Khomeini's *fatwa* against Rushdie and spells out the harm caused by it. Originally written in Urdu, the English translation has four appendices on OIC resolutions and memorandums to the publishers.

SARDAR, Ziauddin and DAVIES, Merryl Wyn
Distorted Imagination: Lessons from the Rushdie Affair
London: Grey Seal, 1990, 303pp.

An excellent and well-documented work perceiving the Rushdie affair as a question of cultural identity. Holds Orientalism responsible for the distorted image of Islam and Muslims in the West. Discusses the issues of freedom of expression and the intolerance of Western secularists. Khomeini's *fatwa* is seen as completely indefensible under Islamic law.

SHERBOK, Dan Cohn (ed.)
The Salman Rushdie Controversy in Inter-Religious Perspective
Lampeter, UK: The Edwin Mellen Press, 1990, 151pp. £29.95.

Contributed by eight scholars of Muslim, Christian and Jewish persuasion, it views the Rushdie affair in a broader and multi-faith perspective. A balanced and insightful work.

SMITH, F. Lagard
Blasphemy and the Battle for Faith
London: Hodder & Stoughton, 1990, 208pp. £2.99.

Commenting on the religious scene in Britain in the wake of the Rushdie affair, it focuses on the constituents of blasphemy, heresy, religious interests and poses some searching questions about the role of religion in life itself.

UK ACTION COMMITTEE ON ISLAMIC AFFAIRS (UKACIA)
The British Muslim response to Mr. Patten
London: UKACIA, 1989, 16pp.

Published by the UKACIA, the main representative body of the British Muslims in the campaign against *The Satanic Verses,* it reproduces the British Home Office Minister, Mr. John Patten's letter to leading British Muslims and the UKACIA's rejoinder. Central to the correspondence is the point that either the blasphemy law should be extended to protect the Muslim sanctities or a new law should be enacted to protect the religious sentiments of all faiths.

WALTER, Nicolas
Blasphemy: Ancient and Modern Rationalist Press Association
London: Rationalist Press Association, 1990, 96pp.

Written from a blatantly psuedo-rationalist viewpoint it argues for a total abolition of the law of blasphemy, viewed as sheer anachronism.

WEATHERBY, W.J.
Salman Rushdie: Sentenced to Death
New York: Carroll & Graf, 1990, $19.95.

A sympathetic biography of the author of the blasphemous novel by a foreign correspondent of the British daily *The Guardian.* Tracing Rushdie's privileged life through Bombay, Rugby, Cambridge and London, it sheds interesting light on the exotic literary life of the author, suggesting that the Rushdie affair is a test case in the confrontation between fundamentalism and modernism, between Islam and the West.

WEBSTER, Richard
Brief History of Blasphemy: Liberalism, Censorship and the 'Satanic Verses'
Southwold, UK: Owell Press, 1990, 112pp. £3.95.

Offers a detailed examination of the concept of blasphemy and freedom of expression and its history. Calls on both liberals and Muslims to exercise restraint in that the controversy has already strained badly race relations in the UK.

WELDON, Fay
Sacred Cows
London: Chatto & Windus, 1989, 43pp.

An offensive piece by an activist of Rushdie's Defence Committee. Full of sheer abuse hurled with mindless crudity against Islam and its followers.

B. **Special Issues of Journals**

Discernment (A Christian journal of inter-religious encounter), 4/2 (1990): Focus on the Salman Rushdie Affair.
London: British Council of Churches, 1990, 49pp.

Contains a number of articles discussing blasphemy, free society, the Muslim campaign and underlying issues. Includes a select bibliography on the Affair.

Focus on Christian-Muslim Relations: The Rushdie Affair – Responses and Reactions, 3 (1989), 11pp. The Islamic Foundation, Leicester (UK).

Documents statements of the Archbishop of Canterbury, the Inter-Faith Network, UK and World Conference on Religion and Peace. Also contains excerpts from Christian magazines on the Rushdie Affair.

Impact International (London), 18/20 (28th October–10th November 1988).

The first Muslim magazine in Britain to draw attention to Rushdie's sacrilege. Apart from quoting some offensive passages from *The Satanic Verses* it contains articles by Manazir Ahsan and Ali Ashraf.

——, (London), 20/4 (23rd February–8th March 1990).

Focusing on *The Satanic Verses* Affair it offers a broad and deep analysis of the whole affair in the articles contributed by Shabbir Akhtar, Atam Vetta, Ziauddin Sardar, A.R. Kidwai and Ali Ashraf.

Radiance Viewsweekly – Reply to Rushdie, 24/39 (May 1989), Delhi, 42pp.

Explains why Muslims all over the world demand the total withdrawal of *The Satanic Verses.* Contains articles by Gandhi, Shahnaz Begum, G.R. Malik, Munawar A. Anees and Ali A. Mazrui.

Research Papers – Muslims in Europe: The 'Rushdie Affair – A Documentation', 42 (June 1989). Centre for the Study of Islam, Selly Oak Colleges, Birmingham (UK), 40pp.

A brief documentation covering the public debate in the print media in Britain up to March, 1989 and a highly informative survey of the Affair in Europe.

Third Text: Beyond the Rushdie Affair (Special Issue), 11 (Summer 1990). Third Text, London, 144pp.

Contains seven articles on broader aspects of the Rushdie Affair such as migration, secularism, post-modernism and race relations in Britain.

C. **Articles**

ABU-SHARIF, Ibrahim
'Everything You Always Wanted to Know About Islam, But Were Afraid to Read in English'
Islamic Horizons (Plainfield, Indiana), 18/1–4 (1989), pp. 44–9.

Apart from analysing the offence caused by Rushdie's work, it looks also at several Western popular writings which depict distortingly Islam and Muslims. Calls for proper Islamic education, particularly for the future generations of Muslims in the USA.

AFSHARI, Reza
'Ali Mazrui or Salman Rushdie: The Satanic Verses and Islamist Politics'
Alternatives, 16 (1991), pp. 107–14.

Written by an erstwhile Muslim who has 'lost his religious identity', it heaps applause on Rushdie's iconoclasm in having written *The Satanic Verses.* Accuses Mazrui of playing into the hands of Islamist 'pundit-ocracy' and 'militants' for his criticism of the sacrilegious novel. Alarmingly warns in a hysterical tone against the Islamists' bid for power. Believes that the 'intellectual route to secularism, democracy and freedom' in the Muslim world 'passes through blasphemy'.

AHSAN, M.M.
'The "Satanic" Verses and the Orientalists'
Impact International (London), 18/20 (1988), pp. 17–18.
Also published in *The Kiss of Judas,* op. cit., pp. 6–10, *The Radiance* (Delhi) and in Zakaria Bashier's book *The Makkan Crucible* (Leicester, The Islamic Foundation), 1991, pp. 223–34.

Originally published in *Hamdard Islamicus,* 5/1 (1982) and *Islamic Quarterly* 24/3–4 (1980), this scholarly article exposes the malicious story about the so-called 'Satanic Verses' fabricated by Makkan polytheists and circulated by Orientalists, which Rushdie has scandalized in his *The Satanic Verses.*

AKHTAR, Shabbir
'An Open Letter Concerning Blasphemy'
Newsletter (Centre for the Study of Islam and Christian-Muslim relations), (Birmingham), No. 21 (1989), pp. 18–21.

Describes the Muslim campaign against *The Satanic Verses* as their attempt to transmit and preserve the faithful heritage. Explains also the nature and dimension of the Muslim protest.

——,
'Art or Literary Criticism?'
In: Dan Cohn-Sherbok (ed.), *The Salman Rushdie Controversy in Interreligious Perspective.*
Lampeter, UK: The Edwin Mellen Press, 1990, pp. 1–24.

Being the second chapter of Akhtar's *Be Careful with Muhammad,* it brings out the offensive nature of *The Satanic Verses* and the Muslims' resolute challenge to such an outrageous work designed to abuse and ridicule their deeply held convictions.

——,
'Holy Freedom and the "Liberals" '
Impact International (London), 20/4 (1990), pp. 9–11.

Scrutinizes the response of the political, literary and media establishment to the Muslim demand for equal treatment. Provides instances of the liberal fundamentalists' Inquisition of Muslims for expressing their anger and sorrow.

Also published entitled 'Is Freedom Holy to Liberals? Some Remarks on the Purpose of Law'. In: S. Mendus (et al.), *Free Speech: Report of*

a Seminar. Organized by the Commission for Racial Equality and the Policy Institute, September, 1989.
London: Commission for Racial Equality, 1990, pp. 18–27.

——,
'Back into the Fold'
Africa Events, 7/2 (February 1991), pp. 36–7.

Cogently argues why a complete withdrawal of *The Satanic Verses* is essential to end the controversy following Rushdie's reported conversion to Islam.

ALI ASHRAF, Syed
'Nihilistic, Negative, Satanic'
Impact International, 20/4 (28th October–10th November 1988), pp. 16–17.

Sees Rushdie following in the footsteps of 'vicious missionaries and theologians of the Middle Ages' in attacking the Islamic sanctities. Dismisses the work as 'Satanic'.

——,
'On the "Satanic Verses" '
Al-Islam (Dhaka), 5/6 (1989), pp. 2–8.

Views *The Satanic Verses* as part of the vicious conspiracy to malign Islam and the Prophet. Examines the episode of the so-called 'Satanic Verses' in historical works.

ALI, Ausaf
'The Westernization of a Nice Muslim Boy'
The Universal Message (Karachi), 12/10 (March 1991), pp. 25–32.

Asks Rushdie 'to apologize to Muslims at once and forthwith' and 'Muslims to show him the true Islamic spirit'. Examines how to keep the Muslim youth away 'from going Western unashamedly, guiltily or secretly'.

ALIBHAI, Yasmin
'Satanic Betrayals: Is There Anyone There for Multiculturalism?'
New Statesman and Society (London), 2/38 (February 1989), p. 12.

Refers to British Muslims as 'uncompromising and at times separatist', partly because of the global assertion of Islamic fundamentalism and partly owing to the political pressures and tendencies within Britain. Reports how 'Muslim' has tended to become a word of abuse in schools.

——,
'Beyond Belief'
New Statesman and Society (London), 4/138 (February 1991), pp. 17–18.

Looks at the Rushdie Affair in retrospect with special focus on the sufferings British Muslims had to undergo for protesting against the blasphemous book. Calls for a positive, reconciliatory response from the Muslim community to Rushdie's embracing of Islam.

ALLY, Muhammad Mashuq ibn
'The Muslim Response (to Rushdie Affair)'
In: S. Lee (et al.), *Law, Blasphemy and the Multi-Faith Society: Report of a Seminar.* Organized by the Commission for Racial Equality and the Inter-Faith Network of the UK, September 1989.
London: Commission for Racial Equality, 1990, pp. 21–9.

Points out several instances of censorship in today's Britain while British Muslims are told to respect the freedom of expression. Argues for equality for all religious communities.

——,
'Stranger Exiled from Home'
In: Dan Cohn-Sherbok (ed.), *The Salman Rushdie Controversy in Interreligious Perspective.*
Lampeter, UK: The Edwin Mellen Press, 1990, pp. 131–49.

Identifies Rushdie as 'a typical hybrid, the product of the bastardization of Indian culture, which began with the Christian missionary . . . ' Points to the intolerance in Britain towards minority culture, modes of behaviour and religion and concludes that 'democracy has yet to embrace the concept of cultural diversity'.

ASAD, Talal
'Ethnography, Literature and Politics: Some Readings and Uses of Salman Rushdie's "The Satanic Verses" '
Cultural Anthropology (Washington, DC), 5/3 (1990), pp. 239–69.

Considers *The Satanic Verses* as a 'political act' and an 'encounter between Western modernity' and a non-Western Other. Brings out its political setting and deplores the pious horror of liberals over the book's symbolic burning in Bradford in the face of other instances of public burning of publications and legislative documents.

——,
'Multiculturalism and British Identity in the Wake of the Rushdie Affair'
Politics and Society (Stoneham, MA), 18/4 (1990), pp. 455–80.

Examines why the British government took such a harsh stand on the peaceful protests by British Muslims against *The Satanic Verses,* in perceiving them as a threat to the British identity. Studies the whole affair as yet another symptom of British post-imperial identity in crisis.

BENNETT, Clinton
'The Rushdie Affair: Some Underlying Issues'
Discernment (London), 4/2 (1990), pp. 3–11.

Perceives the Rushdie Affair as a catalyst for the crucial issue of the position of Muslims living outside the House of Islam. Endorses the masterly (!) survey of Ruthven in *A Satanic Affair.*

BENTON, Sarah
'Do We Really Want Freedom?'
New Statesman and Society (London), 2/39 (March 1989), pp. 12–13.

Commenting on 'attitudes to freedom of expression', it points out that 'it is not just some Muslims who want to silence unwelcome voices. It is quite a common wish in Britain'.

BHABHA, Homi
'Novel Metropolis'
New Statesman and Society (London), 3/88 (1990), pp. 16–18.

Analyses the issue of migration in *The Satanic Verses.* Also explains the migrants' aversion to 'assimilation' as the basis for integration in a national or global community.

BHARUCHA, Rustom
'The Rushdie Affair: Secular Bigotry & the Ambivalence of Faith'
Third Text (London), No. 11 (Summer 1990), pp. 62–8.

Affirms that 'Rushdie cannot pretend to disguise his irreverence because it is written into the very fabric of the book'. Brands certain passages of *The Satanic Verses* as 'clearly the mischief of a non-believer'.

BILGRAMI, Akeel
'Rushdie and Reform of Islam'
Economic and Political Weekly (Bombay), 25/12 (1990), pp. 605–8.

States that 'Reformation' which would have relegated religion to the private realm has not occurred in Islam hence the Muslim outcry over *The Satanic Verses*.

BILMORIA, Purusottama
'The Jaina Spirit in Salman Rushdie'
South Asian Bulletin (New York), 9/2 (1989), pp. 57–64.

Discovers the Jaina doctrine of Anekanta-vada (against one-sidedness) in Rushdie's works! Points to the resemblance between Nagachandra's apocryphal *Ravanic Verses* written in 1100 CE and *The Satanic Verses* in that both of them oppose the orthodoxy.

'Blasphemy Today: The Satanic Verses in the High Court'
New Humanist (London), 105/1 (May 1990), pp. 12–14.

Summarizes the British Muslims' attempt to prosecute *The Satanic Verses* under the criminal law; the appeal heard by the Queen's Bench Division of the High Court from 26th February to 5th March, 1990 in London and the judgement that neither the common law of blasphemy nor of sedition could apply to *The Satanic Verses*.

BOYD, Andrew
'A Look at the Blasphemy Law', Parts 1 and 2.
Prophecy Today (London), 5/5–6 (September/October and November/December 1989), pp. 6–7 and 10–11.

Examines in the wake of the Rushdie Affair the Muslim demand for changes in Britain's blasphemy law, with the conclusion that rather than extending the law, it should remain as it is. Reports that 'National Front members planned to burn a copy of the Koran in Dewsbury.'

CAUTE, David
'Prophet Motive'
New Statesman and Society (London), 3/88 (1990), pp. 18–19.

Brings out the unwillingness of writers and intellectuals to advance their understanding of British Muslims. Studying the Rushdie Affair it affirms: 'The underlying issue is not only freedom of expression but the vast pain of integration within the disdainful host society.'

CHRYSSIDES, George
'Fact and Fiction in the Salman Rushdie Affair'
Discernment (London), 4/2 (1990), pp. 21–2, 23.

Holds that *The Satanic Verses* could not be published in the name of artistic freedom and regrets the inadequacy of British law which allows one to malign a deceased religious leader without fear of any legal consequences.

'Conclusions (of the Discussion on British Blasphemy Law and the Rushdie Affair)'
In: S. Lee (et al.), *Law, Blasphemy and the Multi-Faith Society: Report of a Seminar.* Organized by the Commission for Racial Equality and the Inter-Faith Network of the UK, September 1989.
London: Commission for Racial Equality, 1990, pp. 56–62.

Among the options considered to deal with the issues generated by *The Satanic Verses* controversy the contributors to the Seminar discuss the extension of the law of blasphemy and some new provision to cover incitement to religious hatred and group libel.

COTTLE, Simon
'Reporting the Rushdie Affair: A case study in the orchestration of public opinion'.
Race and Class (London), 32/4 (1991), pp. 45–61.

An in-depth account how public opinion is constructed and orchestrated. With pointed reference to the media story of a Muslim rally in Birmingham against *The Satanic Verses,* it shows how its 'conflict' and 'trouble' aspects were exaggerated.

DAWKINS, Richard
'A Deplorable Affair'
New Humanist (London), 104/2 (May 1989), p. 9.

Laments that 'our whole society is soft on religion. Even secular activists are incomprehensibly soft when it comes to religion. Our best weapon is education, especially education in the scientific world-view'.

DAY, Michael
'The Salman Rushdie Affair: Implications for the CRE and Race Relations'
In: S. Mendus (et al.), *Free Speech: Report of a Seminar.* Organized by the Commission for Racial Equality and the Policy Studies Institute, September, 1989.
London: Commission for Racial Equality, 1990, pp. 104–10.

Analyses the main reasons of the Muslims' grievance and concedes that they have cause for complaint. Studies the Rushdie Affair in the context of Race Relations and presses for a meaningful dialogue.

DECTER, Midge
'The Rushdiad (Rushdie Affair)'
Commentary (New York), 87/6 (1989), pp. 18–23.

Condemns Rushdie's 'hounding' (!) and makes an impassioned plea for regaining faith in the power of words. Describes how American writers rallied against the forces of obscurantism.

'Discussion (on British Blasphemy Law)'
In: S. Lee (et al.), *Law, Blasphemy and the Multi-Faith Society: Report of a Seminar.* Organized by the Commission for Racial Equality and the Inter-Faith Network of the UK, September, 1989.
London: Commission for Racial Equality, 1990, pp. 47–55.

Discusses the main components of the Muslims' grievance: Rushdie hurting their religious sensibilities and degrading them in their own eyes and in the eyes of others. Takes note of the issue of 'group libel' in this context.

DYSON, Anthony
'Looking Below the Surface'
In: Dan Cohn-Sherbok (ed.), *The Salman Rushdie Controversy in Interreligious Perspective.*
Lampeter, UK: The Edwin Mellen Press, 1990, pp. 59–69.

Disagrees with the view that any real progress to counter blasphemy can be made by developing the law. Stresses 'the need for strengthening of the bonds between the different religious bodies in Britain'.

EASTERMAN, Daniel
'A Sense of Proportion: The Rushdie Affair'
Index on Censorship, No. 4 (April 1990), pp. 9–11.

A former lecturer in Islamic studies gives vent to his deep aversion to Islam, Islamic law and religious orthodoxy. Demands of British Muslims tolerance and reasonableness (!).

FARUQI, M.H.
'The Saṭanic Verses: Publishing Sacrilege is Not Acceptable'
Impact International (London), 18/20 (1988), pp. 12–14.

Deplores the freedom to publish and spread obscene sacrilege and make a business out of it. Describes the Muslim demands as quite reasonable.

——,
'The Satanic Verses: Dear Mr. Baker, Please do not Rush to Judgement'
Impact International (London), 19/3 (1989), pp. 7–8.

Written in response to the British Secretary of State for Education and Science Mr. Kenneth Baker's article 'Argument before Arson' (*The Times,* 30th January 1989), it absolves the British Muslims of Baker's charge of being arsonists and explains their stance on freedom of expression and culture.

——,
'The Author as the Stooge'
Impact International (London), 20/4 (1990), pp. 16–18.

Holds that the Rushdie Affair has remained unresolved basically because of the dismissive attitude of the publishers Viking-Penguin to consider the Muslim demands.

FISCHER, Michael M.J. and ABEDI, Mehdi
'Bombay Talkies, the Word and the World: Salman Rushdie's Satanic Verses'
Cultural Anthropology (Washington, DC), 5/2 (1990), pp. 107–59.

Examines *The Satanic Verses* as a modernist writing and explains away the controversy generated by it with reference to the immigrant politics in Britain, the rivalry between Saudi and Iranian fundamentalism, communal politics in India and anti-Benazir politics in Pakistan. Endorses some of the fabrications in *The Satanic Verses* about Islamic history and Muslims.

GANOUSHI, Rashid
'Europe and Islam – Co-operation or Confrontation?'
In: T.A. Linstad and S.E. Maoula (eds.), *International Seminar on Islam: Debates on the Rushdie Affair.*
Oslo, Norway: Muslim Magazine, 1990, pp. 35–40.

Surveys the relations between the West and Islam and finds the Western attitude towards Islam marred by distortion and exploitation. Calls for a new, healthy dialogue between Muslims and the West for future good relations.

GOERINGER, Conrad
'Lessons from The Satanic Verses'
American Atheist (Austin, TX), 31/9 (1989), pp. 32–6.

By the Director of the Tucson Chapter of American Atheists, it strongly condemns the Muslim campaign and attempts to make a case for unbridled freedom.

GREEN, S.F.D.
'Beyond the Satanic Verses'
Encounter (London), 74/5 (June 1990), pp. 12–20.

Views the Rushdie Affair as a conflict between the conservative religion and the liberal society and as the beginning of a militant Islamic presence in British public life. Studies the issue also in the context of multi-culturalism and multi-faithism.

HAMMAD, Ahmad Zaki
'Between Fairness & Freedom'
Islamic Horizons (Plainfield, Indiana), 18/1–4 (1989), pp. 40–3.

Greed and hate, it is concluded, lie at the heart of *The Satanic Verses* controversy. Rushdie's work is seen as a deliberate exploitation of religion for commercial purposes.

HARTLEY, Anthony
'Saving Mr. Rushdie?'
Encounter (London), 73/1 (1989), pp. 73–7.

Concedes that *The Satanic Verses* does contain much that is profoundly offensive to a believing Muslim. Exaggerates the threat to Rushdie's life in the wake of the *fatwa.* Calls the *fatwa* 'a monstrous infringement of national sovereignty'.

HERRICK, Jim
'The Might of the Pen: Rushdie's Imaginative Novel'
New Humanist (London), 104/1 (May 1989), pp. 6–7.

Sees Rushdie's novel as 'a courageous tribute to the power of imagination' and discovers that the 'humanist spirit pervades the novel'. Points out that not only Muslim sanctities but others too are satirized in *The Satanic Verses.*

HUSSAIN, Mushahid
'The Rushdie Affair: A Muslim's Perspective'
Index on Censorship, No. 4 (April 1990), pp. 12–13.

Relates the concern and anguish of Muslims in the wake of the Rushdie Affair and sees no artistic merit in *The Satanic Verses.* Records the Western countries' officially sponsored violence on foreign soil.

INAYATULLAH, Sohail
'Understanding the Postmodern World: Why Khomeini wants Rushdie Dead'
Third Text (London), No. 11 (Summer 1990), pp. 91–8.

Frames the Khomeini/Rushdie discourse in a politics of divergent construction of the real. Points to several similarities between the two (!).

IRVING, T.B.
'The Rushdie Confrontation'
Islamic Order (Karachi), 11/3 (1989), pp. 43–51.

Summarizing the contents of *The Satanic Verses* it is dismissed as a 'simply bizarre' work written in 'offensive and utter poor taste'.

JAIN, Madhu (et al.)
'Salman Rushdie: Satanic Storm'
India Today (15th March, 1989), pp. 14–24.

Based upon a special correspondent's analysis, it surveys the Muslim and non-Muslim reaction to the publication of Rushdie's book and the Ayatollah's *fatwa* in Bombay, Islamabad, Srinagar, New Delhi, London and New York.

JONES, Peter
'Respecting Beliefs and Rebuking Rushdie'
British Journal of Political Science (Cambridge), 20/4 (1990), pp. 415–37.

Examining 'whether a principle of "respect for beliefs" can provide adequate reason for limiting freedom of expression', it finds 'this principle untenable', for there cannot be a sound 'basis for setting limits to freedom of expression'.

JUSSAWALLA, Feroza
'Resurrecting the Prophet: The Case of Salman, the Otherwise'
Public Culture (Philadelphia PA), 2/1 (1989), pp. 106–17.

Analysing the novel it shows how Rushdie tries to 'escape the responsibilities of the monstrosities he perpetuates' and how he hides his real political motives behind the veil of modernism.

KING, Preston
'Rushdie and Revelation'
In: S. Mendus (et al.), *Free Speech: Report of a Seminar.* Organized by the Commission for Racial Equality and the Policy Studies Institute, September 1989.
London: Commission for Racial Equality, 1990, pp. 28–48.

Provides a brief history of the Western attitude towards revelation and regards the Rushdie Affair as closely tied to the religious and revelatory question. Holds that Islam will survive Rushdie's assault as Christianity and Judaism have survived similar assaults in the past.

KING-HAMILTON, Alan,
'Legal Position of Blasphemy'
In: S. Lee (et al.), *Law, Blasphemy and the Multi-Faith Society: Report of a Seminar.* Organized by the Commission for Racial Equality and the Inter-Faith Network of the UK, September 1989.
London: Commission for Racial Equality, 1990, pp. 40–3.

Spells out the difficulties in the extension of the law of blasphemy to protect religions other than Christianity. Agrees that religious feelings of individuals should be protected.

LEE, Simon
'Free Speech and Religious Freedom'
In: S. Lee (et al.), *Law, Blasphemy and the Multi-Faith Society: Report of a Seminar.* Organized by the Commission for Racial Equality and the Inter-Faith Network of the UK, September 1989.
London: Commission for Racial Equality, 1990, pp. 4–20.

Points to a whole range of restrictions on free speech in Britain. Treks through a brief history of blasphemy and explores possible solutions for the Rushdie Affair. Calls for rationalizing the law of blasphemy and incitement to religious hatred.

LEWIS, Bernard
'Behind the Rushdie Affair'
American Scholar (Washington, DC) (Spring, 1991), pp. 185–96.

Sets forth the Islamic legal and historical issues raised by Ayatollah Khomeini's *fatwā*. Sifting Islamic history, it examines precedents, particularly from the life of the Prophet, for actions taken against apostates, and blasphemers and those guilty of insulting the Prophet. Calls into question Khomeini's jurisdiction in judging a citizen of a non-Muslim country. Also discusses at length the socio-legal implications for Muslims living in a non-Islamic society.

LEWIS, Philip
'From Book Burning to Vigil: Bradford Muslims a Year On'
Discernment (London), 4/2 (1990), pp. 26–34.

Focuses on the Bradford Muslims, their profile, their campaign and why they played such a key role in the affair. Surveys also the part played by the majority community, particularly the Bishop's role in the controversy.

LICHTENSTEIN, Leonie
'Rushdie, Steiner, Sobol and Others: Moral Boundaries'
Encounter (London), 73/3 (1989), pp. 34–42.

Rules out that *The Satanic Verses* compounds blasphemy with betrayal. Points to Rushdie's 'Marxist leanings'. Refers constantly to the Muslim 'anathema, danger and their (!) breach of peace'.

LYNCH, James
'Cultural Pluralism, Structural Pluralism and the United Kingdom'
In: S. Poulter (et al.), *Britain: A Plural Society: Report of a Seminar.* Organized by the Commission for Racial Equality and the Runnymede Trust, October, 1989.
London: Commission for Racial Equality, 1990, pp. 29–43.

Elaborates the meaning of cultural pluralism and its relevance in Britain and how far the needs of minority communities should be accommodated.

McEWAN, Ian
'Do You Dare Like This Book?'
New Statesman and Society (London), 2/39 (March 1989), pp. 11–12.

Insinuates that the poison of intimidation is infecting the free exchange of ideas. Speaks disparagingly of the Ayatollah and endorses Rushdie's ravings.

MAITLAND, Sara
'Blasphemy and Creativity'
In: Dan Cohn-Sherbok (ed.), *The Salman Rushdie Controversy in Interreligious Perspective.*
Lampeter, UK: The Edwin Mellen Press, 1990, pp. 115–30.

Defends *The Satanic Verses* for being an attempt to explore what belief, or faith, is and why it matters. Dismisses religion, be it Christianity, Islam or any other, as 'just a myth, a social construct' . . . and 'the concept of legal blasphemy as theologically stupid'.

MAZRUI, Ali A.
'The Satanic Verses or A Satanic Novel'
Also published in *Africa Events* (London), 5/7 (July 1989), pp. 30–40, and 5/8 (August 1989), pp. 37–41; *Alternatives*, 15/1 (Winter 1990), pp. 97–121.

'The Satanic Verses: Novelist's Freedom vs Worshipper's Dignity'
Impact International (London), 19/7 (1989), pp. 10–15.
Also published entitled 'Satanic Verses or a Satanic Novel' in *The Kiss of Judas,* op. cit., pp. 61–90; in *Free Speech: Report of a Seminar,* op. cit., pp. 79–103; in *Third World Quarterly* (London), 12/1 (1990), pp. 116–39; in A.A. Mazrui, *Cultural Forces in World Politics* (James Currey, London, 1990), pp. 83–98; and its abridged version in *The Rushdie File,* op. cit., pp. 220–8.

The Satanic Verses is seen as a grossly anti-Muslim work written out of basically financial and mercenary motives. Demonstrates how it is sheer 'hate literature'.

——,
'Witness for the Prosecution: A Cross-Examination on the Satanic Verses'
Third Text (London), No. 11 (Summer 1990), pp. 31–40.

Deals with the Rushdie Affair in the context of the following issues: death punishment, incitement to violence, hate literature, sacrilege and blasphemy, freedom of expression, libelling the dead and censorship.

——,
'A Testimony'
Africa Events 7/2 (February 1991), pp. 37–9.

In this interview Mazrui explains the Muslim insistence on withdrawing *The Satanic Verses* completely from circulation, as a logical outcome of Rushdie's announcement of embracing Islam. Asks Rushdie not to be a beneficiary of commercialized blasphemy, if he is a sincere Muslim.

MENDUS, Susan,
'The Tigers of Wrath and the Horses of Instruction'
In: S. Mendus (et al.), *Free Speech: Report of a Seminar.* Organized by the Commission for Racial Equality and the Policy Studies Institute, September 1989.
London: Commission for Racial Equality, 1990, pp. 3–17.

Discovers the following themes at the heart of the Rushdie Affair: rationality versus sanctity, choice versus tradition and the sovereignty of the individual versus the identity of the group.

MODOOD, Tariq
'British Asian Muslims and the Rushdie Affair'
The Political Quarterly (Oxford), 61/2 (1990), pp. 143–60.

With the focus on the ethnic history of British Muslims in Bradford and Birmingham, it discusses their conservatism, religious devotionalism and defensive traditionalism. Refutes the charge of fundamentalism against British Muslims.

——,
'Muslims, Race and Equality in Britain: Some Post-Rushdie Affair Reflections'
Third Text (London), No. 11 (Summer 1990), pp. 127–34.

Points out that 'it was not the exploration of religious doubt but the lampooning of the Prophet that provoked the anger'. Re-echoes Ruthven, *A Satanic Affair,* in saying 'the anger over *The Satanic Verses* is not so much a Muslim response but a South Asian Muslim response rooted in its reverence of the Prophet'.

MULLEN, Peter
'Satanic Asides'
In: Dan Cohn-Sherbok (ed.), *The Salman Rushdie Controversy in Interreligious Perspective.*
Lampeter, UK: The Edwin Mellen Press, 1990, pp. 30–1, 33–5.

Condemns the arrogance of the liberal attitude towards the religion and holds that 'Rushdie has done a disservice to us all. By his clever derogatory remarks in *The Satanic Verses* he has undermined our evaluation of what is supremely valuable in the religious tradition . . .'

MURRAY, John G.
'The Right to Disrespect'
American Atheist (Austin, TX), 31/9 (1989), pp. 4–10.

Rules out any respect for religious doctrines and argues for even legalizing it. Its anti-religion stance borders on gross tendentiousness and hysteria.

NAIR, Rukmini Bhaya
'Text and Pre-Text: History as Gossip in Rushdie's Novels'
Economic and Political Weekly (Bombay), 24/18 (1989), pp. 994–1000.

Rushdie's work is seen as a creative re-organization of the received narrative of Islam and gossip as a literary weapon against the claims of historical truth and religious morality. Tries to explain the Muslim reaction.

NAIR, Rukmini Bhaya and BATTACHARYA, Rimli
'Salman Rushdie: Migrant in the Metropolis'
Third Text (London), No. 11 (Summer 1990), pp. 17–30.

Posits that opinions in the metropolis are generally articulated in two main centres – media and academia – and the collusive interaction between the two is quite evident in the Rushdie Affair.

NEUREITER, Anton (et al.)
'Blasphemy is Enlightenment'
American Atheist (Austin, TX), 31/9 (1989), pp. 47–52.

Surveying the Muslim protest against Rushdie's abusive work, it brands it as 'Inquisition' and condemns the cowardly and bigoted states that banned *The Satanic Verses*. Discovers in the whole affair the ebbing away of the Enlightenment.

NEWBIGIN, Lesslie
'Blasphemy and the Free Society'
Discernment (London), 4/2 (1990), pp. 12–18.

Contributed by a renowned theologian it traces the creation of the free society and its elimination of the sacred and concludes that a society without a sense of the sacred is bound to dissolve into nihilism. Vindicates stoutly reverence for the sacred.

O'HAIR, Madalyn
'Red Herring Rushdie (A Chronology)'
American Atheist (Austin, TX), 31/9 (1989), pp. 12–31.

Documents news and events related to the Rushdie Affair up to 14th February, 1990 with a marked bias in Rushdie's favour.

———,
'The Theopolitics of the Rushdie Case'
American Atheist (Austin, TX), 31/9 (1989), pp. 57–8.

Sees the Rushdie Affair as the attempt of a growing religion to protect itself from new ideas. Warns against the threat of Muslim fundamentalism.

PAPASTERGIADIS, Nikos
'Ashis Nandy: Dialogue and the Diaspora – A Conversation'
Third Text (London), No. 11 (Summer 1990), pp. 99–108.

Focuses on the Rushdie Affair in terms of its broader consequences – the contemporary position of the artist, the relationship between the secular and the sacred in modernity, the distinction between high art and popular culture, non-Western cultures branded as bearers of fundamentalism and fetishization of freedom.

PAREKH, Bhikhu
'Between Holy Text and Moral Void'
New Statesman and Society (London), 2/42 (March 1989), pp. 29–33.

Examines *The Satanic Verses* in the context of the migrant experience and discusses its impact on fellow immigrants. Recognizes that some of its passages 'do demean Muslims in their own and others' eyes'.

——,
'The Rushdie Affair and the British Press'
Social Studies Review (Oxford), 5/2 (1989), pp. 44–7.

This masterly survey of the British press demonstrates how it 'made little attempt to articulate and understand the Muslim complaint against *The Satanic Verses* and sought instead to bludgeon the protesters into silence'.

——,
'Britain and the Social Logic of Pluralism'
In: S. Poulter (et al.), *Britain: A Plural Society: Report of a Seminar.* Organized by the Commission for Racial Equality and the Runnymede Trust, October 1989.
London: Commission for Racial Equality, 1990, pp. 58–77.

Dealing, in the main, with the effects of post-war immigration on the British society and the future direction the pluralistic British society should take, it makes passing references to the Rushdie Affair.

——,
'The Rushdie Affair and the British Press: Some Salutary Lessons'
In: S. Mendus (et al.), *Free Speech: Report of a Seminar.* Organized by the Commission for Racial Equality and the Policy Studies Institute, September 1989.
London: Commission for Racial Equality, 1990, pp. 59–78.
Also published in Dan Cohn-Sherbok (ed.), *The Salman Rushdie Controversy in Interreligious Perspective.*
Lampeter, UK: The Edwin Mellen Press, 1990, pp. 71–95.

Critically examines both the liberal and conservative British newspapers' reaction to the Rushdie Affair and censures their insensitivity and self-righteousness. Criticizes also their campaign for the inviolability of free speech.

——,
'How Shall We Talk About Rushdie?' (Review Article).
Futures (special issue on 'Islam and the Future'), 23/3 (April 1991), pp. 322–7.

While reviewing Kabbani's, Shabbir Akhtar's and Sardar's and Davies's books on the Rushdie Affair, it notes four distinct discourses on the Affair: the Muslim, the religious, the racial and the diasporic. Asks Muslims to learn lessons from the West's surrender to the forces of secularism and modernity.

PIPES, Daniel
'The Ayatollah, the Novelist and the West'
Commentary (New York), 87/6 (1989), pp. 9–17.

The Ayatollah's *fatwa* is perceived as a challenge to 'some of Western civilization's deepest values'. Recounts the Muslim campaign worldwide but concentrates on the Ayatollah's motives in pronouncing the *fatwa* and concludes that he 'succeeded in imposing his will on the West in a temporary and partial way'.

PISCATORI, James
'The Ruşhdie Affair and the Politics of Ambiguity'
International Affairs (Cambridge), 66/4 (1990), pp. 767–89.

Examines Rushdie's challenge to Islamic tradition in questioning established religious and political authority. Analysing the Muslim responses to *The Satanic Verses,* it concludes that the idea of an Islamic force in international relations is misleadingly simplified.

POULTER, Sebastian
'Cultural Pluralism and its Limits: A Legal Perspective'
In: S. Poulter (et al.), *Britain: A Plural Society: Report of a Seminar.* Organized by the Commission for Racial Equality and the Runnymede Trust, October 1989.
London: Commission for Racial Equality, 1990, pp. 3–28.

In the wake of the Rushdie Affair it aims at scrutinizing the concept of a multi-cultural Britain and cultural pluralism in English law, education, employment and religious observances and on the question of differential treatment it argues for a careful analysis of issues and some flexibility.

PRISKEL, Peter
'The Rushdie Case and the Cowardice of the West'
American Atheist (Austin, TX), 31/9 (1989), pp. 55–6.

Describes the European reaction to the Rushdie Affair and their appeasement of Muslim fundamentalism as an omen of the intellectual repression.

REZUN, Miron
'The Internal Struggle: The Rushdie Affair and the Prospects for the Future'
In: M. Rezun (ed.), *Iran at the Crossroads.*
Boulder, CO: Westview Press, 1989, pp. 201–18.

Sets forth the reasons why the Ayatollah issued the *fatwa* against Rushdie and its internal and international dimensions. Looks also at the fall-out of the Rushdie Affair.

ROSE, Aubrey
'Difficulties in the Extension of the Blasphemy Law in Britain'
In: S. Lee (et al.), *Law, Blasphemy and the Multi-Faith Society: Report of a Seminar.* Organized by the Commission for Racial Equality and the Inter-Faith Network of the UK, September 1989.
London: Commission for Racial Equality, 1989, pp. 44–6.

Disapproves any extension of the existing law of blasphemy, for new revelations through medical and scientific discovery (!) may make today's blasphemy tomorrow's accepted doctrine.

SARDAR, Ziauddin
'A Postmodern War of the Wor(l)ds: Putting Rushdie and His Defenders Through Their Paces' (Review Article)
Muslim World Book Review (Leicester), 10/3 (1990), pp. 3–17.

Surveys the writings on the Rushdie Affair, such as those of Akhtar, Fay Weldon and Anees and brings home the main points of the Muslim outrage over the publication of *The Satanic Verses*.

——,
'The Rushdie Malaise: Orthodoxy of Doubt in the 'Little Room' of Postmodernist Fiction' (Review Article)
Muslim World Book Review (Leicester), 11/1 (1990), pp. 3–19.

A remarkably insightful critique of writings, particularly of Ruthven on the Rushdie Affair. Apart from vindicating the Muslim stance on the issue, it explores in detail many dimensions of the Affair such as Orientalism, Western literary establishment and post-modernism, etc.

——,
'Secularism's Grand Project'
Impact International (London), 20/4 (1990), pp. 12–14.

Elaborates the assaults of secular fundamentalists on Islam and Muslims, concluding that 'positive change is not possible unless Western society learns to tolerate pluralism other than on its own terms'.

'A Satanic Venture'
Al-Tawhid (Tehran), 6/2 (1989), pp. 10–18.

Perceives the publication of *The Satanic Verses* as a conspiracy of Western imperialism and explains why the Ayatollah and Iran took such a firm stand on the issue.

SIDDIQUI, Kalim
'Islam – A Universal Message? What Europe can Learn from Islam'
In: T.A. Linstad and S.E. Maoula (eds.), *International Seminar on Islam: Debates on the Rushdie Affair.*
Oslo, Norway: Muslim Magazine, 1990, pp. 26–34.

Restates the European confrontation with Islam and elucidates the message and agenda of Islam. Perceives the publication of *The Satanic Verses* as the start of a final crusade.

SMOKER, Barbara
'Fundamentalist Moslem Violence in Britain'
American Atheist (Austin, TX), 31/9 (1989), pp. 37–46.

Alarmingly reports that 'fundamentalist Moslems in Britain are carrying out acts of violence and inciting one another to murder . . . for the banning of a work of fiction'.

SPIVAK, Gayatri Chakravorty
'Reading the Satanic Verses'
Public Culture (Philadelphia, PA), 2/1 (1989), pp. 79–99.

Apart from containing a literary critical plot summary of *The Satanic Verses* it discusses the cultural politics of its (mis)reading with pointed reference to 'the anti-Enlightenment' behaviour of the Ayatollah.

SULERI, Sara
'Contraband Histories: Salman Rushdie and the Embodiment of Blasphemy'
The Yale Review (New Haven, CT), 78/4 (1989), pp. 604–24.

Considers *The Satanic Verses* as 'a deeply Islamic book' and constantly attempts to relate its episodes to Muslim history yet it deplores the 'furore that greeted its publication'.

'Summary of the Discussion'
In: S. Mendus (et al.), *Free Speech: Report of a Seminar.* Organized by the Commission for Racial Equality and the Policy Studies Institute, September 1989.
London: Commission for Racial Equality, 1990, pp. 111–18.

Most of the conclusions on the Affair are drawn in the contexts of the deprivation of the British Muslim community and of the press and writers' defence of Rushdie and treatment of Muslims as forces of darkness.

TAHERI, Amir
'The Rushdie Affair: Reflections on an Invalid Fatwa'
Index on Censorship, No. 4 (April 1990), pp. 14–16.

Written by a rabidly anti-Khomeini, an Iranian exile, it is solely preoccupied with discrediting the Islamic revolution of Iran and the Ayatollah Khomeini. Describes the freedom of expression as man's most vital victory through centuries which the Islamic tyrants intend to snatch.

TAYLOR, Charles
'The Rushdie Controversy'
Public Culture (Philadelphia, PA), 2/1 (1989), pp. 118–22.

A cogent piece arguing for limits on free speech and respect for religious feelings. It asks the Western liberal mind to learn to look outside its narrow worldview.

THURSBY, Gene R.
'Rushdie, Rajpal and Religious Controversy in British India'
Proceedings of the Eleventh International Symposium on Asian Studies (Hong Kong), 1989, pp. 423–34.

Points to the similarities in *The Satanic Verses* and a number of polemical offensive works that appeared in British India in the 1920s which Muslims regarded as painfully unacceptable. Provides also a brief history of the prosecution of such polemical writers in British India.

TWEED, James
'True Faith'
New Statesman and Society (London), 4/138 (February 1991), p. 19.

A brilliant piece detailing restrictions on the freedom of expression in the West even in the post-*The Satanic Verses* period: Robert Maxwell pulping 20,000 copies of *True Faith* in deference to the wishes of the Evangelist Alliance and protests by feminists, including Fay Weldon, against Ellis's *American Psycho.*

UNTERMAN, Alan
'A Jewish Perspective on the Rushdie Affair'
In: Dan Cohn-Sherbok (ed.), *The Salman Rushdie Controversy in Interreligious Perspective.*
Lampeter, UK: The Edwin Mellen Press, 1990, pp. 97–114.

Dwells on the religious differences among Jews, Christians and Muslims. Disapproves Chief Rabbi Jakobovits's view that a work such as *The Satanic Verses* should not be allowed, by law, to be published. Finds it ironic that Muslims have attempted to prosecute Rushdie under the blasphemy law, for it could prohibit the publication of certain Islamic writings on the grounds of objections from members of other religions.

VEER, Peter Van Der
'Satanic or Angelic? The Politics of Religious and Literary Inspiration'
Public Culture (Philadelphia, PA), 2/1 (1989), pp. 100–5.

Sees *The Satanic Verses* as 'a major political-literary event' with its 'attacks on Islam's moral absolutism and its treatment of women'. Although recognizing the novel as offensive and acknowledging the Muslim outrage, the author prefers 'to take sides with an apostate Muslim – Rushdie'.

VETTA, Atam
'A Contract with the Devil'
Impact International (London), 20/4 (1990), pp. 5–8.

Quoting some of the blasphemous sentences from the book, the author explains why *The Satanic Verses* is offensive even to an agnostic Hindu like himself. Strongly argues for its withdrawal for it is seen 'as a continuing provocation'.

WALTER, Nicholas
'Blasphemy Ancient and Modern'
New Humanist, 104/4 (1990), pp. 9–11.

Surveys the historical development of the blasphemy law and argues that the most desirable thing to do with this law is to abolish it as its '. . . extension could open up Pandora's box'.

——,
'Blasphemy: Punishment is Worse than Practice'
Index on Censorship, (April 1990), pp. 21–2.

As an official of the Rationalist Press and Secretary of the Committee against Blasphemy Law, Walter attempts to defend absolute freedom of expression and condemns any legal protection for religious feelings.

WARD, Keith
'The Nature of Blasphemy'
In: S. Lee (et al.), *Law, Blasphemy and the Multi-Faith Society: Report of a Seminar.* Organized by the Commission for Racial Equality and the Inter-Faith Network of the UK, September 1989.
London: Commission for Racial Equality, 1989, pp. 30–9.

Addressing the main components of blasphemy, its place in today's society and the law of blasphemy, it concludes that 'from a Christian point of view a law of blasphemy is actually rather difficult to sustain'.

WEALE, Albert
'Freedom of Speech vs. Freedom of Religion?'
In: S. Mendus (et al.), *Free Speech: Report of a Seminar.* Organized by the Commission for Racial Equality and the Policy Studies Institute, September 1989.
London: Commission for Racial Equality, 1990, pp. 49–58.

Considers the principles defining and limiting the practice of freedom of expression. Suggests the setting up of an independent council, rather than extending the law of blasphemy, with powers to decide whether a publication was blasphemous or not.

WEIR, Stuart
'The Sound of Silence'
New Statesman and Society (London), 2/38 (1989), pp. 10–11.

Holds that 'Khomeini's incitement to murder Rushdie strikes at the very heart of our freedom. Inquires into the silence both of the Conservative government and Labour opposition, in expressing their outrage and finds baser interests at work in the body politic'.

——,
'Death Sentences'
New Statesman and Society (London), 4/138 (February 1991), pp. 16–17.

Considers the resumption of diplomatic relations between Iran and Britain as an act of 'betrayal' by the British government. Censures the Conservative and Labour parties, the Church of England and several writers on not defending the freedom of expression.

WELLER, Paul
'Literature Update on the Salman Rushdie Affair'
Discernment (London), 4/2 (1990), pp. 35–41.

A useful annotated bibliography of some books, press statements and articles on the Rushdie Affair till February 1990.

——,
'The Rushdie Affair, Plurality of Values and the Ideal of a Multi-Cultural Society'
Navet Papers 2 (October 1990), pp. 1–12.

Holds that the 'debate about the relationship of free speech and social responsibility is central to the Rushdie Affair. Emphasizes the need for more considered public debate in a calmer atmosphere for strengthening a multi-faith society such as that of Britain.

——,
'The Rushdie Controversy and Inter-Faith Relations'
In: Dan Cohn-Sherbok (ed.), *The Salman Rushdie Controversy in Interreligious Perspective.*
Lampeter, UK: The Edwin Mellen Press, 1990, pp. 37–57.

States the Inter-Faith Network's position on the Affair. Records also the stances of radical Christians, Chief Rabbi, Lord Jakobovits and the World Conference on Religion and Peace.

'Words for Salman Rushdie (Writers Support Rushdie)'
New Statesman and Society (London), 2/43 (1989), pp. 24–30.

Contributed by a host of literary figures it demonstrates their unqualified support for Rushdie. The lone voice of dissent is Rana Kabbani, holding

Rushdie responsible for resurrecting medieval prejudices against Islam and Muslims.

ZAFAR, S.M.
'Islam and the Freedom of Speech'
In: T.A. Linstad and S.E. Maoula (eds.), *International Seminar on Islam: Debates on the Rushdie Affair.*
Oslo, Norway: Muslim Magazine, 1990, pp. 19–25.

Outlines the limits of the freedom of speech in Islam which bars one from ridiculing others, particularly their religious beliefs and sanctities.

Index